STRANGERS & SOJOURNERS
AT PORT ROYAL

PLATE I

MONUMENT TO JAMES II AND VII IN THE COLLÈGE DES ÉCOSSAIS,
WHERE HIS BRAIN WAS BESTOWED

Part of the inscription reads: "Haec domus quam pius princeps labantem sustinuit et patriè fovit cui etiam ingenii sui monumenta omnia scilicet sua manu scripta custodienda commisit eam corporis ipsius partem qua maxime animus viget religiose servandam suscepit."

STRANGERS & SOJOURNERS AT PORT ROYAL

Being an account of
the connections between the British Isles and the
Jansenists of France and Holland

by

RUTH CLARK

Professor of French at Wellesley College

OCTAGON BOOKS

A DIVISION OF FARRAR, STRAUS AND GIROUX

New York   1972

First published 1932

Reprinted 1972
by permission of the Cambridge University Press

OCTAGON BOOKS
A DIVISION OF FARRAR, STRAUS & GIROUX, INC.
19 Union Square West
New York, N. Y. 10003

Library of Congress Cataloging in Publication Data

Clark, Ruth.
    Strangers & sojourners at Port Royal.
    Reprint of the 1932 ed.
    Bibliography: p.
    1. Jansenists. 2. Port Royal. 3. Great Britain—Church
history—Modern period. 4. Jansenists—Bibliography.
    I. Title.
BX4730.C55   1972   284'.84'0942   72-6953
ISBN 0-374-91664-0

Manufactured by Braun-Brumfield, Inc.
Ann Arbor, Michigan

Printed in the United States of America

To

MRS FREDERICK G. ATKINSON
*First Vice-President of the American Association of
University Women, whose generous interest
made the writing of this book possible,
in very grateful appreciation of her
help and encouragement*

Contents

List of Plates

Preface

O F late years a number of books have dealt with Jansenism in countries other than France. Books on Jansenism in Italy have been particularly frequent, as for instance: E. Fabri, *I Giansenisti nella conversione della famiglia Manzoni*, 1914; A Parisi, *I riflessi del giansenismo nella letteratura italiana*, 1919; N. Rodolico, *Gli amici e i tempi di Scipione dei Ricci, Saggio sul giansenismo*, 1920; F. Landogna, *Il giansenismo ligure alla fine del secolo XVIII*, 1926; A. C. Jemolo, *Il giansenismo in Italia prima della Rivoluzione*, 1928; F. Ruffini, *I giansenisti piemontesi*, 1929. Jansenism in Spain is treated by M. F. Miguelez in *Jansenismo y regalismo en España*, 1895, and Jansenism in Germany and Austria by W. Deinhardt in *Der Jansenismus in deutschen Landen*, 1929.[1] Jansenism in Holland is almost inseparable from Jansenism in France. English readers were introduced to the subject a number of years ago by J. M. Neale's *History of the so-called Jansenist Church in Holland*, 1858, and, more recently, by the Rev. C. Beaufort Moss in a sketch, *The Old Catholic Churches and Reunion*, 1927.

But what of England and Jansenism? Does the question arise at all? "Do you find any material whatever?" the writer has been frequently asked. It is quite obvious that a book dealing with England and Jansenism will perforce be very different from a work dealing with Jansenism in a Catholic country, and this will account in part for the episodic character of the book.

The material found has resolved itself into three distinct types, though in practice it was, of course, not feasible to keep the results of investigations in three compartments. From French sources, chiefly, it was possible to write about certain individuals who, living abroad, came under the influence of Port Royal and the Jansenists. This will be found to be the most complete part of the book, as no important source, it is hoped,

---

1 See also Préclin, *Les Jansénistes du 18e siècle et la constitution civile du clergé*, 1929 pp. 432–4, Autriche; pp. 434–7, Italie.

has been overlooked. It is also the part that first suggested itself to the writer a number of years ago when, preparing a biography of Anthony Hamilton, the author of the *Mémoires de Grammont*, she was struck, as she could not fail to be, by the charity which Port Royal extended to all those who took refuge in France.

English memoirs and letters, translations of Jansenist books, mostly by Protestants, made it possible to ascertain how well Port Royal and Jansenism were known to seventeenth- and eighteenth-century English readers, and furnished sources for chapters on the attitude of English Protestantism toward Jansenism, an attitude practically always most favourable. The material to be examined was vast and the results often rather meagre. It will no doubt be possible to add to them, for no one person could investigate every source.

Finally a third class of material brings one to the question of Jansenism and the Roman Catholics of the three Kingdoms, and here this study is fragmentary when compared with some of those dealing with Jansenism in other countries. From the very circumstances of the Roman Catholics in England, a minority frequently harassed by penal laws and persecutions, a Church leading a precarious existence, it was impossible that Jansenism could assume the importance it had on the continent or that the clergy could always practise the watchfulness expected of them. In 1706, at the time of the Bull *Vineam Domini*, Bishop Giffard writes: "I have been for sixteen months tossed about by continued perturbations and perils, so as scarcely to find anywhere a place to rest in safety", and in 1714 he says he has been obliged to change his lodgings fourteen times in five months. Thrice he has been in prison and now daily expects a fourth prison in which to end his life. He has received the Constitution *Unigenitus*, but could signify it to a few only of the clergy.[1]

When Dom Gerberon published his history of Jansenism in 1700 he gave it the title *Histoire générale du Jansénisme contenant ce qui s'est passé en France, en Espagne, en Italie, dans les Pays Bas, au sujet du livre intitulé "Augustinus Cornelii Jansenii"*; but no mention was necessary of England. When the Cardinal de Bissy

1 Brady, *Episcopal Succession*, ii, pp. 151-3.

brought together in 1718 his *Témoignages de l'Église Universelle en faveur de la Bulle Unigenitus*, he was able to print a number of attestations from Roman Catholic bishops in other countries, but all he could do in the case of England was to give short extracts from the informal letters of three of the vicars-apostolic whose names he cautiously omitted.

The printed sources are therefore not very numerous. Gillow's *Biographical Dictionary* is among the most important, and there are a few controversial books. The manuscript sources are yet to be explored more fully. The Roman transcripts at the Record Office have been utilized, and the records of Jansenism preserved at St Cuthbert's College, Ushaw, Durham, but there is doubtless further material in the Italian libraries, the archives of the diocese of Westminster, and other places. It is hoped that an adequate general outline has been given here, but the inmost history of Jansenism and the English Roman Catholics can probably be unfolded still further. Generally speaking this story consists in the main of accusations of Jansenism brought against certain individuals and their defence, and relates a phase of the struggle between the regulars and seculars. Jansenism itself was not openly taught in England.

For Scotland the chief source is Sir David Hunter-Blair's enlarged translation of Bellesheim's *History of the Catholic Church in Scotland*; for Ireland, Cardinal Moran's *Memoirs of the Most Rev. Oliver Plunket*. Some additions have been made to this material, but here again there is probably more to be gleaned from private manuscript collections, such as the one at Blairs College. There is little trace of Jansenism in Ireland, but in Scotland there were some friends, men who came from the Scots College in Paris.

From the foregoing it will be seen that this study does not and cannot claim to be an exhaustive history of Jansenism and Great Britain, but it does hope to have accomplished some honest spadework which may help to lay the foundation for some larger treatise, undertaken, possibly, by a theologian. Certain little-known relations between France and England have perhaps been indicated, some fresh light thrown on the circumstances of those forced to live abroad, something observed of the widespread influence of those others who, whether rightly or wrongly, suffered for what they believed to be a righteous cause.

It is a privilege to record the kindness of all those who in various ways have contributed to the writing of this book.

To the Duke of Richmond and Gordon I owe the permission to reproduce the portrait of Ludovic Stuart d'Aubigny at Gordon Castle, Fochabers; to the Duke of Leeds and the Marquess of Ormonde the permission to use manuscript material; to the authorities of Sion College, London, the ready access to Mrs Schimmelpenninck's collection of Port Royal books. The Lady Abbess of St Mary's Abbey, Colwich, Staffs., graciously lent me a copy of the history of the community (privately printed), and Dame M. Margaret, O.S.B., was good enough to answer my questions. I gratefully acknowledge the liberality of the authorities of St Cuthbert's College, Ushaw, Durham, the Right Rev. Monsignor W. H. Brown, President of the College, the Rev. E. Bonney, Vice-President, and the Rev. B. Payne, Librarian, who allowed me to utilize the manuscript collection of the college, and with the utmost goodness did everything in their power to facilitate my researches. I recall with gratitude the exceedingly kind reception given me by various members of the Old Catholic Church of Holland, and I thank His Grace, the Archbishop of Utrecht, Monsignor Kenninck, for permission to consult the archives, and the Rev. President C. Wijker of the Oud-Katholiek Seminarie at Amersfoort, the Rev. E. Lagerwey of Utrecht, and Mr J. Bruggeman of the Rijksarchief at the Hague for all their help so generously given. For advice or information of various kinds I am further indebted to Mademoiselle Cécile Gazier, to Miss I. Thornley of University College, London, to Monsieur J. Laporte, Chargé de Cours à la Sorbonne, to Monsieur Morel-Payen, Conservateur de la Bibliothèque de Troyes, to David Hannay, Esq., to the Rev. C. Beaufort Moss, to Mr W. H. Reade, Librarian of Keble College, Oxford, to Mr A. C. Potter, Librarian of Harvard College Library, and, very specially, to the Rev. Dr H. F. Stewart of Trinity College, Cambridge, who read this book in proof and whose kindness was great to one who had no

PREFACE   xiii

claims on his time. I am under great obligations to the various
libraries in which I have worked—I should like to make at least
some mention of the unfailing courtesy shown at the archives
of the Ministère des Affaires Étrangères to the research worker.
For the plates I am indebted to the Duke of Richmond
and Gordon, the Lord Abbot of Douai, Woolhampton, the
Secretary of the Royal Society, the Trustees of the National
Portrait Gallery, and to Monsieur Georges Roth for procur-
ing the photographs of the Collège des Écossais.
My deepest thanks must go to Mrs Frederick G. Atkinson,
First Vice-President of the American Association of University
Women, whose generosity in establishing a research-fellowship
at Wellesley College enabled me to carry on a study begun long
ago. If anything has been achieved it is in a large measure due
to her initiative and to her interest in the higher education of
women.

RUTH CLARK

WELLESLEY COLLEGE
WELLESLEY, MASSACHUSETTS
1932

Chronology

[A very full Table Chronologique for 1601–1737 will be found on pp. xiii–lxii of Cerveau's *Nécrologe*, vol. 1, Dix-septième Siècle. Many dates are taken from this work.]

1602   Jacqueline Arnauld (la Mère Angélique) becomes Abbess of Port Royal at the age of eleven.

1609   Reform of Port Royal. The so-called Journée du Guichet. Father Pembroke becomes Director of Port Royal.

1610   Murder of Henri IV. Reign of Louis XIII.

1625   Richard Smith consecrated as Bishop of Chalcedon. Port Royal de Paris opened. The nuns move in from Port Royal des Champs.

1629   Richard Smith retires to France.

1632   Publication of *Petrus Aurelius*.

1634   Saint-Cyran becomes director of Port Royal (though known to Port Royal before this date).

1637   M. Le Maître withdraws from the world. The first Solitaries.

1638   Death of Jansenius. Saint-Cyran imprisoned. The Solitaries obliged to disperse.

1640   Publication of the *Augustinus*.

1641   Publication of Conry's *Peregrinus Jerichuntinus*.

1642   Urban VIII condemns the *Augustinus* in his Bull *In eminenti* (not published till the following year). Death of Richelieu.

1643   Saint-Cyran released from prison. Death of Louis XIII. Publication of Arnauld's *Fréquente Communion*. Dr John Sinnich in Rome (till 1645) in defence of the *Augustinus*. Death of Saint-Cyran.

1645   Dr Bourgeois in Rome in defence of the *Fréquente Communion*.

1646   The Little Schools of Port Royal established.

1648   La Mère Angélique and some of the nuns return to Port Royal des Champs. The Solitaries withdraw to the adjoining farm-house of Les Granges. Outbreak of the Fronde.

1649   Cornet formulates the five propositions.

1651   L'affaire des Hibernois. Dr Callaghan attacked by Brisacier.

xvi CHRONOLOGY

1652 The Cardinal de Retz arrested.
1653 The Jansenists provide Charles II with funds, but are accused of intriguing with Cromwell.
The five propositions condemned by Innocent X (Bull *Cum occasione*).
1654 Charles II leaves France. Sends thanks to Singlin and Bernières.
The Cardinal de Retz becomes Archbishop of Paris. He escapes from prison.
1655 Arnauld's *Lettre à une personne de condition* and *Lettre à un duc et pair*.
First draft of the Formulary.
1656 Arnauld censured and excluded from the Sorbonne.
The *Lettres Provinciales* begin to appear.
The Little Schools closed.
The Solitaries dispersed (1655 according to Cerveau).
Miracle of la Sainte Épine.
A Bull of Alexander VII (*Ad sanctam B. Petri sedem*) confirms the Bull of Innocent X (1653).
1657 The *Lettres Provinciales* continue to appear.
The 1655 Formulary adopted by the Assembly of the Clergy (in a slightly modified form).
1658 The Little Schools begin to resume their activities.
The Duke of Monmouth a pupil.
1660 The Little Schools suppressed.
The Restoration.
1661 Death of Mazarin.
Expulsion of the Solitaries (1660 according to Cerveau).
The novices and pensionnaires sent away from Port Royal.
Death of la Mère Angélique.
The Formulary presented to the nuns of Port Royal.
1662 Retz resigns the archbishopric. M. de Marca, his successor, dies. M. de Péréfixe becomes Archbishop of Paris.
Death of M. de Bernières.
Death of Pascal.
1663 Ludovic Stuart d'Aubigny not to become a cardinal.
1664 M. des Touches helps the English Benedictines to buy a house.
Renewed persecutions. A number of nuns carried off captives from Port Royal de Paris.
Francis Jenkins obliged to leave Port Royal de Paris.
1665 Bull of Alexander VII imposing Formulary (*Regiminis apostolici*).
The Bishops of Alet, Angers, Beauvais and Pamiers refuse to conform.

Death of Ludovic Stuart d'Aubigny and news of his cardinalate.

1667 The Mons New Testament published.
1668 The so-called Paix de l'Église.
     Return of the Solitaries.
1669 Separation of Port Royal des Champs and Port Royal de Paris.
1670 Death of M. de Péréfixe. M. de Harlay becomes Archbishop of Paris.
     Publication of the *Pensées*.
1679 Death of Mme de Longueville.
     Renewed persecution of Port Royal. Pensionnaires and novices sent away. Expulsion of the Solitaries.
     Arnauld withdraws to Flanders.
1688 Flight of James II to France.
1689 Arnauld's book against William of Orange.
     The Canons of Beauvais accused of intriguing with England.
1694 Death of Arnauld.
1695 Death of Nicole.
     Death of M. de Harlay. M. de Noailles becomes Archbishop of Paris.
1699 Mme de Gramont forbidden to go to Marly on account of her visits to Port Royal.
1701 Death of James II at Saint-Germain.
1702 The *Cas de Conscience* printed.
1703 Imprisonment of Quesnel at Brussels and his escape.
     Dr Betham, preceptor of the Chevalier de St George, at Saint-Germain, accused of Jansenism.
1704 Dr Hawarden of Douay accused of Jansenism.
1705 The Bull *Vineam Domini*.
1707 English Roman Catholics accused of Jansenism.
1709 Final dispersion of the nuns of Port Royal.
     A papal brief addressed to the Roman Catholics of England, Scotland and Ireland.
1710 Beginning of the demolition of Port Royal.
1713 The Bull *Unigenitus*.
1715 Douay College cleared of the accusation of Jansenism.
     Death of Louis XIV.
     Ordination of Dutch Jansenists in Ireland.
1716 Further ordinations.
1717 Appeal of the Bishops of Senez, Montpellier, Boulogne, Mirepoix, from the Constitution *Unigenitus*.
     Appeal of the Cardinal de Noailles.
1718 Du Pin's Project of Union.

1719 Death of Quesnel.
1720 Noailles retracts his appeal.
1723 Death of the Regent.
1727 Condemnation of Soanen, Bishop of Senez.
1729 Death of the Cardinal de Noailles.
      The Jansenists Le Gros and Étemare visit England.
1732 The cemetery of St Médard closed on account of the convul-
      sionaries.
1736 Scottish missionaries required to subscribe a formulary.
1737 Lercari's report on the Jansenism of the Scots College at Paris.
1739 Lord Edward Drummond (afterwards 6th Duke of Perth)
      imprisoned for being a convulsionary.
1755 Lady Elizabeth Drummond refused the sacraments.

The following résumés may be found useful:

Temps principaux dans l'histoire des persécutions de Port-Royal

1653 La situation, assez belle, se gâte par la condamnation à Rome
      des cinq propositions de Jansénius.
      Persécution continue et croissante, surtout à partir de 1656.
1664 L'archevêque Péréfixe s'y prêtant, la persécution atteint aux
      extrêmes rigueurs.
1664–1668 Il y a véritablement captivité.
1668 La paix de l'Église.
1669–1679 Port-Royal jouit d'un vif et suprême éclat.
1679–1709 Dernière persécution, plus sourde, plus lente,...finit par
      l'entière ruine.   D'après Port-Royal, II, pp. 342–3.

Dispersions des Solitaires

1638 La première.
1656 La plus bénigne.
1661 La plus violente.
1679 La dernière.

D'après Port-Royal, III, p. 172.

The Five Propositions

said to be contained in the *Augustinus*

1. Some of God's Commandments are impossible to the Just according to their present forces, though they have a will, and do endeavour to accomplish them: and they want the Grace, that rendreth them possible.

2. In the state of nature corrupt, men never resist Interiour Grace.

3. To merit and demerit in the state of Nature corrupted, it is not necessary to have the liberty that excludes necessity; but it sufficeth to have that liberty which excludes Coaction, or Constraint.

4. The Semipelagians admitted the necessity of Interiour preventing Grace to every Action even to the beginning of Faith. But they were Heretiques in this that they would have that Grace to be such, as the will of man might resist it or obey it.

5. It is semipelagianisme to say that Jesus Christ died, or shed his blood, generally for all men.

From *An Answer to the Provinciall Letters* (1659), pp. xxiii–xxiv.

The Formulary of Alexander VII

The Pope's Bull for imposing the Formularies..."The best remedie to extirpate the restes of this contagious Maladie, is to cause all the World to sign one Formularie founded on our Autoritie. In pursuit whereof we command that all Ecclesiastiques etc. to subscribe the following Formularie: I, N. submit my self to the Apostolick Constitution of Innocent X dated May 31, 1653, and to the Constitution of Alexander 7th, dated Oct. 16, 1656, the chief Bishops: and I do with a sincere mind reject and condemn the V propositions, taken out of Cornelius Jansenius's Book, named Augustinus, and in the sense intended by the same Author, as the Apostolick seat has by the said Constitution condemned them. And thus I sware. God so help me, and these holy Evangels of God".

Given at Rome, Feb. 15, 1665.

From Gale, *The true Idea of Jansenisme* (1669), pp. 93–4.

CHAPTER I

Early Days

IF anyone were found willing to wrestle with that huge folio, the fateful *Augustinus*, from which sprang such years of strife, after a thousand or more closely printed pages he would reach an appendix with a separate title-page and pagination, not by Jansenius, but by an Irishman, the Franciscan Florence Conry, Archbishop of Tuam. If, undertaking a much easier task, he wished to read the little volume of Jansen's letters to Saint-Cyran, he would have to use a key to the strange names that dot these pages and make these obscure letters even more obscure, and he would learn from the *Dechifrement des Lettres de M. Jansenius* that while "*Sulpice*", "*Boëce*", "*Quinquarbre*", "*Cudaro*" meant Jansenius, and "*Celias*", "*Solion*", "*Durillon*", "*Rongeart*" meant Saint-Cyran, "*Solsti*", "*Philippas*", "*Gemer*", "*L'Illustrissime*", "*Notre Voisin*", all stood for Conry. If he were to take up Dom Clémencet's *Histoire littéraire de Port-Royal* he would first come upon Jansenius, and next upon Conry with the Louvain theologians, or, if he were to glance through the *Dictionnaire des Livres Jansénistes*, his eye might presently alight on a mention of Conry's *Peregrinus Jerichuntinus*, and he would be told by this hostile dictionary that having taught almost the same doctrine as Jansenius, Conry had been condemned with him.[1]

A brief account of Conry will not therefore be out of place here, even though he died before the *Augustinus* appeared, and before the word "Jansenism" had been coined. It may seem as if our narrative were going rather far afield, but Louvain was in a

---

[1] *Dictionnaire des Livres Jansénistes*, III, p. 233. But condemnation by this book need embarrass no one. Even Mme de Sévigné's letters are included (II, pp. 527–34). "Bei den Jansenisten standen die Schriften Conry's in hohem Ansehen; eine ausdrückliche Verwerfung derselben durch den heiligen Stuhl ist jedoch nicht erfolgt." Bellesheim, *Geschichte der Katholischen Kirche in Irland*, II, p. 327.

way the home of Jansenism, and so it is perhaps natural enough that our story should begin at Louvain.

Conry was born in 1561 in Ireland and had been consecrated to his see in 1609, but he spent most of his life abroad in Spain and in the Low Countries, and was never able to visit his province. At Louvain, where a college for the Irish had been founded at Conry's solicitation, Jansenius knew him and realized that he also was deeply interested in St Augustine, for Conry devoted sixteen years of study to St Augustine, reading him more than ten times.[1] But perhaps just because Conry was writing on Grace and Predestination Jansenius was on his guard with him and somewhat uneasy on the subject of this fellow-enthusiast.[2]

The book in which Conry hoped to set forth his ideas concerning man's fall from grace and his redemption was the *Peregrinus Jerichuntinus*, a work which never appeared during his lifetime. In 1621 Jansenius observes that Conry has given up all idea of obtaining an approbation from Rome, yet he hopes that perhaps Saint-Cyran will be able to do something for him in Paris.[3] Another request went from Conry to Saint-Cyran through Jansenius about this time, and that was that Saint-Cyran might help the General of Conry's order in Paris and the Guardian of the Irish Franciscan College in Louvain, Father Hugh MacCaghwell, to obtain permission from Louis XIII to establish a residence for the Irish friars in Paris.[4] This was, of course, long before the days of open controversy, but it is curious to reflect in retrospect on the possibility of an Irish college founded under the auspices of Jansenius and Saint-Cyran.

Conry's *Peregrinus* was not to see the light for many years, but another book by him is foreshadowed in the letters of Jansenius. "Gemer brûle de désir de mettre en lumière un certain ouvrage *De Pœna Parvulorum post hanc vitam*", interesting to Jansenius because it touches the *affaire de Pilmot*, and the *affaire de Pilmot*, shrouded mysteriously in the disguise of this invented name, is

---

1 Arnauld, *Œuvres*, x, p. lxxxvii; xvi, p. 263.
2 Jansenius, *Lettres*, pp. 36, 41–2, 43, 49, 126, 129.
3 *Ib*. pp. 35–6, 38, 45, 46.   4 *Ib*. pp. 47–8 (1622).

to Jansenius the great affair of his life, the treatise he will write some day on the doctrine of St Augustine.[1] A strange grim book was this of Conry's—he undertook, so Gerberon explains,[2] to combat with the aid of St Augustine the error of those who from a wrong sense of compassion, more Pelagian than Christian, exempted little unbaptized children from the pains of hell, and thereby undermined the doctrine of original sin.

The students of Conry's college at Louvain, St Anthony of Padua, were so eager to hear what he had to say that, at their desire, the manuscript was read to them in the refectory during the dinner-hour, and they listened with rapt attention to the harsh doctrine of their master.[3] Jansenius, however, foresaw that the book would bring much opposition to its author and he tried to dissuade Conry from publishing it; but Conry persevered in his design, though he seems to have modified some of his positions.[4]

The book appeared in 1624,[5] and was reprinted several times; it was reprinted in 1640 as an appendix to the *Augustinus*. "Conclusion fâcheuse," remarks Sainte-Beuve, "perspective tout au moins inopportune et révoltante."[6] Both Conry and Jansenius had passed away by this time, Conry in 1629 and Jansenius in 1638.

We are told that Conry left his *Peregrinus Jerichuntinus* to Jansenius, and that Saint-Cyran, greatly impressed by this treatise, caused it to be published with the approbation of several doctors in 1641, shortly after the *Augustinus* had appeared. It will be remembered that Saint-Cyran was imprisoned from 1638 to 1642, and we are therefore not surprised to hear

1 *Ib.* pp. 72, 75, 90.
2 In the notes to these letters. The name of the editor appears as François du Vivier, but this stands for Gerberon (Arnauld, *Œuvres*, x, p. lxxxvii).
3 *Ib.* pp. 90, 96, 114.
4 *Ib.* pp. 117, 126, 129, 131. "Quoique cet ouvrage n'eût pas été condamné à Rome comme le sieur Preville en sa naissance du Jansenisme...l'assure très-faussement et très-imprudemment, les censures, c'est à dire, les jugements particuliers des Theologiens de Rome à qui on le communiqua ne lui furent pas avantageux." (Note by Gerberon, p. 131.)
5 *Tractatus de statu parvulorum sine baptismo decedentium ex hac vita juxta sensum B. Augustini compositus a F. Florentio Conrio...*, Lovani, 1624.
6 *Port-Royal*, I, p. 298.

that he entrusted Conry's book to the care of Arnauld,[1] who not only saw the Latin text through the press, but provided a French translation which appeared in 1645[2] and was also issued in this year by Saint-Cyran's nephew, de Barcos, in a *Recueil de divers Ouvrages touchant la Grâce.*

The Irish residing abroad do not seem to have doubted the orthodoxy of Conry's book, however dubious they felt about Jansenius. One of them writes in 1642 to the famous Luke Wadding, Guardian of St Isidore's Convent at Rome, "Your Paternity will by this time have received the *Peregrinus* of our Tuamensis which circulates here to the immense relief of those who are zealous in the defence of the truth of St Augustine's doctrine", and with this book Hugh Bourke, Commissary of the Irish Friars Minor in Germany and Belgium, sends Wadding other matter "set in order with much care in exculpation of this country for not receiving the prohibition of the work of Jansenius". "I see a cloud threatening our country with grave confusions", he remarks, "if this doctrine receive not judicious consideration; for it is admirably suited to pass as that of St Augustine, victor of Pelagianism.... Jansen's affair needs to be handled with the utmost circumspection, for his doctrine has been passionately embraced by not a few in France and Flanders."[3]

The *Peregrinus* is fully analysed in Clémencet's *Histoire littéraire de Port-Royal*[4] where there is also a list of Conry's other works. It is interesting to note that Pascal made use of the *Peregrinus* in his *Écrits sur la Grâce*, and that, speaking of the number of learned and illustrious defenders of the doctrine of St Augustine with which, as he says, God was pleased to honour the century, he

1 Arnauld, *Œuvres*, x, pp. lxxxvii–lxxxviii; Gerberon, *Hist. générale du Jansénisme*, 1, p. 36; Racine (abbé), *Hist. ecclés.* p. 29.
2 *Florentii Conrii Peregrinus Jerichuntinus, hoc est, de Natura humana feliciter instituta, infeliciter lapsa, miserabiliter vulnerata, misericorditer restaurata* [Edidit Thadaeus Macnamara vel potius A. Arnould], Parisiis, 1641. *Abrégé de la doctrine de S. Augustin touchant la grâce par Florent Conrius... traduit de son livre intitulé Peregrinus Jerichuntinus*, Paris, 1645.
3 *Hist. MSS. Comm., Franciscan MSS. at Dublin*, pp. 117, 119, 124. Bourke also thinks that Dr Edmond Dwyer, Resident on the part of the Bishops of Ireland at the Roman Curia, did well "to eschew the agency of Iprensis book", the party opposing the *Augustinus* being powerful in Rome. *Ib.* p. 116.
4 Vol. 1 (the only one printed), pp. 85–96.

draws attention to the number of forerunners, foremost among whom he places Conry.¹

The other Louvain theologian long remembered by the Jansenists as one of their doughty fighters is the Irishman John Sinnich,² at one time Rector of the University of Louvain. He has his place in the Port Royal *Nécrologes*,³ he is prominent in the Jansenist histories,⁴ his name appears in the *Calendrier des Amis de la Vérité*—an honour accorded only to one other Irishman, an Englishman and two Scotsmen,⁵—and the *Dictionnaire des Livres Jansénistes* condemns him without indulgence, "Hibernois et Janseniste outré", "il étoit un des chefs du parti", "il publia sous des titres extraordinaires et ridicules differens Ouvrages qui sont tous infectés des erreurs Janséniennes".⁶

Sinnich was born in the county of Cork,⁷ educated at the University of Louvain, became president of the greater theological college at Louvain in 1641, a charge which he held for

1 Pascal, *Œuvres*, XI, pp. 104, 143. An account of Conry written by an opponent of Jansenism may be read in Rapin's *Hist. du Jansénisme*, pp. 113–19, 133–4. For more modern estimates of Conry see Renehan, *Collections*, I, pp. 395–401; Bellesheim, *op. cit.* pp. 326–7; *The Catholic Encyclopedia*; and A. Meyer, *Les premières controverses jansénistes en France*, pp. 12, 13, 114, 115, 139, 214.

2 He is called John "Shinnick" in an article in the *Irish Eccl. Record*, 3rd ser., vol. 7, 1886, pp. 732–42.

3 [Le Febvre de Saint-Marc] *Supplément au Nécrologe de l'Abbaïe de Notre Dame de Port-Royal des Champs*, pp. 608–13. [Cerveau] *Nécrologe des plus célèbres Défenseurs et Confesseurs de la Vérité*, I, pp. 99–100; IV (Supplément au Nécrologe), pp. 293–4.

4 Gerberon, *op. cit.* I, pp. 26, 78–105, 116–40, 164–7; Clémencet, *Hist. litt. de Port-Royal*, I, pp. 164–93; Saint-Amour, *Journal*, p. 357, Appendix, p. 270; Arnauld, *Œuvres*, XXII, p. 139; Racine (abbé), *Hist. ecclés.* XI, pp. 24, 34–47; *Hist. du Cas de Conscience*, III, pp. 231–5. On the other side see Rapin, *Hist. du Jansénisme*, pp. 412 (where he is erroneously called Smith), 488, 509–10, and *Mémoires*, I, pp. 14–15, 68–70, 144–6, 297; II, p. 182; III, p. 101. For modern works see A. Meyer, *Les premières controverses jansénistes*, *passim*, especially pp. 134–5, 137; also Vacant et Mangenot, *Dictionnaire de Théologie Catholique*, article "Jansénisme".

5 Printed at the beginning of vol. IV of Cerveau's *Nécrologe*. The other names in question are: "Milord Perth, Seigneur Anglois", "M. Innèse, Prêtre Ecossois", "M. Callaghan, Curé de Cour Cheverny" and "M. Jankins, Solitaire de Port Royal".

6 *Dictionnaire des Livres Jansénistes*, I, p. 504; II, pp. 166, 241; III, pp. 133, 234; IV, pp. 1, 8, 14, 174.

7 About 1603 according to Port Royal sources, in 1593 according to Vacant et Mangenot, *op. cit.* (article "Jansénisme"), which would seem an error. According to his Epitaph, printed in the *Irish Eccl. Record*, 3rd ser., vol. 7, p. 742, he was sixty-three in 1666.

twenty-five years, and in 1643 was elected Rector of the University. At Louvain he certainly knew Jansenius, and according to Gerberon he was one of the first to side with the Jansenists in the controversies that arose upon the publication of Jansen's posthumous book. As early as 1641—the *Augustinus* had appeared in 1640—he published anonymously his *Homologia Augustini Hipponensis et Augustini Yprensis de Deo omnes salvari volente*, establishing a parallel between the doctrine of St Augustine and that of Jansenius, and in December of that year he was one of those who furnished an approbation of the *Augustinus*.[1]

In 1642 the Pope, Urban VIII, issued his Bull *In eminenti* which condemned the *Augustinus* as renewing certain errors of Baius condemned by Pius V and Gregory XIII. The Bull, which also prohibited among other books Sinnich's above-mentioned *Homologia*,[2] was not made public till June of the following year.[3] When it was sent to Louvain, Sinnich, as Rector of the University, made difficulties about receiving it, referred the matter to the council of Brabant, and was ultimately sent to Rome with another doctor, Cornelius de Paepe, to explain why the University found it hard to accept a Bull which seemed to proscribe the doctrine of St Augustine under the name of Jansenius, a Bull which, moreover, by its defects inclined the doctors to believe that it was not a genuine one—the various copies of the Bull showing discrepancies.

Sinnich and his companion left Louvain in September 1643. Jansenist historians relate that the partisans of the Bull sent portraits of Sinnich to various places through which he was to pass, and Sinnich, fearing for his liberty, entered Paris in a closed carriage, partook only of food prepared by his servant or under his servant's supervision, remained incognito in Paris, spending three days and three nights in consultation with M. de Saint-Cyran—then drawing near the end of his earthly career, with his nephew M. de Barcos and with Arnauld, and finally he left

1 Gerberon, *op. cit.* 1, p. 41.
2 *Bullarum Romanorum Pontificum amplissima Collectio, Tomus Sextus, Pars Secunda, Romae*, 1760, p. 275.
3 Gerberon, *op. cit.* 1, p. 67.

again prudently in a *carrosse fermé*. On October 11th Saint-Cyran departed this life.

The deputies arrived in Rome on November 8th. It would be wearisome to give a full account of all their movements, their stay of many months, their visits, their conferences, their audiences, their delays and disappointments, their ponderous dissertations presented to popes and cardinals. One may read of them at great length in Gerberon's history.[1]

One or two incidents may perhaps be mentioned. In an audience which the deputies had with Cardinal Barberini the cardinal asked Sinnich from which country he was. Sinnich answered that he was Irish, and the cardinal remarked that the Irish were as a rule greatly attached to the Holy See, and that far from opposing its decisions they were wont to uphold them. "We do not oppose the Holy See nor its decisions," was Sinnich's reply, "we oppose those that circumvent the Holy See, and we do not look upon this Bull as emanating from the Holy See, but as the work of those who gave rise to it through their impostures."[2] One of the earliest visits of the deputies was to Father Luke Wadding, who received them very kindly.[3] In 1645 M. Bourgeois, a doctor of the Sorbonne, appeared in Rome in defence of Arnauld's book *De la Fréquente Communion*, and he betook himself at once to Dr Sinnich and consulted him in all his deliberations, as long as Sinnich remained in Rome. Presumably Sinnich did not understand French, for they conversed only in Latin.[4] Meanwhile Sinnich's companion had died in

1 An excellent summary is given in a few lines by Sainte-Beuve. "Les Jansénistes selon l'usage où nous les verrons de toujours savoir les intentions des Papes mieux qu'eux-mêmes soutenaient qu'elle [the Bull] avait été, en partie, surprise à ce pontife. Urbain VIII, selon eux, avait pensé que, pour étouffer les disputes, il suffisait de renouveler et de confirmer les Bulles de Pie V et de Grégoire XIII, et il aurait ordonné qu'on dressât une Constitution en ce sens, en défendant d'y nommer Jansénius, mais l'assesseur du Saint Office, Albizzi, d'accord avec le cardinal Patron (on était sous le népotisme des Barberins) aurait dressé la Bulle à l'intention des Jésuites, y nommant à plusieurs reprises Jansénius, et signalant en général dans son livre plusieurs Propositions précédemment condamnées chez Baïus." *Port-Royal*, III, pp. 8–9.

2 *Supplément au Nécrologe de l'Abbaïe de Notre Dame de Port-Royal des Champs*, p. 609. 3 Gerberon, *op. cit.* I, p. 94.

4 Bourgeois, *Relation...contenant ce qui s'est passé à Rome en 1645 et 1646*, pp. 9–10, 31.

September 1644, and in the following year Sinnich, finding that nothing was to be achieved and that the new Pope Innocent X was no more likely to be favourable than his predecessor, asked the university to recall him and returned to Louvain toward the close of 1645.

The years subsequent were filled with much laborious writing and more battling against the Bull.[1] At one time the Internuncio suggested that it might be easy to get rid of Sinnich, not a subject of the King of Spain, but an Irishman,[2] and another time, in 1653, he reported to Cardinal Pamfili that Sinnich and his friends had said they would rather let themselves be torn asunder than abandon their doctrine.[3]

The Jansenist M. de Pontchâteau, who visited Sinnich on a journey to Holland, has left a curiously flat picture of one whom his adversaries have represented as an effervescing busybody: "Un bon homme qui n'avoit rien d'élevé dans l'esprit, qui étoit sans cérémonie, assez simple, laborieux au dernier point et emploiant tout son temps à l'étude pendant laquelle il ne vouloit point être détourné".[4]

A long account of his writings is given in Clémencet's *Histoire littéraire de Port-Royal.*[5] One may note a treatise *Utrum damnandus sit Jansenius* which begins with the words *Nullo Jure* and ends with the conclusion *Non potest damnari Jansenius, nisi ridente Pelagio, plorante Augustino*; further a book which by its title recalls Conry's *Peregrinus Jerichuntinus*, namely *Peregrinus Jerosolymitanus*, which made the *Dictionnaire des Livres Jansénistes* remark that the Pilgrim to Jerusalem was no more orthodox than the Pilgrim to Jericho;[6] a tome of 740 pages that was extensively used by Pascal in the preparation of his *Écrits sur la*

1 Gerberon, *op. cit.* I, pp. 202, 207, 224.
2 Rapin, *Mémoires*, I, pp. 144–6.
3 *Ib.* II, p. 182.
4 *Supplémemt au Nécrologe*, p. 612.
5 Pp. 166–93. See also Gerberon, I, pp. 233, 354–6, 419, 539–40, 548; II, p. 90. M. Maire in his *Bibliographie des Œuvres de Pascal*, II², p. 61, gives Sinnich's *Molinomachia* as a work directed against Jansenism, but a résumé of his work in Clémencet, *Hist. litt. de Port-Royal*, I, p. 191, shows that the book is in defence of Jansenius. See also Maire, p. 131, and the index, where Sinnich appears as a Jesuit!
6 *Dictionnaire des Livres Jansénistes*, III, p. 234.

Grâce[1]—*Sanctorum Patrum de Gratia Christi et Libero Arbitrio dimicantium Trias*, and a work in two folio volumes, *Saul Exrex*, much esteemed by Nicole who referred to it readers of his Wendrock notes on the *Provinciales*, desirous of further arms against the Casuists.[2] Arnauld accounted Sinnich as one of the most learned theologians of Europe in the matter of grace.[3]

Sinnich died in 1666 at the age of sixty-three. The Jesuit Father Rapin speaks of his attachment to the Jansenists as late as 1660,[4] but when, shortly after the Restoration, the Irish Franciscan Peter Walsh presented the *Loyal Remonstrance* (in which a number of Irish Catholics protested their fidelity in terms which now and again recalled James I's Oath of Allegiance, a formulary in which some of the Irish clergy saw a kind of Jansenist opposition to ultramontane authority) the Louvain Theological Faculty was among those who censured it, greatly to the displeasure of Walsh. Foremost among them was " John Synnick, an Irishman,...a Doctor of Divinity and famous and leading in the University of Louvain (forasmuch as he had been their agent at Rome...for the booke or five propositions fathered on Iansenius)". Whether he was so eager about the censure "partly or only wholly to recover himself at Rome by this means" Walsh leaves others to judge,[5] but it certainly marks, on the part of Sinnich, an attitude to the Holy See very different from that of his younger days. His last will shows him in complete submission.[6]

1 Pascal, *Œuvres* (éd. Gr. Écrivains), XI, pp. 104, 108–258 *passim*. "Cet ouvrage est de Sinnich, théologien de Louvain. Une note manuscrite d'Adrien Le Paige ajoute que les titres ont été composés par Arnauld."
2 *Litterae provinciales...A Willelmo Wendrockio...E Gallica in Latinam linguam translatae et Theologicis notis illustratae....Editio quinta....Coloniae*, 1679, pp. 638–48 (*De tribus Casuistarum flagellis....De libro Sinnichii Doctoris Lovanensis*).
3 Arnauld, *Œuvres*, XIX, p. 58.
4 Rapin, *Mémoires*, III, p. 101.
5 *History and Vindication of the Loyal Formulary or The Irish Remonstrance*, p. 101. Father Redmond Caron, at one time Professor of Theology at Louvain, was one of the upholders of the Remonstrance. Gerberon shows him present in 1644 at a conference favourable to Jansenism (*op. cit.* I, pp. 144–131—erroneous paging). For the Irish Friars Minor at Louvain and their sentiments "tout conformes à ceux de l'Augustin d'Ipres", see Gerberon, *op. cit.* I, pp. 23, 276, and Clémencet, *Hist. litt. de Port-Royal*, I, p. 115.
6 *Irish Eccl. Record*, 3rd ser., vol. 7, 1886, p. 741.

Let us leave the Irish Louvain theologians for the present, and turn to an Englishman whose name is linked up with the early years of Jansenism and occurs more frequently than any other English name in Jansenist writings, though he himself was not a Jansenist and had no connexions with Port Royal. This was Richard Smith, Bishop of Chalcedon and vicar-apostolic in England and Scotland. In Cerveau's *Nécrologe*[1] he is preceded by la Mère Eugénie Arnauld and M. Fromond, one of the approbators of the *Augustinus*, and followed by M. Bignon, whose sons were among the first pupils of the Little Schools, and by M. Dugué de Bagnols, solitary of Port Royal.

The full title of Cerveau's work explains in part why the Bishop of Chalcedon is admitted to this company—*Nécrologe des plus célèbres Défenseurs et Confesseurs de la Vérité du dix-septième siècle, contenant les principales circonstances de la vie et de la mort des Personnes...qui ont été recommandables par...leur attachement à la vérité et surtout par les persécutions qu'elles ont essuyées au sujet du formulaire et de la part des Jésuites.*[2] He suffered, says the Jansenist Cerveau, a persecution without precedent in the annals of the Church before the rise of the Jesuits. A brief account of what happened will explain more fully the Jansenist interest in the affair, for not only did the Jansenists speak of Smith as of one who had suffered like themselves,[3] but they were wont to say that Saint-Cyran's quarrel with the Jesuits arose in England.[4] Saint-Cyran himself was, indeed, never in England, though if Richelieu had had his own way, Saint-Cyran would have gone there in 1626 as confessor and almoner-in-chief of the young bride of Charles I,[5] and thus perhaps would never have been director of Port Royal; but he declined the honour which would have removed him from his sphere of work.

Bishop Smith was consecrated in 1625 and soon became in-

---

1 Vol. i, p. 54.

2 One finds also, rather unexpectedly in this *Nécrologe* (pp. 4–5), William Barclay (1546–1605) who is included as one of the defenders of the liberties of the Gallican Church in virtue of his book *De Potestate Papae*.

3 E.g. *Hist. du Cas de Conscience*, v, p. 239.

4 E.g. Racine, *Port-Royal*, pp. 25–7.

5 Rapin, *Hist. du Jansénisme*, pp. 171–4; Clémencet, *Hist. générale de Port-Royal*, ii, p. 99.

volved in struggles with the regulars of England who objected
to his claiming the full prerogatives enjoyed by a bishop in
Catholic countries. The Bishop of Chalcedon was a man of
ardent mind, they said, "addicted to the principles of the Sorbonne and the Gallican Bishops".[1] The Jesuits were bitterly
opposed to his regulation that none should hear confession,
unless he had obtained a licence from the bishop. "Ils étaient
accoutumés à l'indépendance par une trop longue habitude pour
pouvoir consentir à cet affaiblissement de leur liberté", explains
a Jansenist writer.[2] However that may have been, the Pope
condemned some of the bishop's proceedings; in the meantime
the controversy attracted the notice of the English government,
which issued a proclamation for his arrest, and in 1629 he retired
to France under the protection of the Cardinal de Richelieu, and
was never enabled to return.

In the controversy Smith found an advocate in Dr Kellison,
president of the English college at Douay, while on the other
side wrote two Jesuit Fathers, Edward Knott, under the name
of Smith, and John Floyd under the name of Daniel a Jesu.
Their works attracted considerable attention in France, certain
propositions were delated to the Faculty of Theology of Paris
by the English secular clergy,[3] and the works were censured.
Floyd, writing under the name of Loemelius, answered the censure in two books "full of fire and brimstone", to use the Jansenist Hermant's expression,[4] and these in turn called forth a
work most famous in the annals of Jansenism, a defence of the
censure in 752 pages, by one who called himself Petrus Aurelius,
and who is universally assumed to be Saint-Cyran, though he
never openly acknowledged himself to be the author. In all
probability the work was written with the aid of his nephew,
M. de Barcos. "We shall find", writes Father Hunter in 1714,
"that the Abbé St Cyran under the Name of Petrus Aurelius
with other Abettors of Jansenism were the chief sticklers for
Dr Kellison against Father Floyd."[5]

1 *Relation of the Regulars*, quoted in Berington's *Panzani*, p. 264 *n.*
2 Hermant, *Mémoires*, 1, p. 8.   3 *Ib.* p. 10.   4 *Ib.* p. 14.
5 *A modest Defence of the Clergy and Religious*, p. 92. Knott and Floyd are made
to reappear in the *Écrits* inserted in the 1659 edition of the *Provinciales*.

The story of this book has often been told elsewhere—how it obtained the approbation of the French clergy who had the works of Petrus Aurelius reprinted at their expense, and how the English Chapter sent a letter of thanks[1] to Petrus Aurelius— and it need not be recounted here.

The letters of Jansenius and Saint-Cyran are full of allusions to the controversy—the two friends send each other propositions extracted from the books of the English Jesuits and think them very bold; Saint-Cyran asks Jansenius again and again to procure him copies of Daniel a Jesu's (Floyd's) and Smith's (Knott's) writings, and Jansenius, who obtains the books with some difficulty, is of the opinion that "Celias" (Saint-Cyran) should write something in reply. The books of Loemelius (Floyd) confirm Jansenius in his impression that the affair deserves a good answer. Finally he acknowledges, in disguised language, the work written by Petrus Aurelius, "cette medecine qu'on a donné à ce Phrenetique", though he believes that the patient, the Society of Jesus, is too ill to be cured, possessed as he is with the idea that he is in good health, and that his doctors are beside themselves.[2]

At the same time Jansenius is interested in an English priest, Anthony Champney by name, a confessor of the Benedictine nuns of Brussels, who had laid down his office, accused of being one of the thirteen priests who had signed the protestation of allegiance to Queen Elizabeth. Champney consulted the theologians of Louvain, among them Jansenius, and they pronounced in his favour, with the result that the Jesuits charged the authors of this deliberation with being heretics who favoured the Oath of Supremacy. A letter of Jansen's even tells of mysterious threats. One of the "Gophorostes" (Jesuits) sent an emissary to Jansenius to show him a copy of Floyd's *Spongia*, and to tell him that "Quinquarbre" (Jansenius) and his friends would feel their sting—"aculeos suos"—as those of Paris had done.[3] "Je ne sçai", exclaims Jansenius, "par quelle destinée il arrive à

1 April 12th, 1633, signed by John Colleton, Dean, and Edmond Dutton, Secretary of the Chapter. Jansenius, *Lettres*, p. 253; Hermant, *Mémoires*, 1, pp. 20–1.
2 Jansenius, *Lettres*, pp. 243, 244–54 (Gerberon's Commentary), 256, 260, 264, 265, 267, 273, 274, 275, 277, 282, 290.   3 *Ib.* pp. 240, 267.

Boëce (Jansenius) quasi toujours d'être aux mains avec Pacuvius (the Society of Jesus)."[1]

But to return to Bishop Smith. When Saint-Cyran was imprisoned in 1638—on the principle, suggests Rapin, that much harm would have been avoided if Luther and Calvin had been imprisoned betimes—the Bishop of Chalcedon, according to this same author, was one of those who went to plead with Richelieu for Saint-Cyran's liberation. He told him, "trop simplement peut-être", that Saint-Cyran was his friend, that he was a very good man, and one who by his great gifts was destined to be a pillar of the Church, but Richelieu turned his back upon the aged bishop "avec un fort grand mépris", thinking it lamentable that the old man should have been so imposed upon. Saint-Cyran's friends, so Rapin says, had prevailed on Smith to undertake the mission, for they persuaded him he owed it to one who had written in his defence against the Jesuits of England.[2]

The story of Bishop Smith's intervention seems plausible enough, for doubtless in France he had come to know those who had so warmly taken up his cause. We read in Lancelot's *Mémoires* that he came to Saint-Cyran's funeral in 1643.[3] He himself lived on for a few years longer, dying in 1655 in the convent of the English Augustinian nuns, and whoever composed his epitaph must not have been far from the Jansenist way of thinking, for the bishop's fate is ascribed to the treachery of his brethren ...*Domino Richardo Smitheo...a falsis fratribus vendito....*[4]

---

1 *Ib.* p. 240. 2 Rapin, *Hist. du Jansénisme*, p. 382.
3 Lancelot, *Mémoires*, I, p. 258.
4 Epitaph printed in Brady's *Episcopal Succession*, III, p. 103. Bishop Smith's story and his connection with Petrus Aurelius is told from the Jansenist standpoint by Hermant, *Mémoires*, I, pp. 6–24; Guilbert, *Mémoires...sur l'Abbaye de Port-Royal des Champs depuis sa fondation*, II, pp. 424–67; Racine (abbé), *Hist. ecclés.* XII, pp. 450–2; XIII, pp. 624 *et seq.*, and others; from the Jesuit standpoint in Rapin, *Hist. du Jansénisme*, pp. 213 *et seq.*, 281, 381. A modern writer, the abbé J. Laferrière, treats the episode in his *Étude sur Saint-Cyran* (Louvain, 1912), pp. 75–85. Among English Catholic authorities favourable to Smith one may mention Dodd, *Church History*, III, pp. 76–9 and Berington in his Introduction and Supplement to *Panzani's Memoirs*. For a fairly modern account see Brady, *op. cit.* III, pp. 74–103.

❧❧❧❧❧❧❧❧❧❧❧

CHAPTER II

In and about Port Royal

IN the very early days of Port Royal when the youthful abbess, la Mère Angélique, was barely eighteen years old, and struggling to reform her convent, to bring it back to the primitive rigour of the Cistercian rule, we find a director who bears an English name, le Père Archange Pembroke. "Un de ces Directeurs qui m'a plus aidé qu'aucun des premiers", writes la Mère Angélique, "a été le Père Archange Capucin, qui avoit une extraordinaire charité pour moi."[1]

The story of these early times is well known—how the little abbess was touched one evening in 1608 by the sermon of a Capuchin, le Père Basile, a chance visitor; how during months of ill-health and family opposition to her austerities she pondered over the changes she believed it right to make; how she induced her nuns in 1609 to forego all private possessions—even the nun who loved her little garden above all things; and how in that same year she prevailed on them to observe a stricter seclusion,[2] and led the way by excluding her own family in that famous Journée du Guichet, September 25th, 1609, when M. Arnauld père, at first highly incensed by this new-fangled notion, ended by giving in to his daughter who had fainted from emotion behind the grating.

But if Arnauld, the tenderest of fathers, became reconciled to his daughter's wishes, he visited his wrath on the abbé de Vauclair, now confessor of the convent, and had him removed for his indiscreet zeal from a position for which he seemed too young. It is about this time that Father Pembroke became

---

1 M. A. Arnauld, *Mémoires et Relations* (1716), p. 144.
2 "Elle ordonna a la portière de luy porter les clefs de l'abbaye dans sa chambre et d'envoyer au parloir ceux qui demanderoient leurs parentes a qui on avoit accoutumé d'ouvrir la porte pour les aller voir dans leurs chambres." B.N. f. fr. MS. 20945, f. 63.

connected with Port Royal.¹ La Mère Angélique told a priest who was visiting the convent that she lacked spiritual guidance, and he spoke on her behalf to an elderly Capuchin of great reputation who came to see her. M. and Mme Arnauld knew of him and were glad to have their daughter under his direction, for the Marquise de Maignelay assured them that this Père Pembroke was wise and kind and would not let their daughter do anything detrimental to her health.

Little enough is known about him, and sometimes he is confused with a Scottish Capuchin, also Père Archange, George Leslie.² He certainly came of a great family, for he was of the house of Herbert. He was son of "le comte de Pembroke", the Earl of Pembroke,³ la Mère Angélique tells us, and a close friend of the Guise family and the duc de Joyeuse, known in religion as Père Ange. "D'une mine vénérable et majestueuse, digne de la grandeur de sa naissance", she describes her director's appearance.⁴ He was prominent in his order, frequently guardian of his convent and definitor of his province.⁵

Father Pembroke was not able to come very frequently to Port Royal, but he gave much useful advice,⁶ saw to it that others

---

1 Materials for a study of Father Pembroke are found in the *Mémoires et Relations* (1716) by la Mère Angélique, pp. 22–3, 144–7, 167; *Mémoires pour servir à l'histoire de Port-Royal* (1737), III (a biography of la Mère Angélique by her niece, Angélique Arnauld d'Andilly), pp. 45–6, 79, 82, 84–5 (or instead of the two fore-going works see *Mémoires pour servir* (1742), I, pp. 58, 59, 77, 98, 99, 102, 104, 105, 280–2, 287; II, 292–6, 301, 338–9); Guilbert, *Mémoires historiques et chronologiques sur l'Abbaye de Port-Royal depuis sa fondation*, II, pp. 24–5; Ubald d'Alençon, *Les Frères mineurs et les Débuts de la Réforme à Port-Royal des Champs*, where Pembroke's letters are printed. See also Sainte-Beuve, *Port-Royal*, I, pp. 177–9, 181, 214, and Bremond, *Hist. litt. du sentiment religieux en France*, IV, pp. 183–6.

2 E.g. B.N. f. fr. MS. 25046, pp. 201–3. See Ubald d'Alençon, *op. cit.* p. 11. There were also in Pembroke's lifetime two brothers, John and William Forbes, also Capuchins who both went by the name of Archangel.

3 Since the word *comte* is used to translate the word "Earl" (e.g. "Parvenue à Wight la duchesse apprit que le gouverneur de l'île était le comte de Pembrock", Batiffol, *La Duchesse de Chevreuse*, p. 228, referring to Philip, 4th Earl of Pembroke), one wonders whether Father Pembroke could have been Edward, son of William Herbert, 1st Earl of Pembroke (1501–70). He entered the order in 1607, by no means young, for twenty years later he struck la Mère Angélique as venerable.

4 M. A. Arnauld, *Mémoires et Relations*, p. 144.

5 For details see Ubald d'Alençon, *op. cit. passim*.

6 Such as the often quoted "Le premier avis qu'il me donna et qui m'a été très utile ce fut de ne laisser jamais parler nos sœurs à pas un Religieux, ni même aux Capucins quand ils prêcheroient comme des Anges". *Mémoires et Relations*, p. 23.

went in his place and that the nuns were taught their catechism; he wrote frequent letters of guidance, occasionally he acted as confessor; now and then he preached there. One reads in a Port Royal manuscript: "Le P. Pembrok capucin fut celuy de qui Dieu se servit le premier pour toucher la jeune abbesse car lorsqu'elle ne pensoit point encore a se reformer il y precha par occasion et fit un sermon sur les jugements de Dieu tres fort qui toucha la jeune abbesse et ce fut alors qu'elle commença a concevoir des pensées pour se mettre dans son devoir et pour se reformer".[1] This does not tally with other Port Royal accounts according to which la Mère Angélique came under the influence of Father Pembroke only after she had contemplated and begun the reform, and there is some confusion here, but it throws an interesting light on his high repute.[2]

He lived a life of great simplicity, and sometimes la Mère Angélique supplied his temporal necessities by sending to him at his convent the plainest of food, as she said—some bread and meat—and he would reply with affectionate gratitude "Vous êtes mal nommée Madame de Port Royal, votre vrai nom est Madame de Cœur Royal".[3] He went everywhere on foot, and when no longer able to walk long distances he rode, like the physician M. Hamon, on a humble ass.

From his letters, written in long-winded, flowery, foreign French, abounding in suave imagery and quaint conceits, he seems the kindest and most benign of directors. Already in his second letter he crosses out the word "obéissant" in the too formal ending, and substitutes the word "affectionné"—"Votre très humble et affectionné à vous servir en Jésus Christ".[4] He writes in the most paternal way to his young charge, perplexed and tossed about, "agitée parmy les flots et tempestes des difficultez innumerables sensibles et poignantes", as he says.[5] "Je veux...par tendre compassion et affection compatire avec

1 B.N. f. fr. MS. 20945, f. 63 (verso).
2 The writer may have been confusing him with le Père Basile, though the subject of his sermon was not the same.
3 M. A. Arnauld, *Mémoires et Relations*, p. 144.
4 Ubald d'Alençon, *op. cit.* p. 19. The first letter is dated Oct. 31, 1609, and in it he speaks of having known her for a very short time.
5 *Ib.*

notre bonne petite Abbesse laquelle en agge jeune et delicate a esté trouvé digne de suivre son doulx espoulx Jesus en la chemin de la Croix."¹ "Que nostre bonne et petite abesse soit du tout ressemblable a son espoux Jesus-Christ."² "Courrage, courrage, ma bonne petite Abbesse, car sy les eslevations de la mer sont merveilleuse, le seigneur est admirable ez lieuz haultes qui convertera ceste tempeste en une doulx calme."³ "Courrage donc ma petite madame, cy Dieu est pour nous, qui sera contre nous?"⁴ "Dictz donc de rechef, ma petite abbesse: ô Seigneur et cher espoux, je suis ta servante et la fille de ta servante, je te offrera moy-mesme en sacrifice de louange."⁵ "Ma petite madame, sy vous trouvez les difficultez grandes considerez le merite de celuy pour qui vous combattez."⁶

Some of the difficulties still arose from the vexed question of family interference, and always his advice was of the most conciliatory. How far, asked Angélique, was she bound to honour and obey her parents? And he replies: "Sy c'estoyt qu'ilz vous voulussent empescher en l'observation de vos vœux ... alors vous ne debvriez pas les escouter, ains plustost choisir de les contrister".⁷ Yet let her not become unnecessarily estranged from a kind father. "Que si son affection naturelle qu'il ne peult oublyer le portayt à choses dont seulement vous receussiez quelque leger empeschement, comme de vous vouloyr voyr plus souvent que le desir de vostre retraicte et solitude ne vouldroyt permettre je croy quant à moy que pour peu de chose comme celà vous ne debvez facilement l'estranger de vous."⁸ Let her write to her father from time to time—"je vous supplie de luy escripre parfois d'un stil doulx et recognoissant".⁹ And as for her mother, Angélique must not think of her presence as harmful; on the contrary, he believes that her words and prayers will confirm Angélique in the path she has chosen.¹⁰

At Port Royal he saw not only la Mère Angélique but the future Mère Agnès, and he was so much impressed by the

---

1 *Ib.* p. 21.   2 *Ib.* p. 20.   3 *Ib.* pp. 21–2.
4 *Ib.* p. 24.   5 *Ib.* p. 26.
6 *Ib.* All these letters were written in the last months of 1609.
7 *Ib.* pp. 15–16.   8 *Ib.* p. 16.   9 *Ib.* p. 22.
10 *Ib.* p. 17.

fervour and the grave maturity of the young girl that he remarked to la Mère Angélique: "Voyez vous Madame votre
jeune sœur ce n'est qu'une Fille de 14 ans et une Novice, mais
j'ose vous dire que quelque jour ce sera une des plus grandes
Religieuses de France".[1] He remembers her in his letters to
Angélique, "Vous suppliant d'avoir esgarde que vostre petite
sœur ne faict rien par excesse, car j'apprehende que sa ferveur
trop indiscret la conduise en quelque extremité";[2] "Vous
suppliant de saluer nostre petite sœur; le command tousjours
d'avoir esgarde à sa santé".[3]

To another of the Arnauld sisters, the future sœur Anne
Eugénie, he gave the benefit of his wise counsel when she was
contemplating a religious life, and here again one finds him on
the side of moderation.[4]

He remained director of Port Royal till 1612,[5] though a letter
of 1613 still shows him writing affectionately and full of concern
for the health of the young abbess.[6] And yet somehow or other
they drifted apart, and la Mère Angélique outgrew the old man.
From 1618 to 1623 she was away at Maubuisson, occupied with
the reform of the convent, and from 1619 to 1622 Saint François
de Sales was her spiritual guide. The last letter we have from
Father Pembroke, written in 1622, is not addressed to la Mère
Angélique but to la Mère Agnès. He is relieved to hear from her,
for he feared that she might have adopted some headstrong
resolution of her sister whom he can no longer understand:
"Ses lumières sont extraordinaires, aussy sont ses sentementez,
elles ebluissent ma veuë, et mon esprit ne peult estendre jusques
là".[7] And writing many years later la Mère Angélique speaks
condescendingly of him, and remarks that he was good enough

---

1 M. A. Arnauld, *Mémoires et Relations*, p. 147.
2 Ubald d'Alençon, *op. cit.* p. 27.   3 *Ib.* p. 30.
4 M. A. Arnauld, *Mémoires et Relations*, p. 167; *Mémoires pour servir à l'histoire
de Port-Royal* (1737), III, pp. 79, 82, 84-5; see also Sainte-Beuve, *Port-Royal*,
I, pp. 181-2.
5 Besoigne, *Histoire*, I, p. 84.
6 Ubald d'Alençon, *op. cit.* pp. 31-3. The abbé Guilbert remarks that he saw
letters from le Père Archange de Pimbrock which showed that he enjoyed the
confidence of la Mère Angélique from 1609 to 1620 (*Mém. hist. et chron. sur
l'Abbaye de Port-Royal depuis sa fondation*, II, p. 24).
7 Ubald d'Alençon, *op. cit.* p. 34.

for what they were at the time. "Si ce bon Père n'eût point été nourri dans la lecture des Casuistes il ne lui eût rien manqué pour être un parfait Religieux; mais n'ayant point d'étude que celle-là, elle lui a fait grand tort, néanmoins il nous étoit meilleur pour ce tems là que nul autre que nous eussions pû avoir et ses conseils étoient proportionnez à ce que nous pouvions faire."[1] He was still alive in 1620, she remarks casually, as of one very old who at that time could scarcely be expected to last much longer, but he lived till 1631 or 1632, beloved by all the English in Paris.[2]

Pembroke's connection with Port Royal belongs to that earlier period of youth which Sainte-Beuve calls the period of Saint François de Sales. Two or three years after Pembroke's death Saint-Cyran became the director, in succession to M. Zamet, Bishop of Langres, and with him Port Royal takes on a darker hue, and salvation becomes a thing of fear and trembling.

Visitors to Port Royal were sometimes struck by the sight of the gardener—he was tall and taciturn, rather fierce looking, and with something un-French about him.[3] He never addressed the nuns, but toiled on in silence and solitude. If one of the Messieurs spoke to him he replied in outlandish French, as on one occasion when, after much talk of the damage wrought in the neighbourhood by a strange wild beast, Fontaine turned to the gardener and asked him what he would do if he saw it coming into his garden, and the gardener replied resolutely, but with a fine disregard for genders: "Je lui fourrerois mon bêche dans son gueule".[4]

Who was he? Where did he come from? What was his name? All one could learn was that he was called M. François— "Monsieur", to distinguish him from the ordinary servants—

1 *Mémoires et Relations*, p. 23.
2 Aug. 14, 1631, according to B.N. f. fr. MS. 25045, p. 47 and f. fr. MS. 25046, p. 117; Aug. 29, 1632, according to p. 203 in this last MS.
3 Fontaine, *Mémoires*, I, p. 302.
4 *Ib.*

and that he was English, an English nobleman, said some. No one knew his family name.

The years went on, and he grew old in the service of Port Royal, and still nothing was known about him. In 1690, writing to that delightful solitary whom Sainte-Beuve calls the Froissart of the Messieurs, namely Fontaine, M. de Pontchâteau adds a postscript to his letter.

"Je rouvre ma lettre", he says, "parce que je ne puis laisser passer cette occasion sans vous prier de nous donner quelques Memoires de ce que vous avez vu à Port Royal....Vous pourriez nous dire, Monsieur, comment et quand M. Hillerin fut touché....Ne savez-vous rien de M. François qui s'en ira sans qu'on sache même son nom? Je pense néanmoins qu'il est dans les plaidoyers de M. le Maître. Ne connoissez-vous pas M. Charles pour ce qu'il étoit? ...Ne savez-vous rien non plus du détail de la conversion de M. de la Rivière et de celle de M. Bascle et de quelques autres de ces premiers frères et fondateurs de notre solitude?"[1]

But M. de Pontchâteau was never to have an answer to his questions, for death carried him away a few days afterwards, and this same year M. François also departed this life. *Memoriæ Francisci, nobilis Angli*, said the epitaph[2] which M. Dodart composed for him, not knowing what other designation to bestow.

Fontaine mused about him as he wrote his Memoirs. "Vous savez aussi, mon Dieu, combien me revient souvent dans l'esprit l'idée d'un de vos bons serviteurs qui étoit des plus anciens habitans de ce désert. C'étoit un Gentilhomme Anglois qu'on appeloit M. François." But he admits that M. François' exterior was not prepossessing. "J'ouvrois les yeux pour tâcher de voir dans ses habits quelque marque de sa noblesse, mais je ne les avois pas assez éclairés pour découvrir une grandeur intérieure sous cette bassesse apparente."[3] He tells us something about M. François' life at Port Royal, but he left to others the care of searching through M. Le Maître's *Plaidoyers* to find out M. François' family name. Here follows what we have been able to discover about the gardener of Port Royal.

1 Fontaine, *Mémoires*, II, pp. 556–8.
2 Printed in the *Nécrologe*, pp. 393–4.
3 Fontaine, *op. cit.* I, pp. 302–3.

Somewhere about 1635 there died in Paris an aged English secular priest, Dr John Cecil, who had at one time led an adventurous existence as a kind of spy and intelligencer, flitting between Spain and Scotland, working and counter-working, sometimes disguised as a soldier, sometimes going under his own name, or again under that of Snowden, or even of Juan de Campo, but he had eventually settled down in France and had become almoner, so we are told, to a princess royal.[1]

When he died he left his small fortune to his nephew Francis Jenkins, but dying, as he did, a foreigner in a strange country, there were difficulties about his legacy. It seems to have been confiscated in virtue of the *droit d'aubaine*, according to which the monarchy claimed the property of any stranger dying in France without having been naturalized, and this in spite of a recent treaty which had abolished the ruling of the *droit d'aubaine* between England and France.[2] Francis Jenkins went to law about his heritage, and the English ambassador in France interested himself in his cause. It was put into the hands of a young advocate not yet thirty years old, but famous already for his eloquence, M. Antoine Le Maître, a nephew of the Arnaulds. The Chancellor Séguier promised the English ambassador and M. Le Maître that he himself would preside when the case came up for judgment.[3]

But things fell out otherwise. Francis Jenkins died in Paris in 1636,[4] and some time afterwards—it must have been at least two or three years later—his son Francis, a young man of about twenty-one, came to France to pursue the cause.[5] He tried to find M. Le Maître, but M. Le Maître, to the stupefaction and dismay of all interested in his earthly career, had withdrawn from the world and had retired to Port Royal, one of the first of that little group known presently as the solitaries or gentlemen of Port Royal.

---

1 *Scot. Hist. Soc. Miscellany* (1893), I, pp. 3–20; cf. A. Lang, *Hist. of Scotland* (1902), II, pp. 408–9, 443–4.
2 Le Maître, *Plaidoyers*, p. 711.
3 *Ib.* p. 712.   4 *Ib.* p. 733 (note by M. Issaly).
5 "La mort de ses parents l'obligea de venir en France soutenir son procès", *Nécrologe*, p. 393.

Francis Jenkins sought him out in his retreat to ask whether he would engage upon his affair, but M. Le Maître replied that he was engaged in something far more important, namely his salvation, and he told Francis that he also would do well to abandon all for this one thing. The young man resolved to follow his advice. He was no student, and M. Le Maître did not urge him to stay on long at Port Royal des Champs where at this time lived only five solitaries[1]—in 1625 the nuns had left Port Royal des Champs, damp and unhealthy, and had moved into a town house known henceforth as Port Royal de Paris. It was here that M. Le Maître sent him, and he became first the porter, for a year or so, and then the gardener for twenty-one years.

This peaceful laborious existence came to a sudden end. For some years the clouds had been gathering around Port Royal and at last the storm burst. The "little Schools" were suppressed, the solitaries scattered, the confessors removed, the pension-naires and novices sent away, both from Port Royal de Paris and from Port Royal des Champs, whither part of the nuns, too numerous now to stay in the Paris house, had returned in 1648.

Things reached a climax in 1664. The new Archbishop of Paris, M. de Péréfixe, irritated by the obstinacy of the nuns who would not sign the formulary condemning the five propositions, thought himself justified in resorting to drastic means. On August 26th he appeared at Port Royal de Paris with the lieu-tenant civil, the chevalier du guet and a train of armed men.

Twelve of the foremost nuns were told that they must get ready to leave Port Royal at once. Eight coaches had accom-panied the archbishop, and the nuns were then and there carried off to exile, singly for the most part, to various convents where other influences might break their stubborn wills. After the coaches had rolled off the archbishop proceeded to visit the convent to see whether there were any secret issues. Was there any back door to the garden? he inquired. And though the nuns assured him that there was none he preferred to see with his own eyes.

All filed out into the garden. Among the company was M. Chamillard, whom the archbishop had established confessor

1 C. Gazier, *Hist. du Monastère de Port-Royal*, p. 98.

at Port Royal in June. He was intensely hostile to Jansenism, and had doubtless felt that the gardener was a dubious character, for in the garden he whispered into the archbishop's ear and drew his attention to a man at work under the trees. The adversaries of Port Royal were wont to see in every solitary some dangerous individual in disguise, and the archbishop was probably not surprised to learn that this was a gentleman and no ordinary gardener. The man, a tall strapping fellow, was called, and the archbishop noting his stalwart frame told him it was more fitting that he should wield a sword than a spade, and that he was to betake himself off at once. The gardener, nothing daunted, replied that he had served the nuns for twenty-one years without pay, but that since M. de Paris was giving him notice, he would ask him for some retribution. "M. de Paris", however, merely told him to be off immediately—a man of his size could go and serve the king.

Francis Jenkins, at this time about forty-five years old, did not become a soldier; he became gardener to one whose name is famous in the annals of Port Royal, the duc de Liancourt, whose exclusion from the sacraments by a Saint-Sulpice ecclesiastic called forth Arnauld's *Lettre à une personne de condition* and *Lettre à un duc et pair*, these letters in turn giving rise to Arnauld's condemnation and to the *Lettres provinciales*. Jenkins remained with the duc de Liancourt for about ten years, till the duke's death in 1674, and then returned to Port Royal, but not to Port Royal de Paris.

In 1669, after the so-called Paix de l'Église of 1668, the convents of Port Royal de Paris and Port Royal des Champs were definitely separated. At Port Royal de Paris remained those who had signed the formulary, and the convent virtually ceases to exist for the Jansenist historian; at Port Royal des Champs were united all those who had fervently opposed the signature. Here Monsieur François took up his abode, tending the gardens, and here he remained for the last twenty-five years of his life "dans le travail des mains, une solitude continuelle, et un grand désir d'aller à Dieu".[1]

1 *Nécrologe*, p. 393.

At first life was peaceful at Port Royal des Champs; the convent was in a flourishing state, the novices were numerous, pensionnaires were admitted again, some of them daughters of former pupils, as, for instance, la petite Gramont, daughter of Elizabeth Hamilton; the Messieurs returned to the neighbouring farmhouse of Les Granges, visitors flocked to the place from all parts.

But in 1679 death took away the duchesse de Longueville, and in her Port Royal lost its most influential friend. For the sake of Condé's sister Port Royal had been tolerated, and the Paix de l'Église had lasted ten years. A month after her death, on May 17th, the Archbishop of Paris, M. de Harlay, appeared in person at Port Royal and signified to the abbess, la Mère Angélique de Saint-Jean, that all the pensionnaires and postulants must leave at once. Nor was this all. The confessors were also to withdraw. The Messieurs must go. It was not a question of orthodoxy at the moment, or of signing the formulary. The new persecution was political rather in its nature, for the king could never forget that the Messieurs had seemed to side with the Frondeurs.[1]

When the abbess asked what they had done to incur such treatment M. de Harlay replied: "Hé, mon Dieu, ne le voit on pas bien? On parle toujours de Port Royal, de ces Messieurs de Port Royal. Le Roi n'aime pas ce qui fait du bruit....Il ne veut point de ralliement. Un corps sans tête est toujours dangereux dans un Etat. Il veut dissiper cela, et qu'on n'entende plus toujours dire: ces Messieurs, ces Messieurs de Port Royal".[2] All these gentlemen disguised as MM. Pierre, Jean and Jacques must withdraw, said M. de Harlay; these penitents in disguise, even though they cloaked their identities from an estimable motive, were suspicious characters and very dangerous.[3]

In June the archbishop desired information about the solitaries who had remained behind in the capacity of servitors. A memorandum submitted to him named: M. Charles, in charge

1 Sainte-Beuve, *Port-Royal*, III, p. 283; v, p. 154; Gazier, *op. cit.* pp. 331, 335–6.
2 Quoted by Sainte-Beuve, *op. cit.* v, pp. 173–4.
3 Bibl. de Troyes, MS. 2271, p. 137 (quoted in Jovy, *Pascal inédit* (1908), I, p. 320 *n.*).

of a farm; M. Hilaire, a kind of general agent; M. Fontenelle, in charge of the poultry yard, the hay and grain, and the visitors; and finally, M. François, the English gardener. "On a distingué toutes ces personnes d'avec les autres domestiques en les faisant appeler Monsieur pour leur donner plus d'autorité sur les gens qui dépendent d'eux. On les nourrit et on les entretient sans gages. Tous les autres domestiques sont valets ou ouvriers qui sont tous à gages."[1] There was also a doctor, an absolute necessity in this unhealthy place; he is not named, but it was the beloved physician, M. Hamon. This little handful was allowed to stay on at Port Royal des Champs.

The years that followed were sad and quiet. No more postulants or pensionnaires were received. M. Arnauld had withdrawn to Holland. Death reaped a constant harvest among the nuns. Now and then M. François was called from the garden to carry with others the dais in a procession, there being a dearth of ecclesiastics and acolytes. One reads in a Port Royal manuscript record for the Thursday before Easter 1680: "Le daix de la procession fut porté par M. Charles, M. François, M. Hamon et M. Bracqueville",[2] and similarly on Good Friday,[3] and again at Easter of the following year.[4] Sometimes M. François put aside his work to help in the sad task of carrying a friend to his last resting place—M. Brandon, M. de Saci in 1684, brought to Port Royal from Pomponne, M. Grenet, a kind superior, M. Thomas, M. Thiboust.[5] We are not told in this chronicle who helped to carry M. Hamon in 1687, but doubtless M. François was one of the bearers.

And finally the day came when M. François too went his way. He departed on October 7th, 1690, in his seventy-second year, *etiam de nomine ignotus omnibus*. He was buried in the church of Port Royal des Champs at the feet of M. de Pontchâteau "avec les mêmes cérémonies que les Religieuses. Ce fut elles

1 B.N. f. fr. MS. 17779, f. 29. "Il en a pris le memoire qu'il a lu et mis en ses poches, m'en devant rendre reponce au premier jour. Je croy autant que j'en puis juger qu'ils resteront tous" (f. 30).

2 *Ib.* f. 89.

3 *Ib.* f. 90.   4 *Ib.* f. 116.

5 *Ib.* ff. 107, 217, 224, 233, 274.

qui chantèrent tout devant la grille".[1] An epitaph composed by
M. Dodart retraced the events of his life.

But he was not long allowed to rest in peace. When Port Royal
was demolished his remains were dug up with those of others in
1711 and 1712, and flung into a ditch in the cemetery of Saint
Lambert. Here he lies to-day with many other nameless dead.
Here lie also M. de Sévigné, M. Hamon and Jacqueline Pascal.[2]

Were there ever any English nuns at Port Royal? There was
one who had come to Port Royal from Maubuisson with la
Mère Marie des Anges Suireau, and her story and that of her
sister is told in the *Relation touchant les deux Demoiselles Maitteland* in the *Vies Intéressantes et Edifiantes des Religieuses de Port-
Royal et de plusieurs Personnes qui leur étoient attachées.*[3] La Sœur
Magdeleine de Sainte-Candide Le Cerf wrote down the tale in
1665 as it had been told to her by the younger of the Demoiselles
Maitteland, and many years later the more or less unknown
compiler of the *Vies intéressantes* added to it the substance of a
little narrative by la Mère Angélique, for she too had written on
the same subject.

The two Demoiselles Maitteland can be identified fairly easily
as the granddaughters of Sir William Maitland of Lethington,[4]
"secretary of Mary Queen of Scots". Before his son James—
the future father of our demoiselles—was six years old, Sir
William had died in prison, his lands were forfeited, and the
widow and orphans were left in great distress. Eventually
James Maitland became a Roman Catholic and married Agnes

1 B.N. f. fr. MS. 17779, f. 301.
2 For Francis Jenkins see in addition to the authorities already quoted: B.N.
f. fr. MS. 17776, ff. 22, 30 and MS. 20945; B.M. Add. 25043, f. 46; *Hist. des
Persécutions*, pp. 304, 326; *Divers Actes, Lettres et Relations...touchant la persécution*,
p. 108; Gerberon, *Hist. du Jansénisme*, III, p. 131; Besoigne, *Hist. de l'Abbaye de
Port-Royal*, III, p. 141; IV, pp. 43–5; Clémencet, *Hist. générale de Port-Royal*, IV,
pp. 462–4; Guilbert, *op. cit.* II, pp. 248–50; III, p. 125; Cerveau, *Nécrologe des plus
célèbres défenseurs*, I, pp. 254–5; Mlle Poulain, *Nouvelle Hist. abrégée*, III, pp. 54–6
(chiefly a reprint of Besoigne); *Almanach de Pratique pour l'année 1734, ou Calendrier
historique des grands personnages de Port-Royal*, p. 58; *Le Calendrier ecclésiastique*, 1735,
Oct. 7; Gazaignes, *Manuel des Pèlerins de Port-Royal des Champs* (1767), p. 36.
3 II, pp. 312–26.
4 R. Clark, "Les deux Demoiselles Maitteland", *Mod. Lang. Rev.* October
1923, pp. 427–34.

Maxwell, daughter of William, fifth Lord Herries, a prominent Roman Catholic. His wife died early, and most of his later life was spent abroad in exile on account of his religion, chiefly in Brussels and Antwerp, in great poverty, with his son Richard and his two daughters, "strangers in ane strange cuntrie as or warss than banischitt, destitut of our auin meanes withe al wants, witheout the confort or the conversation of freendis".[1] The narrative of la Sœur Candide contains many curious, occasionally rather fantastic, incidents of his early life.

When the two Maitland ladies were grown up they went to visit their Protestant relatives in England. It was hoped that some relief might be obtained from them, especially as the position of Catholics in England had improved with the marriage of Charles I to Henrietta of France, but though the relatives were kind and willing to find a rich husband for each of the ladies, yet they laid down as a condition that they must first become Protestants. When James Maitland heard of this he found means to have his daughters conveyed to France, and there he abandoned them to divine Providence, dying himself not long after this in Brussels in 1639.

The two sisters came to Paris with letters of recommendation from Henrietta to the Queen, Anne of Austria, and at court Mme de Longueville heard of their plight and told la Mère Angélique and M. de Saint-Cyran. Both wrote to la Mère Marie des Anges Suireau, a Port Royal nun who had gone to be abbess at Maubuisson, and she declared herself very willing to take in the English ladies. It was found, however, that the younger Miss Maitland was too delicate for convent life, so M. de Saint-Cyran sent only the elder one to Maubuisson.

This Miss Maitland for some reason or other never managed to learn to read or to pronounce Latin, and she was therefore considered unfit to perform the regular duties of a choir nun. Hence, in spite of extreme disinclination for menial work, she voluntarily became a lay sister under the name of Elizabeth de

---

1 James Maitland, "The Apologie for William Maitland of Lidington" (*Scott. Hist. Soc. Miscellany* (1904), II, where see also an Introduction by Andrew Lang).

Sainte-Ludgarde. When she first arrived at Maubuisson she had, like her sister, a very haughty air, we read, and she disliked even to approach the lay sisters, "les sœurs converses qui faisoient la cuisine et d'autres pareils ouvrages parce qu'il en restait quelque mauvaise odeur dans les habits", but having accepted the situation bravely she toiled for twenty-five years, both at Maubuisson and at Port Royal de Paris whither she accompanied la Mère Marie des Anges Suireau in 1648, and no task was too lowly for her. M. de Saint-Cyran esteemed her very highly, and when she died in 1656, she was much regretted by la Mère Angélique.

As for the younger Miss Maitland, M. de Saint-Cyran obtained a pension for her from the convent of Maubuisson; he found a room for her in Paris, furnished it and looked after her "avec une bonté tout extraordinaire". During the time of his imprisonment from 1638 to 1642 and after his death in 1643, la Sœur Anne Eugénie, one of the sisters of la Mère Angélique, took her in charge and saw that her pension was regularly paid, even after la Mère Marie des Anges had ceased to be Abbess of Maubuisson. Two days before la Sœur Anne Eugénie died, in 1653, she sent for la Sœur Candide, writer of the narrative, and entrusted Miss Maitland to her care as a kind of legacy from M. de Saint-Cyran, who had never taken anything more to heart than "l'assistance de cette personne, ayant toujours appréhendé qu'elle fut exposée à souffrir".

Sometime after this the Abbess of Maubuisson, the successor to la Mère Marie des Anges Suireau, died and the new abbess, Mme d'Orléans, declined to continue the pension in spite of all the entreaties of M. de Bernières, that charitable friend of so many English fugitives. Miss Maitland was destitute, and, to add to her cares, her confessor, a priest of Saint-Sulpice, objected to her connections with Port Royal and threatened to refuse her absolution if she persevered. As she sat talking one day to la Sœur Candide M. de Bernières asked to see the sister. "I was unable to sleep last night", he said, "thinking of Miss Maitland. I will take charge of her and pay her pension as long as God enables me to do so."

M. de Bernières remained true to his promise until he died

in exile in 1662, and after this la Sœur Candide obtained permission to make little wax effigies which were sold for Miss Maitland's benefit. Anyone who has seen the striking wax death-mask of la Mère Angélique, to-day at the little museum of Port Royal des Champs, will know what experts the sisters were in this kind of work. But in 1664 persecution broke out afresh, and at the time of writing, 1665, la Sœur Candide says that she can no longer work for Miss Maitland, as she has been deprived of all means. Miss Maitland herself has had to forego her chief consolation, which was to come and see the sisters of Port Royal, the nuns having been forbidden to receive visitors. Enough money remains for Miss Maitland's support till la Saint-Remi, after which, if she finds no charitable friends, "elle pourra bien mourir de faim", being aged and infirm.

It is pleasant to be able to quote a postscript of 1678 by the Abbess of Port Royal des Champs, la Mère Angélique de Saint-Jean, niece of the great Angélique. "Elle vit encore. Dieu par sa providence a toujours pourvu à ses besoins, et on continue d'ici à l'assister et à lui procurer par des personnes amies de quoi la faire subsister. Elle vit toujours fort retirée et craint beaucoup Dieu." To this the compiler of the *Vies intéressantes* adds that he has been unable to discover the date of Miss Maitland's death. One would like to assume that provision was made for her till the very end, but new measures of repression were put upon Port Royal in the following year, 1679, as we have seen. Yet one can at least say that, however great the stress, the charities of Port Royal would be the last to suffer diminution.[1]

The mother of the demoiselles Maitland had been a Maxwell and it is no doubt therefore a cousin of the Maitlands, also a

[1] Besides the foregoing authorities quoted see also B.N. f. fr. MS. 17797, pp. 502-6, 508-14; B.M. Add MSS. 25043, f. 6.; *Nécrologe*, p. 70; *Lettres de la Mère Angélique*, I, p. 554; III, p. 182; Besoigne, *Hist. de Port-Royal*, I, p. 352; J. Skelton, *Maitland of Lethington* (1888, 2 vols.), I, pp. 330-1; Douglas, *Scots Peerage*, ed. by Sir James Balfour Paul (1907), v, p. 295 *et seq.*; *Cal. St. P. Dom.* 1611-18, p. 193; 1619-23, p. 518; 1623-25, p. 306; 1639, p. 374. A cousin of the Misses Maitland "la petite Demoiselle Banatine" was also for a time at Port Royal. See Brégy, *Modèle de Foi et de Patience ou Vie de la Mère Marie des Anges* (1754), pp. 173-4.

granddaughter of William Maxwell, 5th Lord Herries, whom we find at Port Royal de Paris in 1661, a lay sister attached to the infirmary. In this year the pensionnaires, the postulants, the superior and the confessors had been sent away. The new superior, M. Bail, curé of Montmartre, and M. de Contes, doyen of Notre Dame, were ordered to visit both Port Royal de Paris and Port Royal des Champs. They began with Port Royal de Paris. One by one the inmates were questioned—the prioress, the sub-prioress, the nuns, the lay sisters. Their Interrogatoires can still be read to-day in the *Histoire des Persécutions*, and here follows part of the Interrogatoire of la Sœur Marie de Sainte Elizabeth Mazuelle—the name is also spelled Maxuelle in a Port Royal manuscript.[1] The little dialogue is interesting in its simplicity.

Après avoir demandé la bénédiction Mr le Doyen me dit: Comment vous appelés-vous?
R. Sœur Marie de Sainte Elizabeth.
D. Quel âge avés-vous?
R. J'ai 30 ans, Monsieur.
D. D'où êtes-vous, ma Fille?
R. D'Angleterre, mon Pere.
D. Comment êtes-vous venuë ici?
R. Par la Providence de Dieu, mon Pere.
D. Qui est-ce qui vous a amenée?
R. Une de mes Tantes, parce que Dieu m'avoit donné le désir d'être Religieuse et il y avoit une de mes Cousines qui l'étoit en ce pays.
D. A quel âge êtes-vous sortie d'Angleterre?
R. A vingt ans moins trois mois.
D. Combien avés-vous été à faire ce voyage?
R. J'ai été trois mois en tout, à compter du jour que je suis sortie d'Angleterre, jusqu'au jour que je suis entrée en ce Monastère.
D. Avés-vous apporté beaucoup de bien?
R. Rien du tout, on m'a recuë par charité. Je ne sçavois seulement pas parler, on eut la bonté de me mettre avec les Enfants pour m'apprendre....

After two or three theological questions—were the commandments of God impossible? Had Christ died for all? Was Grace sufficient?—M. de Contes returned to more personal questions.

1 B.N. f. fr. MS. 20945, f. 19.

D. Tous vos parents sont-ils Catholiques?

R. Oui, mon Pere, ils ont été persécutés pour la Foi Catholique et moi aussi.

D. N'avés-vous jamais été Hérétique ni instruite de la Religion Hérétique?

R. Non, mon Pere, je n'ai jamais été instruite que de la Foi Catholique et j'ai toujours été avec des Catholiques.

D. Les Meres et les Sœurs ne vous font-elles point de peine?

R. Non, mon Pere, c'est moi qui leur en fais ne leur rendant pas tous les devoirs que je leur dois.

D. A quelle obéissance êtes-vous?

R. Je sers à l'infirmerie, Monsieur.

D. Eh bien! dites-moi, ne sçavés-vous point quelque chose cachée, soit dans l'infirmerie, dans les Sœurs ou dans les Meres, dont il soit necessaire de nous avertir? n'y a-t-il point quelque secret qu'on ne veuille pas nous dire? dites le nous en confiance, si vous le sçavés?

R. Monsieur, je ne sçai rien sinon qu'il y a partout dans ce Monastere une grande union et beaucoup de charité.

D. N'a-t-on pas moins d'amitié pour vous que pour les autres Sœurs étant d'un pays étranger?

R. Non, mon Pere, au contraire, on m'a toujours témoigné encore plus de charité.

D. N'avés-vous point regret d'être Religieuse?

R. Non, mon Pere, je n'en ai que de la joie, et je me sens toujours portée à remercier Dieu de la grâce qu'il m'a faite d'être Religieuse en cette Maison.

D. Allés, ma Fille.[1]

This sister must have been among those who left Port Royal de Paris to go to Port Royal des Champs, for thirty-six years later, in September 1697, then about sixty-six years old, she was still working at Port Royal des Champs as a lay sister,[2] but she did not live to see the final dispersion—her name is not in the list of nuns still living in 1709.[3]

There were also some English pupils at Port Royal, but of these it will be more convenient to speak later. Something may, however, be said of an ecclesiastic attached to Port Royal, and with him we leave the relative quiet and seclusion of convent life for a warfare of polemics.

1 *Hist. des Persécutions*, pp. 180–1. See also p. xii.

2 B.N. f. fr. MS. 20945, f. 19.   3 Besoigne, *Histoire*, III, p. 200.

In reading the eleventh *Provinciale*, the one dealing *inter alia* with the Jesuit Brisacier's attack on Port Royal, one comes across this curious passage: "Et parle-t-il avec discrétion quand il déchire l'innocence de ces filles, quand il les appelle *des Filles impénitentes, asacramentaires, incommuniantes, des vierges folles, fantastiques, Calaganes, désespérées et tout ce qu'il vous plaira?*"[1] What, one wonders, are "Calaganes"? And if one proceeds to investigate the etymology of this strange appellation one finds that the word is derived from the name of an Irish ecclesiastic, Dr John Callaghan.

This Dr Callaghan or MacCallaghan[2] was born in 1605 in Killone in the county of Cork, the son of Dermot MacCallaghan, very distantly related to Lord Muskerry.[3] He came to France in 1627, studied "rhétorique" at Nantes in the college of the Oratorian Fathers, "philosophie" at Rennes in 1629–30, and theology for four years at La Flèche under the Jesuit Fathers, living not with them however, but in town as tutor to some children of wealthy parents.[4] He went to Paris, became Doctor of the Sorbonne, and finally returned to Ireland, though in 1642 he was back in Paris or still in Paris, not greatly beloved by the Irish Jesuits there who sent complaints about him to Father Luke Wadding at Rome—he was a man full of ambition, they said, who forced acquaintance at every point, thinking some day to wear a mitre; they were displeased by his intimacy with the nuncio in France, he whispered daily "at the Nunce is ears to have more access unto matters of state".[5]

In Ireland he identified himself with the Confederate Catholics, and after the conclusion of the Ormonde peace in 1646 he became a staunch adherent of Ormonde. At Lord Muskerry's solicitation the Supreme Council of the Confederate Catholics recommended Callaghan in 1646 to the see of Cork, but the Nuncio Rinuccini who had come to Ireland a few months

---

1 Pascal, *Œuvres* (éd. Gr. Écrivains, 1914), v, p. 328.
2 He tells us that his name was originally MacCallaghan. Arnauld, *Œuvres*, xxx, p. 394 (Première Lettre de M. Callaghan). Contemporaries also call him O'Callaghan.
3 *Ib.* p. 391.   4 *Ib.* p. 359.
5 *Hist. MSS. Comm., Franciscan MSS. at Dublin*, pp. 151–2, 178, 197–8, 201, 227.

earlier, wrote to Cardinal Pamfili in cipher that this had been done without consulting him and that others had better qualifications. "O'Callaghan is a doctor of the Sorbonne and an excellent man, but at this crisis it would not be wise to promote one so dependent on the Marquis of Ormonde, and frequently with him in Dublin; since those who are independent have more courage."[1]

Callaghan did not therefore obtain the mitre and he returned to France in March 1647, accompanying Lord Muskerry's son as his tutor,[2] while things grew more strained between Rinuccini and the Supreme Council. He withdrew to Port Royal de Paris and remained there for about two years with M. Singlin and M. Rebours.[3] A little anecdote taken from a Port Royal record shows in what esteem la Mère Angélique held Callaghan, though the incident in question took place a number of years after this first stay at Port Royal de Paris. Once when M. Hamon, the doctor, was staying at Port Royal de Paris during an illness of la Mère Angélique he was asked to go back to Port Royal des Champs to see Dr Callaghan who was lying ill there. One of the nuns in attendance on la Mère Angélique demurred and did not want to let him go—it was not necessary, M. Callaghan was not so very ill. "La Mère se tourna vers elle et luy dit: Ouy, ma Sœur, M. de Calagan, un prestre qui vaut mieux que dix mille filles. Elle dit ensuite que M. Hamon s'en allast, qu'il arriveroit d'elle ce qui plairoit à Dieu et que cela ne la feroit pas mourir plus tost."[4]

It would seem that he used some of the time at Port Royal in writing an account of the past events, for in 1650 there appeared a little book usually attributed to him[5] though sometimes it is

1 Rinuccini, *Embassy in Ireland*, p. 170.
2 Arnauld, *Œuvres*, xxx, p. 398; M. A. Arnauld, *Mémoires et Relations*, p. 214.
3 Arnauld, *Œuvres*, xxx, p. 25. And see p. 23, "Il s'estime heureux d'avoir rencontré...dans les dehors du Monastère de Port-Royal à Paris une retraite favorable".
4 B.N. f. fr. MS. 17797, p. 162. Cf. *Mémoires pour servir* (1742), III, p. 189. It is true that there were two Callaghans attached to Port Royal, but only Dr John Callaghan was alive at this time.
5 Thus in Clémencet's *Hist. litt. de Port-Royal* (Bibl. Mazarine, MS. 4535, p. 3); Brisacier, *Le Jansénisme confondu*, 3e partie, p. 33. In his polemics with Brisacier Callaghan neither acknowledges nor repudiates the authorship.

also attributed to Richard Bellings[1], secretary of the Irish
Confederacy—very likely both had something to do with its
writing, though it may be pointed out here that Bellings did not
leave Ireland till December 1650.[2] This little book, a defence of
the Supreme Council of the Confederate Catholics—*Vindiciarum
Catholicorum Hiberniæ authore Philopatre Irenæo Libri duo*, usually
referred to as *Philopater Irenæus* by French contemporary writers
—is doubtless the one which Hyde had in mind when he wrote
in 1652 that the Pope had hitherto been so utterly unpropitious
to the king that his affairs in Ireland had been destroyed "by
the Nuncio's express and passionate opposition: all which is with
greate clerenesse and courage published in a book sett forth by
a sæcular priest of Irelande, printed aboute two years since at
Paris",[3] and elsewhere Hyde speaks of Callaghan as an honest
man who always preached obedience to the people.[4]

In his book Callaghan gave an account of Irish affairs from
1641 to 1649, but chiefly after the coming of the Nuncio
Rinuccini in 1645. He upheld the principle of obedience to
kings and their magistrates of whatever religion, justified the
Supreme Council of the Confederate Catholics who had concluded the afore-mentioned peace in 1646 with Ormonde, the
representative of Charles I and the Protestant Royalists, and
showed the unreasonableness of the nuncio who had excommunicated the Confederate Catholics upon making the treaty
with Ormonde and had at one time imprisoned Bellings and
Lord Muskerry,[5] to both of whom Callaghan was attached. The
second part of the book deals with a diatribe written in 1649 by
the Irish Franciscan, Paul King, against Rinuccini's opponents.[6]
In 1650 Callaghan left Port Royal to become curé prieur of
Cour Cheverny, near Blois, on the recommendation of
Mme d'Aumont, the lady of the place. Mme d'Aumont had

1 Thus in the catalogue at the B.N. Father Ponce addressed his reply to
Bellings, viz. *Richardi Bellingi Vindiciæ eversæ*, Paris, 1653.
2 Bagwell, *Ireland under the Stuarts*, II, p. 243.
3 *Cal. Clarendon Papers*, II, pp. 144–5.
4 *Clarendon State Papers*, III, p. 158.
5 Bagwell, *op. cit.* II, p. 129.
6 *Epistola nobilis Hiberni ad amicum Belgam.*

withdrawn to Port Royal after the death of her husband, and it was there that she met Callaghan.[1]

At Cour Cheverny Callaghan soon came into collision with the Jesuits—they could not forgive him, so we are told by Jansenist writers, for leaving them to go over to MM. de Port Royal, and for joining certain Irish doctors in their opposition to some of the Irish students who had signed a kind of censure of the five propositions.[2] They suspected his rigorism and disapproved of his friendship with M. de Barcos, nephew of Saint-Cyran, established near Cheverny. "Il devint en cette province-là", says Rapin, "un petit patriarche de la nouvelle doctrine."[3]

And so le Père Brisacier—of *Provincial Letter* fame—preached a vehement sermon against Callaghan at Blois in March 1651, in which he called Callaghan and his friends "priests of the devil" and the "gateway of hell",[4] a sermon which brought forth a reply in four parts and eighty pages by a friend and colleague of Callaghan, Étienne Lombard, abbé du Trouillas, afterwards preceptor of Mme de Longueville's son, the comte de Saint Paul.[5] The writer relates that not only had Brisacier attacked Callaghan in his sermons—for there were several sermons of invective—but he had sent a woman to Cour Cheverny to tell the inhabitants of the place that their priest was a heretic, and that Brisacier would shortly come himself and preach in their streets what he had preached in the church at Blois.[6]

Next appeared a Latin satire, *Calaghanus an Satyrus?* which Arnauld, remembering a similar attack on Godeau, Bishop of Grasse, attributed to the Jesuit Father Vavassor. "Ce Jésuite demande *Godellus an Poëta?* Il demande *Callaghanus an Satyrus?*

1 Arnauld, *Œuvres*, xxx, p. ii. According to Rapin, Callaghan was Lady Hamilton's and Lady Muskerry's director, and it was they who introduced him to Mme d'Aumont, but she had known him for the past twelve years. Lady Hamilton did not come to France till the year after Callaghan went to Cour Cheverny. Rapin, *Mémoires*, i, pp. 131–2; Hermant, *Mémoires*, i, p. 565; R. Clark, *Anthony Hamilton*, p. 5.
2 Arnauld, *Œuvres*, xxx, p. ii; Rapin, *Mémoires*, i, pp. 410–11.
3 Rapin, *Mémoires*, i, p. 338.   4 *Response* (see below), p. 25.
5 *Response à un sermon prononcé par le P. Brisacier Iesuite dans l'Eglise de Saint Solene à Blois le 29 mars 1651.*
6 *Ib.* p. 5.

Mais y a-t-il une seule personne pieuse qui n'ait ici la pensée de demander *Jesuita an Christianus?*"¹ Arnauld was, however, mistaken,² and the pamphlet with its allusions to Ireland was probably in part from the pen of some of the Irish, and an attack on *Philopater Irenæus*. The satire with its violent invectives passing from the suggestion that Callaghan be relegated to Ireland amid the swine, to an offer to provide gallows for him,³ created an unfavourable impression, and Brisacier suggested that Callaghan had probably written this libel himself in order to bring discredit on him, Brisacier, to whom it would be attributed.⁴

The Jesuit was none too pleased by the appearance of this little book, for it seemed to cut the ground from under his feet —he himself was writing a reply to the reply to his sermon, and presently there appeared *Le Jansenisme confondu dans l'Advocat du Sr Callaghan.*⁵ This pamphlet attacked Callaghan's person—he was of the dregs of the people—a calumny which Callaghan attributed to Father Ponce; he had arrived at their collège in Quimper in a beggarly condition, he had remained there five or six years as valet, "correcteur" and "balayeur", so much so that his successors, those who chastised the unruly pupils⁶ and those who swept the chapel, were still called "Callaghans"; he had been supported by the Jesuits for eight or ten years and had repaid them with rank ingratitude; he had been banished from Ireland for having leagued himself with the heretics; he was the cause of the misfortunes of Ireland; his work the *Philopater Irenæus* was a mass of falsehoods; his doctrine had been censured in Ireland; he had been excommunicated by the Pope.⁷

It also attacked his Jansenism—"le voyla Iansenius, le voyla S. Cyran, le voyla ce Docteur Callaghan qui sont les lumières nouvelles du monde";⁸ it went on to attack the principal

---

1 Arnauld, *Œuvres*, xxx, p. 68.   2 Sainte-Beuve, *Port-Royal*, III, p. 50.
3 A number of extracts are printed in Arnauld, *Œuvres*, xxx, pp. 68–72.
4 Letter from Brisacier, printed in Arnauld, *Œuvres*, xxx, pp. 74–5.
5 "Par le P. Brisacier de la Compagnie de Jesus. Avec la deffence de son Sermon fait à Blois. Contre la responce du Port Royal", 1651.
6 From Arnauld, *Œuvres*, xxx, p. 76, one infers that a "correcteur" was one who wielded the rod.
7 *Le Jansenisme confondu, passim,* esp. Advis au Lecteur and 3e partie, pp. 33–4.
8 *Ib.* 3e partie, p. 4 *et passim.*

Jansenists and the nuns of Port Royal, adepts of a new religion called "les filles impénitentes, les désesperées, les Asacramentaires,...les Callaghanes" and other names—the original of the religion was at Port Royal and a copy of it at Cour Cheverny under the direction of the sieur Callaghan.[1] The perfection to which the new penitents aspired was to be found in "les idées Callaghaniques, les grotesques de S. Cyran et les fables du Port Royal".[2]

Mme d'Aumont, who had been instrumental in getting Callaghan appointed to Cour Cheverny, complained to the Archbishop of Paris, M. de Gondi, uncle of the future Cardinal de Retz, and Brisacier's book was censured on December 29th, 1651.[3] As for Callaghan, he replied forthwith in a *Lettre à un-docteur de Sorbonne de ses amis touchant les principales impostures du père Brisacier*,[4] giving an account of his family to show that he was not of the dregs of the people. If Lord Muskerry, his distant relative, were in France, he would bear witness to what he said; Muskerry's son was at Caen and could be asked to vouch for him, or inquiries could be made of the Marquis of Ormonde, Sir George Hamilton or Monsieur Bellings, all in Paris. These gentlemen, as well as M. le Chevalier d'Igby, could also say whether he had really been the ruin of Ireland. He was not rich, it was true, but he had never been as destitute as Brisacier reported, he had never in his life been at Quimper, and neither at Rennes nor at La Flèche had he lived with the Jesuits, though he had studied under them. A testimony from Bellings was subjoined, showing that Callaghan was of honourable descent.[5]

A second letter by Callaghan gave an account of a conversation he had had with the Bishop of Chartres to request his protection.[6] Brisacier in the meantime leapt into print again with a *Lettre d'importance sur le livre du Jansenisme confondu composé par le R. P. Brisacier contre le Sr Callaghan* to which Port

---

1 *Ib.* 4ᵉ partie, p. 6 *et passim*.   2 *Ib.* 4ᵉ partie, p. 11.
3 Hermant, *Mémoires*, 1, pp. 564–6; Arnauld, *Œuvres*, xxx, pp. iii–iv.
4 (Jan. 5, 1652.) Also attributed to Arnauld and printed in *Œuvres*, xxx, pp. 391–401.
5 Printed in Arnauld, *Œuvres*, xxx, pp. 403–4.
6 *Ib.* pp. 405–13.

Royal replied by a *Défense de la Censure de M. de Paris*.[1] Then Brisacier produced *Les preuves authentiques et juridiques des qualités de Correcteur et Balayeur exercées...par le Sieur Callaghan ...dans la ville de Quimper Corentin es années 1626–1627*,[2] which Callaghan attacked in a *Troisième Lettre*,[3] and Arnauld in a *Réfutation d'un Ecrit nouvellement publié à Blois par le P. Brisacier*.[4] Finally Arnauld massed all his batteries and delivered an attack in six parts and 340 pages, *L'Innocence et la Vérité défendues*,[5] which Brisacier counter-attacked in *L'Innocence et la Vérité reconnues dans les preuves invincibles de la mauvaise foy du Sr Jean Callaghan, Ibernois*.[6]

It would be futile to analyse all these polemics.[7] One notes *en passant* that Brisacier in his *Preuves authentiques* has reduced the five or six years at Quimper to one, but he has collected a number of letters to testify to Callaghan's presence at Quimper. We are no longer told that, like the Pharaohs and Caesars of old, Callaghan had given his name to a dynasty, the Callaghans, cleaners and disciplinarians, but a witness relates that at La Flèche the Jesuits gave Callaghan a large loaf of bread once a week and soup every day, and that the stone on which Callaghan sat awaiting his soup was called a "Callaghan" to this day— more than twenty years after![8] Brisacier's *Innocence et Vérité reconnues* seems practically a reprint of the *Preuves authentiques* with some additional matter,[9] though the story of the Callaghan stone has disappeared.

Callaghan too collected letters of attestation, among them one of Charles II declaring him to be a faithful subject and not

1 Printed in vol. xxix of Arnauld's *Œuvres* ("On varie sur l'Auteur de cette Défense", p. vii).

2 May 1652, a pamphlet of 8–10 pp. No copy seems in existence, but it is described in Arnauld's *Réfutation* (*Œuvres*, xxx, pp. 431–55).

3 May 1652, Arnauld, *Œuvres*, xxx, pp. 414–24.   4 *Ib.* pp. 431–55.

5 July 1652, reprinted in *Œuvres*, xxx, pp. 1–378. A copy of this was among Ormonde's books at Kilkenny (*Hist. MSS. Comm.*, *Ormonde MSS.*, N.S., vii, p. 525).

6 1653. This last pamphlet was not known to Arnauld—he learned of its existence only a short time before his death. *Œuvres*, xxx, p. ix.

7 Arnauld, *Œuvres*, xxx, p. 452.   8 Two of them are known by name only.

9 One infers this from Callaghan's *Troisième Lettre* which seems directed against *L'Innocence et la Vérité reconnues*, but is earlier in date and deals with the testimonials of the *Preuves authentiques*.

responsible for the ruin of Ireland,[1] but he found more difficulty in getting letters from Rennes where people hesitated about helping one "enfoncé dans le Jansénisme jusques par dessus la tête".[2]

The probable explanation of the controversy, as far as the Quimper episode goes, is one of mistaken identity, since even Brisacier's witnesses speak of a second Callaghan attached afterwards to Lord Muskerry's son,[3] a description fitting our Callaghan, who in turn speaks of having known another theological student John Callaghan in France, and of there having been at one time three priests by the name of Callaghan in Paris. There were two Callaghans attached to Port Royal.[4] The virulence of the attack on Callaghan is no doubt due to the fact that it came jointly from two quarters—the Jesuits who saw in him a Jansenist, and the Irish ecclesiastics of the Rinuccini party, especially Father Ponce, who saw in him an opponent of the nuncio.

At the time that Brisacier's last-named book appeared Callaghan was busy with other things—nothing less than plans for a mission to Rome on behalf of Charles II. It will be more convenient to treat of this in the next chapter, and it will be sufficient to note here that his Jansenism helped to bring the mission to nought.

Callaghan died on May 19th, 1664, aged 59; he desired to be buried at Port Royal de Paris, but this was impossible on account of the persecution then at its height.[5]

---

1 Printed in Arnauld, Œuvres, xxx, p. 381. Paris, March 4, 1652.
2 Ib. p. 450.
3 L'Innocence et la Vérité reconnues, p. 21 (two mentions).
4 "Milord de Muskry...ayant déjà quelque connaissance à Port Royal par le moyen des deux Messieurs de Callaghan, Prêtres de son Pays, dont celuy qui est vivant a été précepteur de son fils." M. A. Arnauld, Mémoires et Relations, p. 214. Refers to the year 1655. Dr John Callaghan did not die till 1664.
5 Bibliothèque Mazarine, MS. 4535 (Clémencet's Histoire littéraire de Port-Royal, vol. III, 24ᵉ pièce, pp. 2–3). See also pp. 1–13 of this manuscript for a general account of Callaghan. Also in addition to the foregoing references: Supplément au Nécrologe de Port-Royal, p. 626; Mémoires pour servir (1742), II, pp. 100–4; Cerveau, Nécrologe des plus célèbres Défenseurs, I, pp. 92–3; Gerberon, Hist. du Jansénisme, I, pp. 484–8, 512 et seq.; II, pp. 68 et seq.; Besoigne, Hist. de l'Abbaye de Port-Royal, IV, pp. 383–4; Clémencet, Hist. générale de Port-Royal, III, pp. 177 et seq.; Hermant, Mémoires, I, pp. 496, 532–3, 564, 567, 576, 580, 581; Arnauld, Œuvres, xxxv, pp. 100–16; Rapin, Mémoires, I, pp. 130–1, 338, 410–12; III, p. 301.

CHAPTER III

Port Royal and the Exiles
(1647–1656)

" IT is true", remarked the Nuncio Piccolomini, writing from Paris to Cardinal Chigi in September 1661 about Charles II, "that the Jansenists are supposed to enjoy the king's friendship, they having rendered him some services while he was in France and having supplied him with funds."[1] And it is very true that Port Royal, persecuted itself, had shown much kindness, not only to Charles, but also to the other exiles who were more or less dependent on the charity of pious benefactors.[2]

As early as July 1647 la Mère Angélique wrote to her friend the Queen of Poland, Marie de Gonzague, "Outre nos miseres nous participons encore à celle de l'Angleterre, y ayant ici une grande quantité d'Ecossois et d'Anglois si miserables qu'ils font une extrême pitié".[3]

All joined in helping the fugitives—the nuns of Port Royal, the Messieurs, the duc de Luynes, a fervent Jansenist who had built himself the country-house of Vaumurier near Port Royal des Champs, M. de Bernières, another of the *amis du dehors*, Mme d'Aumont, and the convent of Maubuisson under la Mère Marie des Anges Suireau, herself Abbess of Port Royal from 1654 to 1658. "Quantité...d'Hybernois et d'Anglois... ruinez par les guerres ont été tirez de l'extrémité de la misère par cette bonne Abbesse",...:"il est incroyable combien elle en a nourris et pourvus."[4]

1 Vatican, *Nunz. di Francia*, vol. 120, quoted by Cl. Cochin, *Bulletin du Comité flamand* (1908), p. 340.
2 The pages that follow are not intended to minimize the charitable effort of others, such as M. Olier who was anxious to help Charles both in spiritual and temporal matters. *Vie de M. Olier*, II, pp. 320–2, 326.
3 M. A. Arnauld, *Lettres*, I, p. 337. For one or two examples of her charity see B.N. f. fr. MS. 17797, pp. 130, 132.
4 M. A. Arnauld, *Mémoires et Relations*, p. 46; *Lettres*, II, p. 562; cf. Brégy, *Modèle de Foi et de Patience*, p. 165.

The Queen of England was invited to stay at Port Royal de Paris, but she preferred to found a community of her own at Chaillot—which was perhaps just as well, judging from an outspoken but cryptic remark of la Mère Angélique: "Je suis bien aise que la visite de la reine d'Angleterre se soit bien passée. Que Dieu par sa grâce nous préserve de son retour".[1]

In the spring of 1651 Sir George Hamilton left his country, Ireland, for France with his wife, Ormonde's sister, and their seven children—one of these was Anthony, the future author of the *Mémoires de Grammont*. Hamilton had lost everything and was totally ruined, so that one finds him applying for relief to the French court through Lord Jermyn, failing which he would be "a very unseasonable and unwilling burden upon His Majesty's care who, God knows, had need bestow it wholly upon himself".[2]

What help Sir George obtained from the French court we do not know, but it is very likely at this time that Port Royal came to the rescue, and in all probability Dr Callaghan, who had been tutor to Lady Hamilton's nephew, young Muskerry, acted as intermediary. The gentlemen of Port Royal helped Sir George and his sons, and the sons of his brother-in-law, Lord Muskerry, who was still in Ireland; the nuns looked after Lady Hamilton and her sister, Lady Muskerry, and their daughters; Elizabeth Hamilton, the future Madame de Gramont, and one of her sisters, Helen Muskerry and possibly also one of her sisters, became pensionnaires at Port Royal des Champs, and since Port Royal was in straitened circumstances, the duc de Luynes, Mme d'Aumont and M. de Bernières contributed funds for their subsistence. The little girls remained there for seven or eight years, wearing the cast-off clothing of those who had taken the

1 Baillon, *Henriette-Marie de France* (Paris 1884), p. 279; J. Cartwright, *Madame* (London 1894), p. 25; M. A. Arnauld, *Lettres* (May 19, 1651), 1, p. 558. A nun of a community prejudiced against Port Royal, on hearing of this visit, remarked "qu'il eût autant valu que cette Princesse eût été à Charenton " (Arnauld, *Œuvres*, xxix, p. 564), Charenton being a Huguenot place of worship, showing once more how often Jansenism and Calvinism were compared.
2 *Hist. MSS. Comm., Ormonde MSS.* N.S. 1, p. 259; Clark, *Anthony Hamilton*, pp. 5–8.

veil. Helen Muskerry was left at Port Royal till 1661, when she was forcibly removed with the other pensionnaires. Lady Hamilton and Lady Muskerry stayed for a while at Vaumurier with the duc de Luynes and later at Port Royal de Paris.[1]

As for their master, Charles II, "leur prince comme eux recevait des assistances".[2] La Mère Angélique was very favourably impressed by what she heard of him. "On dit beaucoup de bien de ce roi, et même (mais cela est fort secret) il a quelque bonne disposition à se faire catholique."[3] The possibility of such a conversion made it doubly desirable to help him. Charles, so la Mère Angélique relates, told a friend of Port Royal that he was desirous of sending an emissary to the Pope, to ask for his help in return for the promise to give freedom of conscience to the Catholics upon his restoration, but that he had no funds wherewith to finance such a mission. Port Royal would have furnished the money for such a worthy cause, but it had to be put off, "à cause de quelque chose qui est arrivé", she says mysteriously,[4] though the complications were probably greater than she knew.

Among the Clarendon Papers is a letter from Dr Callaghan, dated 1653, in which he urges recourse to the Pope as the only sure means for the king's restoration, but requests that the proposal be kept secret.[5] Charles had already tried to negotiate with Rome, and with but indifferent success;[6] he seems to have accepted Callaghan's proposal rather half-heartedly,[7] but in March Sir Edward Hyde announced that Lord Taaffe and Dr Callaghan were to be dispatched shortly to Rome;[8] early in April they were almost ready to start,[9] and since their departure was bound to attract much attention Hyde thought it best to explain the nature

---

1 B.N. f. fr. MS. 17797, p. 47; MS. 20945, ff. 69, 70; *Mémoires pour servir* (1742), iii, p. 12; Guilbert, *Mémoires hist. et chron. sur l'Abbaye de Port-Royal des Champs*, iii, pp. 267–8.
2 B.N. f. fr. MS. 20945, f. 69.
3 M. A. Arnauld, *Lettres* (May 1, 1653), ii, pp. 317–18.
4 *Ib.*
5 *Cal. Clarendon Papers*, ii, p. 179.
6 Scott, *The King in Exile*, pp. 173, 284, 294–5, 374.
7 R.O. *Roman Transcripts*, vol. 103, pp. 7–8.
8 *Cal. Clarendon Papers*, ii, p. 183.   9 *Ib.* p. 190.

of the mission to Secretary Nicholas. "You must know many of the clergy, the Bishops and the Ulster Irish are very busy at Rome to solicit the Pope to recommend them the Protection of some foreign Prince, alledging that the King hath withdrawn his protection from them and left them to be destroyed by English rebels. Many other of the most considerable Irish Catholics have besought the King to send some person to Rome to inform the Pope how untrue all these suggestions are, and how wickedly his Nuncio and some of the Bishops have behaved themselves." Callaghan and Taaffe had no other commission than "to make the truth of the proceedings in Ireland appear", and so Hyde conceived that no wise men could take scandal at this journey, unless they wished the king to renounce all help from Catholic princes "which sure none but the Presbyterians can desire".[1]

The nuncio in Paris, without knowing the inmost reasons for this mission, suggested to Charles that it would be better to find out first of all whether such an embassy would be acceptable to the Pope, before dispatching the emissaries, but Charles replied that everything was decided and requested a letter of recommendation for Callaghan and Taaffe which the nuncio could not well refuse.[2]

But a week later the nuncio writes home again in some alarm —"il Calegano", so he had just heard, was going to Rome at the instigation of some Jansenists and provided with their funds.[3] An even stronger letter had already gone from Father Ponce to Massari, secretary of the De Propaganda Fide. This Father Ponce, an Irish Franciscan whom we have already met as an adherent of the Nuncio Rinuccini in Ireland, had dispatched a certain Dr Tyrrell to Charles to point out to him the unsuitability of sending persons who could not possibly be acceptable to his Holiness, but Charles again said that everything had been settled in his Council and that he could not act otherwise. The truth, explains Father Ponce, is that Dr Calla-

1 *Clarendon State Papers*, III, pp. 158–9; cf. *Cal. Clar. Papers*, II, pp. 200–1.
2 R.O. *Roman Transcripts*, vol. 103, pp. 7–8.
3 *Ib.*

ghan, a Jansenist, had procured "un buon viatico" for himself and Taaffe from Jansenist sources under the pretext that he, Callaghan, could accomplish great things for the Jansenists in his dignity of "Agente d' un Re", which king, although a heretic, was nevertheless, so Callaghan had explained to the Jansenists, inclined to become a Catholic in return for help. Since the king had not money to give to those he wished to send, he was determined to send those that could go at their own expense. His Holiness, Ponce urged, should be informed of all this, so that these men might accomplish nothing either for the king or for the Jansenists, nor should they even be received. For not only was Callaghan a Jansenist, but he had written "infamemente" against the Nuncio Rinuccini.[1]

And so one is not surprised to hear that because of the "false and pestilential reports" as Hyde calls them, the "discourses and calumnyes raysed and scattered by persons of all religion" the mission had to be abandoned;[2] for not only did the religious orders and the Jesuits oppose Callaghan's going on account of his Jansenism, but the Protestants were alarmed by the terms that Callaghan and Taaffe were said to be empowered to offer,[3] and Nicholas thought the king wise to have given up the mission, "albeit some say it hath been principally the Queen's doing because they were to have gone upon the account of the Jansenians of which profession that Doctor is a chief man".[4] Dr Callaghan, who probably knew from what quarter opposition had arisen, at once set about to "undertake Father Pontius in earnest", and Hyde believed that he would handle him as he deserved.[5]

1 R.O. *Roman Transcripts*, vol. 95, no. 79 (April 4, 1653); cf. Bellesheim, *Geschichte der Katholischen Kirche in Irland*, II, p. 452.

2 *Cal. Clarendon Papers*, II, p. 197.

3 *Nicholas Papers* (Camden), II, pp. 7–8.

4 *Ib.* p. 10. In return Hyde wrote back that the Queen would never forgive him, Hyde, nor Ormonde, for proposing Taaffe and "O'Calloghan" for the mission to Rome rather than her confessor, the Abbé Montagu. *Cal. Clarendon Papers*, II, p. 201.

5 *Cal. Clarendon Papers*, II, p. 202. On p. 267 Hyde speaks of the death of Callaghan, but according to Port Royal records he lived till 1664. Either this must have been a wrong report, or it may refer to a second Callaghan—there were two connected with Port Royal, as we have seen.

All this time, ever since 1649, the battle over the five propositions was being waged. In May of this year, 1653, Thurloe, Cromwell's secretary of state, was informed from Rome that "the difference touching the Jansenians" was not yet ended "though congregations do daily sit, and very intricate is the matter".[1] The Bull of Innocent X condemning the five propositions ("Cum occasione...") was published in Rome at the end of the month and received in Paris a month later. "At last the pope declared his mind against the Jansenists", says a letter from Paris preserved among the Thurloe papers, "and sent his bull of excommunication hither to his nuncio by the last post against the said Jansenists, that they shall not teach or meddle in that opinion concerning the 5 points which were sent to you long since"—it is interesting to note the five points being sent to England. "The lord nuncio had audience last Thursday before the king, queen, Mazarin, and the whole court, shewing them that bull which they accepted willingly....I do not yet know what they will make of it in the university, for I believe there may be a quarrel about it soon."[2]

"What a strange transmutation is here!" writes Thomas Cordell from Paris to Sir Ralph Verney, "above 100,000 hereticks made with a word of Innocentus' mouth."[3] Hyde notes with interest a week later that "already divers little discourses are printed against the Pope's Bull against the Jansenists",[4] and he does not think the Jansenists likely to acquiesce in "the Pope's determination".[5] Condemnation of the Jansenists is so rare among Englishmen other than certain Roman Catholics that one is surprised to find a royalist divine, Richard Watson, "exceedingly glad the Jesuits have got the better of the Jansenists at Rome, for Christianity's good sake; the latter are a pack of villains, worse ten times, if possible, than the Puritans".[6]

---

1 *Thurloe Papers*, I, p. 238. See also *Journal of Sir John Finch, Hist. MSS. Comm., Finch MSS.*, p. 66.
2 *Thurloe Papers*, I, p. 319, July 5, 1653.
3 *Hist. MSS. Comm., Appendix to 7th Report*, p. 459.
4 *Cal. Clarendon Papers*, II, p. 224.   5 *Ib.* pp. 226–7.
6 *Ib.* p. 232. Wesel, July 29th. Richard Watson was Lord Hopton's chaplain.

But in spite of these hard times the Jansenists did not forget Charles, and when in December 1653 an Irish leader, O'Sullivan Beirne or Beara, left Paris for Ireland "with some relief to Col. O'Brian", that relief, according to intelligence sent to Thurloe from Paris, "was had only from the charity of some congregation here of the late condemned Jansenists, and that by the privy advice of R. C. [i.e. Charles]". The assistance sent was not above two thousand pounds sterling, "but more is promised".[1] Reports also reached England about this time that Charles himself was much given to the Jansenistic opinion "by reason some of them promise to help him with monies and his defenders".[2]

And yet, at this very moment when the Jansenists were helping Charles, they were accused of intriguing with Cromwell. Port Royal, it was said, was full of individuals who consorted together under a cloak of penitence but had dealings with all the enemies of the State. Their emissaries were trying to get Cromwell to France to make war on the French king for the benefit of their party; they had promised him six thousand armed men on his arrival, they wanted to establish a government in France not unlike the one which Cromwell had established in England.[3]

"Imaginez-vous, Monsieur," exclaims la Mère Angélique with consternation, "qu'on va jusqu'à cet excès de nous accuser d'avoir intelligence avec Cromwel, cet horrible monstre parricide de son Roi",[4] and her brother, le grand Arnauld, recalls the accusation in a letter of 1662: "On n'a pas eu honte de porter jusqu'aux oreilles de la Reine Mère que j'avois une étroite intelligence avec Cromwel", he writes. "J'ai sujet de m'attendre", he continues in a half humorous strain, "que l'un de ces jours on publiera que j'en ai avec le Grand-Visir et que nous pensons à nous retirer en Hongrie, sous la protection du Grand-Turc."[5]

1 *Thurloe Papers*, I, p. 626, Dec. 17, 1653. The expedition had to be abandoned eventually, O'Brien having been forced to lay down his arms. Scott, *The King in Exile*, p. 413.   2 *Thurloe Papers*, I, p. 618, Dec. 10, 1653.
3 Hermant, *Mémoires*, II, pp. 110, 314, 351, 357, 533, 535, 536; Gerberon, *op. cit.* II, p. 174; Des Lions, *Observations sur le Jansénisme*, quoted in *Port-Royal*, III, p. 592.
4 M. A. Arnauld, *Lettres*, II, p. 435, Feb. 28, 1654.
5 Arnauld, *Œuvres*, I, p. 301.

Early in 1654 diplomatic relations were resumed between England and France. Charles was no longer recognized in France as a reigning sovereign and withdrew, first to Flanders, then to Cologne, "exilé en quelque sorte dans la Flandre", says a Port Royal writer, "où le grand crédit de celui qui avoit fait coupper la teste au Roy son père l'avoit obligé de se retirer".[1] Before Charles left Paris he instructed Ormonde, a Protestant, but a brother-in-law of Sir George Hamilton and Lord Muskerry, to go and thank M. Singlin and M. de Bernières for all they had done for him and to recommend his Catholic subjects to their charity. M. Singlin was at this time director of the nuns of Port Royal, and M. de Bernières, a lay friend, had given up for the care of the poor all earthly ambition. According to Hermant[2] he had devoted himself specially to the relief of the exiled English Catholics, and Du Fossé tells us[3] that he was a particular friend of "the King of England".

The two Messieurs were not at the time in Paris, so Charles commanded Ormonde to write from Spa in July, and Ormonde with infinite trouble put together a French letter, though he was not sure that it could be called French. Bad as it was, he said, the letter had taken up six times the time he thought a letter could do, but he preferred to write himself knowing that "la secresie", as he called it, was as necessary to the success of the undertaking, as it would be acceptable to Port Royal. The letter is so curious in its quaint, laboured language, and so little known, that it deserves to be given in full.

Monsieur:

Le Roy mon maistre rencontrant en toutes les viles où il a tant soit peu demuré depuis qu'il est sorti de Paris tant d'objects pitoyables des miseres de ces subjects Catholiques d'Irland qu'ils soufrent par la cruauté des Rebelles d'Angleterre qui les tiranirent avec tant de barbarité qu'ils les contreignent de quiter leur pais et biens, eux, leur femes et enfants en un estat peu convenable à l'age, à la qualitè et à la naisance de quelques uns, sa Majestè en est si sensiblement touché de pitiè que ill regret l'usurpation de ces estats et de son pouvoir beaucoup moins pour la gloire et le grandeur que le suivent que pour ce que en estant depouillè il se trouve destituè des moins de

---

1 Du Fossé, *Mémoires*, II, p. 103.   2 Hermant, *Mémoires*, IV, p. 635.
3 Du Fossé, *loc. cit.*

secourir et venger ces subjects contre l'inhumanitè de leur opresseurs. Mais avec la pitiè et le regret ces spectacles de desolation font ausi naistre ou plustost redoubler en luy une firme resolution de chercher par tout et un desir ardent non sans espoir par la grace et misericorde de dieu de trover a la fin quelque remede a des maux si afligeantes, pourquoy il m'a comandè mesme devent qu'il partit de Paris de vous aler trover de sa parte non seulement pour vous tesmoigner qu'il avoit et aura toutjours un souvenir tout particulier et recognoisante des obligations qu'il vous a, mais ausi de vous recomender le deplorable estat de ces subjects Catholiques a fin que quand un occasion se pouvoit presenter vous voulier exercer vostre charitè en leur endroit; ce que ne pouvent faire pour ce que vous n'esties pas a Paris il m'a comandè de le faire par escrit de quel comandement je scay que je me suis fort mal acquitè, mais j'ai plustost choisi de luy obeyer en une affaire si digne de vostre pietè et si proportionè a mes sentiments que de failir ou d'emprunter la main d'un autre, sachant que la secresie est ausi necessaire pour le bien de l'affaire que pour vous plaire en la methode de l'avancer, si je me suis fait comprendre et si vous me pardoner la peine que je vous done ce tous que je doibts attendre qui suis, Monsieur, vostre tres humble et tres affectionè serviteur.

Ormond.

(Endorsed: A copy of the letter for Mons. Bernier and Mons. Singlin.[1])

This letter was sent to Sir George Hamilton—it was not superscribed, but Hamilton was to direct it "in an unknown hand" to one or other or both of the gentlemen, or to one in the absence of the other. However, Ormonde was so little satisfied with this letter, all of his own writing and inditing, as he said, that he could not believe it would satisfy anyone else, and therefore he also wrote an English one, sending this to a certain Dr Kelly "intended by the help of his interpretation to Monsieur Bernier and Monsieur Singlin".[2]

•This Dr Kelly, later prominently connected with the Irish College, is denounced to the Propaganda Fide as a rabid Jansenist, "Jansenista arrabbiato",[3] and le Père Rapin who writes with a vitriolic pen where Jansenists are concerned, gives a very

1 *Hist. MSS. Comm.*, *Ormonde MSS.*, N.S. 1, pp. 297–8 (reprinted by permission).
2 *Ib.* pp. 298–9.
3 Bellesheim, *op. cit.* 11, p. 609. This is probably the priest "Kellis" who is attacked in 1653 as a Jansenist according to Hermant (*Mémoires*, 11, pp. 251, 292).

unflattering portrait of him, "un ecclésiastique hibernois, grand janséniste,...homme hardi, intéressé...qui s'étoit fourré à l'hôtel de Longueville où il s'était acquis du crédit par ses intrigues et s'étoit rendu considérable par sa hardiesse. Jamais homme n'a mieux fait le dévot et d'un ton plus radouci, sans aucun principe de dévotion".[1] He had formerly been confessor to Marie de Gonzague, now Queen of Poland,[2] the friend of la Mère Angélique, and was at one time director of the daughter of the comtesse de Brégy, la Sœur Anne Marie de Sainte Eustoquie, a nun of Port Royal.[3] For this Dr Kelly Sir George Hamilton requested a letter authorizing him to act for the king and this letter Ormonde sent also, enjoining secrecy—"it would be very inconvenient to the king, if it should be fruitlessly known".[4]

Ormonde's French letter arrived safely. "Your letter was received with very great expressions of friendship", writes Sir George Hamilton, "and I find that person and the other to whom the authority was sent very desirous to bring somewhat to a perfection. Within this four days they are to bring me to speak with some other private friends whom I will study to satisfy as much as I hope these other two are already."[5]

And a few days later he writes again: "As to our business, it is now with much industry brought to a resolution, and something will be done very speedily, but as yet I know not what, or by what name I am to mention it, though I believe I shall be instructed tomorrow afternoon when I am to meet with our friends to that purpose. Seriously, my Lord, Doctor Kelly has behaved himself in this not only like a friend and well affected subject, but likewise with extreme great discretion and understanding". Their hopes were not "concluded" by the present they were now to receive—evidently some financial help was forthcoming again, and more might be looked for. Another

1 Rapin, *Mémoires*, III, pp. 254–5.
2 See his Epitaph, printed in Belleisheim, *op. cit.* III, pp. 754–5, or in Boyle, *Irish College*, p. 229.
3 Rapin, *loc. cit.*
4 *Hist. MSS. Comm., Ormonde MSS.* N.S. I, p. 299, July 18–28, 1654.
5 *Ib.* p. 300, Aug. 4–14, 1654.

CJ

"letter of authority" was requested for Kelly, and for an interesting reason—Sir George Hamilton feared that Kelly might be sent from town as an adherent of the Cardinal de Retz then in disgrace, though, as Hamilton said, Kelly had no other relation to him than as his bishop. The Jansenists, however, were suspected of siding with Retz. The first letter of authority had contained some particulars that would not be fit to appear, but let something be sent with all speed under the king's hand to remain with Dr Kelly "whereby he might appear to have some credence as one employed by His Majesty". But once more, "la secresie"—the authority must on no account relate in particular to the business now in hand, nor must it mention their friends who, writes Hamilton, "are so cautious as they will scarce have me that deals with them take notice what they do or of the manner they proceed",[1] an interesting picture, this, of the Jansenists, all their doings shrouded in prudence, mystery and humility; but indeed caution was necessary.

It is difficult to discover the exact nature of the "business", but one comes to the conclusion that it had something to do with an expedition to Scotland to help Sir John Middleton, and one is confirmed in this hypothesis by finding Sir Edward Hyde writing in December of the same year about "Scotland where there is argument in abundance for the charity intended, and therefore the King hopes for the return of Sir George Hamilton".[2] Eventually the money was used for something else, no doubt for the projected rising in England. By the end of February (1655) Charles disappeared quietly from Cologne and proceeded to Middelburg in Zeeland to join his friends in England, but before he went he left a message to be sent to Dr Kelly and his friends. As Hyde wrote to Dr Kelly from "Cullen" on February 28th, the king, being obliged to withdraw suddenly and privately from this place, desired to let him know his sense of the affection of Kelly's friends and of his own services for which he gave hearty thanks. Sir George Hamilton would communicate all particulars about the non-applying of the

1 *Hist. MSS. Comm., Ormonde MSS.* N.S. 1, p. 304.
2 *Ib.* p. 311.

supply to the place for which it was intended and its disposal to another part. A copy of the same letter was also sent to Richard Bellings, another friend of the Jansenists.[1] But nothing came of the Salisbury rising, and the Jansenist funds were probably swallowed up in the general disaster.

In these years, 1654 and 1655, la Mère Angélique took a special interest in Lord Muskerry, Ormonde's brother-in-law. Although reported in 1654 as having been condemned, hung, drawn and quartered in Ireland[2], he was acquitted and allowed to withdraw to the continent with a large number of retainers. Safety was precious, but now arose the question of daily bread! After having gone on a fruitless errand to Portugal he returned to Paris, and having already some connection with Port Royal through the two "Messieurs" Callaghan, one of whom, the Doctor, had been tutor to his sons, he was befriended by the duc de Luynes; "il fut puissamment assisté par la charité de Mr le Duc de Luines qui lui fournit toute la dépense pour se faire honnêtement habiller". At Port Royal des Champs he found his daughter Helen, a pensionnaire, as well as his nieces, the Hamiltons.

La Mère Angélique seems to have suggested his going to Poland to offer not only his services, but those of his five thousand men who were in an "extrême misère", and on November 20th, 1654, she writes to the queen, Marie de Gonzague, from Port Royal de Paris, asking whether the king could use Muskerry. By March 1655 Muskerry had decided to go to Poland to plead his own cause and with him went Richard Bellings,[3] the former Secretary of the Irish Confederate Catholics, who had shown his friendship for Port Royal by translating the Latin translation of Arnauld's *Fréquente Communion* into English for his fellow-countrymen.[4] He was to speak for Muskerry "entendant très

1 *Cal. Clarendon Papers*, III, p. 18. 2 *Ib.* II, p. 298.
3 Who, one wonders, was "M. de Bel-Air, Gentilhomme Anglois", whom Besoigne (*Histoire*, III, p. 549) describes as one of those who came from time to time to see M. Le Maître at Port Royal? He gives an account of a M. de Belair elsewhere (IV, pp. 122–3) but there is nothing English about him. The real name of the "Gentilhomme Anglois" does not seem to have come down to us. It is not impossible that Bellings went to see M. Le Maître.
4 Marie-Angélique Arnauld, *Lettres*, II, p. 591; cf. pp. 569–70.

bien le Latin et un peu le François". Muskerry having read *The Frequent Communion* was deeply impressed by it, and made a renewed profession of faith. La Mère Angélique, touched by his patience in affliction and by his courage, speaks of him as "ce bon Seigneur que je révère singulièrement comme un vrai Chrétien".

"The Lord Musgray and old Mr Bealing are gone for Poland" we hear in April.[1] The expense, at least as far as Muskerry was concerned, was borne by the duc de Luynes, while Charles contributed a letter of recommendation to the king, John Casimir.[2] In July news came of their safe arrival, and la Mère Angélique writes many letters full of gratitude to the queen. "J'apprends, Madame, toutes les bontés et les soins que vous prenez pour le pauvre Milord qui ravit par le récit qu'il en fait ici à ses amis."

Unfortunately—the chronicle of the Stuart exiles is one of perpetual futility and disappointment—the journey led to nothing, and in August Muskerry returned to France again.[3] Later—in 1656—M. Arnauld d'Andilly, the eldest of the Arnauld brothers and sisters, seems to have taken him up, recommending him to the Marquis, presently Maréchal, de Fabre. Along with his letters about Muskerry went copies of certain famous pamphlets, the *Provinciales*, and while Fabre is not optimistic about Muskerry's prospects, foreseeing nothing advantageous in what he is undertaking, each of the *Provinciales* is received more enthusiastically than the last.[4]

There is little doubt that copies of the *Lettres Provinciales* were sent to Charles himself in 1656 and 1657, along with other edifying writings, for M. de Bernières, with a touching faith in Charles' higher nature, tried not only to provide him with earthly help but with spiritual sustenance. "Comme il scavoit que le Roy prenoist un goût particulier à lire pendant ce temps

1 *Nicholas Papers* (Camden), II, p. 256.
2 A copy is preserved at the Bibliothèque de l'Arsenal, MS. 6034, f. 102, Cologne, April 24 (1655).
3 M. A. Arnauld, *Lettres*, II, pp. 534, 569-70, 571, 583, 591, 606, 614, 618, 623, III, pp. 24, 28, 36, 40, 50; *Mémoires et Relations*, pp. 213-17; *Mémoires pour servir* (1742), II, pp. 387-91.
4 Arsenal, MS. 6035, f. 130, Dec. 7, 1656. Cf. Oct. 18.

de son affliction les écrits qui se faisoient pour deffendre les Religieuses de Port Royal et leurs amis, qui étoient dans l'affliction comme luy, il avoit soin de luy envoyer en Flandre tout ce qu'il jugeoit pouvoir contribuer à le consoler en quelque sorte et à l'instruire de plus en plus sur les grands principes de notre Religion."[1] Certainly others took it upon themselves to provide refutations of the *Provinciales*. Father Peter Talbot sent Ormonde the "answers to the Jansenian calumnies against the Jesuits",[2] and getting no acknowledgment, he expressed a hope some weeks later that the "answer to the Jansenian libels" had been received.[3]

From M. de Bernières came doubtless also the copies of Arnauld's *Lettre apologétique de M. Arnauld à un evesque* and M. Le Maître's *Lettre touchant l'inquisition qu'on veut établir en France*, both of which were translated into English by John Nicholas, the son of Sir Edward Nicholas,[4] and from the same source came very likely also Ormonde's copies of M. de Saci's *Enluminures du faux Almanach* and Arnauld's defence of Callaghan, *L'Innocence et la Vérité défendues*, which in 1684–5 were still preserved in the library of Kilkenny Castle, along with Arnauld's *Lettres* and his *Tradition de l'Église*.[5]

It was probably also M. de Bernières who provided Charles with a servant by the name of Pantiot. This Pantiot with his master, M. de Saint-Gilles d'Asson, had come to know Port Royal, and after having been employed as a watchman at Port Royal during the Fronde, he entered the service of Charles, remaining in it for about thirty years. He was a most exuberant person, in spite of his connection with Port Royal, and Charles probably enjoyed his hilarity, though it was seasoned at times with moral precepts, "plaisantant toujours à son ordinaire, et

1 Du Fossé, *Mémoires*, ii, pp. 104–5.
2 *Cal. Clarendon Papers*, iii, p. 158, Aug. 12, 1656.
3 *Ib.* p. 174, Sept. 21, 1656.
4 *A letter from a clergyman to his Bishop touching subscribing the form made by the Assembly of the Clergy*, 16 folio pages. *A letter from an advocate of the Parliament to a friend touching the inquisition which is endeavoured to be established in France upon occasion of the late Bull of Pope Alexander VII*, 13½ folio pages. *Cal. Clarendon Papers*, iii, pp. 292, 299–300.
5 *Hist. MSS. Comm.*, *Ormonde MSS.* N.S. vii, pp. 520, 525.

luy disant cependant bien des vérités qui pouvoient luy estre utiles. Car quelque bouffon qu'il fust, il avoit un très bon fonds et aimoit beaucoup la vérité quoiqu'il ne la prattiquast pas toujours".[1] When he came back to France in 1685 after the death of Charles, he was judged to have lost somewhat in spiritual fervour. "Ayant passé plus de trente ans à bouffonner et à plaisanter auprès d'un prince, on peut bien juger qu'il avoist plutost recullé qu'avancé dans la connoissance et la prattique des choses de la Religion."[2]

Before closing this chapter some reference must be made to a curious and interesting tentative undertaken by an Anglican divine, a tentative of which we know nothing beyond a few lines in Wood, namely that Dr Richard Steward, Dean-designate of St Paul's and Provost of Eton "with that public-spirited man Sir George Ratcliffe did go very far in making an accommodation between the Jansenists and the Reformed party, our author being then chaplain to his Majesty King Charles II".[3] Steward died in Paris in October 1651, *Moriens nihil aliud inscribi voluit Epitaphium quam quod Vivens Assidue Oravit pro Pace Ecclesiæ*, and so nothing came of this projected rapprochement, nor would anything probably ever have come of it, but it is interesting to note this first attempt, in view of the attempted union with the Gallican church in the eighteenth century. Sir George Radcliffe probably kept up relations with the Jansenists; in any case he associated with Dr Kelly.[4]

1 Du Fossé, *Mémoires*, I, pp. 185–8.
2 *Ib*. III, p. 313.
3 *Athen. Oxon.* (ed. Bliss), III, p. 296; cf. N. Pocock, *Life of Richard Steward* (1908), p. 179; T. D. Whitaker, *Life of Sir G. Radcliffe* (1810), p. 287.
4 See e.g. Carte, *Original Letters* (1739), II, pp. 73–4.

CHAPTER IV

Port Royal and the Exiles (*continued*)
(1656–1660)

THE year 1656 was an eventful one for the Jansenists. Arnauld's *Lettre à un Duc et Pair*, a treatise of 254 pages, was being examined by the Sorbonne. "As for that business of Jansenius", Thurloe, Cromwell's secretary of state, is informed in January, "it remains undecided in the Sorbonne",[1] but by the end of the month Arnauld had been censured, he had been excluded from the Sorbonne, and in March the solitaries were dispersed and their schools, the Petites Écoles, broken up. Orders were about to be given for the removal of the novices and the nuns' pupils.[2] From Paris Thurloe hears that the Pope, Alexander VII, "did intend to authorize the condemnation which has been given by those of Sorbonne against the partisans of Jansenius; whereupon the King has prohibited their assembly which was held in St James street at a house called port royal from whence they are gone to hold their congregation out of this city",[3] and Sir Richard Leveson learns that the Pope "has proclaimed a Jubilee with plenary indulgence and general pardon...to them that shall visit so many churches...and pray for rooting out the new heretics sprung up in the Catholic Church (he meaneth those that uphold Jean Sanius opinions)".[4]

Two events put a temporary stop to persecution, one was the extraordinary success of the *Provinciales* which had begun to appear in January in defence of Arnauld; the other, in March, the miraculous cure of Pascal's niece Marguerite Périer, the "miracle de la Sainte-Épine". Years later, we are told, when the abbé Stuart d'Aubigny, almoner of Catherine of Braganza,

1 *Thurloe Papers*, IV, p. 438.
2 Racine, *Abrégé de l'Histoire de Port-Royal*, p. 77.
3 *Thurloe Papers*, IV, p. 645, Mar. 25–April 4, 1656.
4 *Hist. MSS. Comm., App. to 5th Report*, p. 144, April 8, 1656.

made the queen in her illness touch a relic said to be a part of the crown of thorns, he pointed out to Charles where the thorn of Port Royal had been cut, and both the king and the Duke of York, remembering the cure of the little girl, said they had believed in it. The duke added that he had been persuaded of its truth by Turenne. Port Royal friends heard of this with satisfaction and Hermant remarks: "On peut voir avec étonnement que le roi d'Angleterre et les Protestants rendoient plus de justice à la Sainte-Epine de Port-Royal que les jésuites de France".[1]

Yet even in that year—1656—Charles appears to have looked for some help from the Jansenists. Ormonde tells Hyde in August that "Mr Moyle" seemed confirmed in thinking that his friends would do something considerable and "believed Dr Kelly and Mons. Berriere to be the first persons to be written to"; Ormonde could "fit Kelly with a letter to set the business on foot"; moreover Moyle had received "extraordinary civilities from the Duke of Luyine", which Ormonde thought the king should acknowledge in a letter to the duke "which may do some honour to Moyle and some good to the main design".[2] "Moyle" is difficult to identify—the name is one of those fictitious ones which abound in the correspondence of the time. Hyde, the recipient, has deciphered it by substituting "Mr Mat.", but we are none the wiser, though one may note that "Mr Matome" is used as a pseudonym for Charles II.[3] Probably Moyle stands for Lord Muskerry, for certainly the Duke had helped Muskerry even to the extent of clothing him, as we have seen. On August 18th Charles himself writes from Bruges to Henry Bennet: "I hear nothing yet of Jansenius which I wonder at since 'tis so long since he set forth and the Wind as 'tis now always good" which one might take to refer to assistance from the Jansenists, though one is puzzled by the sentence which follows, "when he comes I will tell him of the Request you have made in his behalf and give him the assurance of the place".[4]

1 Hermant, *Mémoires*, VI, pp. 575–8.
2 *Cal. Clarendon Papers*, III, p. 158.   3 *Ib*. pp. 291, 317.
4 Brown, *Miscellanea Aulica*, p. 118. The date is erroneously given as 1655 instead of 1656.

"The Jansenists grow dayly in reputatione", so Cromwell's ambassador, Lockhart, writes home to Thurloe in November, "but the story concerning them must be so long, as I shall deferr it till my arrivall in London."[1]

Arnauld and his friends were busy with their pens and their polemics. The *Lettres Provinciales* were followed by a whole host of tracts and pamphlets, some of which are to be found in the earlier editions of the *Provinciales*—the various *Écrits* of the curés de Paris and the curés de Rouen. "The curates of Paris whoe are peradventure moste of them Jansenians", reports Colonel Bampfylde, "oppose themselves violently to the Jesuits, not openly upon any principle of Jansenius, but agaynest the Jesuites new doctrine published in their moral theologye. The quarrell is soe great betwixt them, and the subject soe plausible, that it may produce more trouble then is generally foreseen."[2]

Our exiles seem to have followed the controversy with interest. "There is come forth in print an excellent peec lately published by the curats of Paris", writes a royalist from Paris to Hyde at Bruges.[3] "If I find that the packet when it is made up, be not to bigg, you may receave it by this poast, if I do, you shall by the next", and another time he sends him "this factum of the curats of Roen".[4] Or again, "You will receave with these a sixt peece sett forth by the Curats of Paris"—tradition ascribes the sixth "peece" to Pascal—"Certainly these late differences have been the occasion of much good. All they write is edefying and excellent; and this is admirable. This copy may be layd by unsullyed, to be added to the rest in the last volume of your books".[5]

The correspondence between the English and the Jansenists is kept up in 1657. A letter from Dr Sinnich, the Louvain theologian who had been dispatched to Rome in 1643 in connection with the *Augustinus* and its condemnation, brings Arnauld the king's thanks, and requests Arnauld to write to the king to tell him that he, Sinnich, had carried out all his behests,

---

1 *Thurloe Papers*, v, p. 610. 2 *Ib.* p. 585.
3 "Mr Kingstonn to Mr Laurence", i.e. to Hyde, *Ib.* 1, p. 736.
4 *Ib.* p. 740. 5 *Ib.* vii, p. 325.

while Arnauld speaks with affection and pity of the exiled king and of his hopes of a restoration, *optamus illud et precibus a Deo exposcimus,* of his friends' correspondence with the king's household, *non raro ad Aulæ ipsius primores scribunt,* of the help given, *aliquas etiam pro viribus suis amici quidam nostri sublevarunt,* of the king's gratitude out of all proportion to the *officiorum mediocritas.*[1]

But soon after this some kind of misunderstanding seems to have arisen, and after 1657 one does not find many traces of direct dealings between the Jansenists and Charles. In June some sort of proposition was made by them through Bellings, but the king's answer did not prove acceptable. Letters from Dr Kelly and Lady Muskerry informed Ormonde that the friends at Paris were not satisfied with the king's first answer to their proposition, and that Lord Muskerry, who at this time had gone to Spain with Sir George Hamilton to obtain help for an attempt upon Ireland, could no longer look for supplies from that source. Ormonde writes as if the friends undervalued Charles' promises of toleration to the Roman Catholics[2] and considered them "insatisfactory". "Those friends, I doubt, are lost", he adds, "and that principally by means of the Nobleman who put that extravagance into their head, though he hath been well assisted by some that write strangely of the King's person and how he passes his time"—it was scarcely avoidable that the Jansenists should sooner or later be disillusioned in their regard for Charles.[3]

It would seem almost certain that the proposition in question was in some way connected with a plan for the conversion of the Duke of Gloucester, suggested precisely at this time by the abbé Stuart d'Aubigny in whose Paris house M. de Bernières lived.[4] In 1654, it will be remembered, a first attempt had been

1 Arnauld, *Œuvres,* i, p. 153, Feb. 12, 1657.
2 Part of the secret treaty between Charles and Philip IV of Spain, but not inserted in it on account of the need for secrecy.
3 *Clarendon State Papers,* iii, p. 347. In this letter the words "these people" and "these men" coming before and after the sentence about the friends in Paris, do not of course refer to the Jansenists but to the Spaniards. Cf. *Cal. Clarendon Papers,* iii, p. 308, where the summary is somewhat misleading. See also *Ib.* pp. 110, 315, 387.
4 Du Fossé, *Mémoires,* ii, p. 103.

made to induce the duke to change his religion, under the auspices of the queen-mother, her confessor the abbé Montagu, and the Jesuits. This time, it would appear, the conversion was to take place under Jansenist auspices, or at least at the desire of the Jansenists, though one cannot help feeling that Aubigny's personal ambitions had much to do with the matter. More will be said about Aubigny in a later chapter.

It was Bellings who brought Charles the proposition from Aubigny, nine and a half closely written folio pages. In order to win support from the Catholics some kind of guarantee must be offered, "promises of princes in your majestie's condition are not easily relyed on". The assurance most satisfactory to Catholics would be Charles' yielding to the duke's conversion "to which your majesty seemed formerly to have been avers, because he was to be compel'd...to live with the Jesuits, whose very name is extremely odious in England". This conversion was to be carried out with the aid of the Cardinal de Retz "your majestie's very real friend", Monseigneur Banny and the Cardinal Barberini, the latter to provide suitable maintenance for the duke at Rome. A scheme for bringing together the Catholics and Cromwell was under contemplation, but the duke's conversion would help to bring this rapprochement to naught. Aubigny himself would gladly undertake the charge of the duke. No force, no compulsion was to be used. "His conversion, that it may be perfect, must be the work of grace." The proposal must be kept secret from the English queen-mother and the French court. Ormonde and Hyde might alone be taken into confidence. If news leaked out before the conversion had taken place the queen would leave nothing undone to have some creature of her own about the duke "wherein she will be powerfully seconded by the Jesuits who will not fayle to have a finger in the matter".[1]

---

[1] *Thurloe Papers*, I, pp. 740–4; *Cal. Clarendon Papers*, III, p. 325. Incidentally the correspondence shows that Charles was not a Roman Catholic at this time. In connection with Ormonde's observation about the people who made derogatory remarks about the king, it is interesting to note that Aubigny, who was probably the "Nobleman" in question, spoke about a year later of "the dislike he once had of the King's way of living, and other impressions given him to his disadvantage". *Thurloe Papers*, I, p. 737.

The king sent Bellings on to Louvain to see Dr Sinnich,[1] possibly in this connection. Bellings also went to see Hyde at Bruges, and Hyde, gravely disapproving, drew up a kind of answer for the king to Aubigny's proposal, in the form of instructions to Bellings. In his refusal Charles asked that Aubigny would dispose his friends to continue the same good wishes towards him, and for the advancement of his service which they had always professed—he hoped this of their ingenuity, generosity and integrity—" and if any of that kindness be abated I shall be very sorry for any occasion that induced that person to make this proposition to me".[2]

Meanwhile things were not going well for the Jansenists. A Bull from Alexander VII confirmed the Bull of Innocent X condemning the five propositions, and the young king, Louis XIV, insisted on the Parlement of Paris receiving the Bull. " The poor Jansenists are condemned in parliam[t] this day", so Cromwell's ambassador, Lockhart, reports on December 9th. Everything, he said, was to be done with great solemnity in presence of the king and cardinal, " all public ministers are invited and places kept for them. I have excused myself upon the account of my wife's indisposition".[3] The same news went to Sir Edward Nicholas in Flanders, from a different source. " The King upon Wedsonday last went to y[e] Parliament to passe an arrest against y[e] Jansenistes in order to a late sentence given by the Pope for condemning severall of theire writings; y[e] particulars whereof in short I have in print and if your Honour please, shall send them by the next."[4]

In this same year, 1657, "Mrs Barlow", *alias* Lucy Walter, a former mistress of Charles, had established herself in Brussels with her son, the future Duke of Monmouth, her appearance causing much talk and trouble. After a certain struggle the child was taken out of her hands—early in 1658—and it must have been at this time that he was entrusted to Aubigny, and

1 *Cal. Clarendon Papers*, III, pp. 315, 318.
2 *Thurloe Papers*, I, p. 744; *Cal. Clarendon Papers*, III, pp. 326, 327.
3 R.O. *State Papers, France*, vol. 113, f. 318, Dec. 9–19, 1657; see also *Cal. Clarendon Papers*, III, p. 398.
4 *Nicholas Papers* (Camden), IV, p. 28, Dec. 21, 1657.

through him to M. de Bernières who placed the child in one of the "Petites Écoles", the one at his country house of Le Chesnay, where he was brought up under the care of M. Walon de Beaupuis, another friend of Port Royal who was in the habit of staying with Aubigny when he came to Paris.[1]

It is usually stated that the child's tutors were first an Oratorian father, Dr Stephen Goffe or Gough, and later, when Charles had resolved to send for him to come to England, the Protestant, Thomas Ross; but before passing into the hands of Goffe the child undoubtedly received for a short period the instruction of Port Royal. "Le Duc de Montmouth n'a point étudié sous M. Nicole," says one of Arnauld's letters, "mais il a été quelque temps chez M. de Bernières au Chenai proche de Versailles où était une autre troupe d'enfants de qualité instruits par de jeunes gens qui étoient sous la conduite des Ecclésiastiques de Port Royal. Cela fut dissipé par un ordre de la cour et alors M. d'Aubigny qui en avoit le soin le mit à Juilly chez les Pères de l'Oratoire."[2] The Petites Écoles—the three chief ones being at Les Granges, Le Chesnay and Les Trous—had been broken up a first time in 1656, but a temporary calm allowed a certain resumption of activities in 1658. The final dispersion came in 1660.[3] The average age of the pupils was from ten to twelve years, and the duke was about nine or ten on his arrival. There were four classes at Le Chesnay, and one imagines that he was put into the first and lowest, "trois ou quatre Ecoliers que l'on mit sous la conduite de M. Guyot".[4]

Many years afterwards a little note-book of M. Walon de Beaupuis was found, giving the names of the pupils, about thirty in number. We are told that according to this little book there were several Dutch and English children at Le Chesnay "sans que l'on y voye cependant le celebre Duc de Monmouth que l'on a sçu de M. de Beaupuis même avoir été quelque temps

1 *Vies intéressantes et édifiantes des Amis de Port-Royal*, p. 120.

2 Arnauld, *Œuvres*, ii, p. 561; cf. Du Fossé, *Mémoires*, ii, p. 105.

3 Barnard, *The little Schools of Port Royal, passim*; Gazier, *Hist. du mouvement janséniste*, i, p. 123.

4 Nicole, *Continuation des Essais de Morale. Tome Quatorzième. Première Partie contenant la Vie de M. Nicole*, Luxembourg, 1732, p. 30.

au Chesnay".[1] The writer goes on to say that doubtless the Journal, as he calls it, did not give the name of all the "Etudians"; a possible explanation is perhaps that Monmouth was entered under the name of Crofts by which he then went. In any case his stay, which at the very most could have been but two years, was not long enough to make any lasting impression. The little note-book itself has disappeared again[2]—it would have been interesting to have known the names of the other English children at Le Chesnay.

At last came the Restoration. Port Royal, though in the throes of persecution, rejoiced with Charles. "Ces Messieurs avec qui j'étois", so Fontaine, M. de Saci's secretary, records in his *Mémoires*,[3] "...aimoient tellement la justice et l'ordre qu'ils ne purent s'empescher dans les peines de leur tristesse de ressentir de la joye de cet evenement." But though some of their friends would fain have gone to England to witness the king's return, such was not the desire of the solitaries. "Ils avouoient que c'estoit une chose belle à voir, mais pour eux ils n'auroient pas voulu faire un pas pour aucunes de ces Magnificences de ce monde." Other friends, animated with missionary zeal, consulted them about the advisability of proceeding to England at once, in the interests of the Church, but the Messieurs counselled prudence and moderation—"il étoit dangereux d'aller si viste... ils ne croioient pas encore que rien pressat, que le Roy d'Angleterre etoit trop sage pour se commettre d'abord qu'il ne pouvoit rien changer dans ces commancemens touchant la religion, s'il n'y trouvoit le monde extrémement porté" which, as they sagely remarked, was very hard to believe. Perhaps the would-be apostles struck the solitaries as more ardent for the cause than fit for their calling, for they were advised to make quite sure of their own salvation first:

1 *Vies intéressantes*, pp. 86–7.

2 Even Mademoiselle Gazier, who probably knows more about Port Royal sources than anyone else, has never come across it.

3 All that follows is taken, not from the printed *Mémoires*, but from the manuscript copy preserved at the Bibliothèque Mazarine. It was Mademoiselle Gazier who kindly drew my attention to the fact that there were omissions in the printed text, and who suggested my collating it with the manuscript.

que ces personnes si zelees devoient voir auparavant ce qui etoit utile pour leur salut propre et aprés voir ce qu'ils croient capables de faire pour celuy des autres mais qu'on devoit touiour se considerer le premier... outre qu'il falloit avoir une capacité, une verve et une sagesse très grande pour gouverner la religion catholique en Angleterre dans un temps où il falloit la faire renaitre presque de nouveau par une puissance et une grâce presque apostolique sans laquelle on ne pouvoit rien faire qu'en apparence... qu'il falloit pour le present se contenter de prier beaucoup pour cette affaire qui était alors une des plus importantes de l'eglise.

There were also some English ecclesiastics of high birth—no doubt the abbé Stuart d'Aubigny is one of those meant—who felt that they must go to England, but came to consult the Messieurs about "the Oath" which they would be obliged to take and which was worrying them. The Messieurs thought the terms of the oath harsh and subject to misinterpretation, but they believed that it could be taken if it were understood in a certain sense.[1] They thought, however, that there would doubtless be plenty of time to consider the matter, for they remained convinced that the king would not be able to re-establish the Catholic ecclesiastics at an early date, however good his intentions might be; he would have to face many difficulties "qu'il feroit beaucoup s'il pouvoit soutenir les evecques protestants comme il sembloit y estre obligé par ce qui s'étoit passé"—if he could do this he would have more liberty to proceed afterwards, but first he must establish his authority.[2]

[1] Fontaine is very long-winded here, and it is not quite clear whether he is speaking of the Oath of Allegiance or the Oath of Supremacy. "Il sembloit qu'on ne pretendoit attribuer qu'au Roy le pouvoir de commander et de faire des Loix et des ordonnances dans les choses même ecclesiastiques avec droit de contraindre et de punir temporellement les contravenans comme par amende, prison, et autres punitions extérieures—ainsi si c'étoit seulement l'intention de ce serment ils ne le trouvoient pas illicite étant certain que le pouvoir de contraindre et de punir de la sorte extérieurement et temporellement les suiects n'appartient proprement qu'aux Roys et aux Princes et non a l'Eglise qui n'a receu la puissance que d'imposer des peines purement spirituelles et de conscience dont l'excommunication est la plus grande et la derniere, et si elle passe plus avant elle exerce une puissance qui approche plus de la politique extérieure, elle ne l'a que par la concession des Rois qui la luy pouvoient oster pour de petites raisons comme ils la luy ont donnée volontairement et de gré." Bibl. Mazarine, MS. 2466, pp. 730–1.

[2] Bibl. Mazarine, MS. 2466, *Histoire très curieuse et très édifiante de Messieurs de Port-Royal des Champs par Monsieur Fontaine*, ii, pp. 729–31. (MS. 2465 is vol. i.)

And so those whom Port Royal had befriended returned to England. One young girl was left behind at Port Royal des Champs—Helen Muskerry. Marguerite Périer, Pascal's niece who had been so miraculously healed in 1656, was her fellow-pensionnaire; Pascal's sister Jacqueline was sub-prioress and mistress of the novices. Helen Muskerry was evidently very happy there, and her parents, now become the Earl of Clancarty and Lady Clancarty, hoped that she might eventually become a nun of Port Royal, but all this came to a sudden end with "la grande persécution de 1661".

In April of this year the king gave orders to remove all pensionnaires and novices from both houses, Port Royal des Champs and Port Royal de Paris. On May 5th the lieutenant-civil, M. d'Aubray, returned to Port Royal des Champs to find out whether the order had been obeyed and he discovered that four of the twenty-seven pensionnaires—Helen Muskerry was one of them—had not yet gone. The prioress, la Mère du Fargis, a cousin of the Cardinal de Retz, explained that the parents of the three French girls were expected hourly to take the children away, and that as for Mademoiselle Muskerry, he might see for himself that it was impossible for them to hear so soon from her parents to whom they had written. No—the pensionnaires must be handed over at once. The prioress pointed out that she had no clothes for them, "lesquelles Pensionnaires n'ont point l'habit seculier, ayant seulement un petit habit blanc comme des novices avec lequel il seroit indecent de les transferer", and if three or four days could be granted, she would inform the abbess, la Mère Agnès—before the time of separation of the two houses the abbess was at Port Royal de Paris and the prioress at Port Royal des Champs—hoping that in the meanwhile the parents of the French girls would come, and Mademoiselle de Muskry (sic) could be entrusted to a "dame de condition" until news was received from her parents. All was of no avail, and the four pensionnaires in tears were removed to the convent of the Ursulines of the Faubourg Saint-Jacques.[1]

1 B.N. f. fr. MS. 17774, ff. 4, 7, 15; *Hist. des Persécutions*, pp. xiii, 4, 10, 11; Hermant, *Mémoires*, IV, p. 651; la Mère Agnès Arnauld, *Lettres*, I, p. 500.

We have a quaint picture of the little girl-prisoners, so childlike in some ways, so wise beyond their years in others, discussing theology with the Ursuline nuns. They were asked whether Christ had died for all, and when they replied in the affirmative, saying that they had never been taught the contrary, they were told that at Port Royal it was said that he died only for the elect. Was contrition necessary when you went to confession? "Yes", said the girls. "No, it was sufficient to have attrition and receive absolution." One of the girls, a child of eleven, replied, "Ma mère, je ne le croy pas, car si cela estoit on seroit donc sauvé sans aimer Dieu et c'est ce qui ne se peut".

Then they were made to recite the prayers they said at Port Royal, morning and evening, but when they came to a passage "si jamais nous avons fait quelque bien, c'est vous, mon Dieu, qui l'avez fait en nous", they were interrupted, "Il ne faut pas dire comme cela, mes enfants, car vous cooperez", and they were taught to say other prayers in the place of the Port Royal prayers. But the girls used to recite the Port Royal prayers at night, when they had gone to bed, in order not to forget them, and every night too they recited part of M. de Saint-Cyran's catechism in bed, though they had been told all kinds of things about him and about M. d'Ipres (i.e. Jansenius) who was "le pavé de l'enfer".[1]

About five weeks later, on June 12th, la Mère Agnès writes, "Les enfans qui etoient aux Ursulines sont sorties hormis mademoiselle de Muskri que l'on n'a pas voulu rendre parce que l'on n'a pas ordre de monsieur son père et de madame sa mère qui seront dans la dernière affliction de la violence que l'on a faite à mademoiselle leur fille que nous avons élevée depuis l'âge de sept ans".[2] At the end of the month Helen was still there, and was to remain there for another two months, in spite of all the efforts of several "personnages de condition",[3] but that she should not be a burden to the Ursulines Louis XIV

---

1 B.N. f. fr. MS. 17774, f. 16; cf. *Hist. des Persécutions*, pp. 10–11.
2 *Lettres*, I, p. 500.
3 Manuscript cited.

gave them 300 livres, "pour la pension et les habillements de la demoiselle de Mousery, Irlandoise".[1]

About the time that Helen Muskerry left, la Mère Angélique died,[2] in her seventieth year, and Port Royal was never quite the same again. Two months later died Jacqueline Pascal, of a broken heart, it is said, for having signed the Formulary, and in the following year, 1662, Pascal himself departed this life.

Perhaps one of the personages approached on Helen's behalf was the young Duchess of Orleans, Charles' youngest sister Henrietta, who had married Monsieur in March 1661. Her mode of living was not an austere one, but she certainly had some adherents of Port Royal among her friends—M. de Tréville, Turenne, Madame de Sablé, Gondrin, the Archbishop of Sens;[3] and Rapin, speaking of the crowds that flocked to hear the sermons of a Jansenist, the famous Père Desmares—"la princesse de Conti, la duchesse de Longueville, Liancour, Arnault, Nicole, toute la cabale s'y trouva"—tells us that Madame also attended his sermons "sur quoy sa reputation redoubla de moitié dans le party".[4]

Years later, in 1678, Charles was reminded of Port Royal by some one very far removed from its austere virtues—no less a person than the Duchess of Cleveland. The duchess, somewhat fallen from royal grace, had left England, and had established herself in Paris with two of her daughters. During a temporary absence in England she had left her daughter Anne, the young wife of the Earl of Sussex, at a convent in Conflans, but Anne was "never...two daies together" at the convent, was out every day with the English ambassador, Ralph Montagu, whom the duchess considered attached to herself, and finally Anne, at Montagu's instigation, left this convent for one inside Paris.

The duchess, highly incensed, demanded the king's help, and Charles evidently sent directions for Lady Anne to return to Conflans, but this did not satisfy her mother, Lady Anne having gained the abbess there with presents.

1 Boislisle, *Mémoriaux*, II, p. 78.   2 Aug. 6, 1661.
3 Cartwright, *Madame* (1894), pp. 188–9.
4 Rapin, *Mémoires*, III, p. 499. This was in 1669.

"You are pleasd", she writes, "to command my Lady Sussex to stay in the monesstery at Conflans: I bege of your Ma^ty not to command her that, but that which I would propos to you is that you would writ a letter in french which may be showed to the Arch Bishop of Paris in which you desier she may be put into the Monestry of Portroyall at Paris, and that she may have to nuns given her to wayet on her, and that she cares no sarvants with her, that she stires not owet nor reseaves no visits what so ever withowet a leter from me to the Abes: for whar she is now all pepel visits her and the Embasodor and others careys consorts of museke every day to entertan her...this Portroyall that I propos to you is in great reputation for the piete and regularety of it, so that I thinke it much the best place for her."[1]

That the king readily assented to Lady Anne's transfer we gather from the account of one who found "my Lady Cleveland...very possitive about her goeing to port royall and she had ye King of her own side",[2] though whether Lady Anne actually went is not known. Her health was indifferent, she had to take "physicke" and Lady Northumberland suggested one might represent to the king that "a strange monesterie where she knew noebody was but a mallincolly place to doe it".[3]

The Port Royal that Lady Cleveland praises so highly, Port Royal de Paris, was by this time entirely separated from Port Royal des Champs, and the Jansenist historians have little more to say about it, but it is interesting to note that its reputation continued as of old, and that it was known to the English as a place that contrasted favourably with other convents.

1 Sergeant, *My Lady Castlemaine*, pp. 232–3 (from B.M., Add. MSS. 21505).

2 A letter from Lady Northumberland to Ralph Montagu, preserved in the collection of the Duke of Leeds, formerly at Hornby Castle, Bedale, Yorkshire. My grateful thanks are due to His Grace the Duke of Leeds, and to Mr Ward Soame of Rudd Hall, Catterick, Yorkshire, for a copy of this letter. The entry in the *Eleventh Report of the Hist. MSS. Comm.* Part VII, p. 19, is misleading, viz.: "a letter...about the intention of the Duchess of Cleveland to retire to Port Royal in accordance with the King's wishes".

3 From the above letter.

CHAPTER V

Les Bénédictines Anglaises

LET us turn aside, for a space, from the controversies and agitations of the day to a brief record of charity and friendship. "Il y a un petit Couvent d'Angloises qui ne sont que huit, toutes de grandes Maisons qui nous sont venues voir", wrote la Mère Angélique in May 1653. One of the English nuns who, she said, was truly "un ange de corps et d'esprit" would gladly have remained at Port Royal. Their poverty was equalled only by their humility. "Elles n'ont quoi que ce soit que ce qu'on leur donne et elles ne demandent qu'à l'extrémité et se passent de si peu qu'on voit en cela leur vertu et leur bon cœur."[1]

This was the community of the English Benedictines, to-day residing at the Monastery of our Lady of Good Hope at Colwich in Staffordshire. Originally founded at Cambrai in 1623 by the Fathers of the English Benedictine Congregation, the increase of members made it desirable in 1651 to transfer part of the community to Paris under Dame Clementia Carey, though this was done against the advice of the abbé Montagu who pointed out the poverty of the English court, incapable of rendering any assistance, and the unsettled condition of the city of Paris, at this time of civil war.

In Paris they made many friends. Among them was the abbé Stuart d'Aubigny whom they call one of their "best patrons" or even their "exceeding great Patron". He was the first "extern superiour", and their first choice of a house belonging to "Mr Hulose" in "St Dominick's Street" was due to the fact that Aubigny lodged near by.[2]

1 Marie-Angélique Arnauld, *Lettres*, II, p. 318.
2 *A Sketch of the History of the Benedictine Community now residing at St Benedict's Priory, Colwich, Stafford*, pp. 6, 41 *et passim*. The Lady Abbess was good enough to lend me a copy of this sketch (privately printed), and I should like here to express to her once more my very grateful thanks for her kindness without which this chapter could not have been written.

Death soon visited the little community—a lay sister, Elizabeth Gertrude Hodson, died on October 7th, 1652, and was buried at Port Royal de Paris at her own request. She is remembered in a manuscript *Nécrologe*.

Octobre. Le 9, 1652, fut enterree en notre monastere de paris sœur gertrude de St Laurent, relig. benedictine Angloise conuë dans le monde sous le nom de d^elle Elizabeth hodon etant sortie de son païs avec plusieurs autres relig. pour sauver leur foi elle mourut a paris le 7 dans une petite maison où elles s'etoient retirees ensbles et où elles vivoient dans l'observance de leur regle mais cõe il n'y avoit point la de lieu de sepulture elle souhaita l'avoir parmi nous.[1]

Their first confessor was Father Serenus Cressy, O.S.B., "well known to Lord Aubigny", obtaining for them "many Benefactours by his acquaintances and Interest with many Learned Persons, particularly with the Messieures de Port Royal".[2]

They changed houses several times, but in 1664 they settled down to a sixth and last house, where they remained until their departure from France at the time of the Revolution. How they came to live in this house is a story which would have enchanted Sainte-Beuve, and one wishes he could have known these pages written by Dame Theresa Cooke, not only to show forth "the Infinite Mercy and Providence of God", but also "out of Gratitude and memory of the Goodness and Liberality of our Worthy Benefactours the Messieurs of Port Royal".[3]

Obliged to remove from their fifth house the Prioress Dame Brigid More, a great-great-granddaughter of Sir Thomas More, went out several times, together with Mother Clementia Carey, afoot and disguised, to look for a new house, but nothing suitable could be found. Added to this was their great poverty —there was no money to pay the rent of the house in which they

---

1 B.M., Add. MSS. 25043, f. 46. See also *A Sketch*..., p. 6, and *Catholic Record Society Publications*, vol. 13, p. 47.

2 *A Sketch*..., chapter VII.

3 *Ib.* pp. 8–13. Most of the narrative was reprinted recently (1929) in Eaton's *Benedictines of Colwich*, pp. 34–9. The story was also related in Dodd's *Church History* (folio ed.), III, pp. 181 *et seq.*; only here M. des Touches and M. Singlin are prudently called Monsieur de T—— and Monsieur S——. See also Daumet, *Notice sur les Établissements religieux*, Première Partie, pp. 42–5.

lived; there was no money to pay for their removal. In this difficulty Mother Clementia turned to the Messieurs of Port Royal. Mother Clementia, it may be noted, "spoke french in perfection, knowing well how to treat with all sorts of persons, of what condition or quality soever". The Messieurs at once sent a gentleman with money for the rent, and the promise that a house should be sought out for them.

A few days later the house was found, and a coach came on March 12th to carry Mother Clementia and some others to the rue du Champ de l'Alouette in the Faubourg St-Marcel to see it. "Mr Anthony Singline, who was the chief of all the Messieurs", was there with some friends, all disguised in secular clothes, "by reason they were much persecuted in those days", also lawyers, notaries, architects and masons, and the nuns were "wonderfully surpriz'd" to see so many people, not knowing who they were. M. Singlin conducted them aside, to another room, and after giving them his benediction pronounced a little homily. Finally he told them that he had chosen the place for its quiet, but if they did not find it convenient they should tell him, and he would look for another place. Then the architects and masons were called in, and the nuns were led through the house, so that they might decide where the chapel, the choir, the refectory, and other places should be. With the architects and masons had come in a plain young ecclesiastic who now and then made some suggestions to Mother Clementia, as they went on their round. Mother Clementia thought he was a "Studiant" and did not lay much store by what he said, in fact she thought he rather intruded into the conversation, "so that when he spake...she did not at all mind him, but hearkened and acquiesc'd to Monsr de Singline in all, wondering what made the other so forward to give his opinion". And when the visit of inspection was over, and orders had been given to the masons to begin their work on the morrow, and to the lawyers and notaries to draw up a contract for the buyer, Monsieur des Touches—the nuns to give what they could and when they could—then M. Singlin once more took the nuns apart—and also the ecclesiastic who had been mildly ignored.

"My Reverend Mothers," he said, "you do not yet know your Benefactour, but think it is I who am indeed nothing but a poor Instrument. It is this Gentleman who has done you this Charity." Then Mother Clementia and her companions were "all abash'd and in great confusion and Mother Clementia begged of him a Thousand Pardons for our seeming neglect and disrespect of him, assuring him that we should have an Eternal Memory of this our obligation to him for his great Charity".

Monsieur des Touches,[1] for it was he, took charge of all the alterations, and defrayed the costs, not only of the rebuilding, but also of the removal into this house. On April 2nd they were able to move in, though all the necessary changes were not completed for another three months. They had only been in the house for a fortnight when they were saddened by the death of M. Singlin.

Things gradually grew worse for the Jansenists. "About a year after we were settled here", writes Dame Theresa Cooke, "this our worthy Founder and all the rest of our Benefactours, the Messieurs of Port Royal, were so persecuted and dispersed, that we had not the satisfaction of seeing Monsr de Touche, or the rest in many years after. Yet sometimes we received Charities from them."

The list of the French benefactors is an interesting one. First come Louis XIV and his queen, but immediately afterwards Port Royal appears.

II. Besides the Messieurs of Port Royal...Mr Bernier, a Secular Gentleman and one of them, gave us 400 livres tournois for 14 years time

III. Monsr de Touche, besides what has bin before said of him, was likewise wont for many years together, to give us 400 livers tournois, besides other Charities, and as if all this had yet bin nothing, was pleased to contribute to our late building, as his owne private Charity ye summe of — .

---

1 Paul Le Pelletier, seigneur des Touches (1622–1703). He had become acquainted with Port Royal through Saint-Cyran. Singlin was his director and confessor.

IV. The Religious of the Monastery of Port Royall de Champs have bin very extraordinarily Charitable to us, especially in the 2 former Abbesses time, viz. Mother Angelique and Mother Agnes de Arnaud.

V. Mr de Sevignie, one of the Messieurs of Port Royal, was likewise our great Friend and Benefactour....[1]

But the oppression of Port Royal told on the English Benedictines. "Being deprived of ye helpe of o^r cheife Benefactors, the Messuers of Port Royall y^t then lay under sever persecutions and we living in this retired place, having few acquaintance wth ye french o^r v. R^d Mo: prioress found things goe so very hard ye first foure years that we were forced to sell or pawne o^r plate and linning." Yet assistance came "in the great charitys procured us by our worthy freind and Benefactor Mon^r de St Mar^t one of the Messuers of Port Royall *in absconditum*".[2]

At that time M. de Sainte-Marthe, one of the confessors of Port Royal, lay concealed near the house of the Benedictines and often came " with a secular gentleman called M. Petitier"—doubtless M. de la Petitière, one of the solitaries—to celebrate mass in their little private chapel. Through a visitor, a Mrs Swift, the prioress, Mother Justina Gascoigne, asked M. de Sainte-Marthe to dispose of a pair of holland sheets. Mrs Swift merely said that the sheets belonged to persons of quality who were reduced to dire straits and forced to dispose of them for money to buy food. M. de Sainte-Marthe listened with compassion, gave her four louis d'or and told her to keep the sheets till they were called for, but guessing to whom the sheets belonged he took steps to make someone else do what he could not—approach the Archbishop of Paris, M. de Péréfixe, on behalf of the English nuns. Their needs were made known and relief obtained.[3]

One finds M. de Sainte-Marthe also helping in other ways. Some of the "Benefactors"—doubtless Port Royal—objected against the Constitutions of the English Benedictines, thinking

1 *A Sketch*..., p. 51. The names of other French benefactors follow.
2 *Catholic Record Society*, vol. 9, p. 358.
3 *A Sketch*..., p. 55.

LES BÉNÉDICTINES ANGLAISES 73

them not rigid enough. Mother Justina Gascoigne endeavoured
to satisfy them, but in vain, until she sent for M. de Sainte-
Marthe, and explained to him "upon what mature deliberation"
the Constitutions had been composed. M. de Sainte-Marthe approved whole-heartedly and undertook to satisfy the objections
of the benefactors, "afterwards they had much more kindness
and value for us than they had before".[1]

Poverty continued to be the lot of the nuns. The year 1693
was a terrible year of hardship. We read in a Port Royal
history: "Les Bénédictines Angloises de Paris étoient dans une
telle pauvreté pendant la famine qui désola la France en cette
année 1693 que personne ne vouloit plus leur vendre de pain à
crédit. Comme elles étoient étrangères les secours ne pouvoient
être abondans chez elles. Elles se souvinrent dans cette ex-
trêmité que la charité de Port Royal étoit de toute nation, et elles
écrivirent leur état à la Mère Abbesse".[2]

At this time Racine's aunt was abbess.[3] She assembled the
community at once—money there was none to spare, but they
decided to send a very beautiful chalice immediately to Paris, to
be sold for the benefit of the Benedictines. The lady who undertook this errand was fortunate enough to get far beyond their
expectations from an ecclesiastic who was touched by the story
of the poverty of the Benedictines. When she brought the
money, the English prioress, Dame Agnes Temple, said with
gratitude: "On ne peut être plus obligé que nous le sommes
à nos sœurs du Port Royal. Jamais secours n'est venu plus à
propos: il n'y a point un morceau de pain dans notre Maison et
personne ne veut nous en prêter. Actuellement toute notre
Communauté est prosternée au pied de Jesus Christ le vrai pain
de Vie pour lui demander le pain matériel dont nous avons
besoin".[4]

A few years later Port Royal des Champs had ceased to exist,
and so we come to the end of this story, but before leaving the
Benedictines it is interesting to note that the English Benedictine

1 *Ib.* p. 57.
2 Guilbert, *Mémoires hist. et chron. sur l'Abbaye de Port-Royal*, III, p. 153.
3 Agnès de Sainte-Thècle Racine.
4 Guilbert, *op. cit.* III, pp. 153–4.

fathers were well known to Port Royal de Paris. At the
time of the persecution of 1661 the king appointed M.
Bail, curé de Montmartre, to be the superior of Port Royal—"ses cheveux
se hérissaient au seul nom de Port-Royal", says Racine[1]—and
one of his first decisions was that all the confessors must go—
M. Singlin, M. de Saci, M. de Sainte-Marthe and others.[2] The
abbess, la Mère Agnès Arnauld, then asked whether they might
have as their confessors the English Benedictine fathers "qui
disent la Messe ici", and permission was given at first, but in a
few days M. Bail returned and withdrew it saying that "ces
Religieux estoient suspects parce qu'ils estoient estrangers",[3]
and indeed when one remembers that Port Royal had been
variously accused of schism and sedition, of a spirit of political
independence, of siding with the malcontents during the Fronde,
of intriguing with Cromwell, of befriending the Cardinal de
Retz, of being too partial to foreigners, one can understand that
a relationship with fathers who were Englishmen was bound to
be viewed with disapproval.

1 Racine, *Abrégé de l'Histoire de Port-Royal*, p. 127.
2 *Ib.* p. 131.
3 B.N. f. fr. MS. 17774, f. 26. May–June 1661.

CHAPTER VI

Ludovic Stuart d'Aubigny and his French Friends

AT Gordon Castle near Fochabers hangs the portrait of a fair-haired youth in clerical dress sitting at work among his books.[1] "Lodowych Stewart, Abbé d'Aubigny," we read in the catalogue,[2] "a beautifully finished picture, small full length, seated at a table writing. He wears a priest's black robe with deep white collar and ruffles at the wrist. His fair hair is cut square across the forehead. On the table, which is covered with a Turkish cloth, are writing materials, a large open book, lamp, bell and large crucifix. A gold drapery over his head, and in the background a large bookcase filled with volumes.... Painter unknown, but in soft French style."

One who knew Ludovic in his youth—not a Jansenist—bears witness to his personal charm. "Il avoit un esprit rare, une grâce singulière dans ses discours, son visage estoit beau et on pouvoit dire de lui que Dieu l'avoit enrichi de dons naturels."[3] Another, a Jesuit Father, noted the advantages conferred on him by his birth and gentle bearing, "Sa qualité jointe à une douceur naturelle qui luy séioit extrêmement, luy servoit d'un grand charme pour s'insinuer dans les cœurs".[4] Years later Saint-Évremond—no mean judge of men—wrote in his praise " Avec lui, la joie est de tous les pays et de toutes les conditions; jusque là qu'un malheureux y devient trop gai, et perd sans y penser la bienséance d'un sérieux que l'on doit aux infortunes".[5] Disillusioned as Saint-Évremond was in all things, he was deeply attached to Aubigny, but three years younger than he, and Aubigny's premature death left him desolate. Like Montaigne

1 Cust, *Stuarts of Aubigny*, p. 108. The portrait was exhibited in the Stuart exhibition of 1889.

2 I gratefully acknowledge the kindness of His Grace the Duke of Richmond and Gordon who was good enough to send me this description.

3 Bibl. Sainte-Geneviève, MS. 1480 (*Vie de M. du Ferrier*), f. 188.

4 Rapin, *Mémoires*, I, p. 170.

5 Saint-Évremond, *Œuvres* (éd. Giraud), III, p. 35.

grieving for La Boétie, Saint-Évremond remembers Aeneas lamenting the anniversary of Anchises' dying day. "Parlant du jour que mourut M. d'Aubigny," he writes, "je dirai toute ma vie avec une vérité funeste et sensible:

Quem semper acerbum,
Semper honoratum, sic Dii voluistis, habebo."[1]

And yet there are darker sides to the picture of one who could inspire such affection. Evelyn is disparaging in his judgment, and says that Aubigny was "a person of good sense, but wholly abandoned to ease and effeminacy",[2] and indeed Aubigny alludes more than once to his own indolence.[3] Burnet shows positive dislike, but is doubtless biassed in his verdict by his distrust of a Roman Catholic. "The Lord Aubigny", he tells us, "maintained an outward decency and had more learning and better notions than men of quality who enter into orders generally have. Yet he was a very vicious man; and this perhaps made him the more considered by the King who loved and trusted him to a high degree. No man had more credit with the King."[4] The Quaker Latey heard that "the way of the Lord was evilly spoken of".[5] And though disapprobation by the Jansenists is not necessarily a valid condemnation of a man, the fact remains that they were disappointed in him. A curious, complex personality is that of Ludovic Stuart d'Aubigny, and so intimately is he connected with certain ecclesiastical affairs of the early years of the Restoration, that an account of him may well be given in these pages.

The Stuarts of Aubigny were established in France from 1422 till 1672, the seigneurie of Aubigny in Berry having been conferred on Sir John Stuart by Charles VII as a reward for help against the English.[6] They resided, however, not infrequently in England and Scotland, and it was in London that Ludovic was

1 Saint-Évremond, Œuvres (éd. Giraud), I, p. 106.
2 Evelyn, Diary, I, p. 360.   3 Hermant, Mémoires, V, p. 356, and VI, p. 575.
4 Burnet, History (ed. Airy), I, pp. 242–3.
5 R. Hawkins, Life of Latey (1851), p. 36.
6 For this and the next few paragraphs see Cust, op. cit. passim. For a description of the town and château of Aubigny, and of the château of La Verrerie, also belonging to the Stuarts of Aubigny, see L. Boucher, Aubigny sur Nère en Berry (Rouen 1926).

born at March House, Drury Lane, on October 14th, 1619, the fourth son of Esme Stuart, seventh seigneur d'Aubigny and of Katherine Clifton, daughter of Sir Gervase Clifton. Esme Stuart having been made a peer of England in the year of Ludovic's birth,[1] and succeeding his brother as third Duke of Lennox, could not continue to hold Aubigny as a vassal of France, therefore his second son Henry was chosen to take his place. Henry and his younger brothers, George and Ludovic, were all sent to Aubigny to be educated, being also naturalized in France. Ludovic was but five years old when he was brought across in 1624, the year of his father's death. The three boys were placed under the charge of their grandmother, Catherine de Balzac d'Entragues, widow of the first Duke of Lennox, sixth seigneur d'Aubigny.

It is often said that Ludovic was brought up at Port Royal,[2] but it must be remembered that he could not have been a pupil of one of the Petites Écoles which did not yet exist in his boyhood. In his youth he certainly came under the influence of Jansenist ecclesiastics, notably the abbé de La Lane, and though for a while he appears to have left them, choosing M. du Ferrier of Saint-Sulpice to be his director, later on Jansenist influences seem to have reasserted themselves. Nevertheless M. du Ferrier and Aubigny always remained friends.[3]

At the age of twenty or twenty-one, early in 1640, the fairhaired youth had thoughts of becoming a cardinal, and went to see the English ambassador, the Earl of Leicester, in this matter. Richelieu, so he represented, would use his influence, if Charles I in turn would allow Bishop Smith, the Roman Catholic Bishop of Chalcedon, to return to England, but the king would have none of this bargaining; and if Ludovic was excused for his presumption it was only on the grounds of a "youthfull Inconsideration".[4]

1 As Lord Stuart of Leighton Bromswold and Earl of March.
2 E.g. *Vies intéressantes et édifiantes des Amis de Port-Royal*, I, p. 120.
3 Bibl. Sainte-Geneviève, MS. 1480, ff. 187–93; cf. Faillon, *Vie de M. Olier*, II (4th ed.), pp. 312–19, 350–4.
4 Collins, *Letters and Memorials of State*, II, pp. 632, 633, 635, 637, 647; *Thurloe Papers*, I, p. 743.

His brother Henry, eighth seigneur d'Aubigny, had died in Venice in the meanwhile, and his brother George, ninth seigneur, fell at the battle of Edgehill. Ludovic therefore took possession of Aubigny in 1643, and, at the age of twenty-four, wrongfully became the tenth seigneur, the property belonging not to him, but to his brother's orphan, a little boy of two. However, as Lady Cust suggests, in the confusion caused by the English civil wars the existence of this child was perhaps overlooked in France.[1]

In 1647, so Rapin tells us, Mazarin, who had more claimants to satisfy than rewards to bestow, and who feared his enemies more than he esteemed his friends, put Aubigny off with a very small living, the Abbaye de Hautefontaine, which Aubigny, not highly elated, was able to exchange a few years later—in 1653—for a canonry of Notre Dame.[2]

Aubigny soon found himself involved in party matters—the young ecclesiastic was elected to preside over the "Congrégation de la Propagation de Foi", a congregation founded in 1632; the election was evidently carried on on partisan lines, and Aubigny was sponsored by the Jansenists. His modest refusal was not accepted, and his election was confirmed by the Archbishop of Paris, Gondi, uncle to the Cardinal de Retz, but Mazarin, so one hears, dissolved the congregation rather than let the election stand.[3]

As a Canon of Notre Dame Aubigny became one of the upholders of "the Coadjutor", the Cardinal de Retz, in captivity

1 Cust, *op. cit.* p. 107. The friends of the dispossessed heir presented a petition in his name as "Charles, Lord Aubigny" to the House of Lords in 1646 which states that "his uncle Ludovic now liveth in France and most wrongfullie detaineth the estate of your petitioner there" (see also p. 112). Eventually a friendly arrangement seems to have been made that Lord Ludovic Stuart should not be disturbed at Aubigny, and in 1658 the young nephew came to live for two years with his uncle.

2 Rapin, *Mémoires*, I, p. 171. His version seems to me to conform more to reality than that, diametrically opposed, given in Faillon's *Vie de M. Olier*, II (1st ed.), p. 185. In this book, based on the MS. life of M. du Ferrier, Aubigny is consistently idealized. Father Dumas in *Études*, v, p. 206, points out how absurd is one of the statements made concerning Aubigny. Faillon answers in *Olier*, II (4th ed.), pp. 350–4, but by quoting M. du Ferrier, who had too charitable an opinion of Aubigny.

3 Faillon, *op. cit.* II, 460–2; Hermant, *Mémoires*, II, pp. 258–62, 295.

since December 1652 for his political intrigues, and for his participation in the Fronde. In August 1654 Retz, who in the meantime had become Archbishop of Paris, escaped from his prison. The chapter of Notre Dame showed its joy by having a Te Deum sung, and the court retaliated by sending *lettres de cachet* to some of those who had taken part in the manifestation. Aubigny narrowly escaped inclusion, but he was finally exempted, so a Jansenist historian tells us, out of consideration for the Princess Palatine, Anne de Gonzague, and Turenne, who were both much attached to him.[1] In his *Mémoires* Retz acknowledges Aubigny's loyal support,[2] and the cardinal's companion, Guy Joly, remarks that M. Stuart d'Aubigny, a relative of the King of England, everywhere upheld the cardinal's cause vigorously.[3]

But Aubigny was not so much taken up with the affairs of the Cardinal de Retz as not to be deeply interested in the affairs of his countrymen, many of whom were now taking refuge in France. His attitude to Charles was at first one of disapprobation which gradually gave way to a warm desire to serve him.[4] He corresponded with Charles when the latter left France,[5] to drift about in other countries, and in 1657 he submitted to him, as we have seen, a proposal for the conversion of the Duke of Gloucester. He was also able to give information and advice to English friends in Paris.[6]

The history of the relationship between Charles and Retz is very involved and obscure. Aubigny was certainly implicated; in the years that followed the cardinal's escape from prison, he acted as a link between him and Charles.[7] It may be convenient to deal here briefly with Burnet's suggestion that Retz and Aubigny had much to do with the king's conversion.[8] Burnet says that this took place before Charles left Paris, but even after

---

1 Hermant, *Mémoires*, II, pp. 575, 584, 585.
2 Retz, *Œuvres* (éd. Gr. Écr.), V, p. 133.
3 Joly, *Mémoires* (éd. Michaud et Poujoulat), p. 124, see also pp. 125 and 135.
4 *Thurloe Papers*, I, p. 737; *Nicholas Papers* (Camden), II, p. 113.
5 *Thurloe Papers*, I, pp. 742, 745.
6 *Ib.* I, pp. 732 *et seq.*, VI, pp. 765, 891–3, VII, pp. 325–7. *Cal. Clarendon Papers*, IV, 45, 622, 667.   7 *Ib.* I, pp. 735, 737, 741.
8 Burnet, *History of My Own Time* (ed. Airy), I, p. 133, where see also a long note on Charles and Roman Catholicism.

Charles had left, Aubigny continued to have a very ill opinion of him and his way of living;[1] his proposals for the conversion of the Duke of Gloucester show that he did not look upon Charles as a convert, and though the long years of sojourn abroad doubtless made Charles a Roman Catholic at heart, yet the documents published by Boero in 1863[2] tended to show that no formal abjuration had taken place in Aubigny's lifetime.

"I think 59 hath very sincear desires to serve 242," writes a Royalist from Paris, "yet those take him not up so fully, as not to doe somewhat in order to himself."[3] And indeed "59", Aubigny, though deprecating the vanity of his youth when he wished to be cardinal, proposed himself to take charge of the Duke of Gloucester, wanted to be sent to Rome in the king's ("242") behalf, and was quite pleased to tell him that the Roman Catholics in England had earnestly solicited him to become their bishop, if an attempted rapprochement between Cromwell and the Catholics took place.[4]

After the Restoration Aubigny went to England, in the autumn of 1660, and in November strange reports began to reach the French court, joining the names of Retz and Aubigny. Where Retz was, no one knew, but Aubigny, the cardinal's good friend, was in close touch with him; the way in which he spoke of the cardinal showed that they were in constant communication and that Aubigny enjoyed the cardinal's utmost confidence. He often talked to the King of England of the cardinal, and was responsible for the king's goodwill to the fugitive. "Let Aubigny's person be watched, his valets followed, his correspondence intercepted, and some light might be thrown on the enigma."[5] In December it was rumoured that the cardinal was in England and that, thanks to Aubigny, he had been very well received.[6]

1 *Nicholas Papers*, ii, p. 113; *Thurloe Papers*, i, p. 737.

2 In *La Civiltà Cattolica*, April–Sept. 1863.

3 *Thurloe Papers*, vi, p. 765, Kingston to Lawrence (i.e. to Hyde), Feb. 8, 1658 (N.S.).   4 *Ib.* and i, pp. 741–2.

5 Aff. Étr. Corr. *d'Angleterre*, vol. 73, f. 67 (Nov. 4), f. 92 (Nov. 6), f. 178 (Dec. 2, 1660); vol. 72, f. 100 (Nov. 8). Dispatches from the Agent Bartet.

6 *Ib.* vol. 73, ff. 198–9; vol. 74, ff. 654 *et seq.* (quoted in Ogg, *The Cardinal de Retz*, pp. 258–64); R.O. *France*, vol. 115, f. 175, Justel to Oldenburg; Joly, *Mémoires*, p. 142.

PLATE II

LUDOVIC STUART D'AUBIGNY

Such news was not acceptable to the court of France, and one is not surprised to find a message sent in March 1661 to Bartet, the French agent in London—Aubigny is on no account to come to France at this juncture "où les partisans du cardinal de Retz se font entendre qu'ils attendent son retour pour l'avancement des affaires du dit cardinal".[1] Mazarin had died three days before, the friends of Retz were in great hopes, and a daring move on their part was to be expected. Bartet had, however, left before the royal command arrived,[2] so, three weeks later, Aubigny was the object of another message. This time the Earl of St Albans, the English ambassador in France, was desired to write to the King of England, asking him to hinder Aubigny's return to France.[3] "The adherents to that Cardinal have carried themselves in these latter times in such a manner that his Majesty is pleased to let them know that the Lord d'Aubigny shall not come to France as they did imagine." The request was complied with, although "in many ways a little inconvenient".[4]

About the same time Bartet, who had been giving the French government all the private information about Aubigny, was dismissed from office—Joly says he was clapped into the Bastille—he had played the government false. Two of Aubigny's Jansenist friends, sharing in Bartet's disgrace, were condemned to exile. Aubigny was the unwitting cause of their misfortune.

The story of what happened is complicated enough, but it would seem that upon Mazarin's death Aubigny, who knew Bartet extremely well, had won him over to the side of Retz and had sent him to Paris with Meade, a gentleman of his household, to meet the cardinal's friends in Paris, while Retz, awaiting the outcome of events in Valenciennes,[5] sent his man Malclerc to Paris to confer with them. Bartet was seized in Paris, letters

1 Boislisle, *Mémoriaux*, i, p. 29, March 12, 1661.
2 *Ib.*
3 *Ib.* p. 151, April 5, 1661.
4 *Clarendon State Papers*, iii, Suppl. pp. iii–iv; Lister, *Life of Clarendon*, iii, p. 124.
5 Joly, *Mémoires*, p. 144.

CJ   6

from the Cardinal de Retz were found on his person, and he was consigned to prison.[1]

Now Bartet had consorted with Jansenists during his stay in Paris; he lodged in Aubigny's house, upstairs lived M. de Bernières. Spies reported Bartet's going to the duchesse de Longueville's and conferring with her secretary, Taignier, one of the ecclesiastics attached to Port Royal. Bartet must be a Jansenist himself. Letters from Aubigny were intercepted. It happened that M. de Bernières had recommended the Irish Catholics to Aubigny's care; M. Taignier had written the letter for him, using prudently only the most general of terms, and Aubigny had replied just as prudently that the King of England would look after the matter recommended by M. de Bernières through M. Taignier. That letter was opened, the vague expression coming as it did from Aubigny could mean one thing only— Retz; the Jansenists were known to be friendly to Retz though he repaid them but ill for their help,[2] Bernières and Taignier were intimate with Bartet who was discovered to be in the cardinal's interests, "on crut que ces Messieurs tramaient une grande intrigue en Angleterre en faveur du cardinal de Retz". M. de Bernières was relegated to Issoudun in Berry, and Taignier to Castelnaudary in Languedoc.[3] The latter, a poor little asthmatic hunchback, felt unable to undertake the long journey and went into hiding,[4] though orders were issued against him to have him put into the Bastille,[5] but M. de Bernières quietly accepted his destiny.

Bernières' friends hoped much from Aubigny's intervention,

1 Boislisle, *Mémoriaux*, I, p. 151, *n*. 8; cf. R. de Chantelauze, *Le cardinal de Retz et ses missions diplomatiques à Rome* (1879), pp. 11–13. "I am sure you will not believe that I have gone a sharer in any intriegue with Bartett"—the Lord Chancellor Hyde to the Earl of St Albans, Lister, *op. cit.* III, p. 121.

2 On this point see Chantelauze, *Le cardinal de Retz et les Jansénistes* in Sainte-Beuve, *Port-Royal*, v; Gazier, *Les dernières Années du cardinal de Retz*; Cochin, *Retz et Port-Royal* in *Supplément à la correspondance du cardinal de Retz* (*Œuvres*, éd. Gr. Écr.).

3 Hermant, *Mémoires*, IV, pp. 634–5; Rapin, *Mémoires*, III, pp. 109–10. According to Rapin the duchesse de Longueville had written to Aubigny, to recommend an Irish Catholic gentleman, and Aubigny's reply to her was intercepted.

4 Hermant, *Mémoires*, IV, p. 636.

5 Boislisle, *Mémoriaux*, I, p. 166.

Aubigny "l'occasion de sa disgrâce".[1] It was true he was not a *persona grata* at the French court, but was he not a cousin of the King of England? and certainly M. de Bernières deserved much of that country. Letters from Aubigny reached Taignier in his seclusion,[2] while Dr Holden, an English doctor of the Sorbonne, who evidently knew of Taignier's hiding place, forwarded his letters to Aubigny. The utmost caution was necessary, for Aubigny knew that their letters were opened— he himself did not write in his own hand. One does not see, however, that he is doing anything for M. de Bernières. Instead he tells Taignier negligently, " Si vous entendez parler sur mon sujet de choses magnifiques, j'y suis plus passif qu'actif, et je laisse faire ceux qui ont droit d'agir et de disposer de moi".[3] And what was fortune holding out to Aubigny? A bishop's mitre perhaps, a cardinal's hat—it remained to be seen; certainly he would be the future queen's Grand Almoner.[4] Taignier and Bernières began to fear that Aubigny was too much wrapped up in this world's vainglory. " Ses emplois me font trembler pour lui", writes Bernières in November, and Taignier penned grave letters to their absent friend.[5]

The weeks went on, and M. de Bernières heard nothing from Aubigny. He is reminded of the description of those who, unlike John the Baptist, wear soft clothing and are in kings' houses—*Mollibus vestiuntur et in domibus regum sunt.* M. d'Aubigny, far from his Jansenist friends, has no one "pour lui parler et lui dire qu'il prenne garde de tomber".[6] In London at this time Aubigny was showing Evelyn with pride his "elegant lodging", his "wheelchair for ease and motion", his curios;[7] he was supping at Whitehall,[8] he was participating, as he thought, in state affairs. The French ambassador, d'Estrades, had arrived in July of that year, 1661, and Aubigny had at once busied himself

---

1 Hermant, *Mémoires*, v, p. 356.
2 *Ib.* pp. 230, 356. 3 *Ib.* p. 358, Autumn 1661.
4 Aff. Étr. *Corr. d'Angleterre*, vol. 75, f. 135, Sept. 1, 1661.
5 Hermant, *Mémoires*, v, p. 360. 6 *Ib.* pp. 386–7, Dec. 1661.
7 Evelyn, *Diary*, i, p. 360.
8 Aff. Étr. *Corr. d'Angleterre*, vol. 74, p. 654 (quoted in Ogg, *The Cardinal de Retz*, pp. 262–3).

bringing compliments from the ambassador to the Lord Chancellor,[1] being present at their meetings, serving as interpreter,[2] carrying messages from the king to the ambassador.[3]

Naturally Louis was not pleased to find "le sieur d'Aubigny", one of whom he disapproved, coming suddenly into such prominence.[4] In reply Estrades pleads his own ignorance, and his desire to do everything for the Catholics of England who looked upon Aubigny as their foremost man.[5] Besides the King of England honoured Aubigny with his friendship, and entertained great projects for him,[6] in fact Aubigny was indispensable—"Si le Roy entre en quelque traité de liaison avec le Roy d'Angleterre on ne sçauroit se passer de Mr d'Aubigny".[7] All of which drew forth a somewhat grudging permission to utilize the services of Aubigny;[8] still the tone that pervades the French state correspondence continues to be one of general distrust where he is concerned.[9]

"Il y a longtemps qu'il ne m'a écrit," writes Bernières of his

1 *Clarendon State Papers*, III, Suppl. p. xi.

2 Aff. Étr. *Corr. d'Angleterre*, vol. 75, f. 71, July 21, 1661; cf. *Mém. et Doc.* vol. 23, ff. 92, 170, vol. 27, f. 80.

3 Aff. Étr. *Corr. d'Angleterre*, vol. 75, f. 69, July 21, 1661; cf. *Mém. et Doc.* vol. 23, f. 89, vol. 27, f. 76.

4 Aff. Étr. *Corr. d'Angleterre*, vol. 75, f. 85, July 29, 1661; cf. Boislisle, *Mémoriaux*, II, p. 265.

5 Cf. "Il se fit hier au soir une assemblée pour les Catholiques chez M. d'Aubigny où assistèrent l'ambassadeur d'Espagne, le marquis d'Ormond, le comte de Bristol, l'abbé de Montaigu et plusieurs autres seigneurs de qualité". Aff. Étr. *Corr. d'Angleterre*, vol. 72, f. 110, Nov. 26, 1660 (from Bartet). In 1661 "A general assembly was this year held, but under an apprehension that some umbrage might be given to the government, lord Aubigny was requested to acquaint His Majesty that the design of their meeting was merely to settle some private concerns and to procure a bishop for their superior, but that he might be assured they would well chuse such a man for the office as should be well principled and his loyal subject. The King consented to their meeting and sent this answer... not to accept any extraordinary authority from Rome." Panzani, *Memoirs*, pp. 303–4.

6 Aff. Étr. *Corr. d'Angleterre*, vol. 75, ff. 102, 135, Aug. 1661; B.N. *Mélanges Colbert*, vol. 106, ff. 122, 124.

7 Aff. Étr. *Corr. d'Angleterre*, vol. 75, f. 143, Sept. 5, 1661.

8 *Ib.* f. 156 (the same in vol. 76, f. 228; *Mém. et Doc.* vol. 23, f. 142; vol. 27, f. 27); for Charles' good opinion of Aubigny see vol. 75, f. 170. See also *Mém. et Doc.* vol. 23, f. 167.

9 See e.g. Aff. Étr. *Corr. d'Angleterre*, vol. 76, ff. 254–5; cf. vol. 77, ff. 55, 62, 63, 80; Boislisle, *Mémoriaux*, III, pp. 168–9. Nor was Aubigny made aware of Charles' inmost negotiations. See *Notes which passed at the Privy Council*, p. 37.

friend in December 1661, "j'ai seulement appris par une lettre qu'il a écrite à un homme du cloître qu'il prendra son temps de parler de moi. Car il est fort bien et de çà et de là; et mes amis jugent que je dois le laisser faire et quitter toutes les autres médiations que l'on a voulu prendre." But there were to be no concessions on Bernières' part, no compromise, no signing of formularies. "Si par hasard vous lui écrivez," he says to Taignier, "vous lui manderez qu'il ne faut rien faire pour moi qui ne soit pur et simple, c'est-à-dire sans aucune condition ou de signer quelque chose que je ne pourrais."[1]

The days went on, and Bernières thought more of the spiritual dangers to which Aubigny was exposed than of the help that might be expected of him. "L'autre me fait compassion", writes this exile of his prosperous friend, though he is glad to note a certain firmness in one of his letters.[2] As for Aubigny's promised intervention he awaited it patiently. "C'est la seule porte qui m'est ouverte comme mon frère me le mande, à moins que de donner du nez en terre comme les autres et fléchir le Père Annat par la lâcheté de ma plume."[3]

A new year began—1662. *Ad te levavi oculos meos qui habitas in cælis.* When would Bernières and Taignier meet again? And yet too great a price would be paid for such a reunion, if it meant any compromise through Aubigny. "Il faut examiner plus que jamais à quoi il tend et quel (*sic*) est la disposition de son cœur.... Etant au milieu d'une nation perverse on ne saurait être trop sur ses gardes.... Il me fait dire qu'il va travailler pour moi. Je le laisse faire et m'abandonne à l'ordre de Dieu."[4]

M. d'Aubigny was very busy going backwards and forwards between the king and the French ambassador, or the chancellor and the ambassador; he was entertaining Saint-Évremond; he was planning to go to France to buy furnishings for the new queen's chapel; he was negotiating for permission to have his coach enter the Louvre, as befitted the rank of a Scottish prince.[5]

1 Hermant, *Mémoires*, v, p. 387.
2 *Ib.* p. 388. 3 *Ib.* 4 *Ib.* pp. 426–7.
5 Aff. Étr. *Corr. d'Angleterre*, vol. 76, f. 253, vol. 77, f. 13, vol. 81, ff. 8, 31, 43, 50, 60, 62 (many copies in other volumes); *Mém. et Doc.* vol. 23, f. 189; *Notes which passed*, p. 57.

M. de Bernières' friends hoped anew for Aubigny's intervention, now that he seemed reconciled with the French court. "J'attends avec patience le succès de la négociation de notre ami", writes Bernières in February. And surely Aubigny would not forget Taignier? "Je ne peux croire que notre ami ne veille pour vous-même malgré vous. Il n'y est pas moins obligé que pour moi." Yet Bernières is still haunted by the fear that some condition will be imposed that he cannot accept, some signing of the formulary, but he was not an ecclesiastic and no layman had been required to sign.[1] "Ce serait me noter d'infamie", he exclaims, "que je fusse le seul du royaume de qui l'on eût tiré cette servitude." Surely when Aubigny "fera parler par une recommandation si puissante"—one is inclined to see in this an allusion to Charles—they would not have the temerity to exact such a condition? Bernières' friends, elated by the "powerful protection", are already congratulating him on his return, but Bernières is saddened by the persecution closing in around Port Royal, "la maison que nous aimons", and this takes from him all desire to return to Paris, that Babylon which will indeed be nothing but a Babylon to him, if he comes back to find his true friends gone.[2]

But still nothing came from England. Aubigny could scarcely be expected to find time to take up his friends' case—he was getting ready for the queen's arrival from Portugal; he was discussing literature and the play—le théâtre, ô Port Royal!— with Saint-Évremond; he was helping Saint-Évremond, along with the Duke of Buckingham, to write the comedy of *Sir Politick would be*;[3] he was marrying Charles and Catherine of Braganza;[4] he was Grand Almoner.

"Je n'entends point parler de l'ami d'outre mer", Bernières writes in July, and a note of wistfulness creeps into his letters. "Je crains que le souvenir qu'il doit avoir de nous ne soit

1 "Nul laïque, à moins d'être maître d'école ou enfant de chœur, n'est soumis à cette loi." Hermant, *Mémoires*, v, p. 435.
2 *Ib.* pp. 435-6.
3 Des Maizeaux, *Vie de Saint-Évremond*, in Saint-Évremond, *Œuvres mêlées*, VI, p. 35.
4 Evelyn, *Diary*, II, p. 186; Burnet, *History* (ed. Airy), I, p. 307. In May 1662.

englouti dans les vagues. Prions pour lui du meilleur de notre
cœur, et pour tous les autres qui nous ont abandonnés....*Si
Deus pro nobis, quis contra nos?*"[1] And yet perhaps Aubigny was
not as forgetful as his friends thought, for ten days later came
an order from the French court, giving Bernières permission to
withdraw from Issoudun to a country property of his. But the
permission came six hours after M. de Bernières' death. God
had ended his banishment in a better way, says Hermant,
bringing him to a true country.[2] A curiously similar incident
overtook Aubigny, as we shall see.

1 Hermant, *Mémoires*, v, p. 498.
2 *Ib.* p. 500. Sainte-Beuve takes up Bernières and Aubigny in *Port-Royal*, IV,
Appendice, pp. 555–63.

CHAPTER VII

Aubigny and the Cardinalate

L E T us leave Aubigny's humble friends and, turning back for a moment, examine some of the projects that had perhaps made him forgetful of the plight of his former companions. He was still the same man who had wanted to be a cardinal in his youth; he was now contemplating a bishopric; he had thoughts of becoming Bishop of Dunkirk. The town of Dunkirk, it will be remembered, belonged to the English from 1658 to 1662 when it was sold to the French.

In 1661 Aubigny presented his friend, the ambassador Estrades, with a document which he asked him to transmit to the nuncio in France. This document, dated August 24th, 1661, dwelt first on the necessity of providing the Catholics of England with a bishop to put an end to their discussions. The king did not, however, wish a bishop *in partibus*, and a Roman Catholic Bishop of Canterbury, York, or London, or even of Great Britain was out of the question—it would rouse the Protestants and expose the Catholics to new persecutions. The creation of a bishopric of Dunkirk would solve all difficulties, it would not offend the susceptibility of the Protestant bishops, since the see of the new bishop, though in an English possession, would not be in England itself. Moreover, the document went on to say, it would help to detach the Catholics of Dunkirk from Spanish influences, the clergy being entirely governed by Spanish prelates. But great haste and secrecy were necessary—everything must be settled in two months, before Parliament met in November. Who the bishop was to be, was, of course, not mentioned, but a week later Estrades informed Brienne of the king's friendship for Aubigny and his family—the king wanted Aubigny to be cardinal and Bishop of England including Dunkirk.[1]

1 Aff. Étr. *Corr. d'Angleterre*, vol. 75, ff. 135–6, Sept. 1, 1661. The document itself is preserved in the Archives of the Vatican. (See following page, *n.* 1.)

Estrades, a former governor of Dunkirk, forwarded the document at once to Paris, accompanied by a warm letter of recommendation, and from Paris it was sent to Rome to be examined. But the French court did not approve of Aubigny, as we have seen, tainted as he was through his relationship with Retz, and Estrades, reprimanded for his intimacy with Aubigny, declined to forward another memoir to the nuncio.

The first memoir had gone its way, however, and the Nuncio Piccolomini, on the strength of Estrades' affirmations, had also written to Cardinal Chigi to tell him that Aubigny was not a Jansenist—that was an "imposture" set afoot by the late Cardinal Mazarin to discredit Aubigny at Rome. A week later he changed his mind entirely, he had been making inquiries in the meantime, the "abbate d' Obegny" was a great friend of the Jansenists, and the King of England was supposed to favour the Jansenists, they having befriended him during his exile.

The nuncio determined to try Aubigny himself. He sent him the anti-Jansenist profession of faith which Rome had recently received from Aubigny's friend, the Cardinal de Retz, and desired his adhesion. Aubigny was put into an awkward situation. A month went by, and the nuncio expressed surprise that no answer had been received. Six weeks, and he was still waiting, though Estrades, on a visit to Paris, let him hope that Aubigny would subscribe. Three months, and still nothing was forthcoming. In the meantime it had been decided at Rome that Dunkirk should continue to be part of the bishopric of Ypres, doubtless for political reasons, but Aubigny's reputation had not been improved by this episode, and he continued to be regarded as a Jansenist.[1]

Charles was mortified in the extreme by the attitude of Rome, for he had expected Rome to be gratified by his attentions. The

[1] All that concerns this episode is based on an excellent article by the late M. Claude Cochin, "Dunkerque Évêché Anglais" in the *Bulletin du Comité flamand de France* (1908), pp. 331–52. M. Cochin used principally the *Corr. d'Angleterre* for 1661 at the Aff. Étr. and documents of the *Nunziatura di Francia* in the Vatican archives. Cf. Dodd, *Church History*, III, p. 239, "I find him [Aubigny] among the candidates for the mitre an. 1661, with a particular recommendation from King Charles II. However his enemies found means to hinder his preferment by representing him at Rome as a person tainted with Jansenism".

French embassy reported in July 1662 that he was so weary of the "longueurs" of Rome that he would assuredly show his resentment, and that he and the chancellor would "revert to their first threats".[1] Complaints were also sent by Aubigny's friends to the Cardinal de Retz.[2]

In August a new plan was mentioned, "M. Belings" was to leave shortly for Rome "sous pretexte d'aller baiser les pieds de sa Saincteté au nom de la Reyne", but in reality to urge Aubigny's promotion to the cardinalate. "Il a ordre de laisser tout espérer pour cela et de faire tout craindre."[3] Joly tells us that the Cardinal de Retz was given large sums of money to help to bring about Aubigny's promotion, and the cardinal wrote letters, drew up impressive memoirs, or rather made Joly draw them up, took a special journey to Hamburg to urge Queen Christina to use her influence, and bestowed much advice, such as the sending of men-of-war to Civitavecchia to intimidate the Pope.[4]

Bellings left late in October, or possibly in November.[5] He carried various letters from Charles, from the young queen and from the queen-mother. The one from Charles to Cardinal Chigi was decidedly ungracious and grudging in tone. "Mon Cousin," he writes, "si la Reyne ma mère et la Reyne ma famme n'avoient souhaitté que je meslasse quelque chose de ma part dans les civilitez qu'elles font au Pape, ce qui s'est passé entre la cour de Rome et moy depuis que je suis restabli dans mes royaumes auroit pu me persuader de ne les pas faire."[6] The queen writes timidly to Cardinal Orsini, Protector of Portugal, "J'appréhenderois beaucoup les mauvaises suites du chagrin du roy...et de ses ministres si la cour de Rome persistoit à lui refuser la faveur qu'il demande pour son parent monsieur d'Aubigny".[7]

1 Aff. Étr. *Corr. d'Angleterre*, vol. 77, f. 86, July 17, 1662. Letter from Batailler.
2 *Ib.*   3 *Ib.* f. 134, Aug. 17, 1662.   4 Joly, *Mémoires*, pp. 143, 149.
5 Aff. Étr. *Corr. d'Angleterre*, vol. 77, f. 231. For this very curious episode see Lord Acton, *Historical Essays and Studies*; Boero, *Istoria della Conversione alla Chiesa cattolica di Carlo II* (reprint from the *Civiltà Cattolica* for 1863); *Études* (the periodical published by the Society of Jesus), vol. v, 1864 (a discussion of Boero).
6 R.O. *Roman Transcripts*, vol. 99, Oct. 25, 1662 (also printed in *Bulletin du Comité flamand* (1908), p. 352, from the original autograph).
7 Printed in *Études*, v, p. 199, Oct. 25, 1662.

In Paris Bellings visited Retz[1] and also the abbé Montagu, from whom he brought a letter of recommendation to Cardinal Barberini. Montagu assured the latter that any advantage to be hoped for the Roman Catholics of England would depend on the granting of the two queens' request.[2]

Bellings' instructions were to the effect that Aubigny's promotion was an essential condition to any good understanding between Charles and the Pope, and only after he had received satisfaction with regard to Aubigny might he proceed with another very secret part of his mission.[3] Everything was done to secure Aubigny's promotion,[4] a favourable vote was passed on him,[5] but the Pope, Alexander VII, found himself unable to assent. There were various reasons—the Pope did not think it fitting to bestow a cardinal on a country in which penal laws against the Catholics were still in force, and to expose the dignity of the purple to the contempt and the persecution of the heretics. But the first and foremost objection was the person of Aubigny. He was under suspicion, and well-founded suspicion, not to be altogether at one with the Church; he was said not to have shown due deference to the decisions of the Holy See, and even were it true that he had at one time severed connections with the Jansenists, it was reported that he had again joined the "novatori", and familiar letters from him to Arnauld were mentioned.[6]

According to Jansenist sources, when Bellings returned to Paris in May 1663 he said he had been exceedingly well received by the Pope; however, instead of giving him a hat for Aubigny, the Pope had given him two gold medals, one of which represented the Pope seated on St Peter's throne upheld by four doctors of the Church, and the four doctors—but the irony of

1 Aff. Étr. *Corr. d'Angleterre*, vol. 77, f. 321.
2 R.O. *Roman Transcripts*, vol. 137, Nov. 27, 1662.
3 Boero, *op. cit.* p. 17; *Études*, v, p. 200.
4 See Boero, *op. cit.* and *Études, passim*.
5 *Voto in favore della promozione al Cardinalato del Signor d'Aubigny*, Boero, *op. cit.* pp. 19–20; *Études*, v, p. 201; Acton, *op. cit.* p. 115.
6 Boero, *op. cit.* p. 23; Hermant, *Mémoires*, vi, p. 301. Rapin (*Mémoires*, iii, p. 192) says that the refusal was due to political reasons and not to Aubigny's reported Jansenism, but Boero's study disproves this.

the story is too good to be true—were graven to represent
Cornet, Hallier, Morel and Grandin, four virulent opponents of
Jansenism.[1]

But this is an anticipation, for Bellings did not return
at once—he went on with that part of his mission that he was
not to undertake unless he obtained satisfaction in Aubigny's
case. Why he disregarded his instructions is hard to say,
unless perhaps hearing of the vote emitted in Aubigny's
favour, he thought himself sure of success.

The second part of the mission was far more extraordinary
than the first; it was nothing less than a project of reunion, a
proposal from Charles to submit his three kingdoms to the
Church of Rome. The document[2] brought by Bellings begins
with a profession of faith, and what interests us here is that this
profession contains a clause accepting the decision of the last
two Pontiffs with regard to the matter of Jansenism. This must
have proved acceptable—not so, certain other passages where
the king insisted on a degree of independence that the Holy See
could never have granted. "He carefully restricted the papal
jurisdiction both of doctrine and discipline, and reserved to
himself the rights which the Gallican system attributed to secular
power. He even proposed that the Church should abandon
her essential function of judging and defining matters of faith
as occasion should arise."[3] The question of the infallibility of the
Pope was not to be discussed either in the pulpit or in print.[4]

Who helped to draw up this extraordinary Latin document?
Bellings? Bristol? the abbé Montagu? Aubigny? Certainly the
thing was not done without Aubigny's knowledge, Aubigny
who, as the French state correspondence shows us, was so
constantly with Charles. Lord Acton considers it the work of
a Catholic layman, Bellings, and thinks that Aubigny, the only

1 Hermant, *Mémoires*, VI, p. 301. Even Hermant doubts the story about the
doctors, "Éclaircir ce fait" he has written in the margin of his manuscript.

2 Ranke (III, pp. 398–9) analyses this document *Oblatio ex parte Caroli II*. There
are two copies of it at the Aff. Étr. *Corr. d'Angleterre*, vol. 77, ff. 346–57, and vol.
81, ff. 195–211. For a discussion of the document see Acton, *op. cit.* p. 95 *et seq.*;
Études, v, p. 210; Boero, *op. cit.* pp. 25–6.

3 Acton, *op. cit.* p. 95.

4 Ranke, *op. cit.* III, p. 399.

priest liable to be consulted, would scarcely have introduced the clause against Jansenism. But Aubigny was a lukewarm Jansenist, as we shall see, and Bellings, on the other hand, was not without Jansenist sympathies.[1] We may note, however, that it was Bellings who had drawn up the protestation of allegiance which had been adopted by a certain party in Ireland, and that there is a similarity in the ideas of this protestation and the profession of faith.[2] As for Bristol, in his impeachment of Clarendon in July 1663, he showed himself violently hostile to the Aubigny-Bellings mission.[3] Father Dumas[4] thinks Aubigny the probable author, and the present writer is inclined to agree with him, the document showing a close knowledge of French ecclesiastical affairs. Very likely Aubigny realized that it was time to break with Jansenism, if he were to hope for promotion, but his old reputation still served as a stumbling-block.[5]

The offer could naturally not meet with acceptance, and Bellings returned in May 1663 with letters from the Pope.[6] Hostile rumours concerning the mission to Rome had begun to spread in England in the meantime,[7] and, writing some years later about these letters from Rome, Charles himself says that in spite of all the precautions taken by the messenger—Bellings undoubtedly—"ce ne peut (sic) être avec tant de prudence que nous ne fussions soubçonnés d'intelligence avec le Pape par les plus clairvoyans de nostre cour",[8] and he has to admit that in

---

1 Walsh, *History and Vindication*, Fourth Treatise, p. 74. Bellings had translated *La Fréquente Communion* as we have seen.

2 Cf. Acton, *op. cit.* p. 97. Lord Acton thinks that the Bellings who went to Rome was the son of the above Bellings who indeed was secretary to the Queen. Bagwell, *Ireland under the Stuarts*, III, p. 53, takes the messenger to Rome to be the older Bellings, and this seems more likely.

3 *Cal. S.P. Dom.* 1663-4, p. 199; Burnet, *History* (ed. Airy), I, p. 352; Lister, *Life of Clarendon*, III, pp. 246-7; Pepys, *Diary*, III, p. 203.

4 *Études*, V, p. 211.

5 According to Arnauld (*Œuvres*, XXII, p. 214) Aubigny was personally known to Alexander VII, he had been in Rome after his accession (i.e. after 1655) and had been well received by him; on his return he told his Jansenist friends he was but "médiocrement" convinced when the Pope told him "qu'en faisant sa constitution [against the Jansenists] il avait senti sensiblement la présence du Saint Esprit".

6 *Études*, V, p. 471.

7 Aff. Étr. *Corr. d'Angleterre*, vol. 77, f. 306, Nov. 30, 1662.

8 *Études, loc. cit.*

order to stifle these suspicions he stooped down to give Parliament proofs of his aversion to Catholicism.[1] All negotiations were broken off for the present.

In his later correspondence with the general of the Jesuits[2] Charles says that the Pope's refusal to promote Aubigny was given for good reasons, but certainly at the time he was extremely irritated by it and, strange to say, the chancellor even more. In March 1664 the abbé Montagu writes thus to Cardinal Barberini who had evidently favoured the promotion:

Depuis la response de sa Sainteté au Sieur Belins le Roy s'en estant trouvé fort mal satisfait comme d'un delay qu'il entendoit comme temoignage de peu de considération à son esgard, M. le Chancelier s'en est trouvé si offensé qu'il n'a pas manqué de faire paroistre ses sentiments en plusieurs occasions, qui ont touché les Catoliques de bien près. Je scay bien quels ont esté les sentiments de Votre Eminence en cette affaire, c'est pourquoi ie puis vous assurer que s'ils eussent esté suivis les affaires des Catoliques ici s'en seroient mieux trouvés.[3]

Montagu, it may be added, did not himself escape the charge of Jansenism in later years. "Censetur ad Jansenismum et ad opiniones contra sedem Apostolicam propendere", says a note on the *Personae digniores ex clero Anglicano*.[4]

For a time Aubigny, as he himself tells us, was forbidden to have any dealings with Rome, but "ceste mauvaise humeur aiant esté un peu diminué par le temps et par le changement de quelques conjonctures", he obtained leave about a year later to correspond with Barberini again.[5]

One day in September 1664 the king noticed in the queen's apartment a man who looked familiar to him, he looked familiar to the Duke of York also, but neither he nor the Duke of York could remember who he was. They made inquiries and discovered that it was Vecchiis, the internuncio at Brussels—they had seen him in the days of exile. Vecchiis had come over

1 "A demand for new laws to restrain the progress of popery and assent to a proclamation ordering all priests to quit the Kingdom under pain of death." Acton, *op. cit.* p. 97. Cf. Charles' letter in *Études*, v, p. 474.
2 See *passim* Boero, *op. cit.* or *Études* or Acton, *op. cit.*
3 R.O. *Roman Transcripts*, vol. 137, March 26, 1664.
4 *Ib.* vol. 99, Aug. 12, 1672.
5 *Ib.* vol. 137, Aubigny to Barberini, May 19 [1664].

incognito to deal with Father Walsh in the matter of the Irish
Remonstrance, and realizing himself to be discovered he asked
Bellings to request an audience for him, and this was promised
at first, but the thing coming to the chancellor's ears, he would
fain have put him into prison as a spy, and Vecchiis departed
hastily without having been received by the king.[1]

Before he went, however, he had been able to see the queen-
mother and Aubigny, and this interview is described with much
evident enjoyment by the French ambassador Comenge (or
Cominges) who probably had the story from Aubigny himself.
"Il a pourtant veu la Reine Mère et M. d'Aubigni qui luy ont
bien mis le feu soubz le ventre, ne feignant point de luy dire que
presentement le Roy de la Grande Bretagne n'estoit pas en estat
de se vanger du mespris que l'on avoit faict de ses prieres à
Rome, mais qu'il vouloist bien que l'on sceust et qu'il le fit
scavoir aux puissances qu'il n'en perdroit pas l'occasion sitot
qu'elle se presenteroit." One pictures the alarm of the worthy
internuncio who is made to play a slightly grotesque part in this
tale. After these dark threats came something alarming.

"L'on a poussé l'affaire jusques a luy dire que l'on feroit des
evesques en Irlande et a Tanger qui vivroient selon la doctrine
et discipline de l'eglise catholique Romaine, a la seule diference
qu'ils feroient serment de ne recognoistre le Pape non plus au
spirituel qu'au temporel et que ce schisme seroit bien plus
sensible que toutes les heresies qui sont en Europe." Blackloism[2]—Jansenism—this was going to be infinitely worse! The
internuncio feels that something must be done at any cost. "Il
s'est engagé de faire merveilles a Rome pour donner satisfaction
au Roy d'Angleterre quoy qu'on luy ait affirmé que le Roy ne
s'en soucioit en façon du monde et qu'il ne faisoit point son
affaire d'obtenir un Bonnet par graces puisqu'il scait ce qu'ils
coustoient a Rome."[3]

Whether these undignified threats had any effect, or whether
the charges against Aubigny's Jansenism were withdrawn, at

1 Aff. Étr. Corr. d'Angleterre, vol. 82, ff. 192, 195, Comenge to the king and to
Lionne, Sept. 22 and 29 (N.S.), 1664.
2 More will be said about Blackloism in a later chapter.
3 Aff. Étr. Corr. d'Angleterre, vol. 82, f. 195, Comenge to Lionne, Sept. 29
(N.S.), 1664.

any rate little more than a year later Aubigny was to become a cardinal.

He went to France in July 1665.[1] Letters from Courtin, the ambassador, announce his visit, and Lionne is urged to take advantage of his coming, for Aubigny will prove an interesting guest, and one from whom much information can be derived. "Si vous voulez avoir le plaisir d'entendre parler au vrai sur l'état des affaires d'Angleterre, dites à M. le Commandeur de lui donner à dîner avec MM. de Turenne, d'Humière et de Ruvigni: mettes-vous de la partie et ne faites pas trop le ministre et vous aurez contentement." Aubigny is quite a personage at court and should be shown some consideration: "Il meriteroit bien que le Roi le caressast un peu, car il fait ici une très bonne figure, il est parfaitement bien auprès du Roi d'Angleterre, et dans une etroitte liaison avec le chancelier et milord Arlincton". The Spanish ambassador pays his court to Aubigny, and by the way, if Lionne wants to be amused, let him ask Aubigny to mimic the ambassador, he imitates the ambassador's grimaces to perfection.[2]

Aubigny left for Paris on the 20th. "Je vous conseille de chercher les occasions de l'entretenir", reiterates Courtin, for in the English court "il n'y a point d'homme qui soit mieux avec le Roi et M. le Duc d'Yorc".[3] Aubigny could look forward to an excellent reception, and one expects to read glowing accounts of his stay in Paris, but fate willed it otherwise. He fell ill in August, shortly after his arrival,[4] and lingered on till November 3rd when he died in his forty-sixth year, beloved, influential, and nearing the goal of his ambition, for a few hours after his death came the news of his promotion.[5]

---

1 *Cal. S.P. Dom.* 1664–5, p. 474. "Mr d'Aubigni s'en va à Paris pour résigner la Maison qu'il a dans le cloître de Notre Dame." Aff. Étr. *Corr. d'Angleterre,* vol. 85, f. 149, June 14, 1665.

2 Aff. Étr. *Corr. d'Angleterre,* vol. 86, f. 53, July 16, 1665.

3 *Ib.* f. 56, July 20, 1665.

4 B.N. *Mélanges Colbert,* vol. 131 *bis,* f. 1111, Aubigny to Colbert, Sept. 19, 1660. R.O. *France,* vol. 121, f. 89, Aubigny to (? Arlington).

5 Desmaizeaux, *La Vie de Monsieur de Saint-Évremond* in St-Évremond, *Œuvres mêlées,* VI, p. 46. But it is also said occasionally (e.g. Cust, *op. cit.* p. 110) that the news came a few hours before his death.

He was buried in the convent of the Chartreux de Vauvert, a convent destroyed at the time of the French Revolution. A modest epitaph covered his mortal remains, *De se plura ne dicerentur supremis tabulis cavit.*[1] Was Aubigny a Jansenist? "M. d'Aubigny ne fut jamais qu'un janséniste de circonstance et par générosité", replies Sainte-Beuve,[2] and the truth seems to be that Aubigny sympathized with the Jansenists in a general kind of way, but scarcely to the extent of identifying himself with their cause, and that in the years of court life, and under the influence of Saint-Évremond, he drifted very far from them.

It is true that he was under the influence of Port Royal in his early life; that Arnauld, Arnauld d'Andilly, Taignier, Bernières, La Lane, Feydeau, Dugué de Bagnols and Pontchâteau were among his friends;[3] that he took into his household in 1661 at Taignier's recommendation M. Brunetti, an ardent Jansenist, the Italian translator of the *Provinciales* and a devoted friend of Arnauld and the duc de Luynes,[4] and that in this year 1661 he sent assurances of his most sincere affection to all his good friends[5] who considered him "toujours plein de zèle pour ses amis et pour la cause de saint Augustin",[6] for, hearing of the General Assembly of the Clergy and their deliberations against Jansenism, he had written with indignation to M. d'Andilly: "Quelque méchante opinion que j'eusse des gens je ne pouvais m'imaginer qu'ils allassent dans un tel excès".[7]

But their chronicler, Godefroi Hermant, himself admits that Aubigny's reputation of being a Jansenist had no other founda-

1 For this epitaph see E. Raunié, *Epitaphier du vieux Paris* (1901), iii, p. 40 or Cust, *op. cit.* p. 110.
2 *Port-Royal*, iii, p. 586 *n.*
3 In addition to the foregoing pages see Hermant, *Mémoires*, ii, p. 368; Sainte-Beuve, *Port-Royal*, iii, pp. 582, 586, vi, p. 312.
4 Hermant, *Mémoires*, v, pp. 230, 356; *Port-Royal*, iii, p. 560; Maire, *Bibliographie*, ii, p. 376. Brunetti remained with Aubigny till his death. R.O. *France*, vol. 121, Brunetti to (? Arlington), Nov. 25, 1665. Later he was almost sent to America by the Jansenists, "N'ayant pu s'établir dans le Nord [the island of Nordstrand], ils songeoient à faire des colonies dans l'Amérique". R. Simon, *Lettres* (Amsterdam 1730, 4 vols.), ii, pp. 227–8. See also *Port-Royal*, iv, p. 374.
5 Hermant, *Mémoires*, v, p. 230.
6 *Ib.* p. 356.   7 *Ib.* iv, pp. 584–5.

tion than his good nature, "il ne pouvoit souffrir les maux que l'on faisoit aux disciples de saint-Augustin et qu'on les appelât hérétiques"—as for their doctrine, he had never studied it.[1] Aubigny was an extremely kind-hearted man, kind to Quakers in distress,[2] kind to the Jesuits whom he tried to befriend.

"Il faut que je vous dise", he writes to Taignier in August 1661, "que je suis ici fort empêché à tâcher de sauver les bons pères Jésuites d'un furieux et inespéré malheur, qui est que dans l'abrogation des lois pénales que le Parlement a préparé en faveur des catholiques, ils ont déjà dressé l'acte et y ont excepté tous les Jésuites, ce qui est les chasser pour jamais d'Angleterre." Aubigny thought that if they had an English general like the English Benedictines and were independent of Rome they might be allowed to stay. He is himself amused that they should have found such a strange advocate—"no one to plead for the poor Jesuits of England but this M. d'Aubigny who is said to be such a dangerous Jansenist!"[3]

As the months go on Aubigny's letters begin to show a certain kind of detachment; situated as he is, he judges his friends more objectively. He notes on one side a great deal of injustice and passion, and on the other a little too much zeal. He thinks some of their extreme resistance unwise.[4] Yet he hastens to reaffirm his sympathy. "Vous vous tromperez", he tells his old correspondent Taignier, "si vous croyez que j'ai rien changé à l'estime que j'ai toujours faite de cette affaire et de ceux qui la composent."[5]

But little by little the "ami d'outre-mer" turned from his former companions. He had other preoccupations as we have seen, and no doubt their condemnation of the things of this

1 Hermant, *Mémoires*, II, p. 585.
2 Through his intervention two women members of the Society of Friends were delivered from the Inquisition in Malta. Fox calls him a great man, and says he had much reasoning about religion with him. "He was very free in his discourse. I never heard a Papist confess as much as he did" (Fox, *Journal* (1891, 2 vols.), II, pp. 524–6). The Quaker Latey also often saw him—"he was very kind and free" and reasoned with Latey about religion, "like Felix with Paul" (R. Hawkins, *Life of Latey* (1851), pp. 36–9).
3 Hermant, *Mémoires*, V, pp. 230–1, Aug. 1661; *Port-Royal*, IV, pp. 557–8: cf. E. Taunton, *Hist. of the Jesuits in England* (1901), p. 434.
4 Hermant, *Mémoires*, V, pp. 357–8, Nov. 1661.   5 *Ib.*

world was a stumbling-block to one at the court of Charles II, and their austere ways a foolishness to one who frequented the epicurean society of Saint-Évremond; far from them, he forgot their quiet virtues and remembered only their polemics. Before the century was out the friends of Port Royal, touched to the quick, could read the account of a conversation Saint-Évremond once had with Monsieur d'A*** concerning the Jansenists, and though at first all names were mysteriously given in abbreviation, "Monsieur D. G. B.", "Monsieur de L.", "Monsieur A.", "Monsieur de B.", "le J.", "ceux qui mettent le C. au-dessus des P." etc.,[1] everyone knew what these initials represented, and in ten years or so, later editions gave the names in full.[2]

"Nos Directeurs", Aubigny is made to say, "se mettent peu en peine de la Doctrine: leur but est d'opposer Société à Société; de se faire un Parti dans l'Église et du Parti dans l'Église une Cabale à la Cour."

Hypocrisy is one of his charges. "Ils font mettre la Réforme dans un Couvent sans se réformer, ils exaltent la Pénitence sans la faire; ils font manger des Herbes à des gens qui cherchent à se distinguer par des Singularités, tandis qu'on leur voit manger tout ce que mangent les Personnes de bon goût." Their doctrine is attacked for its harshness, their methods are judged repellent. Aubigny does hate the "docteurs faciles et complaisans", but he wants moderation in all things. "Je veux en un mot une Morale Chrétienne ni austère ni relâchée."

What shall we make of this conversation, jotted down from memory, if indeed it really took place? The account of it appeared long after Aubigny's death; there is a certain contemptuous tone about it that does not ring quite true; it is hard to say how much of it is authentic, and how much of it merely Saint-Évremond the epicurean. Sainte-Beuve considered it a reliable document, and he concludes his study of Aubigny by calling him the Saint-Évremond of Port Royal.[3]

<hr/>

1 Thus in vol. III, pp. 158–62 of the 1693 edition (*Œuvres mêlées*, Paris 1693, 5 vols.).

2 *Les véritables Œuvres de M. de Saint-Évremond*, seconde édition revue (London 1706, 5 vols.), II, pp. 48–53.

3 Sainte-Beuve, *Port-Royal*, III, pp. 584 *et seq.*

Some foundation there was doubtless for this conversation, and so our last glimpse of Aubigny is that of a man of the world rather than a man of the cloister, "trop gay pour un janséniste", as a lady is reported to have said,[1] too wise in his interests to be a fanatic, too easy-going to be anything but moderate, too reasonable to go to extremes, too friendly with an *esprit fort* to be an ardent Christian.

1 Rapin, *Mémoires*, i, p. 172, and see pp. 170–2, 208, for Rapin's estimate of Aubigny. Rapin, a Jesuit author, did not think him a genuine Jansenist. "Quoi qu'on le crût de ce parti, il s'en divertissoit."

NOTE

After the death of Charles II two papers on religion were found in his strong-box, in his own handwriting, but manifestly not by him. Burnet attributed these papers to Aubigny or to Bristol, but Lord Acton came to the conclusion that since they were composed by an English ecclesiastic who knew French better than English, and were written in a tone of frankness and familiarity they were probably by Charles' natural son, James de la Cloche. He did not think that they were by Aubigny, because Aubigny had not forgotten his native language, and he quoted a pleasant historiette from Tallemant des Réaux, according to which Aubigny was able to save himself from some English bloodhounds in Paris by speaking English to them! But French was certainly also Aubigny's first language; he lived thirty-five years in France, and only ten in England, and of these ten, five were years of infancy. There is an autograph letter of his at the B.M. (to Lord — ?), it is entirely written in French, about the "marquise d'hontelej" (Huntly), Add. MSS. 22878, f. 5. The papers in question are very likely by Aubigny. Curiously enough a French translation of one of the above papers has been preserved in a MS. collection of letters (copies) from Arnauld, Nicole, M. de Saci, M. de Sainte-Marthe, Mlle de Vertus, la sœur Angélique de St Jean, etc. "Traduction françoise d'un papier écrit de la main propre de feu roy d'Engletaire et trouvé entre les cahyers après sa mort", Bibliothèque de la Ville de Troyes, MS. 1689, f. 132.

CHAPTER VIII

"The Mysterie of Jesuitisme"

and other translations

"Sir,

We have been extreamly mistaken. Nor was I undeceiv'd till yesterday, till which time I simply thought Religion had an extraordinary concernment in the disputes at Sorbonne."[1]

It was in 1657 that English readers were "undeceiv'd"—if indeed they had known anything about the matter—and generally initiated into the disputes of Jansenists and Molinists, for in this year appeared the first English translation of the *Provinciales*. It is true that a certain Father Macedo had already published a book against Jansenism in London, but his book was written in Latin and necessarily reached a limited circle only; here, however, was the book which had stirred all France, cleric and lay alike. As the Provincial remarked to the writer of the *Letters*, they were not only esteemed by Divines, they were well received by those of a lower sphere in the world—nay, they were understood even of women.[2]

The preface[3] to the English edition explained how the letters came to be written when the "Colledge of Sorbonne" had so many extraordinary assemblies about the second Letter of M. Arnauld, "What the Colledge could not do, what all the writings that came abroad on both sides could not satisfie the world of, these Letters did, clearing up the difficulties". The translator would willingly have said something of the author, "but there's no more known of him then what he hath been pleased to afford us of himself".

Who was the translator? According to Wood it was a certain

---

1 *Provinciales*, 1657 translation, p. 1. For bibliographical details of the books described in this chapter see a special list at the end of this book.

2 *Ib.* p. 37.

3 Based largely on Nicole's *avertissement*.

John Davies of Kidwelly;[1] Evelyn is frequently mentioned and a recent hand-list of Evelyn's works assigns the translation to him;[2] Tonge is another possibility; the 1684 edition of the *Provinciales* giving the French, Latin, Italian and Spanish texts, says that the English translation was made by an English Catholic;[3] there is no certainty.

Two things strike us as we examine this and analogous translations. The first is the rapidity with which all material available is translated and printed; the second is the motive underlying this zeal—not so much interest in the Jansenists, as the most violent hatred of the Jesuits, an almost hysterical fear of Popery, in which even such grave people as Evelyn and the Lord Chancellor participate. The translator of the *Provinciales* thought that the "treatise" must needs work a strange alteration in mankind; that the body of Jesuits would be looked on hereafter as the most abominable and most despicable thing in the world, and he praised the author's dialogue form, since thereby the reader became acquainted not only with the maxims of the Jesuits, "but also with the subtile insinuating wayes whereby they poison the world therewith". The curiously sensational title of the translation should be noted—*Les Provinciales or the Mysterie of Jesuitisme*. "These infamous letters", says an adversary of Jansenism, "...banisht all Catholique countreys came for their refuge into England. And they found a translatour who...set them out in an English dresse: And that they might the better please those ears which itch to hear something against the Jesuites, he baptized them by a new name of *the Mystery of Jesuitisme*...he might better have called it the *Misery of Jansenisme*."[4]

To return to our first point, the rapidity with which this controversial material was made available to the English public,

---

1 *Athen. Oxon.* (ed. Bliss), IV, p. 382. Wood also attributes to Davies the translation of *A further discovery of the Mystery of Jesuitism*, and the *Journal of Proceedings between the Jansenists and the Jesuits*. The latter is however signed H. H. (? Henry Holden).

2 (Anon.), *A Handlist of the works of Evelyn* (Cambridge 1916), p. 3.

3 Faugère's Introduction to the *Lettres Provinciales* (éd. Gr. Écr.), p. lxviii.

4 *An Answer to the Provinciale Letters*, Preface. Baxter drew copiously on the *Mystery of Jesuitisme* in his work *A Key for Catholics to open the Jugling of the Jesuites*.

the date of the last *Lettre provinciale* was March 24th, 1657—the letters had been appearing at intervals since January 23rd, 1656 —by the summer of 1657 an English translation was already being sold, if one accepts the date, August 31st, written by Thomason on his copy, now at the British Museum, as the date on which the copy was published, or was bought by him.[1]

Faugère points out[2] that this translation is based on the quarto edition of the *Provinciales* and almost always on the first printing, and he believes that copies of the *Provincial Letters* were sent to the translator one by one, as they appeared, and that the English translation must have been practically complete when the collected letters first appeared as a whole, in a small duodecimo, in time to let the translator avail himself of Nicole's preface.

The early date of the English translation impresses us all the more when we stop to remember the dates of other translations. The first Italian translation was published after Pascal's death in 1662, but possibly before 1667, a Spanish translation appeared in 1684, a German in 1740, a Danish in 1868 and a Dutch in 1876.[3] The learned in all countries used Nicole's Latin translation which appeared in 1658.

By October of the same year 1657 a book called *Additionalls to the mistery of Jesuitisme* was entered at Stationers' Hall;[4] under this sensational title could be found the "advice of the pastors of Rouen to the pastors of all other places through France" concerning the maxims of the Casuists, translated by a "person of quality".

In 1658 a second and enlarged edition of the English *Provinciales* appeared; the preface had been rewritten, the chapters provided with "arguments"; it contained not only the Letters, but also what was "printed...by way of appendage to the

1 *A Catalogue of the pamphlets, books, newspapers and manuscripts...collected by George Thomason* (London 1908, 2 vols.), II, p. 191. Cf. vol. I, p. xxii: "In the spring of 1641 Thomason began to write on the title page of many of the tracts the date when each came into his possession, or in some instances the date of publication. These memoranda are of the highest value".
2 *Lettres provinciales* (éd. Gr. Écr.), I, p. lxix.
3 A. Maire, *Bibliographie des Œuvres de Pascal*, II.
4 *Registers of the Stationers' Company*, II, p. 150.

Cologne Edition of them in French",[1] including some of the documents issued by "the Reverend the Curez of Rouen" and "the Reverend the Curez of Paris", but penned in many cases by Arnauld, Nicole and Pascal. The translator had gone even farther than the Cologne edition, and had added two pieces, namely the *Factum pour les Curés de Paris* and the *Second Écrit des Curés de Paris*, both possibly written by Pascal, and the second dated April 1658. "The two pieces coming so opportunely to hand...it would have argued a neglect...of the satisfaction to have slipped the present occasion....I had to file them up",[2] the Stationer tells the Reader. He also warns the Reader that the Jesuits are intending to translate *The Apology for the Casuists* to which these pieces are written by way of answer.

This same year 1658 another duodecimo quickly followed up the "discovery" made by "the Authour of the Provinciall Letters (a book better known in England under the title of the Mystery of Jesuitisme)".[3] It called itself *A further Discovery of the Mystery of Jesuitism* and was a collection of six rather worthless pieces, the first two by Pierre Jarrige.

The year 1659 at last brought a rejoinder—this was *An Answer to the Provinciall Letters...made by some Fathers of the Society in France*, a translation of the *Responces aux Lettres Provinciales* written by le Père Annat and le Père Nouet and published in 1658.[4] The translator, said to be Father Martin Grene or Green,[5] added to his translation answers to one or two letters "not made in France", a *History of Jansenisme* taken largely from Préville's *Progresse of Jansenisme* as he tells us, and also replies to "the English Additionals" and to the above-mentioned *Further Discovery*. But his work was printed in Paris "at a time when things were in the greatest confusion here, occasioned by the different designs and conduct of Monk and the Rump. Hence it came to pass that very few copies of it

1 Preface, second English edition. For a list of the documents given see the special bibliography at the end of this book.
2 *Additionals*, p. 15. The Stationer "R. R." is Richard Royston, printer of the *Eikon Basilike*.
3 Preadvertisement, *A further Discovery*.
4 Maire, *op. cit.* II², p. 351.
5 Gillow, *Biogr. Dict. of the English Catholics*, III, p. 51.

could be imported to ballance the influence of that said Mystery, or that of White's disciples in the new Art of Obedience and Government".¹

This year 1659 also saw the translation of what is called the *Septième Factum des Curés de Paris*, a pamphlet attributed sometimes to Arnauld, sometimes to Pascal. It is, as its title says, *A Journall of all Proceedings between the Jansenists and the Jesuits*, from the time of the first publication of the *Lettres Provinciales* to the censure passed by the Faculty of Theology of the University of Paris on a book called *An Apology for the Casuists*, written in answer to the *Provinciales*. The *Factum* is dated February 8th, 1659, the English translation of the same year is dated June 2nd by Thomason.²

The translator, "H. H.", calls himself "a well-wisher to the distressed Church of England". One wonders whether Dr Henry Holden³ appears under this cover, just as Dodd later on attacked the Jesuits in the guise of an Anglican chaplain. "Having told thee who I am", he informs the Reader, "an afflicted Member of a late flourishing Church, I'le tell thee what I offer; a short, but absolutely authentick, history of the present Civil wars (and spiritual too) betwixt the Jesuits and Clergy of France."

The concluding words of the preface are curious in that they touch upon the possibility of union between the Anglicans and the Jansenists, or perhaps it might be better to say, the Gallicans. Speaking of the attacks made on the Casuists by the clergy of France and Rouen H. H. finds in this a cause for gratitude. "So may we, among our distressed hopes, bless God for these happy beginnings, opening a way we never thought on, to check the extravagances on that side, and produce perhaps, in time, an union among us all. Already we see the Clergy...have unanimously condemn'd these exorbitant doctrines of the Jesuits, our most implacable Enemies; who knows how far the hand of Providence may carry on these beginnings, if our mistaking zeal

1 *The Discourses of Cleander and Eudoxe*, Preface.
2 In his copy at the B.M. (E. 985).
3 The allusion to "our University men" would almost show the translator to be a Sorbonne man. More will be said about Holden in a later chapter.

do not hinder it, nor an impertinent pride make us coyly fly farther from them, as they come nearer to us." A plea for discriminating tolerance is made, and we are urged to be "praying continually for a happy successe to such good Endeavours... remembring that Church was once famous for her purity, and may return again to the same perfection; themselves among themselves accomplishing that Reformation, which hath by us been formerly attempted, so ineffectually to them, and so unfortunately to ourselves".

In this year was also published *A Relation of Sundry Miracles wrought at the Monastery of Port Royall*, translated "out of a French Copie published at Paris, 1656" and printed in Paris. The Port Royal miracles were rather carefully sheltered behind a *Holy Life of Philip Nerius* and a *Relation of Miracles* written by St Augustine. After hearing of these the English reader learned how "Margaret Perier...a Pensioner in the Monastery" was cured of her *fistula lachrymalis*, and how others received their health again.

In 1662 came a translation of Arnauld's *Nouvelle hérésie des Jésuites*, published in France that same year, *The new Heresie of the Jesuits Publickly maintain'd at Paris in the Colledge of Clermont*, the new heresy being the Pope's infallibility, not only in questions of right, but also in matters of fact which, as this book said, enabled one to believe with a divine faith that the Book intituled the *Augustine of Jansenius* was heretical, and the five propositions to be of Jansenius, and in the sense of Jansenius condemned.

Arnauld's treatise was again translated by Evelyn who was evidently unaware of the earlier translation. His version appeared in 1664–5 in his book, *Another part of the Mystery of Jesuitism*. It is often said[1] that Evelyn published a translation of the *Provinciales* in 1664. No translation of the *Provinciales* was published in this year, but a book bearing the same general title of the English translation of the *Provinciales* appeared, and this

1 E.g. in Lowndes' *Bibliographer's Manual*, and in Maire's *Bibliographie*, on the authority of Lowndes. Also in Charlanne, *L'Influence française en Angleterre*, pp. 112–13.

book was by Evelyn. Writing to Boyle on November 23rd, 1664, he announces the forthcoming book, "another part of the Mystery of Jesuitism which (with some other papers concerning that iniquity) I have translated and am now printing at Roystons, but without my name—so little credit is there in these days in doing anything for the interest of religion".[1] "This day", he records in his Diary five weeks later, on January 2nd, 1665, "was published by me that part of the Mystery of Jesuitism translated and collected by me, though without my name."[2]

Besides the translation from Arnauld already mentioned Evelyn's book contains four of Nicole's *Imaginaires—Lettres de l'Hérésie imaginaire* to give them their full title, the imaginary heresy being Jansenism—and some minor documents. "The particulars which you will find added after the 4th Letter", so Evelyn explains to Lord Cornbury, "are extracted out of several curious papers and passages lying by me, which for being very apposite to the controversy, I thought fit to annex, in danger otherwise to have never been produced."[3]

When Evelyn first put together his translation only three of the *Imaginaires* had appeared, the last one on April 15th, 1664, and the book was being printed thus, but in the meantime the fourth *Imaginaire* appeared, on June 19th, 1664, and so anxious was Evelyn to make use of all available material that he interrupted the publication of his book, translated the fourth *Imaginaire*, and had it inserted after the third *Imaginaire*.[4]

Before beginning the *Imaginary Heresie* the Reader, in order that he might understand about "the Five Propositions pretended to be in Jansenius", was advised to "cast his Eye upon the Provincials...which the Interpreter of these Papers had

1 Boyle, *Works*, VI, p. 295; Evelyn, *Diary*, IV, p. 148.
2 Evelyn, *Diary*, I, pp. 387–8. The wording of this entry would suggest that the first part of the *Mystery of Jesuitism* (the *Provincial Letters*) was not by him. In a list of his works compiled by him one finds "The Mystery of Jesuitism, 2 parts, 8vo"; the second part one takes to be his book *The pernicious consequences of the new Heresy of the Jesuits against Kings and States*.
3 *Diary*, I, p. 387.
4 The pages of the fourth *Imaginaire* are not numbered; the third *Imaginaire* ends on p. 206, then comes the fourth *Imaginaire*; the following document begins on p. 207. See also Evelyn's note at the end of the fourth *Imaginaire*.

subjoyn'd to them, were they not commonly to be had at every Bookseller's shop, and already translated into English".

How Evelyn came to translate these papers is curious enough —it seems he undertook the work by command of the Lord Chancellor, Clarendon, and his son Lord Cornbury.[1] The day the book was published Evelyn brought a copy to Lord Cornbury. "I came to present your Lordship with your own book[2]: I left it with my Lord your father, because I would not suffer it to be public till he had first seen it, who, on your Lordship's score, has so just a title to it."[3] The book is dedicated to "my most honour'd Friend from whom I received the Copy"— "Sir, I transmit you here the French copy which you were pleased to consign to me, and with it the best effects of your injunction that my weak Talent was able to reach to; but with a zeal so much the more propense, as I judged the publication might concern the world of those miserably abus'd Persons who resign themselves to the conduct of these bold Impostors".

One is inclined to think that the French copies of these documents came to Cornbury's hand from Aubigny; certainly they were all sent to the latter by his Jansenist friends, and Aubigny was on most intimate terms with the Lord Chancellor and his son.[4]

Three weeks after the publication of these pages from Arnauld and Nicole we find the following entry in Evelyn's Diary for January 25th (1664–5): "This night being at Whitehall, his Majesty came to me standing in the withdrawing-room, and gave me thanks for publishing 'The Mystery of Jesuitism' which he said he had carried two days in his pocket, read it and encouraged me".[5]

1 *Diary*, I, p. 387 *n.*, III, p. 149.
2 In the margin is written, "The other part of the Mystery of Jesuitism translated and published by me".
3 *Diary*, III, p. 149, Letter to Lord Cornbury, Jan. 2, 1664–5.
4 "Fort attaché au Chancelier"—Aff. Étr. *Corr. d'Angleterre*, vol. 72, f. 113, 1660; "intime du Chancelier"—*ib.* vol. 73, f. 169, 1660. See also Brown's *Miscellanea Aulica*, p. 369, where we learn from a letter written after Aubigny's death that his will named the Lord Chancellor "his principal Executor with the assistance of my Ld Cornbury".
5 *Diary*, I, p. 389.

The British Museum copy was originally given to Sir Henry Herbert by Evelyn; another copy was given to Dr Thomas Barlow, Bishop of Lincoln, who penned a letter of thanks to the translator. "I received by the hands of my worthy friend Dr Wilkins the last part of the Mystery of Jesuitism; now not more a Mystery; being so well discovered to the world by the pious pains of the Jansenists and yourself....I am exceedingly pleased with those discoveries of the prodigious villainies and atheism of the Jesuits....I perceive by many letters from Paris and other parts of France that the sober French Catholics are strangely alarmed,...that they seek after and read diligently reformed authors to find means against the new heresy...."[1]

So far translators had embarked only on pamphlets and duodecimos, but in 1664 there came, dedicated to the Earl of Elgin, a huge folio of 700 closely printed pages, and indeed, as far as bulk went, it was probably true enough that "A like Display of the Romish State, Court, Interests, Policies, etc., and the mighty influence of the Jesuites in that Church, and many other Christian states" was not hitherto in existence, as the title-page modestly claimed. This was a translation of Saint-Amour's *Journal* which had appeared in 1662. The translator, G. Havers—little or nothing is known of him—must have set to work almost as soon as the French text became available.

The English reader who knew something of the *Provinciales* and of what had happened since the publication of the *Provinciales*, who had possibly also acquired some elementary knowledge of Jansenius, the "Abbott of San Cyran" and "Anthony Arnauld",[2] was now plunged into the year 1646, and was told what passed in Paris with reference to the five propositions in assemblies of the Faculty of Divinity in this and subsequent years; he accompanied M. de Saint-Amour, a doctor of the Sorbonne, to Rome in 1651, in defence of the five propositions, remained there till 1653 if he had patience enough, witnessed audiences, visits, consultations, negotiations, conferences, was presented with letters, tracts,

1 *Ib.* III, p. 143, June 21, 1664. (One wonders whether this is not a mistake for 1665.)
2 From *The History of Jansenisme* in *An Answer to the Provinciall Letters.*

sermons, proposals, memoirs and memorials, and finally left Rome upon the condemnation of the propositions, returning to Paris to "the noise of Molinistical triumphs".

In the meantime Evelyn was busy again with his pen. Lord Cornbury had once more provided him with material from abroad, and Evelyn, having just finished his task of producing "the other part of the Mystery of Jesuitism", obeyed with slight reluctance and weariness. "Being late come home, imagine me turning over your close printed memoirs and shrinking up my shoulders", he tells Cornbury, "yet with a resolution of surmounting the difficulty, animated with my Lord Chancellor's and your Lordship's commands, whom I am perfectly disposed to serve, even in the greatest of drudgeries, the translation of books. But why call I this a drudgery? who would not be proud of the service?" Looking through the "close printed memoirs" Evelyn found God and the king concerned, and he resolved to present Lord Cornbury and the world with the fruits of his obedience cheerfully. "Nor is it small in my esteem that God directs you to make use of me in anything that concerns the Church."[1]

A note by Evelyn tells us that the book in question was his *Mysterie of Jesuitisme, and its pernicious consequences as it relates to Kings and States.*[2] It was a translation of Nicole's *Pernicieuses Conséquences.*[3] About a year later we find him distributing copies of his new book. On March 1st, 1666, the Diary records: "To London, and presented his Majesty my book intituled 'The pernicious consequences of the new Heresy of the Jesuits against Kings and States'".[4] Another copy went to Dr Wilkins, Dean of Ripon. "That I presume to send you the consequence of what I formerly published in English in the controversy betwixt the Jesuits and the Jansenists speaks rather my obedience to a command from that great person, than my abilities to have undertaken or acquitted myself as I ought. I annexed an Epistolary Preface, not to instruct such as you are..., but for

1 *Diary*, III, pp. 149-50, Feb. 9, 1664-5.   2 *Ib.*
3 *Les pernicieuses conséquences de la nouvelle hérésie des Jésuites contre le Roy et contre l'Estat. Par un advocat au Parlement* (1662). See Faugère's Introduction to the *Provinciales* (éd. Gr. Écr.), I, p. lxxi.
4 *Diary*, II, p. 3.

their sakes who reading the book, might possibly conceive the French Kings to have been the only persons in danger."[1]

The translating of this book has been described at some length, because no copy of the translation seems to be in existence; it is not included in any bibliography of Evelyn's works; no one has pointed out that it is a different work from *Another part of the Mystery of Jesuitism*; inquiries made at Wotton House where Evelyn's descendants still reside have been fruitless. Perhaps it was circulated only in manuscript.

With 1667 came another rejoinder from adversaries. This was *The Secret Policy of the Jansenists* from the work by le Père Étienne Agard de Champs or Dechamps, published in May of that year,[2] so this slim little book had been "Englished" with all speed.[3] The reader learned that the Jansenists had a mind to bring Calvinism into the Catholic Church, and was told how they proposed to set about it.

A more amusing work appeared in the following year, 1668. This was a description of a strange land, *A Relation of the Country of Jansenia*, the translation of a text that had been published in 1660. As in Mlle de Scudéry's romance, *Clélie*, where there was a map of "le pays du Tendre", there was here a map of Jansenia showing how that country lay betwixt Libertinia and Desesperia, with Calvinia on the north, and a tempestuous sea on the south. The customs, manners and religion of its inhabitants were explained, and one may note what is said of the sacrament of communion, viz. that "they suffer Lay people to receive under one kind, but many among them affirme that the contrary would be much coveted. 'Tis believed that this light was brought to them from England with other Merchandizes, whereof they make no brags, because they were liable to Confiscation".[4]

The year 1670 brought two more translations of Jansenist onslaughts on the Jesuits,[5] one, *The Moral Practice of the Jesuites*,

1 *Ib.* III, p. 192.   2 Maire, *Bibliographie*, II², p. 53.
3 By Thomas Fairfax, S.J., according to Gillow.   4 *A Relation*..., p. 82.
5 Books of which Sainte-Beuve remarks, "Après la victoire décisive des *Provinciales* cela me fait l'effet du gros train et des fourgons qui, en traversant le champ de bataille, achèvent les blessés et broient sous leurs roues les morts...il y eut la *queue* de Pascal, comme il y a eu la *queue* de Voltaire". *Port-Royal*, III, pp. 216–17.

was a translation of Pontchâteau's work, "a collection of those Learned and Pious Doctors of the Sorbonne to inspire the World, and the Jesuites themselves with horror at their detestable Morality",[1] the other was *The Jesuits' Morals*, translated according to Evelyn[2] by Tonge, of Popish Plot fame. This book was by Perrault and had an introduction by Varet, but the translator whose ideas concerning Arnauld and Pascal were slightly muddled conjectured that the advertisement seemed to be Father Arnold's, the preface and the work itself by "his Nephew (!) Monsieur Pascal", who was supposed to have written the *Provincial Letters* "not without his Uncle's Privity and assistance: whose head and hand could not be wanting to this work also, if his". "The style much differing"—indeed it did!—"and Lewis Montalt affirming himself to be no Doctor" made the translator suspect "a third hand to have been made use of in drawing up these Letters."

It may be convenient to note here that Nicole's Essays, so much admired by Madame de Sévigné, began to appear in France from 1671 onwards, and that soon after, certainly before 1680, probably in 1672, Locke began to translate some of these, though his translation was not printed till 1828. His manuscript was dedicated to Margaret Countess of Shaftesbury, and while he remarked that it was a bold thing for one who had but begun to learn French to attempt a translation out of it, he thought he could not meet in all France anything fitter to be put into her hands.[3]

But if Locke's translation did not see the day, a translation by a "Person of Quality", sometimes conjectured to be Boyle, began

1 *Preface.*

2 *Diary*, II, pp. 125–6. In Evelyn's Library at Wotton House are three volumes in duodecimo on the subject of Jesuitism, uniformly bound in Morocco: (1) *Les Provinciales or The Mystery of Jesuitisme* (second edition). (2) *Another part of the Mystery of Jesuitism* (Evelyn's work). (3) *The Moral Practice of the Jesuites*. See Evelyn's *Miscellaneous Writings* (1825), p. 500, where it is also stated, on the strength of Evelyn's *Diary*, that the translation of *The Moral Practice* was by Tonge. But Evelyn was speaking of *The Jesuits' Morals* which is a different book and could not have been bound uniformly with the others, as it is a small folio. However, it is quite possible that Tonge translated both books.

3 Locke, *Discourses: translated from Nicole's Essays*, Dedication, pp. xxiii–iv; H. R. Fox Bourne, *Life of Locke*, I, p. 294.

PLATE III

JOHN EVELYN

to appear in 1677. A second volume, translated by the person who in 1674 had translated Arnauld's *Logic* into Latin, came in 1678, a third volume followed in 1680. An edition in four parts appeared in 1696, and another edition in four volumes in 1724, as well as a volume of *Moral Thoughts* in 1701.

To return, however, to the *Mystery of Jesuitism*: the Popish Plot brought with it a flood of pamphlets and books directed against the Jesuits, and one is therefore not surprised to see a new edition of the *Provincial Letters* appear in 1679. The title of *Les Provinciales* which had been retained in the first and second English editions had disappeared, and nothing was left but the sensational name which the first translator had bestowed on his work in addition to the French one. The second English edition of the *Provinciales*, and Evelyn's collection of papers, *The other part of the Mystery of Jesuitism*, had been adorned with a large folding picture of Loyola flanked by Suarez and Mariana on one side, and by Vasquez and Escobar on the other, but in this latest edition Vasquez and Escobar have changed names without changing features—they are now called Garnet and Parsons, the better to inflame the English mind!

And since the Popish Plot has been mentioned, it may be noted that when Tonge was asked whether he knew the author of the manuscript giving imaginary details of the plot, he replied he did not, but he suggested that the man had been set on by secular priests or by the Jansenists.[1]

Though the English translation of the *Provincial Letters* had appeared almost as soon as the French text, it was eighteen years before the *Pensées* were translated, not till 1688. Even so the English translation was one of the earliest, the Dutch translation alone preceding it by two years.[2] The English translator, Joseph Walker, had "heard by a Judicious Person that Monsieur Pascall's work would be well accepted", so he "got one of the books" and "used his Endeavours about it". He dedicated his work to Boyle, comparing the virtues of Pascal and Boyle in a flattering Epistle; more interesting is a passage in which he suggests that the *Pensées* had been somewhat arranged by the pious editors. With *Monsieur Pascall's Thoughts* Walker also translated *The Life of Monsieur Pascall writ by Madam Perier his Sister*, and thus made available to the English reader that touching little biography. The *Discours sur les Pensées de M. Pascal* by Filleau de la Chaise was also translated by him. As Mme Périer's life of her brother was first printed in the 1684 edition of the *Pensées*,[1] Walker must have used an edition published between this year and 1688.

A second translation of the *Pensées* came sixteen years later, in 1704, from the hand of Basil Kennet, younger brother of White Kennet, Bishop of Peterborough. It was probably written while he was fellow and tutor of Corpus Christi College, Oxford —he had been almost insensibly engaged in his delightful task, he said, and was afterwards induced "to communicate the satisfaction", "knowing there were still many Persons of Learning and Judgment who continued Strangers to the Language of the Original, either as neglecting so easie a Conquest or as despising an Attainment which has now become rather Vulgar than fashionable".[2] The year before he had translated Godeau's *Pastoral Instructions*. Kennet died in 1715 shortly after having been elected president of his college. A second edition of his translation appeared in 1727, with a lengthy quotation from the *Spectator* on the title-page, a third edition followed, and a fourth one appeared in 1741.

Kennet had not included Mme Périer's life of her brother, so one finds another translation of the life appearing separately in 1723, the publishers quoting Bayle with obvious satisfaction. "An 100 Volumes of Sermons are not worth so much as this single Life.... The extraordinary Humility and Devotion of M. Pascal gives a more sensible Mortification to the Libertines of the Age than if one was to let loose upon them a dozen of Missionaries."[3]

---

1 Maire, *Bibliographie*, IV, p. 116.
2 In his translation of the *Pensées* Kennett omitted "some lines which directly favour'd the distinguishing Doctrines of those of the Roman Communion".
3 Advertisement, at the end of the second edition of Kennett's translation of the *Pensées*.

And finally in 1744, almost seventy years after the last edition,[1] almost ninety years after their first translating, we come at last to a translation of the *Provincial Letters* that is not styled the *Mystery of Jesuitism*—it is a *Life of Mr Paschal, with his Letters relating to the Jesuits*, and though the translator, William Andrews, a non-juror, obsessed with the idea of suppressing the Jesuits, is glad to contribute his mite to so salutary an end, yet the grimness of the earlier editions is gone—we are in a different age, and we are told that the editors of the *Spectator* and of the *Lady's Library* recommend Mr Paschal to the perusal of our English Ladies. "And it is with pleasure, I believe, that such recommendation will have its influence among the fair sex, in families where piety, ingenuity or good sense remain."[2]

1 Lowndes (*Bibliographer's Manual*) mentions a reprint of Evelyn's 1664 translation of the *Provinciales* in 1688, but as we have seen Evelyn did not translate the *Provinciales* in 1664 and it is doubtful whether he ever translated them. 1688 is the year of the first edition of the English translation of the *Pensées* which perhaps accounts for the confusion. I know of no existing copy of a 1688 edition of the *Provincial Letters*.

2 Andrews admired Pascal's "great Purity of Life and zeal according to what he could discern through the Mists of Superstition", for it had to be confessed that he was "a strenuous Papist".

CHAPTER IX

News from Abroad

(1664–1714)

WE have just seen that translations of Jansenist books, or of books directed against the Jansenists, supplied the English reader with some information about the controversy raging abroad. Another occasional source of information may be seen in those correspondents who made it their business to supply news in an age in which the news-letter was a valuable supplement to the gazette and often provided material for it. Eager for this kind of news was Henry Oldenburg, the first secretary of the Royal Society, and one finds him writing in 1664 to his friend and fellow-member, the excellent Mr Boyle:

> I have lately offered me a new correspondence at Paris for all the news and curiosities of France and Italy.... It is a person of quality and philosophically given.... He expects nothing for a return, but the communicating to him what considerable books are continually printing in England...and some general account of the progress and performances of the Royal Society.[1]

Oldenburg's correspondent, who was almost certainly the Protestant Henri Justel,[2] began by sending him some "polemical" books.

"I had on Tuesday last the first fruits of my new correspondence with the Parisian gentleman", writes Oldenburg. "He sent me a pretty big packet, containing both pamphlets and books, all polemical, both in divinity and philosophy. Those of divinity concern the contest betwixt Jansenists and Jesuits whereof the former fall upon the latter without mercy and seem to me to do them more mischief than was ever done to them by the whole body of protestants since the reformation. One piece of this kind is called *Examen de la lettre circulaire de l'assemblée tenue à Paris* Oct. 2, 1663, which layeth the pope's infallibility so much contended for by the Jesuits upon mere

1 Boyle, *Works*, VI, p. 173, Nov. 5, 1664.
2 See e.g. *ib.* VI, p. 285; R.O. *News-letters*, Bundle 14, *passim*.

political grounds as flat as protestants could do. Another is entitled *Les pernicieuses consequences de la nouvelle heresie des Jesuites contre le roy et contre l'estat.* This must needs make all kings, princes and states more afraid of this order and the seeds they sow than ever they were. The third is, en vers burlesque, under the name of *Onguent pour la Brulure ou le secret pour empescher les Jesuites de brûler les livres.*"[1]

These news-letters from the "Parisian gentleman" Oldenburg used to copy out, not only for Boyle, but also for Joseph Williamson,[2] another member of the Royal Society and at that time secretary to Sir Henry Bennet (afterwards Lord Arlington), Secretary of State. Williamson, himself a future Secretary of State, was one of the founders of the *London Gazette* in 1665–6, and was well supplied with news by his friends and others. French news-letters came to Williamson himself,[3] accompanying various French *Gazettes*[4]—even the *Gazette burlesque* and the *Gazette en vers*[5]—and occasionally these news-letters conveyed additional information about the Jansenists.[6] In this chapter are brought together some of the more interesting references to Jansenism in the letters preserved at the Record Office.

Sometimes the English ambassador in France notices the Jansenists in his dispatches. Holles, the stubborn old stickler for etiquette, was interested in the formulary and the "Jansenian points". The question of a formulary[7] condemning the five propositions had first come up in 1655. A Bull of Alexander VII in 1656 confirmed the 1653 Bull of his predecessor, Innocent X, condemning the five propositions, and the French clergy accepted the Bull at their assembly of 1657. But since this

1 Boyle, *Works*, VI, p. 177, Nov. 17, 1664. (By Arnauld, Nicole, and Barbier d'Aucourt.)
2 E.g. R.O. *News-letters*, Bundle 14; *S.P. France*, vols. 123, 126, 149; *Cal. S.P. Dom.* 1667, p. 509.
3 These are at the R.O., sometimes among the bundles of News-letters, sometimes among the State papers (France).
4 "Nous n'avons presques point de nouvelles ici à présent qui ne soient dans les Gazettes cy-jointes." R.O. *News-letters*, Bundle 13, Dec. 5–15, 1663: cf. Nov. 28–Dec. 8. The French *Gazette* itself dates from 1631.
5 See references to them in *News-letters*, Bundle 13.
6 E.g. for 1663 see R.O. *S.P. France*, vol. 117, f. 137; *News-letters*, Bundle 13, Oct. 5, 19.
7 For this see especially Vacant et Mangenot, *Dictionnaire de Théologie Catholique*, under "Jansénisme".

Bull made no mention of formulary or signature, the clergy added to the Bull a circular letter with the 1655 formulary slightly modified, the formulary to be signed by all the clergy. However, for various reasons there was relative calm between 1657 and 1660. In 1660 the question again came before the assembly of the clergy, who once more prescribed the signing of the formulary in 1661, and this formulary was also presented to the nuns of Port Royal. In 1662 and 1663 the rigour was somewhat relaxed, but not for long. A news-letter written early in January 1664 announces, "J'apprens que le Roy va faire poursuivre les Jansenistes sans relasche",[1] and in April Holles writes at some length from Paris,

[The King] was yesterday at ye Parlament; passed there a Declaration against the Jansenists, enioyning all under B^{ps} that have Ecc^{all} promotion to subscribe a forme of abiuration of those Jansenian points or to be putt out; the B^{ps} are taken pro concesso to have all subscribed (though five or six have not and doe absolutly refuse) so ye Declaration runs that every B^p shall tender it to the Clergy in his Diocese and proceede against the refusers: the Abiuration was drawen and framed by ye B^{ps} here in an Assembly and not confirmed by the Pope though often desired of the K^g and upon that ground the dissenting B^{ps} deny subscription as they pretend, but it is believed that in truth they dislike the thing.[2]

A news-letter of the same date explains to the English reader that the formulary condemns the five propositions in the sense in which they were to be found in Jansen. "Ces Mots de Sens de Jansenius faisoient toute la dispute, car les Jansenistes demeuroient d'accord de les condamner, mais non pas dans le sens de Jansenius pretendant qu'il ne les a jamais escrites en ses livres d'Augustinus Cornelii Jansenii."[3]

Louis XIV now wrote to the Pope asking him to impose the signature, and the Pope complied by his Bull of February 1665, which contained a formulary[4] analogous to the one prescribed by the clergy, "all wch is grounded upon ye Pope's Infallibility",

1 R.O. *News-letters*, Bundle 13, Dec. 26–Jan. 5, 1663–4.
2 R.O. *S.P. France*, vol. 118, f. 166, April 20–30, 1664.
3 R.O. *News-letters*, Bundle 13, May 2, 1664; cf. April 22 and May 6.
4 An English translation is on p. xix of this book.

remarks Holles, "because yᵉ Pope hath declared the five Propositions to be in Jansenius".¹ The wary old diplomat believed that the king had been too hasty in the admission of a Bull virtually establishing papal infallibility, for presently the king clashed with the Pope over this very point. "He playes his aftergame better than he did the foregame" is Holles' opinion.²

A news-letter of May 1666 tells of the imprisonment of several Jansenists,³ in whom one recognizes M. de Saci, Fontaine and the two brothers Du Fossé, while in 1667 we hear of the dissenting bishops, the Bishops of Alet, Angers, Beauvais and Pamiers, through Oldenburg's correspondent, the Protestant Justel, as we suppose.

"Le Pape devant que de mourir", says this letter, copied out for Williamson, "a envoyé une Bulle contre les evesques Jansenistes qui ne veulent point signer le Formulaire qui a fait tant de bruit. Il nomme 12 Evesques pour leur faire leur proces, quoiqu'ils soient les plus raisonnables et qui menent une vie exemplaire. Il semble qu'en ce siecle la probité soit un crime."⁴

The death of the Pope, Alexander VII, brought some relief to the Jansenists. Public opinion was with the dissenting bishops, and the new Nuncio Bargellini was instructed to work for reconciliation. "Les Jansenistes reviennent de tous costez malgré les Jesuites", writes the Parisian gentleman to Oldenburg who passes on the information. "Tout le monde va voir Monsʳ Arnaud a qui on rend des hommages comme a un Saint. La bigoterie augmente plus que iamais et ceux mesmes qui ne croyent rien sont les premiers a fair plus de grimaces."⁵

This year 1667 also saw the Port Royal translation of the New Testament, known as the Mons New Testament from having been supposedly printed at Mons. It was received with enthusiasm by a large number of pious readers, and even by the world of fashion, but it encountered much ecclesiastical opposition.

1 R.O. S.P. France, vol. 120, f. 192, June 3–13, 1665; cf. f. 148, May 6–16.
2 Ib. f. 192.
3 R.O. News-letters, Bundle 14, May 18, 1666.
4 Ib. May 11, 1667.
5 R.O. S.P. France, vol. 123, f. 51, Oct. 24, 1667.

"The Port Royal translation of the New Testament is censured at Rome," writes Oldenburg to Williamson, "12 doctors of the Sorbonne are examining it and may perhaps condemn it through complaisance, though there are only little faults in it."[1] Other news comes from a traveller abroad.

The King of Ffrance being not yet arriv'd at Paris, the City is very Barren of newes, only this, whilst the Army is in its winter quarters, the clergy is all in a flame. Ffor the Jansenists have lately printed the new testament in the french tongue which hath so enrag'd the Jesuists that they salute them with no lesser names then Hereticks from the pulpet, and have laid aside all other subjects to exercise their witt in invectives against them. And yet the Jansenists have proceeded farther and have a council to meete in a little City (I cannot recall the name) in Languedoc and all Bishops of their opinion who are unwilling to appear in person will have their representatives at this Assembly. To hinder this meeting is now the great businesse of the Jesuists which they endeavor to do by engaging the King in the quarrell but the successe of this not yet being knowne as soon as it is you shall receive it.[2]

The year 1668 tells us of a new blow dealt to the New Testament—"L'Archevesque de Paris a excommunié tout de nouveau tous ceux qui débitaient le Nouveau Testament en François de la traduction de Messieurs du Port Royal".[3] But most of the news, and very abundant it is, concerns the four dissenting Bishops, "two of wch are mighty popular men, B^p of Alet and Angers".[4] Nothing is added to what we already know of this complicated affair from original sources, or from Sainte-Beuve's masterly account,[5] but it is interesting to find so much information being sent to England.[6]

1 *Cal. S.P. Dom.* 1667, p. 509, Oct. 5: cf. Boyle, *Works*, vi, p. 245.
2 R.O. *S.P. France*, vol. 123, f. 263, W. Allestree (to Williamson?), Oct. 19-29 (1667). See also for this year f. 300 (Dec. 10) and *News-letters*, Bundle 14, April 2.
3 R.O. *S.P. France*, vol. 149 (unbound documents), Aug. 25 (1668)—a news-letter copied out by Oldenburg and sent to Williamson. See also *News-letters*, Bundle 14, May 9, June 2.
4 R.O. *News-letters*, Bundle 15, July 11, 1668.
5 *Port-Royal*, vol. iv.
6 R.O. *News-letters*, Bundle 15, June 29, July 4, 7, 11, 21, 25, 28, Aug. 18, 25, Sept. 1, 11, 22, Oct. 17, 26, 27, Nov. 27.

The so-called peace of the Church was concluded in September 1668, and on January 1st, 1669, a medal was struck commemorating the event, with the inscriptions *Gratia et Pax a Deo* and *Ob restitutam Ecclesiae Concordiam*. On one side of the medal was the effigy of Louis XIV, on the other an altar with an open book on which lay diagonally crosswise (*en sautoir*) the Pope's keys and the king's sceptres.[1] The medal caused not a little ill-feeling in some quarters, and a French correspondent, not Oldenburg's friend, sends a copy of a hostile interpretation of the medal to England. The open book, it said, represented the *Augustinus*.

Il est certain que Mrs de Port Royal taschent par tous moyens de persüader a tout le monde que le livre ou la Doctrine de Jansenius qui a esté condamné par Innocent dixie. et Alexandre septie. a esté depuis approuvé par Clement neufvie. d'ou il suit que ce livre qu'ils representent dans leur medaille n'est ni ne peut estre autre que la Doctrine et le livre de Jansenius puisque c'est en effet ce livre là qui a esté fermé par la condamnation de sa doctrine et qui est maintenant ouvert a ce qu'ils pretendent par l'approbation de la mesme doctrine.[2]

The medal was contrary to truth, and also offensive to the Holy See:

Non seulement en ce que par le Sautoir esgalement composé des clefs de l'Eglise et des marques de la puissance Royale et posé sur un livre de Doctrine ecclesiastique et controversée elle semble vouloir partager l'authorité spirituelle et pontificale entre le Pape et le Roy. Mais encor par le nom de Paix et de Concorde qui ne se donne qu'a la reconciliation de deux puissances esgalles et qu'elle donne néantmoins a la soubmission que les quatre Evesques ont faicte en les dispensant selon leurs prieres des penitences canoniques qu'ils avoie. encourues.

And finally the medal was offensive to the king in that it tended to pass him off as an abettor of a doctrine condemned by the Holy See. Moreover the medal had been struck without his

1 The second sceptre being the so-called "main de justice". For a picture of the medal see Guilbert, *Mém. hist. et chron. sur l'Abbaye de Port-Royal des Champs depuis la Paix de l'Église*, vol. ii, or Lanson, *Hist. de la litt. fr.* (illustrated ed.) i, p. 352. For a history of the affair see Guilbert, *op. cit.* ii, pp. 22–37.
2 R.O. *S.P. France*, vol. 128, f. 166. Endorsed "The new Medall".

knowledge—"a son insceu et par surprise elle se fabrique et se debite publiquement dans la monnoye de Sa Ma^té sans avoir esté préalablement communiquée au Nonce de sa Saincteté".[1]

To this commentary the French correspondent adds a story of his own.

M^r le Nonce fut vendredy après diner au Louvre et sans avoir faict demander audience au Roy il demande a luy parler. Il l'obtint et la il fit de grandes plaintes contre cette medaille. Le Roy qui n'en avoit pas ouy parler luy dit qu'il verroit ce que c'estoit et en effet il en parla dans le Conseil a ses Ministres avec du ressentiment qui dura jusqu'a ce que Mr Colbert prist la parole et dit que Mr le Nonce prenoit la mouche pour peu de chose et qu'il avoit tort d'expliquer ce livre ouvert plustost pour le livre de Jansenius que pour la Bible, que ce n'estoit point les Jansenistes qui avoie. faict fa^re cette Medaille, que c'estoit luy mesme qui avoit donné cet ordre a Varin et qu'il l'avoit faict pour eternizer la Memoire de cette Reconciliation des Jansenistes avec l'Eglise dont il avoit crû que la gloire appartenoit a sa Ma^té et la dessus il fit croire au Roy tout ce qu'il luy plût si bien que le succez fut qu'on y traduisit M. le Nonce en Ridicule. Il a envoyé un Courrier expres a Rome pour en donner advis a sa Saincteté. Mais il aura de la peine a reusir parce que les trois Ministres sont pour les Jansenistes et la Medaille dont il s'est vendu 3000 a 12 francs la piece n'a esté faicte que dans le sens de l'explicaõn sus^d.... J'obmettois de dire sur le sujet de la Medaille que lorsque M. le Nonce en a faict plainte il ne croyoit pas qu'elle eust esté faicte par l'ordre de Mr Colbert et que ce dernier a crû que M. le Nonce en disant que la Medaille avoist esté faicte par les Jansenistes le vouloit fa. passer pour Janseniste dans l'esprit du Roy. Voila pourquoy il a pris la chose a cœur en dizant qu'il prenoist a tache de laisser a la posterité des marques de tout ce qui se passe de plus memorable pendant son Reigne. Cela fera que le Nonce qui estoit desia fort mal etably dans l'estime des Ministres trouvera encore plus de peine dans le reste de ses negotiations.[2]

Shortly after the Peace appeared the first volume of Arnauld and Nicole's "grande" *Perpétuité de la Foi sur l'Eucharistie* dedicated to the Pope. "C'était comme une solennelle inauguration de la Paix," remarks Sainte-Beuve, "les Calvinistes en payaient les frais."[3]

1 R.O. *S.P. France*, vol. 128, f. 166.
2 R.O. *News-letters*, Bundle 16, April 20–30, 1669.
3 *Port-Royal*, IV, p. 445.

Oldenburg's correspondent writes of it sourly:

tout le monde parle du livre de M. Arnaud auquel on respondra fort bien; cependant on triomphe. La presse est si grande pour en avoir qu'on a de la peine a en acheter. Je ne doubte point qu'on ne l'ayt envoyé en vtre cour, ces messieurs l'ayant envoyé partout. Jamais il n'y eut moins de religion, mais il y a longtemps qu'on n'a eu plus de passion qu'on a icy astheur p^r l'avancement de la religion romaine.

"I pray, Sir," adds Oldenburg, copying out this letter for Williamson, "name not ye Author of these particulars though you may guesse who it is. It might spoile his communicãons in ye future."[1] Once before he had written, "Sir, I must desire you that you would not name the person that writes these French particulars to anybody at any time, he having made it his earnest sute to me to forbeare naming him".[2]

Oldenburg's correspondent was doubtless alluding to the Huguenot Claude when he confidently announced an answer to Arnauld's book. Claude was Arnauld's greatest adversary on the Protestant side, and a strange poem found its way to London this year, *M. Arnaud entre deux Larrons*. "The verses I send you", writes Perwich, the English agent in Paris, "are by Arnaud ag^t Pere Anata the King's Jesuitical Confessor and Mr Claude the Huguenot minister."[3]

> ...La vanité d'Annat sans mesure et sans regle
> Le pousse le premier dans le combat nouveau
> Mais il esprouve enfin que la plume de l'aigle
>   Mange la plume du corbeau.
>
> Claude de ce vaincu reprend les noires armes
> Mais il ne songe pas que jusque dans nos temps
> La verge de Moyse aneantit les charmes
>   Et devore les fiers serpens....[4]

But whoever wrote this Jansenist poem, one can at least affirm that it was not Arnauld.

One is surprised to find among the state papers for 1669 a beautifully written copy of the long letter of February 19th

1 R.O. *S.P. France*, vol. 126, f. 39, March 8, 1669.
2 *Ib.* f. 22, Feb. 2, 1668–9.
3 *Ib.* vol. 127, f. 81, Aug. 28–Sept. 7, 1669 (to Arlington?).
4 *Ib.* vol. 130, ff. 136–7, 11 verses.

which the nuns of Port Royal des Champs, the ones who had opposed the formulary, addressed to the nuns remaining at Port Royal de Paris, the ones who had accepted it. The letter which, judging from its appearance, is a genuine Port Royal copy, invites the sisters of Port Royal de Paris to make peace with their sisters of Port Royal des Champs and to forget the past— "Le comble de nostre joye seroit de vous embrasser toutes... ce que nous souhaitons avec...ardeur est de voir nos ruines reparées par vostre reunion".[1]

But the reunion never took place, and the two houses continued apart.

"Le Roy a enfin determiné de luy mesme", reports a French correspondent, "qu'il vouloit absolument que la mère Dorothée[2] (anti-janseniste et establi par M^r l'archevesque superieure de Port Royal de la ville pendant la Rebellion des autres filles Jansenistes) continuast a demeurer Abbesse a vye dans led. couvent et le Roy en a uzé ainsi parceque demandant il y a 10 ou 12 jours a Mon S^r l'archevesque s'il estoit enfin resolu de restablir dans Port Royal les Jansenistes puisqu'elles s'estoient du moins apparemment remises a l'obeissance Mond. S^r l'Archevesque luy respondit que M^r le Prince [i.e. Condé] l'en sollicitoit si fortement et luy avoit rendu tant de visites pour cela qu'il ne pouvoit plus resister. Le Roy voyant que M^r le Prince y prenoit part et craignant qu'il ne se fit un parti dont il fut le chef luy respondit et ensuite a M^r le Tellier qu'il vouloit que lad. Mere Dorothée demeurast. Au moyen de quoy Port Royal qui estoit la forge du Jansenisme est osté a ce party quoy que Madame de Longueville ait tesmoigné qu'elle y voudroit bien faire retraicte pourveu qu'on y mit une autre superieure. Mais tout cela fait encore plus apprehender le party."[3]

It is curious to see how "le party" continues to be suspected as a potential centre of opposition, and how calumny enveloped even their powerful friend Mme de Longueville, Condé's sister.

"Je scay de bonne part", writes the same correspondent who furnished the anecdote about the medal, "qu'il y a quelques iours que

1 R.O. S.P. France, vol. 126, ff. 32 A, 32 B. This letter was also printed as a four-page tract (B.N. Ld.⁴ 468).
2 La Mère Marie de Sainte-Dorothée Perdreau.
3 R.O. News-letters, Bundle 16, April 14-24, 1669.

M. le Nonce fut a St Germain pour representer fortement au Roy qu'il avoit appris d'original et de beaucoup d'endroits qu'on faisoit des assemblées tres frequentes a l'hostel de Longueville où on avoit proposé de chercher les moyens pour fa. un Patriarche en France pour y ruyner entierement l'authorité du St Siege. Et la dessus il luy fit apprehender de quelle consequence il estoit d'estouffer de bonne heure cette rebellion, non seulement parce que cela estant tout se dispose manifestement au schisme, mais parce que ces changemens ne se peuvent faire sans alterer et mesme esbranler bien souvent les Constitutions des Estatz."

"Quoy qu'il en soit," he continues, "je scay d'original qu'on observe par ordre secret du Roy tous ceux qui frequentent a l'hostel de Longueville et que Mme de Longueville se deffiant d'un de ses domestiques parent d'un Jesuite que je connois le fit sortir vendredy dernier de sa maison sur un autre pretexte."[1]

Adversaries deemed that the Jansenists were growing too bold and influential. The correspondent just quoted has more to say a few days later on the same subject: "La publication du Missel traduit en François par un certain Bourdelois nommé Voisin cy-devant Aumosnier du Prince de Conti fait veoir le credit des Jansenistes et le peu de respect qu'on commence a avoir icy pour le St Siege". After explaining that the missal had been condemned in 1661 and subsequently, the writer goes on to say:

Le Missel qui contient dans sa traduction pretendue infidele tous les erreurs du Jansenisme se publie et se vend publiquement depuis 8 jours. Le Nonce qui est intimidé dizant qu'il appartient à l'Archevesque de Paris de pousser cette affa. et Mr l'archevesq. qui est trop courtisan soustenant au contraire que c'est au Nonce a s'en plaindre. Cependant le Jansenisme s'establit et a la premiere occasion qui sera favorable ce fera infailliblement un parti d'Estat.[2]

A week later he goes on in the same pessimistic strain:

Le livre de la frequente Communion de Mr Arnauld qui fit tant de bruit il y a 2 ans recommence a paroistre sous une nouvelle impression, personne ne dit mot, et la Cour ou complice ou mal conseillée souffre ainsi le restablissem[t] du Jansenisme. Les sages mondains disent qu'avec ce phantosme on intimidera Rome et on la captivera tousiours a fa. ce que nous voudrons. Mais cependant le mal qu'on laisse croistre par politique deviendra si grand que quand on le voudra

1 *Ib.* April 27–May 7, 1669.   2 *Ib.* May 1–11, 1669.

esteindre par raison d'estat il faudra par la mesme politique le souffrir.[1]

Yet from about 1670 onwards there is little or no mention of the Jansenists in the French news-letters. Port Royal was enjoying a brief respite before the end. The venerable M. d'Andilly, the eldest of the Arnauld brothers, was graciously received by the king and queen at Versailles. "Dans l'anti-chambre...on luy presenta un bouillon par ordre de sa ma^té pour le fortifier à cause de son grand âge."[2] His son, M. de Pomponne, was made a minister, and the English ambassador extraordinary, Ralph Montagu, remarks: "All the Jansenists are extreamly exalted at this preferment of Mr de Pomponne, all his relations being the head of that party and consequently the Jesuits very much mortified".[3]

Instead of controversies we now hear rather of books. One of the clerks of the embassy, a certain Francis Vernon, is evidently instructed to send Williamson all the interesting things he can find, as well as "the little news" or gossip. "I searche all the stores", he says.[4] Packets of books go home by Lord Hamilton or Lord Oxenford, Mons. Puffendorf or Mr Porter;[5] "Mons. Claude's answer to Arnaud",[6] "two fables of Monsieur de la Fontaine from my Lord Ambassador",[7] the two *Bérénices*[8] ("one written by Monsieur Racine, the other by Corneille of wch that of Racine seems to take much and the Ladies melt away at it and proclaim them hard hearted who do not cry"[9]).

One day he sends "a small Pacquet wherein there is a treatise wch hath gained a great esteeme among the Judicious here wch discourseth concerning the Education of a Prince". "It is written by one Monsieur Nicol a Jansenist", he explains, "and

1 R.O. *News-letters*, Bundle 16, May 8–18, 1669. For news of the Bishops this year see *ib*. Jan. 12, Feb. 6.
2 *Ib*. Bundle 18, Sept. 17, 1671; cf. Sainte-Beuve, *Port-Royal*, v, pp. 8–9.
3 R.O. *S.P. France*, vol. 132, f. 9, Sept. 12, 1671.
4 *Ib*. vol. 131, f. 15.   5 *Ib. passim*.
6 *Ib*. f. 23, Jan. 31, 1670. Justel also sent a copy to be presented to the king, *ib*. f. 125, June 6: cf. f. 112 and f. 127.
7 *Ib*. vol. 133, f. 83, May 8, 1672.
8 *Ib*. vol. 131, f. 27, Feb. 4, 1671.
9 *Ib*. vol. 130, f. 246, Dec. 3, 1670.

one of the ablest of them and who lives in the house wth Monsieur Arnaud. I suppose it will find as kind a reception abroad as it doth at home."[1]

Another day—in January 1671—a priceless little book is dispatched to England through Mr Gee, my Lord of Northumberland's steward:

Monsieur Pascal's booke about religion wch is only a designe of a great work he intended to finish upon that subject, butt because of the Eminency of the author they have published it imperfect as it is and all ye court, Madame Montespan, Valiere, the King, Marechal Turenne all buy it, there are 500 sould since St Stephen's day and Desprez is going to print another edition.[2]

What, one wonders, became of this copy of the first edition of the *Pensées*?

A young Oxford student travelling in France, Henry Smith by name, looks upon Williamson as a kind of patron and in return sends him information about the *litterati* and *virtuosi* which, he believes, will interest Williamson.

"In Divinity", he remarks, "I thinke there is none to be compared to Mr Arnaud among the Papists who was formerly expell'd the Sorbonne for not recanting a booke which he writt in defence of the Jansenists; his brother being one of the 4 dissenting B^ps, he is at present deeply engaged with Mr Claud (the learnedst of the Hugenot) in the long controverted question of the perpetuity of the faith of the church concerning the point of the Eucharist."[3]

Another time he writes about the Cartesianism of the Jansenists; incidentally it is interesting to hear of the vicissitudes of Cartesianism in the seventeenth century.

Upon the first day of every month the Sorbonne doctors hold an Assembly wherein they censure all bookes which are destructive of Religion or good manners; upon Monday last being the first of June it was Descartes his misfortune to be called to the barr, where he found many ennemys and many Advocats, amongst these latter was the B^p of Condome Tutor to the Dauphin [i.e. Bossuet]. The debate was very long and sharp, some argueing that his philosophy was not contrary to their Religion, others were of the opinion that allthough

1 *Ib.* f. 118, Sept. 15, 1670.
2 *Ib.* vol. 131, ff. 15–16, Jan. 15–25, 1670–1.
3 *Ib.* f. 47, early in 1671.

it were contrary, yet it ought not to be condemn'd lest thereby the young men should applye themselves more earnestly to the study of it; the very condemnation being a great motif to their curiosity, but after all this heat they came to no resolution insomuch that the issue is not yet known, but I believe I can give some small conjecture of the cause.

The explanation follows:

There was a monck about a month agoe who printed a little pamphlet touching the present controversy of the Euchariste, wherein he uttered many things not over favourable to the opinion of transubstantiation showing that the notions of Aristotles philosophy applyd to divinity had caused the greatest part of our disputes; but this was not all, for had he rested there peradventure he alone might have undergone the censure, and Descartes remained secure, but his main dessigne was to prove that a Cartesian could never believe transubstantiation... [paper torn] ... [Mr Arnauld that] hath undertaken the defence of this point against Mr Claud is a notorious Cartesian and having been formerly expelled the Sorbonne for Jansenisme is like to suffer a second censure for Cartesianisme; they need no other proof against him for matter of fact but his own Logick wch he hath published under the title of L'Art de Penser which is all built upon Descartes his methode. And certainly the Jesuites will not fail to pursue the businesse to the uttmost, seeing their sworn ennemys (I mean those of the porte royale) are so deeply concerned in this businesse being universally Cartesians.[1]

Another young man, a certain Gaillard, is travelling as tutor to Sir Philip Perceval in 1676–7, and also supplies Williamson with information. He and his charge are at Angers where are also "le marquis de Montross et my lord Kingston d'Irlande", and at Angers Gaillard goes to call on the brother of le grand Arnauld, the venerable bishop, Henri Arnauld, who was evidently known to Williamson.

A mon arrivée icy je fus chez Monsr d'Angers luy faire vos baisemains qu'il receut avec beaucoup de marques de respect et d'estime, c'estoit après un voyage qu'il venoit de faire a pied de plus de 50 lieues en visite de son diocese et cependant il est entré en sa 80e année.

1 R.O. *S.P. France,* vol. 131, f. 127, June 16, 1671. For the Cartesianism of the Jansenists see Besoigne's *Histoire de Port-Royal,* IV, pp. 290–1; F. Bouillier, *Histoire de la philosophie cartésienne* (Paris 1868, 2 vols.), *passim,* especially I. pp. 432–4, II, pp. 208–26; see also Brunetière, *Études critiques,* 4e série, " Jansénistes et Cartésiens".

This Arnauld had just had a lengthy struggle with the University of Angers and the chancellor, the abbé de La Barre; difficulties had again arisen in connection with the formulary:

> On luy a depuis peu donné bien de la paine au subiect du Jansenisme et pour de certaines thèses qu'il avoit approuvé et il a eu besoin de la considération de son age et de tout le credit de Mr de Pomponne pour se maintenir et divertir le coup qui est tombé sur deux chanoines de St Maurice.[1]

In the same letter we hear of a quarrel between two famous grammarians, their *Observations* and their *Remarques* being embittered by the fact that the authors belong to two different theological camps.

> Il y a un autre Jesuiste nomme le Père Bouhours qui est aux prises avec l'Abbé Menage au subject d'un livre de remarques que ce dernier avoit fait sur la langue françoise. Le Jesuiste luy a contredit en bien des choses et a meslé du fiel dans son encre, mais l'Abbé s'en est deffendu avec beaucoup d'aigreur et c'est depuis 6 semaines que son livre a paru. Comme Mr Menage est Janseniste l'inimitié est plus forte dans le cœur de ces deux Antagonistes.[2]

The Pope, Clement X, died in 1676, and of the new Pope, Innocent XI, Williamson learns that if he is not a Jansenist, he is at least a friend of the Messieurs.[3] Sir Robert Southwell also receives a letter from Gaillard on the same subject.

> The late kind answers of the Pope to several heads of the Jansenists in France who had congratulated his assumption to the popedom, make everyone in France say he is a Jansenist. I take the freedom to trouble you with the copies of those several answers.... The Bishop of Angers has done me the favour to show me a copy of his letter to the Pope and the answer to it, but is resolved to give no copy of it.[4]

Copies of the replies to the Jansenists were also promised to Williamson.[5]

---

1 For this complicated affair see Claude Cochin, *Henri Arnauld, Évêque d'Angers* (1921), pp. 261–91.
2 R.O. *S.P. France*, vol. 141, f. 306, Dec. 3–13, 1676.
3 *Ib.* vol. 142, f. 44, June 2, 1677.
4 *Hist. MSS. Comm.*, *MSS. of the Earl of Egmont*, II, p. 64, June 6, 1677: "Now the Bishop is past eighty years, brother to Mr Arneud (*sic*) and uncle to Mons. de Pomgrone". The last should read "Pomponne".
5 R.O. *S.P. France*, vol. 142, f. 44, June 2, 1677.

Nothing of great importance can be gleaned from the letters in the following years—the fate of the Huguenots was a subject of far greater interest to the English. We hear of Jansenists being sent to prison in 1681;[1] of the arrest of le Père du Breuil and ten or twelve Jansenists in 1682, guilty of helping to bring in some of Arnauld's books;[2] of a certain change of attitude as evinced by the famous articles of the clergy in 1682 affirming the liberties of the Gallican church, "On a bien changé de sentiment depuis quelques années que ceux qui tenoient que le Pape n'estoit pas infaillible meme aux questions de fait estoient traités d'heretiques et perdoient leur benefice s'ils ne vouloient pas signer le formulaire".[3]

The Archbishop of Paris, Harlay, died in 1694, and his successor Noailles was inclined to be lenient to the Jansenists; one is not therefore surprised to find a certain M. de Chenailles writing to Sir William Trumbull, Secretary of State, that "Jansenism is reviving among respectable people", though it is curious to be told in this connection that "a reformation on English lines is likely in France".[4] But the respite was brief, and we are not far from the condemnation of Quesnel's *Moral Reflections* and the Bull *Unigenitus*. Matthew Prior, on a mission in Paris, writes home occasionally about the Bull, and with him we begin to hear again of dissenting bishops.[5] The controversy over the Bull *Unigenitus* went on for many years, and there are probably some echoes of it in the English state papers sent home from France, but it is a vast and complicated affair, lacking the interest of the earlier controversies, complicated enough as they are; the later Jansenism involves Gallicanism, and it hardly seemed profitable to pursue chance references.

A very curious document preserved among the state papers for 1666 has not yet been mentioned, as it is of an entirely

1 *Cal. S.P. Dom. Charles II*, 1680-1, p. 447.
2 R.O. *S.P. France*, vol. 144, f. 152, Oct. 31, 1682, Lord Preston to Mr Wynne. Cf. *Hist. MSS. Comm., App. to Seventh Report*, p. 273.
3 R.O. *News-letters*, Bundle 20, April 4, 1682. For other references to the Jansenists in the eighties see *ib.*, May 15; Bundle 21, March 13, 1683; Feb. 5, 1684.
4 *Hist. MSS. Comm., MSS. of the Marquess of Downshire*, 1, pt 2, p. 584.
5 L. G. Wickham Legg, *Matthew Prior* (1921), pp. 192, 193.

different nature. It is not a news-letter, it is not a letter in the ordinary sense of the word, it is an anonymous plan to stir up unrest in France for the benefit of the English. England had been at war with the Dutch since 1665, and in 1666 France found herself obliged to side, rather unwillingly, with the Dutch. The author of the document, whoever he may be, boasts of knowing most of the malcontents in France who can help his main design, "intimider la cour", "reprimer l'orgueil intolerable de la cour". And first of all he remembers the Jansenists and their reputation—they are said to form a faction, a centre of disaffection and unrest—it would be easy to give the impression that the Jansenists had secret relations with England.

"Le Roy des François", says this paper, "est jaloux des trois corps de son Roiaume et surtout des Jansenistes qu'on luy a persuade estre une faction naissante fomentée par les princes et grands de son roiaume pour restablir leur authorité qui se trouve tout a fait diminuée depuis l'uniformité de l'estat et l'entier abaissement des huguenots. La cour apprehende cette faction plus qu'elle ne fait semblant et fait ses efforts pour l'esteindre, elle craint leur intelligence en angleterre, il y a moyen de la leur persuader en escrivant aux evesques notés de cette faction. Je les connois....

Je connois tous ceux qui ont entrepris contre le Roy. J'entens les chefs des provinces. Je connois les principaux mescontenps.

Je connois encore dans toutes les provinces ceux qu'on apprehende parmy les huguenots.

Des lettres hazardées aux uns et aux autres dont le sens sera ambigu et supposera une plus grande intelligence quand mesme elles seroient renvoyées à la Cour, si elles sont bien conceues donneront de l'inquietude...."

All kinds of possible means are suggested, above all recourse to the states general, and then, toward the end of the paper, the writer returns to the Jansenists.

Pour l'intelligence des Jansenistes je scay un moyen infallible de la persuader et connois tant de mecontenps qu'il sera aisé de tirer quelque avantage de tout ce qu'il y a dans les memoires.

Je suis asseuré de pouvoir rendre public par tout le royaume tout le contenu. Il n'y faut qu'un secret particulier et que les memoires soint veus de peu de personnes.[1]

1 R.O. *S.P. France*, vol. 122, ff. 248–9. Endorsed in pencil "Sept. 1666".

There is nothing to show that this document was ever taken seriously, but it is interesting for the light it throws on the reputation of Port Royal as a place of possible intrigues and cabals. In the eyes of Louis XIV the Jansenists were a republican party, in the state as well as in the Church. A few years later, in 1679, when the pensionnaires were sent away from Port Royal des Champs and the gentlemen dispersed, the archbishop, Harlay, gave as one of the reasons for this disciplinary measure, "Ces Messieurs de Port Royal entretiennent un commerce avec les estrangers de toute sorte de pays".[1] We have already seen how, in 1653, the Jansenists were accused of intriguing with Cromwell. It is convenient to mention here another accusation, although strictly speaking it does not belong to this chapter.

France was at war with England in 1689: Louis XIV was supporting James II against William, when suddenly, to their utter amazement, some worthy ecclesiastics, canons of the cathedral of Beauvais and Jansenists by reputation, found themselves lodged in the prison of Vincennes; a former canon of Beauvais, now at Boulogne, was even thrust into the Bastille. What had happened was this—a fellow-ecclesiastic, a certain Raoul Foi, whom they had rebuked for his manner of living, had avenged himself by accusing them of an understanding with England. He gave out that he had discovered a "horrible" conspiracy; the English were to be admitted into Boulogne, the "nouveaux convertis" of Brittany were to be incited to revolt, and as a proof he produced some letters in cipher, all addressed to Arnauld, then in Holland.

The ecclesiastics were watched for a while; nothing of a suspicious nature was discovered. They were seen to pass from their houses to the cathedral, and from the cathedral back to their houses. But the informer was so insistent, even naming the witnesses he could adduce, that it was decided to imprison five or six of those whom he accused. Other arrests, including that of Godefroi Hermant, were to follow. The list of those involved included, besides Arnauld, other Jansenists of note, such as M. de Pontchâteau and M. Feydeau. M. Walon de

1 B.N. f. fr. MS. 17779, f. 13; cf. Sainte-Beuve, *Port-Royal*, v, p. 182.

Beaupuis, then in Beauvais, was advised by his friends to go into hiding. The accusation, however, proved groundless, the prisoners were liberated, and the villain hanged. But not everything ended so happily for the Jansenists.[1]

---

1 The chief source for this is found in Du Fossé's *Mémoires*, III, pp. 343–9. See also Arnauld, *Œuvres*, III (Lettres), pp. 255, 258, 262, 267; *Supplément au Nécrologe*, p. 675; Racine (abbé), *Hist. eccl.* XI, pp. 541–2.

CHAPTER X

"The better kind of Papists"

WE have seen in a preceding chapter how a certain number of Jansenist books were translated, chiefly, though not exclusively, those that could foster the traditional Protestant hatred of the Jesuits; in another chapter we have seen some of the news that reached Williamson, Oldenburg and their circle from correspondents in France. We may now ask ourselves what interest, if any, was shown in the Jansenists themselves by various seventeenth-century Anglican and Puritan divines and writers, other than translators.

There is not a very great deal of evidence, but what there is shows, on the whole, considerable though condescending sympathy with the Jansenists as being the "better" and "more serious kind of Papists", and with Jansenism as being "an inroad made into the Kingdom of Darkness and Error which might open a way to further light and knowledge among the Papists themselves".[1] Esteem is shown for anything that is considered akin to Protestantism—the Jansenist's simplicity, their severity, their use of the Scriptures, their independence, their distrust of papal infallibility. At the same time the controversy between Jansenists and Jesuits is eagerly used to prove that the much-vaunted unity of the Church of Rome does not exist.

Some knowledge of the Jansenists was not infrequently gained by sojourn abroad. Thus Archbishop Bramhall had been made acquainted with the contentions while residing at Antwerp during the Commonwealth, and though he declines to meddle with the merit of the cause, he notes with some approbation the independence of the Archbishop of Malines and the Bishop of Ghent who refused to receive a certain Bull, and of the Council

1 Owen, Preface to Gale's *True Idea of Jansenisme.*

of Brabant which forbade the prelates to appear at Rome whither they were cited.[1]

In 1654 Isaac Barrow arrived in Paris, having sold his books to provide himself with a viaticum,[2] and presently he wrote back a long letter to the Master and Fellows of Trinity College, Cambridge—*reverendissimi et ornatissimi viri*—telling them of the warfare that was being waged at the Sorbonne. He does not begin at the beginning which, as he remarks, would be most tedious, but he speaks with obvious sympathy of Arnauld (*nomen vestris opinor auribus non ignotum*), Arnauld who had answered the Jesuits' writings *docte et eleganter*, and who was now accused of temerity for having said he could not find in Jansenius the five propositions condemned by the Pope. "Ridiculous!" exclaims the young scholar impatiently. If these things were really in Jansenius, then Arnauld's adversaries were stupid not to point out the exact place where they occurred; if they themselves could not find the place, then they either stood convicted of falsehood, or were guilty of the crime they imputed to Arnauld.[3] Like others after him[4] Barrow seizes upon this controversy to cast aspersions on the Church of Rome—those who boast so greatly of their unity he sees split up into hostile factions, and those who arrogate all brotherly love to themselves he sees fighting each other fiercely.

Dr Morley, afterwards Bishop of Winchester, had also seen something of the Jansenists in France, and like Dr Steward and Sir George Radcliffe he had turned his thoughts to union. When Baxter met with him in 1660, hoping to find out "whether Concord was really intended" between the Presbyterians and Anglicans, Morley was evasive, merely talked of moderation in general, "He told me at last", says Baxter, "that the Jan-

1 Bramhall, *Works* (1842–5, 5 vols.), I, pp. 236–7. He uses this as one of his arguments in his "Vindication of the English Church", one of his contentions being that "all princes of the Roman communion have acted on the same principles as the English Church has done in its attitude to Rome" (W. J. S. Simpson, *Archbishop Bramhall* (1927), pp. 160–1).
2 Hill, *Life of Dr Barrow*, prefixed to Barrow's *Works*, I, p. xliii.
3 Barrow, *Works*, IX, pp. 111–19, Feb. 9, 1655.
4 E.g. the translator of Saint-Amour's *Journal*, Owen's Preface to Gale, Baxter's *Key for Catholics*, etc.

senists were numerous among the Papists, and many of the French inclined for peace, and on his knowledge, if it were not for the hindrances which Calvin had laid in the way, most on this side the Alp would come over to us."[1] Baxter, it may be added, had read "the Jansenians'" *Mysterie of Jesuitism*, and "Montaltus the Jansenist" was to supply him with many an argument for his polemic *A Key for Catholics to open the Jugling of the Jesuits*.[2]

One who wanted to see the Jansenists and did not succeed was Burnet. A young man of twenty-one, he went travelling in 1664, and after a stay in Holland he proceeded to France through Flanders. In Flanders he was under a great constraint, so he tells us, by reason of the company of many Scotsmen that travelled with him from Holland to Paris, and he was afraid they might have made stories in Scotland if he had conversed much or freely with any papists. But at Paris he was more at liberty, and he heard many sermons of the popish clergy. He did not like the way of preaching of the Jesuits and the Friars, and thought it had too much of the stage in it, but the secular priests pleased him more and he took "a good tincture of their way".

"The way of preaching in which I still hold", he writes about twenty years after his journey, "is (as some that have observed it well have told me) very like the way of the secular clergy of the Port Royal." Not that he had seen anything of this clergy. "While I was at Paris I could not get into acquaintance of any of the Jansenists; they were run down and were very reserved, so that it was not easy to get into any familiarity with them."[3] "The Jansenists were then so much depressed that they kept themselves in great retirement, and so I could not find a way to be admitted to see any of them."[4]

But a friend of Burnet found access to them, at least in Flanders. This was Archbishop Leighton, accounted a saint from his youth up, as Burnet tells us.[5] In his early life he had spent some years in France between 1631 and 1641; he had

1 Baxter, *Narrative of his Life and Times*, Book I, Part II, p. 218.
2 Baxter, *A Key*, pp. 64, 75–80, 159, 165, 269, 277, 363, 414, 415, 430.
3 Burnet, *History of My Own Time*, Foxcroft's *Supplement*, pp. 95–7.
4 *Ib.* p. 468.
5 *History of My Own Time* (ed. Airy), I, p. 239.

relatives among the Roman Catholic clergy at Douay, not so far from Ypres; he spoke the language like one born there, and it is not unlikely that he then heard of Jansenius and Saint-Cyran. In later years when he was principal of Edinburgh University he went travelling in vacation time.

Sometimes he went over to Flanders to see what he could find in the severall orders of the church of Rome. There he found some of Jansenius's followers, who seemed to be men of extraordinary tempers, and who studied to bring things if possible to the purity and simplicity of the primitive ages, on which all his thoughts were much set.[1]

He was much taken with these men, we are told by Burnet,[2] and one wonders whether he had not in mind the solitaries of Port Royal when, with a wistful longing, he regretted that the Protestant Churches had "no retreat for men of mortified tempers", and thought "the great and fatal error of the Reformation was that more of those houses and of that course of life, free from the entanglements of vows and other mixtures was not preserved".[3] Certainly the quiet contemplative life of the solitaries was in harmony with his aspirations, and their spirit of self-effacement was deeply akin to his "who had no regard to his person unless it was to mortify it".[4]

As for his theological views, one of his biographers remarks that it is impossible to read his sermons and his University lectures without perceiving how closely he was in sympathy with the teaching of Jansen and Saint-Cyran, and he considers that Leighton "unquestionably received from the Jansenists ideals and impulses which modified his early position and which he treasured throughout life".[5] In his library were to be found three volumes of Saint-Cyran's *Lettres Spirituelles*, Arnauld's *Fréquente Communion*, M. d'Andilly's *Vie des Saints Pères*, the *Constitutions du Monastère de Port-Royal* and Pascal's *Pensées*.[6]

1 *Ib*. pp. 243–4.
2 Foxcroft's *Supplement*, p. 13.
3 *History of My Own Time*, I, pp. 246–7.
4 *Ib*. p. 239. Cf. W. G. Blaikie, *The Evangelical succession*, series 2 (1883), p. 184.
5 Butler, *Life and Letters of Robert Leighton*, pp. 95–6. See also pp. 78–9, 83, 88 *n*., 277–8, 544–5.   6 *Ib*. pp. 591–2.

In general it may be said that considerable influence was exerted in seventeenth-century Protestant Scotland by Jansenism and Pascal's works.[1] As early as 1656 one finds a professor of theology and future Principal of the University of Glasgow, Robert Baillie, writing to his cousin William Spang, minister at Middelburg in Zeeland, "Whatever is to be got of...the Jansenists pro et contra, let us have it".[2]

A churchman who doubtless had a deep regard for the Jansenists was Bishop Ken, whom we perhaps remember best to-day as the author of two famous hymns for morning and evening—"Awake my soul and with the sun" and "Glory to Thee, my God, this night". He travelled in France in 1675 with the younger Izaak Walton; and Dean Plumptre, his biographer, describing the route taken, believes that this journey brought him "within range of the saintly Nicolas Pavillon, Bishop of Alet, then nearly four-score, to whose character and life his own presented so striking a parallelism".[3] Ken's library contained, besides the works of Jansenius, Saint-Cyran's *Lettres* and the *Provinciales*, a copy of Pavillon's *Statuts Synodaux du Diocèse d'Alet*,[4] and Plumptre after studying the *Statuts Synodaux* came to the conclusion that the administration of Ken's own diocese was largely modelled on this.[5] Ken had started on his travels "with a keen sense of the shortcoming of the pastoral work of the English Church....He would naturally ask himself whether he could find this better ordered elsewhere....At Alet he could find one who would seem to him, as he did to others, to revive the simplicity and the earnestness of the days of the Apostles".[6] There are a few rather far-fetched details in this biography of Ken, still the suggestion is a most interesting one; so is the one that the sisterhood at Naish was probably a reproduction of Pavillon's "Regents" in the diocese of Alet.[7]

---

1 The Rev. Prof. G. D. Henderson in an article on "The Foreign Religious Influences in Seventeenth Century Scotland", *Edinburgh Review*, April 1929, p. 351.
2 Baillie, *Letters and Journals* (Publ. of the Bannatyne Club, 1841–2, 3 vols.), III, p. 324.
3 Plumptre, *Life of Ken*, I, p. 110 *n*.
4 *Ib.*, also II, p. 298.   5 *Ib.* I, p. 258.
6 *Ib.*   7 *Ib.* II, p. 169 *n*.

Jeremy Taylor commended Arnauld's *Fréquente Communion*.
"I am well pleased", he writes, "that even amongst themselves
[the Roman Catholics] some are so convinced of the weakness of
their usual ministries of repentance that as much as they dare they call
upon the priests to be more deliberate in their absolutions....
Monsieur Arnauld of the Sorbon hath appeared publicly in reproof
of a frequent and easy communion without the just and long prepara-
tions of repentance.[1]

The greatest interest in Jansenism was naturally shown, not
by Anglicans, but by those whom the Jansenists were accused
of resembling in doctrine, the Calvinists. In the early 'sixties a
young nonconformist, who had been tutor at Magdalen, Oxford,
during the Commonwealth, spent two years in Caen whither he
had accompanied the sons of his patron, Philip fourth Baron
Wharton. The boys went to the Protestant "collège" of the place,
and their tutor, Theophilus Gale, came to know the learned pastor, Bochart. The pastor had a good opinion of the Jansenists;
indeed, discussing with Gale[2] one day the imminent downfall of
Antichrist, he gave as one of the reasons for its approach the
multiplying of the Jansenists and the "orthodoxalitie" of their
opinions. Gale became interested in the Jansenists; he was able,
he tells us, to "informe himself from the personal conversation
among the different Parties concerned in this Controversie"; he
consulted "the best Memoires he could procure from one and
t'other Partie";[3] among the books he read were the *Augustinus*
—no light task—Saint-Amour's folio, Saint-Cyran's *Lettres*,
the *Provinciales*, pamphlets such as *La simple Vérité opposée à la
fausse Idée du Jansénisme*, the *Refutation de la fausse Relation du
P. Ferrier*, etc. Saint-Cyran he admired especially, and confessed that he had been "much recreated" in reading his *Epistles*
"sparkling with that Divine fire which burned in his heart",
"letters full of choice and sublime instructions".[4]

---

1 J. Taylor, *Works* (1850–4, 10 vols.), VII, p. 14. From *Unum Necessarium*
(1655). Taylor also quotes Jansenius in VI, pp. 24, 65.
2 I assume that the "English Gentleman" mentioned by Gale is Gale himself.
The true Idea of Jansenisme, p. 97.
3 *Ib.* (*A Premonition*).
4 *Ib.* pp. 15, 160.

Finally, after almost losing his books and papers in the Great Fire of London—they were saved by mere chance—he produced in 1669 a little book which he entitled *The true Idea of Jansenisme*. Being "a person disinteressed" he thought he could with greater liberty and exactitude of spirit give an account of the affair, as a historian, not a disputant, but it is not difficult to recognize his preferences when he deals with the Jansenists "oppressed by calumnies and sinister dealings".[1] Nevertheless this little book is interesting as the first English study of Jansenism.

Gale divided his treatise into two parts. In the first part, *The Historick Idea of Jansenisme*, he gave an account of the rise and progress of the controversy, spoke of Baius at Louvain, of Jansenius and his "immense desire of Truth and indefatigable Studie", Jansenius "greatly esteemed and beloved by the more serious Papists",[2] of Saint-Cyran, his "Sanctitie", his "Humilitie", his "Christian Constancy", of his "great reputation among the more serious Catholicks",[3] but a large part of Gale's narrative being based on Saint-Amour's enormous *Journal*, most space is given to the stormy period treated by Saint-Amour, viz. the years immediately preceding the condemnation of the five propositions, 1651 to 1653.[4]

We next come to the formulary imposed upon the clergy, and here our nonconformist author who had lost his preferments is keenly interested in a situation that had some analogy with his own.

"This formularie", he writes, "great numbers in heart Jansenists, are induced, by virtue of some mental reservations, to subscribe unto, but such as are thorough paced and professed Jansenists, look upon it as their great glorie and Interest to passe for Non-Conformists, though with the losse of their Dignities and preferments, yea with incurring the censure of Excommunication."[5]

A few more pages bring us to the close of the historical part, and he concludes a summary of the present state of affairs on the familiar note of "the Jansenists' acceptation with serious Papists

1 P. 19.   2 Pp. 7-12.   3 Pp. 13-16.
4 Pp. 21-71.   5 P. 72.

and Protestants".[1] Not only have they "many and great friends amongst the more serious and sober of the Nobles, clergy and people of France", but "the Protestants generally have a great favour and kindness for the Jansenists".[2] Gale is somewhat mistaken in his conception of the Jansenist attitude toward Protestantism when he assumes a latent cordiality which never existed—"And albeit the Jansenists hitherto have not dared to professe any great affection for or inclination towards those of the Reformed Religion: yet 'tis conceived they want it not, but rather the opportunitie".[3] He notes with interest that the great crime of which the Jesuits accuse the Jansenists is their "symbolizing with the Calvinists", but he has to admit that the Jansenists, to vindicate themselves from this imputation, now and then write a book against the Calvinists.[4]

The second and shorter part of the treatise is a *Dogmatick Idea of Jansenisme*, and consists of an account of Jansen's doctrines as exposed in the *Augustinus*. In conclusion Gale "discourses a little" on Jansenism. He is glad to observe with all Protestant writers of the time that the "Jansenists generally begin to have a good esteem of the Sacred Scriptures"; he approves of their dislike of "sufficient Grace which the Molinists do so much Idolize", and he tells a curious story of how the Jansenists "in a Shew at Paris framed a Chariot wherein sat two Virgins; the one with fair and beautiful fruit in her hands without use, which they called sufficient Grace; the other with fruit useful and nourishing, which they stiled Grace Efficacious".

But this above all:

The Jansenists seem good friends to Justification by Free Grace and Faith in the blood of Christ, without any regard to human merits as abused in the Popish sense. 'Tis true they make use of the name merit, but in no other sense than it was used by Austin, without any approbation of the thing as the ground of Justification.

To this conclusion Gale comes not only from reading the Jansenists' books but from observing their practice.

It was the usual method of Jansenius, for the comforting of afflicted consciences, to send them to the blood of Christ alone: and

1 P. 95.　　2 P. 97.　　3 *Ib.*　　4 P. 98.

Mr St Cyran seems mighty warme and pressing on this point. The like instances I have had touching others of this persuasion in France, who, being to deal with dying persons, insisted much upon pressing them to have recourse to the blood of Christ.

Speaking of the "practical Theologie" he remarks that Jansenius and Saint-Cyran seem to have had a very deep broad spiritual light and insight into the Mysteries of the Gospel and true Godliness.

They presse with some affectionate importunitie, to the renouncing our own righteousnesse, strength, wisdom, wills. They greatly commend to us spiritual povertie, soul humilitie, heart-mortification, self emptinesse.... These things they insist upon, not according to the Monkish mode of external mortification, but in a Gospel strain, with so much meeknesse of wisdom, yet with so much spiritual passion and warmth, as if their words were but sparks or ideas of that Divine fire which burned in their hearts.[1]

Finally their principles of Church Discipline are examined and Gale commends their "very moderate and favorable persuasions", their disavowal of the Pope's infallibility.[2]

To this book a famous Puritan divine, Dr John Owen, who had been Dean of Christ Church in Cromwell's time, contributed a lengthy and bellicose preface, not in defence of the Jansenists, nor greatly attacking the Jesuits, but resorting to the favourite device of challenging the unity of the Church of Rome by means of this controversy, and pouring contempt on those who were "so blindly zealous as to endeavour to fix and gild the weathercock of Papal Personal Infallibility, yea, in matters of Fact, on the top of that Tower the visible rottenness of whose Foundations threatened them with a downfall every moment".

Coming at length to the subject-matter of the book:

"There are very few, I suppose, amongst us", he says, "who so little concern themselves in Religion...who have not taken notice of the discourses and reports concerning Jansenisme from the Neighbour Kingdom of France. To some, it may be, it is a murmur, which they know not well what to make of, nor what is intended by it. Others, in general, conceive it to be an expression of some differences in Religion: but of what nature, importance or tendency;

1 Pp. 156–60.   2 Pp. 161–6.

how or by whom agitated or maintained they know not.... It is not only considerable as a Controversie in Religion; on which account contemplative persons or men of Learning, professing the Gospel, esteem themselves obliged to inquire into it to the utmost: but also ...it hath an influence into the Civil affairs of that Kingdom."

He believed that both Divines and Politicians would be much relieved and assisted by Gale's narrative, and as for the system of Doctrines that went by the name of Jansenism, he thought them in general agreeable to the Scriptures.

Before leaving Owen it may be pointed out that he used Jansenius in his writings,[1] and that his library contained not only works by Jansenius and Saint-Amour's *Journal*, but also books on the other side, such as the *Answers to the Provincial Letters* and *Cornelius Jansenius Iprensis suspectus*.[2]

To return to Gale, he continued a warm admirer of Jansenius, "that great Patrone of Free Grace, Impugnator of Free Will"[3] and in his erudite work *The Court of the Gentiles* there are frequent references to Jansenius—"as Jansenius acutely demonstrates", "we find it excellently observed by Jansenius", "this is excellently well explicated by Jansenius", "as Jansenius has incomparably well demonstrated", "we find a great account hereof in Jansenius".[4]

None, he assures us, have been more bold and successful in the Roman Church for the overthrowing of the proud Pelagian Idol than the pious and great Cornelius Jansenius. Yet with a characteristic Protestant distrust of the Roman Church Gale marvels to find so much good in one of her sons.

It is or ought to be, the great wonder of pious souls that in this Age wherein so many Professors of the Reformed Religion have turned their backs on the Doctrine of Free Grace and imbibed so many Pelagian Infusions which are the very vital spirits and heart of Antichristianisme, God has raised up, even in the bosome of Antichrist, Jansenius and his Sectators, who in vindication of Augustin's Doctrine, have proved themselves such stout Champions

1 E.g. Θεολογούμενα Παντοδαπά (Oxford, 1661, pp. 42, 444, 515, 516, 519).
2 *Bibliotheca Oweniana* (Catalogue, 1684).
3 *The Court of the Gentiles*, III, p. 145.
4 *Ib.* pp. 29, 30, 37, 38, 40, 41, 130, 132, 133, 143, 144, 145–7, 158, 160, 162; Part IV, pp. 24, 27, 79, 100, 400, 415, 422, 423, 428, 430.

and Assertors of Free Grace against al Pelagian Dogmes. O! what mater of admiration wil this be unto al Eternitie.[1]

Gale's ideas were not allowed to go altogether unchallenged. "The controversie of Predetermination of the acts of sin was unhappily shared this year—1677—among the Nonconformists", writes Baxter. The occasion was "a sober modest book of Mr How's to Mr Boil", viz. *The Reconcileableness of God's Prescience* by John Howe, written at the instance of Boyle. "And two honest, self-conceited Nonconformists Mr Danson and Mr Gale wrote against him unworthily"—Gale had attacked Howe in one of the concluding parts of his *Court of the Gentiles.* "And just now a second book of Mr Gale's is come out", says Baxter, referring no doubt to another part of the *Court of the Gentiles*, "wholly for Predetermination...falsely reporting the sense of Augustin... and notoriously of Jansenius." Baxter thought of publishing a reply as an antidote against the poison of Mr Gale's book and the scandal it brought on the nonconformists. However "Mr Gale fell sick and I supprest my answer lest it should grieve him. (And he then dyed.)"[2]

Gale's death occurred early in 1678: he had bequeathed his valuable library with the exception of some philosophical books to Harvard College where for long his books constituted more than half the library.[3] Doubtless his *Augustinus* went overseas, and almost certainly it was the first copy of the work received in America, but it is impossible to prove this, as Harvard Hall was burned to the ground in 1764, and with it the library and Gale's books, nor is there any list or catalogue of his bequest in existence.[4]

In connection with the attack on Gale's ideas mention may be made of a pamphlet published in 1677 by an anonymous clergyman of the Church of England, attacking the doctrines of Calvin and Jansenius whom he brackets together,[5] and for the sake of convenience, although it is anticipating by almost

1 *The Court of the Gentiles*, Part III, pp. 146–7.
2 Baxter, *Narrative*, Part III, pp. 152–3, 185.
3 A. C. Potter, *The Library of Harvard University* (3rd ed., 1915), pp. 14–15.
4 *Ib.* and information kindly given me by Mr Potter, Librarian-in-chief.
5 *Omnes qui audiunt...*, 1677. See list at end of this book.

PLATE IV

ROBERT BOYLE

thirty years, attention may be drawn here to another pamphlet by a churchman in which Jansenius finds himself in the company of Puritan Divines, Twisse and Baxter.[1]

In 1688, Edmund Calamy, grandson of the "Smectymnuus" Calamy and the future biographer of nonconformity, was studying at Utrecht. "I have conversed with some of the Romanists who are of the Jansenistical sort", he writes, and he adds what is to him the highest of praise, namely that they appeared to him to have as good notions of many points in religion, and to be as sober in their lives as any of the Protestants.[2]

Gale had commended the Jansenist "esteem of the sacred Scriptures", and indeed this attitude of theirs was one which had obtained universal approbation from English Protestants. The Jansenist translation of the New Testament in 1667, known as the Mons New Testament, had aroused much interest, and when that Christian gentleman, the excellent Mr Boyle ("like whom, in his way, the age affords not any", as the Bishop of Meath remarked to Dr Narcissus Marsh[3]), decided to have the Bible translated into Irish, he bethought himself of the Jansenist New Testament and of the valuable preface which the gentlemen of Port Royal had contributed to it. This preface,[4] he thought, would be a fitting introduction to the Irish New Testament.

He mentioned his plan to Andrew Sall, his helper, a former Jesuit and convert to the Church of England, and Sall replies on October 16th, 1680:

I fully approve of your motion to apply in the preface what you yourself and those other worthies shall think fit, of that used by the Jansenists in their French version and am not a little joyed to hear so great an advance to right in the Romish church as to suffer the word of God to come into vulgar tongues.[5]

A few months later Boyle writes to the Bishop of Meath, Dr Henry Jones, that the most intelligent divine he has consulted in London is very earnest to have the Jansenist preface

1 *Animadversiones...*, 1706. See list at end of this book.
2 Calamy, *An historical Account of my own Life*, I, p. 171.
3 Boyle, *Works*, I, p. clxxvi.
4 Chiefly by M. de Saci.
5 Boyle, *Works*, VI, p. 595.

inserted. This preface being "a piece of great learning and piety and much esteemed by the better sort of Romanists themselves, it was judged that if it were published in English with the fewest possible alterations and additions it might very much recommend the introduction of the Irish Testament to the better sort of Papists themselves" for whose benefit it was chiefly made. A Mr Reily who was "correcting the press" for the Irish Testament would also undertake the translation, he having been bred in France, and as soon as he had accomplished his task, the translation would be sent to the bishop for his opinion.[1]

The bishop, awaiting the translation, replies very favourably:

As to that preface of the Jansenists, premised to their translation of the New Testament,...considering their very refined principles, and even that very design of their publishing the holy scripture in vulgar tongue; and that that preface passeth among the better Romanists themselves,...it having also the approbation you mention of those eminent among us,...though I have not yet seen it, yet can I not but well approve.[2]

However, a little later the bishop began to question the wisdom of using this preface.

"In former letters from that worthy person Mr Boyle", so he informs Dr Marsh, Provost of Trinity College, Dublin, "I found him zealously intent on prefixing the Jansenists' late prefaces of the New Testament in French to the Irish New Testament now under his hand in the press, hoping thereby (I conceive) to gain more in the world, in joining so far with those of that persuasion, they drawing toward us, although not closing with us."

But now the bishop had procured himself a copy of the Mons New Testament; he had had the prefaces translated for his better information, being himself a stranger to the French, and he foresaw some difficulties, chiefest of them harsh reflections on some of the more eminent Protestant reformers. There were objections both to the inclusion and to the exclusion of such passages. The objections he gives to the former are obvious, those to the latter are more interesting. "Professing to give the world a true transcript of those the Jansenist prefaces, whether

1 Boyle, *Works*, I, p. clxxiii, April 8, 1681.   2 *Ib.* p. clxxiv, May 3, 1681.

it would be ingenuous by picking and chusing, to omit any part thereof, on a private account? And whether such omissions might not disgust the Jansenists themselves, whom we would indulge?"

He confessed himself inclined to lay these prefaces aside, though if, on further consideration it should be found advisable "to take notice of them", then they might be prefixed to the Old Testament or the Common Prayer Book in Irish when published.[1] Dr Marsh fully concurred with the bishop[2] who sent this reply with his own reflections to Boyle, suggesting that Dr Sall might prepare a preface for the New Testament.[3]

Boyle willingly accepted this advice, explaining that, as to the preface, he must candidly confess that his copy of the Mons New Testament having been got from him by a person of quality before he had read more than here and there some passages of the preface, he had in recommending it relied less on his own judgment than that of a very learned and famous divine, and some other persons of eminent parts. He asked for one thing only, namely that use might be made of some of the passages of the Jansenist preface, "not as it is a preface, but as it contains the public avowed sense and eloquently exhibits the reasons of famous and eminent divines of the Roman church for the translating and studying the New Testament in vulgar tongues".[4]

Sall gladly complied with this last suggestion. In his preface, which begins with charming simplicity, "Here you have, dear Countrymen, the New Testament of our blessed Lord and Saviour Jesus Christ presented to you in your country garment", he makes some use of the Port Royal preface, but in particular he tells his readers that if any should say this precious treasure ought to be reserved for the learned in the original languages, the learned doctors in divinity of the University of Paris have reprinted of late the New Testament in the French language, following therein the doctors of Louvain in the same faculty.[5]

1 *Ib.* pp. clxxvi–clxxvii, Aug. 1, 1681.
2 See his reply in *ib.* VI, p. 601.
3 *Ib.* I, p. clxxviii, Sept. 3, 1681.
4 *Ib.* p. clxxix, no date.
5 *Ib.* p. clxxxv. Cf. VI, pp. 596–7.

This preface pleased not only Boyle, but "some ingenious Romanists" to whom Sall showed it,[1] from which one might infer that there were possibly at that time some friends to Jansenism in Ireland.

Here, for the present, we will leave those who saw in the Jansenists their brothers afar off, and perhaps someone will identify the very learned and famous English divine who was so eager to have the Jansenist preface inserted in the Irish New Testament.

1 Boyle, *Works*, VI, p. 597.

CHAPTER XI

The English Roman Catholics and Jansenism
(Seventeenth Century)

TO what extent was Jansenism favoured by the Roman Catholic clergy in England? Was Jansenism ever taught in England? Educated as so many of the English priests were in France, was it not inevitable that they should become "infected with the heresy" and help to spread it in England?

Plentiful accusations were certainly brought against the clergy, especially at the beginning of the eighteenth century; the English college at Douay[1] was not infrequently attacked, but all these accusations met with indignant protests. The story of Jansenism in England is mainly one of rumours and contradictions, of charges made and refuted; it is an aspect of the struggle between seculars and regulars, a phase of anti-Jesuitism, of opposition to the Ultramontanes; the controversy was not so much on Jansenism itself as on the question whether anyone in England gave support to the doctrines of Jansenius. Now and again, not often, one comes upon the traces of someone who was not unfriendly to the cause, and there was one man who showed utter unconcern when he was labelled a Jansenist.

When Hobbes was an old man he often visited a friend in Westminster, a friend even older than himself, and the friend would often come to see him, but they seldom parted in cold blood, "for they would wrangle, squabble and scold about philosophical matters like young sophisters, though either of them was over eighty years of age". Hobbes was obstinate and could not brook contradiction, and the friend had a lively temper of his own. The scholars who were sometimes present at their wrangling disputes held that the laurels were carried away by Mr Thomas White,[2] for thus the friend was called,

---

[1] "Douai" in modern French, but the other form has more associations for the English reader.

[2] Wood, *Athen. Oxon.* (ed. Bliss), III, p. 1247.

though he was known by other names too—Albius, Anglus, Candidus, Vitus, Leblanc, Bianchi, Blackloe (or Blaclo or Blacklow)—and indeed the busy pen of the controversialist had made the last name quoted far more famous than his real name, and had even given it to a kind of heresy, Blackloism.[1]

To relate the story of his life would be beyond the scope of this study; to enumerate his works "which made a great noise"[2] would require several pages; suffice it to say that, a man of un-common learning, he taught for a time at Douay and was "a kind of enterprizer in the search of truth and sometimes waded too deep",[3] that his works aroused great resentment, especially in as far as they attacked papal infallibility[4] "in soe spightfull a manner as not any heretique writer hath used expressions of a more Satyricall bitternes against it",[5] that he was accused of Jan-senism, and that his works were censured. Bourgeois, the Jan-senist doctor, was certainly one of his friends,[6] and in 1650, when preparing a book to be published with the help of Sir Kenelm Digby, he remarked that in these papers were some things which, he believed, would make the Jansenists in part side with him,[7] and he thought it a propitious time to publish his work "now when the Jansenists begin to print bookes without approbation".[8]

1 "Even after his decease Blackloism continued to be a word of war. In-considerately it was too often given to every clergyman who advocated the appointment of a bishop in ordinary, who disbelieved the pope's personal in-fallibility, who declared against his deposing power, who recommended allegiance to the powers that were, who rightfully or wrongfully resisted any pretension of the regulars, or who argued against any ultramontane extravagance." Butler, *Historical Memoirs*, II, p. 432. See also Canon Flanagan's *History of the Church in England* (London 1857, 2 vols.), I, pp. 354-5.

2 Dodd, *Church History*, III, p. 286. Dodd's list of Blackloe's works contains 48 items. See pp. 287-8.   3 *Ib.* p. 286.

4 *Ib.* p. 351; Butler, *Historical Memoirs*, II, pp. 428-31. A book that gave special offense to the English, whether because of his religion or otherwise, was *The Grounds of Obedience and Government*—"Blackloe's damned booke dedicated to Sr Kellam Digby" (*Nicholas Papers*, III, pp. 71, 120). This was written during Cromwell's protectorate, was supposed to advocate passive obedience to whatever government was in power, and was designed, so his enemies said, to flatter Cromwell (Dodd, *op. cit.* III, p. 286).

5 *A Letter written by G. L. to Mr Andrew Kingh. and Mr Tho. Med.*, p. 2.
6 Pugh, *Blacklo's Cabal*, pp. 13, 19.
7 *Ib.* p. 102. The book was doubtless his *Mens Augustini de gratia Adami...Ad conciliationem gratiae et liberi arbitrii in via Digbeana accessorium* (Paris 1652).
8 Pugh, *op. cit.* p. 107.

We find him submitting his work to "the Cheifest Doctor" of Louvain, a Jansenist, for his opinion, and it is said that the Jansenist was astonished that such learning should be spread abroad and not censured.[1] An adversary joins the names of Calvin, Jansenius and Blackloe—happy had they never taught their doctrine, but left it in hell![2]

In 1654 Blackloe crossed swords with Father Macedo on the subject of Jansenism. Father Macedo was a "Portugues", as Peter Walsh said, one with whom Walsh had been acquainted in "Oliver the Usurper's time", in London, "at the first Portingal Embassadour's".[3] He was one of the first to write in England against Jansenism and the five Propositions,[4] "and by occasion thereof against Mr White alias Blacklow". Walsh speaks of his earnest endeavour to stifle Jansenism in England, and Macedo tells us that he wrote his book in England at the entreaty of many Catholics. He found that all parties needed to be enlightened—some who were inclined to favour Jansenius carped at the censure, others, too severe, tended to exaggerate it; the Protestant heretics laughed it to scorn, some upholding the condemned propositions, others, Semipelagians, thinking that more should have been condemned.[5] Blackloe replied in his *Sonus Buccinae*, or rather in the appendix which, as a writer from London informed the internuncio in Flanders, was a "condemnatio condemnationis Pontificis quinque propositionum Jansenii" by a certain priest, "Blacklot".[6] And indeed in this pamphlet Blackloe says that he willingly acknowledges himself to be a disciple of Jansenius, though he remarked that some of his writings would show he did not follow Jansenius blindly.[7]

1 *An Epistle Declaratorie...* by G. L., p. 24.
2 *Letter from a Gentleman to his friend in London*, p. 23.
3 Walsh, *History and Vindication*, p. 43.
4 In his *Mens divinitus inspirata Sanctissimo....Innocentio Papae X super quinque Propositiones C. Jansenii....*Londini 1653 and in his *Lituus Lusitanus contra tubam Anglicanam....*Londini 1654.
5 *Mens divinitus*, Epistola Dedicatoria, pp. 7–8.
6 R.O. *Roman Transcripts*, vol. 52, Nuntiatura di Fiandra, London, March 6, 1654.
7 *Appendicula*, pp. 199–200, and especially p. 214. The Appendix is not to be found in the 1654 ed. at the B.M., though the above-mentioned London letter speaks of its existence in 1654. It is, however, contained in the 1659 ed. at the B.M. See also a letter from Petrus Hoburgus to Cardinal Barberini, printed in

Independence was ever Blackloe's chief characteristic, and he is criticized by Molinists and Jansenists alike.¹ An adversary of his observed that he contemned "all of Pope, Cardinals, Nuncio, his own Bishop" and would "onely bend the knee to the Baal of his own Fancy".²

In 1657 appeared his *Tabulæ Suffragiales*, and in September Hyde was informed from Rome "Divers books and letters written by the Jansenists are this morning forbidden, amongst the rest *Tabulæ suffragantes* of Mr Blaclo or Mr White".³ Forbidden also were this same month the *Provincial Letters*, a work of which Blackloe had a great opinion. A more useful book had not seen the light that century, he thought, and far from condemning the English translation of the *Provinciales*, he deemed the publishing of such truths more expedient in England than in any part of the world, "nothing being more importantly conducible to the reduction of our separatists than the discarding superfluous controversies and contesting with them only necessary doctrines".⁴ He was reproached with indiscretion. "They accuse me...that in a Kingdom averse and separated from the Communion of the Catholic Church I have printed a book or two from which they conceive Hereticks may take occasion to reproach us with intestine dissensions in religion", but he retorted that the wars waged in Catholic countries upon the subject of efficacious grace and Jansenism were common knowledge in England.⁵

Before the French Ambassador Estrades left for London in

Ch. Plowden, *Remarks on a Book entitled Memoirs of Gregorio Panzani* (1794), p. 369. Blackloe and his *Quaestio Theologica* appear in the *Bibliotheca Antijansenia* (no date, publ. between 1650 and 1654), p. 101: *Supplement de quelques livres imprimez par les Jansenistes et leurs Amys.* Cf. Hermant, *Mémoires*, 1, p. 571. Other works in which Blackloe expresses himself on Jansenism are *Tabulæ suffragiales* (1655), pp. 338 *et seq.; Monumetham Excantathus* (1660), pp. 67–8; *Muscarium ad Immissos a Jona Thamone calumniarum crabrones* (1661), pp. 29–30.

1 Arnauld, *Œuvres*, III, pp. 14, 15; Rémusat, *Hist. de la Philosophie en Angleterre depuis Bacon jusqu'à Locke* (1875, 2 vols.), 1, p. 309: cf. *Cal. S.P. Dom.* 1658-9, p. 229.

2 *A Letter from a Gentleman to his Friend in London*, p. 22.

3 *Cal. Clarendon Papers*, III, p. 361.

4 *Monumetham Excantathus*, p. 48; *A Letter to a Person of Honour written by Mr Thomas White* (1659) (no paging); *Apologia*, pp. 25–7.

5 *A Letter to a Person of Honour written by Mr Thomas White* (no paging).

1661, the nuncio in France came to see him, recommended the Catholics of England to his protection and spoke much against a certain priest "Baquelar", an upholder of the opinions of Jansenius, "homme fort hardi et entreprenant", whom he would like to see driven from England. Estrades replied that he would act "avec chaleur", and arriving in England he found, so he said, that people's minds were beginning to be infected by the new opinions of Jansenius, and other opinions, more extreme still, tending to a heresy of which the priest "Baquelau" was the chief promoter. He had found M. d'Aubigny in charge of the affairs of the Catholics, and M. d'Aubigny was hindering the return of this "Blaqeau" who had been desired to leave England.[1]

The abbé Charrier, secretary of the Cardinal de Retz, reported to Cardinal Barberini about the same time or a little later, in December of that year, that as for the matter of Bianchi —another name for Blackloe-White—and Dr Holden, Aubigny would willingly conform to the cardinal's wishes.[2] Aubigny was at this time hoping for a bishopric and was willing to do a great many things.

At what time Blackloe returned to England is not known— books of his were published in London in 1661, in Paris in 1662, in London again in 1663, which would suggest that his absence was not of long duration. Certainly he spent the last part of his life in London, the respected friend of Hobbes. He submitted himself and his writings more than once to the Holy See when in his advanced old age,[3] perhaps, as Rémusat suggests, more from a desire to be at rest than from conviction or repentance.[4] He died in 1676 and was buried almost under the pulpit in St Martin in the Fields.[5]

Two friends of Blackloe deserve a brief mention here—one

1 B.N. *Mélanges Colbert*, MS. 106, f. 122, Estrades to Colbert, Sept. 12, 1661; Aff. Étr. *Corr. d'Angleterre*, vol. 75, f. 139, Estrades to Brienne (Sept. 1661) (Letter printed in *Bulletin flamand*, 1908, pp. 351–2).
2 Retz, *Œuvres* (ed. Gr. Écr.), *Supplément à la Correspondance*, pp. 273–4.
3 Kennet, *Register and Chronicle* (London 1728), p. 625; Dodd, *Church History*, III, p. 351.
4 Rémusat, *op. cit.* I, p. 309.
5 Wood, *Athen. Oxon.* (ed. Bliss), III, p. 1247.

is Sir Kenelm Digby, whose name is inseparable from that of Blackloe, the other is Dr Henry Holden who had been his student at Douay,[1] "a Sun Diall doth not more exactly mark the motions of that Planet then Holden represent the Doctrin of Mr Blacklo".[2]

Of Sir Kenelm Digby, that curious, restless, versatile spirit, amateur philosopher and scientist, it is sufficient for our purpose to note that he shared Blackloe's friendship for Bourgeois, the Jansenist doctor. Sir Kenelm had been sent to Rome in 1645 to collect money for the royal cause. In Rome he met Bourgeois who had come on a very different errand, namely the defence of Arnauld's *Fréquente Communion*. Bourgeois always acknowledged that M. le chevalier d'Igby had been one of those who encouraged him most.[3] Certainly Digby, the man of the world, gave him some useful advice, namely to "boil down" a book of his, one hundred and twenty closely printed quarto pages, which the Pope, Innocent X, did not have time to read. Brevity, alas, was never the soul of Jansenism! Bourgeois reduced the hundred and twenty pages to fifteen or sixteen, but even this still seemed too long to Digby. At last a pamphlet of six or seven pages was achieved and Digby himself, according to Bourgeois, carried this to the Pope, who reasoned with him concerning the objections and answers.[4]

The other friend, Henry Holden, a doctor of the Sorbonne, was somewhat of a *Janséniste malgré lui*. His adversaries describe him as unlearned, presumptuous and rash,[5] but the general impression one obtains of him is rather that of a mild, cautious man.[6] According to Dodd he never sought after preferment, but was content to remain confessor at St Nicolas du Chardonnet.[7]

1 Dodd, *Church History*, III, p. 353.   2 Pugh, *op. cit.*, Introductory Epistle.
3 Hermant, *Mémoires*, I, p. 343, cf. pp. 358, 381, 384.
4 Bourgeois, *Relation*, pp. 24, 25, 31, 57, 86, 87.   5 Pugh, *op. cit.*, *passim*.
6 At the same time, like his friends Digby and Blackloe, he was suspected of being in communication with Cromwell. Sir Edward Nicholas, referring to him as "Dr or Father Holben (*sic*), a secular English priest (who is great with Sir Geo. Radcliffe and many other English)", describes him as a "pestilent agent" of Cromwell, *Nicholas Papers* (Camden), II, p. 303, cf. pp. 226 and 309. Also *Cal. Clarendon Papers*, II, pp. 19–20, 214.
7 Dodd, *Church History*, III, p. 298. Of course it must be remembered that Dodd is not impartial.

A disciple of Blackloe, he could not be very far from Jansenism, but he would fain have remained neutral—he approved neither of the errors of the Molinists, so a Jansenist writer says, nor of the obstinacy of the Jansenists. However, when he set forth in one of those "Letters to a Person of Quality", so characteristic of the times, what he thought might be held concerning sufficient grace and efficacious grace "comme ces sentimens sont ceux des Jansenistes, il n'étoit pas aisé de deviner en quoi il se vouloit distinguer d'eux. Aussi les Jésuites l'ont-ils mis malgré lui au nombre de ces prétendus hérétiques".[1]

In 1655 Arnauld had composed two famous letters, the first, *Lettre à une personne de condition*, was written when the duc de Liancourt had been refused the sacraments on account of his relations with Port Royal; the second, *Lettre à un duc et pair*, was written to justify the first letter. The second letter was examined by the Sorbonne and Dr Holden took a modest part in the debate. He made a conciliatory speech, criticized Arnauld gently and thought that he might be pardoned if he declared the innocence of his intentions and his willingness to submit to the judgment of the bishops. At the same time, for fear of being thought a partisan, he added hastily that he did not know Arnauld, no, not even by sight.[2]

Things went badly, however, for Arnauld. He was censured on January 31st of the following year, 1656, and his name struck from the roll of the doctors of the Sorbonne. Not all the doctors were willing to sign the censure, but Dr Holden conformed.

Rumours had spread in the meantime that Holden was defending the doctrine of Jansenius, and that he would not sign the censure of Arnauld, so M. Féret, curé of St Nicolas du

1 Gerberon, *Hist. générale du Jansénisme*, I, pp. 506–7. Holden's book was entitled *Lettre d'un Docteur en Théologie à un homme de grande condition touchant les questions du temps* and appeared in 1651. Gerberon gives a résumé of Holden's theories concerning grace. He also states that Holden is made to appear as a Jansenist in the Jesuit publication *Bibliotheca-Antijansenia*. In this book, attributed to Philippe Labbe, Holden's name is given on p. 101, *Supplement de quelques livres imprimez par les Jansenistes et leurs Amys*, the book in question being Holden's *Divina Fidei Analysis* (1652): cf. Gerberon, *op. cit.* II, p. 517.

2 Arnauld, *Œuvres*, XIX, pp. lii–liii; XX, pp. 440–6. In 1649 one finds Holden, Callaghan, and four other doctors giving an approbation to one of Arnauld's books (Hermant, *Mémoires*, I, p. 496).

Chardonnet wrote to him, expressing his surprise. As one of Holden's detractors put it: "The Pastor of St Nicholas warned him to keep out of his Church rather than infect any of his Penitents with Jansenism and unwarrantable novelties".[1]

Holden replied in a letter of February 5th to M. Féret, protesting his innocence, but what he said about doctrinal matters pleased Arnauld so much that he sent Holden a letter of thanks in which he sought to show him that they really thought alike, and that the reasons which Holden brought forward to justify the signing of the censure were groundless. So favourable did Arnauld consider Holden's letter that he forwarded copies to Cardinal Barberini and the Cardinal of St Clement, copies of what seemed to him to be a *pièce justificative* coming from an impartial source. Holden answered in May rejoicing that there was so little divergence of opinion between them, regretting only Arnauld's unwillingness to admit the term of "sufficient grace" in the sense that the Thomists used it.[2]

What happens to many worthy moderate people, unwilling to offend either side, happened to Holden—neither party held him in high esteem. Arnauld's adversaries charged Holden with "ficklenesse and inconstancy...subscribing in publick to the condemnation of Jansenisme, to the high dissatisfaction of his owne party, and then owning that Heresie still in private to regain their good wills", and as for his letter to M. Féret, "in his pittiful Epistle thereupon to the Pastor of St Nicholas, he so played the John of both sides, that his Epistle and he were commonly hissed at".[3] Arnauld's friends allude to him in a slightly contemptuous fashion:

Le pauvre M. Holden...fut si effraié de cette censure et des menaces qu'on faisoit à ceux qui n'y souscriroient pas, que non seulement il donna sa signature, mais qu'il écrivit le 5e jour de février une lettre pour se déjanséniser où il declaroit qu'il condamnoit Jansenius qu'il n'avoit jamais lu et les cinq propositions.[4]

1 *A Letter from a Gentleman*, p. 27.
2 Arnauld, *Œuvres*, XIX, pp. lxiv–v; XX, pp. 78–84 (Arnauld's Letter to Holden); Gerberon, *op. cit.* II, p. 286; Dumas, *Histoire des Cinq Propositions*, I, pp. 134–6; *A Letter written by Mr Henry Holden...touching the Prohibition at Rome of Mr Blackloe's Book intituled tabulae suffragiales.*
3 *A Letter from a Gentleman*, pp. 32–3.   4 Gerberon, *op. cit.* II, p. 286.

Blackloe and Holden were accused of bringing disrepute upon the English clergy.

The clergie's honour and reputation...in forreigne parts....was extreamely eclips'd by the temerarious writings of those two chiefe members from thence being infer'd that the whole English clergy roote and branch was addicted to scandalous Novelties and infected with dangerous doctrines.[1]

The story ends, however, with complete orthodoxy, as far as Holden and Jansenism are concerned. The Jansenists regretted to see that M. Holden's "illusion" about the fitness of Arnauld's censure continued to the day of his death—in 1662[2]—and shortly before he departed this life he wrote, in 1661, a *Defensio Formulae Fidei adversus haereticam calumniam,*[3] in which he joined the ranks of those that upheld the formulary condemning the five propositions.

Another friend and schoolfellow of Blackloe, Mark Harrington, who died in 1657, is accused of maintaining Jansenism to the end.[4]

In 1660 when the English clergy were renewing their appeal to Rome for a bishop—the Bishop of Chalcedon, Richard Smith, having died in 1655—the Dean of the Chapter, Ellis, presented to a dozen of his priests a formulary which included a condemnation of Jansenism: *Nos infra scripti testamur totum clerum Anglicanum esse in fide unanimem et fraterna charitate coniunctum et cum debita obedientia subordinatum Decano et capitulo, quod autem spectat ad errores Jansenii et quorumcunque aliorum illos detestari et Epūm a Sanctmo D. N. flagitare.*[5] This formulary was, however, rejected by four out of the twelve priests, not because they favoured Jansenism—on the contrary—but because they entertained doubts as to the authority of the chapter, and because they knew that Ellis and his friends favoured Blackloe, while

1 G. L., *An Epistle Declaratorie*, p. 17.
2 Arnauld, *Œuvres,* xix, p. lxv. Dodd gives the date of Holden's death as 1665, but Arnauld, Du Pin, Gillow and other authorities give it as 1662.
3 Gerberon, *op. cit.* ii, p. 517.
4 *A Letter from a Gentleman*, p. 41: cf *An Epistle Declaratorie*, p. 41; Dodd, *Church History*, iii, p. 304.
5 R.O. *Roman Transcripts*, vol. 98, a letter written to the Internuncio Vecchiis in Brussels, London, Sept. 21 (O.S.), 1660 (Nuntiatura di Fiandra).

Blackloe, as we have seen, was not averse to Jansenism. Ellis, one of Blackloe's former students, had been asked to sign a condemnation of Blackloe and had refused.[1]

Rinuccini, writing some time between 1660 and 1665, speaks of the dissensions rife among the clergy. "The divisions among them are so great that I could not look on without shame and sore distress of mind. The heads of the Catholic clergy in London are very much incensed against the Jesuits, while the Jesuits and the Benedictines bear very little love to each other. Charges of heresy and Jansenism are made and retorted with fury".[2] Blackloe speaks of the "Antijansenistae" in England in 1661[3]—these doubtless far outnumbered the "Jansenistae", of whom Aubigny, as we have seen, was a very lukewarm one.

A letter sent from Paris to Rome on November 13th, 1668, mentions the disappointment of the English Catholic clergy at not obtaining a bishop, and the rumour that a "novelty" was to be attempted with the assistance of an English doctor of the Sorbonne, formerly inclined to Jansenism, the novelty being the creation of a bishop as in the primitive church with the sole approbation and on the nomination of the aforesaid clergy.[4]

Little is heard of Jansenism in the following years, though accusations are not wanting. A letter written in 1676 intimated that all the English chaptermen were either Blackloists or Jansenists,[5] and the writer, said to be Prior Hitchcock, O.S.B.,[6] remarked of Cardinal Howard, the Cardinal of Norfolk as he was called, that he was "much of his Uncle Aubigny's Spirit, a sufficient Jansenist". Without designating the cardinal by that term we may note that the Dutch Bishop Neercassel, a friend of Port Royal, also looked upon Howard as a friend, corresponded with him, and writing to Arnauld about his own book, the *Amor Poenitens*, attacked as a book of Jansenist tendencies, he

1 R.O. *Roman Transcripts*, vol. 98, a letter written to the Internuncio Vecchiis in Brussels, London, Sept. 21 (O.S.), 1660 (Nuntiatura di Fiandra). See also letters of Oct. 8 (N.S.), 1660, Nov. 4 (N.S.), 1660.
2 Rinuccini, *Embassy*, p. 546 (fragment of a Memoir).
3 Blackloe, *Muscarium*, p. 30.
4 R.O. *Roman Transcripts*, vol. 130, Nov. 13, 1668.
5 Dodd, *Church History*, III, p. 392.
6 *Cath. Record Soc. Publications* (1925), vol. 25, p. 3.

observes with satisfaction, "Cardinalis de Noordfolkia admodum nobis favet".[1] Certainly Arnauld and his friend M. du Vaucel were in touch with some of the English Catholic clergy.[2]

In 1685 the first Roman Catholic bishop after many years was elected, and accusations of Jansenism were taken into consideration by the Holy See.[3] Of Dr Bonaventure Giffard it was said that he had studied in Paris with others suspected of adhering to Jansenism,[4] but though Dr John Leyburn, and not he, became vicar-apostolic of all England, he was made vicar-apostolic of the Midland district three years later, which would show the charge to have been largely unfounded. The charge of Jansenism was also brought against his brother Andrew, who complains that when put in charge of a chapel in Lime Street, London, in 1686, with two other priests, James Dymock and Christopher Tootell,

We had not been there for a month when we were defamed as Blackloists and Jansenists, and this bad reputation was spread all over London, and was the general discourse of all people, and at last had its intended effect, for in less than six months time we were turned out of house and chapel and no recompense made for all our charges, and one Father Kanes [Keynes] a Jesuit was introduced with other companions. ...As to Jansenism I was so far averse to it that I always taught the opposite opinions and this the Jesuits themselves...own to be true, yet when a fit occasion offered and a good situation was to be gained, I was presently rendered a rank Jansenist....No manner of regard ought to be had to their alarms of Jansenism, because...they fix that character, not where it is most deserved, but where it is most convenient.[5]

It is in the eighteenth century, however, that a regular offensive is undertaken against the English clergy as a body. With the eighteenth century begins a new chapter of Jansenism in France, the smouldering hostilities are fanned to a blaze, the warfare breaks out afresh, and even spreads to England. Of this something will be said in the next chapter.

1 Arnauld, Œuvres, IV, p. 178. 2 Ib. II, pp. 516, 719; III, pp. 163, 171, 172.
3 Guilday, English Catholic Refugees, p. 331 n.
4 R.O. Roman Transcripts, vol. 100, f. 515, Jan. 5, 1685 (Nuntiatura di Fiandra).
5 Kirk, Biographies, pp. 98–9; Gillow, Biographical Dictionary under "Giffard", "Tootell": cf. also Kirk, op. cit. p. 34, article on John Brian.

CHAPTER XII

The English Roman Catholics and Jansenism
(Eighteenth Century)

THE ENGLISH COLLEGE AT DOUAY

MADAME DE LONGUEVILLE, the influential friend of Port Royal, had died in 1679. Her death had been followed by renewed measures against Port Royal des Champs, and Arnauld deemed it wise to withdraw from France. Still the period that followed was relatively quiet. The last twenty years of the seventeenth century took away many of the older Jansenists, Arnauld and his brother, the Bishop of Angers, Nicole, M. de Saci, M. Hamon, M. du Fossé, M. de Sainte-Marthe, Bourgeois, Pontchâteau, Le Nain de Tillemont, the duc de Luynes. The nuns of Port Royal were slowly diminishing in number as death carried them off one by one. No novices were allowed to take their places.

In 1702 the *Cas de Conscience*, as it was called, revived the vexed question of the formulary, the question *de fait et de droit*. The problem raised by an indiscreet Jansenist was the following: "Can a confessor absolve one who declares that he condemns the five propositions in the sense that the Church condemned them, but as for attributing these propositions to Jansenius, he believes a respectful silence to be sufficient?" Forty doctors of the Sorbonne replied in the affirmative, and this marked the beginning of a violent controversy. The Bull *Vineam Domini* given in 1705 condemned respectful silence. Port Royal des Champs went under this time; the persistent refusal to conform proved its undoing; in 1709 the few remaining nuns were evicted and presently the buildings were destroyed to their very foundations, the dead dug up and carted away.

A tempest gathered around another book, just as in the preceding century when the *Augustinus* had been the great storm centre. Arnauld's mantle had fallen on the shoulders of Quesnel, living in exile in Brussels, and a work of Quesnel's, the *Réflexions morales*, a commentary on the New Testament, first published in 1671 and reprinted many times since with additions, was attacked and finally condemned in 1713 by the famous Bull *Unigenitus* as containing one hundred and one heretical propositions. The Bull was by no means received with universal favour in France; four bishops stood out again in 1717, the Bishops of Boulogne, Mirepoix, Montpellier and Senez. They appealed against this condemnation to a general council, and a large number of doctors of the Sorbonne, of the clergy of Paris and others became "appellants" like themselves. It is not for this book to give an account of the struggles which lasted through the eighteenth century; the object of the preceding page or two is to point out the importance of the Jansenist controversy in France in the beginning of the new century, and to account thereby for the fact that the question of Jansenism assumed certain proportions in England at the time.

The beginning of the century was marked by the publication of several translations from the French. A reply to the *Provinciales* had appeared in France in 1694, *Les Entretiens de Cléandre et d'Eudoxe* by the Jesuit Father Gabriel Daniel. This book was translated, perhaps as early as 1694,[1] by Father William Darrell, but certainly in 1701 when a translation saw the light at Cologne. In 1704 this translation was reprinted in London, a translation of the *Lettre de l'Abbé...à Eudoxe* was added, also an interesting preface which incidentally casts some light on Pascal's reputation in England. It will be remembered that the *Pensées* were translated anew this year. Darrell comments on the fact that Pascal's so-called conversation with the Dominicans and the Jesuits was an invention—there was no truth whatever in it.

"I am sensible", he remarks, "how surprizing this word may be, especially to the Ladies, however I am bold to say that whatever such may have heard from their refined Teachers of the sincerity of Monsieur Pascal, whatever they may have observ'd he says himself of his own exactness in reporting,...yet it is true he went to neither

1 Date given by Gillow who, however, does not seem very sure of it.

Convent nor College....Zeal may prompt the Shee-Wits to cry out Calumny, Calumny on this occasion; and their little witty Masters who have Pascal at their Fingers' ends will be apt to tell them, this is Vera Crux and Dellacrux all over."

Elsewhere Darrell relates that "Pascal is to be met...gay and brisk in the Ale and Coffee Houses and nothing wanting to make his Letters as authentick as Fox's Martyrologe, but to be chained to the Board's end".

In 1702 appeared the *Secret Policy of the Jansenists*,[1] doubtless a reprint of the early translation, but made more up-to-date by the inclusion of a *Short History of Jansenism in Holland* which is attributed to the Jesuit Father Thomas Fairfax—it is, however, in the main, a translation of Doucin's *Memoire touchant le progrez du Jansenisme en Hollande* (1697). "Fr. Fairfax was the first to begin printing and publishing these books of controversy concerning Jansenism", says Andrew Giffard, the priest who complained in 1686 of being charged with Jansenism, and this, he says,

was the first origin of the liberty which others took afterwards. I have no doubt he thought it was necessary to sound the alarm, and guard the Catholics of this country against the infection of that heresy, yet, at the very time it is most certain that no people were ever more averse to Jansenism than the English clergy. It was never mentioned nor spoke of amongst us, before these unhappy controversies. We knew nothing at all of the matter; so that I may assuredly affirm that there were not so many as five priests in all England who so much as knew the five propositions, perhaps not so much as one of them; so little concern we had in this business.[2]

"After they had sufficiently blasted us with ye ignominious name of Jansenists", says this same writer, doubtless with some exaggeration, "and spread this opinion of us fare and neare and deeply fixed it in ye minds of men, then they presently printed a book and dispersed it through most of ye catholick familys in England: in wich book they

---

1 "In the year 1703 you industriously dispers'd a Book through the whole Kingdom call'd the *Secret Policy of the Jansenists*; which you pretended was written by a converted Doctor of Sorbon, but indeed was penn'd in the year 1657 by a skulking French Jesuit, Etienne de Champs and translated by you with a Preface and some Additions relating to the Jansenists in Holland, and fitted for your present design." Dodd, *Secret Policy*, p. 263.

2 Gillow, under "Fairfax" (from the MSS. collection at Ushaw College).

give ye caracter of a Jansenist and show unto people what sort of men Jansenists are.... This was sufficient to give all ye world a horror of us and laid us under ye blackest imputations of ye worst of crimes.... These divisions have passed from ye Priests to ye People who hereupon are divided into party upon party."[1]

Father Fairfax, who is described as "one of the chief anti-Jansenists in the country or next to it",[2] also translated in the following year 1703 the *Case of Conscience... with some Remarks upon it proper to clear the whole matter.*

About this time serious accusations of Jansenism began to be brought against Douay College, first against one, then against the majority of the professors—an account of this will be given presently.

The Catholics in England were put on their guard against Jansenism "with such effect in some quarters that an illustration is given of one lady, being in danger of death and her good Father not at hand, choosing rather to die without the sacraments than have a neighbouring secular clergyman".[3]

In 1707 Bishop James Smith was given to understand that a charge had been made against the English secular clergy, namely that they were Jansenists and that they corresponded with the Dutch Jansenists "to carry on the good old cause".[4] A copy of an information made about 1709 was transmitted back into England "that the accus'd might clear themselves if innocent". It was said that the pictures of Arnauld and Saint-Cyran were exposed in chapels belonging to the clergy, that books had been recently translated from the French, books openly Jansenist or bordering on Jansenism, and that the converts made by the English secular clergy were taught to speak disrespectfully of the Pope, of indulgences and the invocation of saints. A certain Mr S—— was accused of expounding the *Provincial Letters.*[5] Quesnel's works were being circulated, the bishops in England were doing nothing against Jansenism "besides ordering a

1 MSS. coll. at Ushaw Coll., 1.
2 Gillow, *loc. cit.*
3 Gillow, under "Hawarden".
4 Dodd, *Church History,* III, pp. 519–20; Gillow, under "Jenks".
5 Dodd, *ib.* III, p. 519, cf. Dodd, *Secret Policy,* p. 266.

small book to be printed against it", and a certain Dr Short was mentioned as a "Jansenist without restriction".[1]

"The libells of yᵉ schismaticks in Holland so injurious to yᵉ holy see were publickly sould",[2] said another. Yet another absurd "information" was to the effect that the three bishops and the clergy kept a constant correspondence with the Jansenists in Holland, that they frequently sent priests over to Holland to confer with the Jansenists "to advance yᵗ wicked end", and that by these means Jansenism was more largely spread and more deeply rooted in England than in France or Holland, which accusation, it was said, made Cardinal Caprara write to the bishops that "yᵉ gate of hell was opened against them".[3]

Most of these accusations seem entirely unfounded, and there are no traces of an assiduous correspondence in the archives of the Chapter of Utrecht. There were a number who were not unfriendly to the Jansenists, but few went beyond this point. In earlier years Cardinal Howard had corresponded with Neercassel, the Archbishop of Utrecht,[4] and with his successor Codde, but this was before Codde's interdict.[5] A canon of the London chapter, "J. Wetenhal"[6] by name, had written to Van Erkel, a canon of Utrecht and later dean of the chapter, but this was before Van Erkel was excommunicated.

Dr Richard Short, it is true, had a profound admiration for the clergy of Utrecht. He had studied philosophy at Douay and medicine at Montpellier, and subsequently practised in London, where he "spent both his money and labours in yᵉ assistance of the poor [and] therefore died poor himself".[7] He had read the *Provincial Letters* with lively interest, and from these he passed

---

1 Dodd, *Secret Policy*, p. 267.
2 MSS. coll. at Ushaw College, I, No. 81. April 3, 1710 (accusation reported by Andrew Giffard).
3 MSS. coll. at Ushaw College, I, No. 83. Feb. 20, 1710/11 (accusation reported by J. Coles).
4 Under the title of Archbishop of Castoria.
5 J. Bruggeman, *Inventaris van de Archieven, passim*.
6 This is the spelling in the copy preserved in the archives of the Chapter of Utrecht, a copy said to be in the hand of the Jansenist Ernest Ruth d'Ans.
7 MSS. coll. at Ushaw College, I, No. 75. Gillow, under "Short".

on to other writings on the same subject.¹ How he came to know of the Dutch clergy he tells us himself.

My first Admiration for the Church of Holland began in the person of Mr Neercassel...his Book de la lecture de l'écriture Sᵗᵉ gave me a particular value for him as did his Amor poenitens. Hearing that he took a particular care to educate his clergy in the Doctrine of the fathers I found that whereas in the Gallican Church there's here and there a choice divine, in the Church of Holland there's hardly any but such.²

A book called *La foy et l'innocence du clergé de Hollande defendues*³ came into his hands,⁴ and sending to Holland for more books he made the acquaintance of "a Bookseller of Delft Monsʳ Van Rhyn, educated in the university of Louvain in all sorts of learning in order to an ecclesiastical state but by health forced to take up this calling" in which he rendered great service to the public such as printing "the Apology of the Provinciall letters (wᶜʰ we want in English)".⁵ Van Rhyn sent Short a large number of French and Latin pamphlets in defence of the Dutch clergy, and Short ordered still more books in return. "Mettez aussi à mon compte", he writes in February 1706, "quelques Livres Hollandois touchant votre incomparable clergé....En vérité tout ce que vous m'avez envoyé est convaincant et n'a servi qu'à augmenter en moi l'amour et l'admiration".⁶

What struck him in the Dutch clergy was their courage and unity, "the making head agᵗ loose Casuistry, not by making articles which cost nothing, as the Gallican church did, but by exposing themselves to the last extremity and by standing up like one man against the exorbitant power of Rome".⁷ Of the condition of the Roman Catholic church in England he gave Van Rhyn a black picture: "S'étant une fois lâchement rendue aux Jesuites à discretion [elle] n'a jamais eu le cœur de secouer

1 Quesnel, *Correspondance*, II, pp. 267–9.
2 MSS. coll. at Ushaw College, I, No. 91 (about 1706), Letter from Short.
3 By Quesnel.
4 MSS. coll. at Ushaw College, I, No. 92, Letter from Short.
5 MSS. coll. at Ushaw College, I, No. 91, Letter from Short.
6 *Recueil de divers Témoignages*, p. 108.
7 MSS. coll. at Ushaw College, I, No. 96, Letter from Short (no date). Cf. *Recueil*, p. 108.

ses chaînes. L'ignorance fleurit ici presqu'autant qu'à Goa, et si la Sorbonne dessille les yeux à quelque peu de Prêtres elle ne les guérit pas de la timidité. Nos maux paraissent sans remède ".[1] Van Rhyn rejoiced in the praise Short gave the Dutch clergy, and wrote back to say that many of them had copied Short's letter, happy to find some appreciation at a time when they were beset by so many enemies.[2]

Short had also read some of Quesnel's writings, and he now asked Van Rhyn to let him know whether Quesnel was still alive. He was convinced that Quesnel maintained the truth and, since he considered it the duty of every Christian to stand by the truth, he resolved "with all humility to present him with some guineas", knowing, he said, that the calumnies of his enemies obliged him to great expenses. Van Rhyn replied that Quesnel was now in Holland, but he was uncertain in what town he could be found; he corresponded with him through a third person, and through this intermediary he sent Quesnel Short's offer. An answer came back presently—Quesnel, while most grateful, was not in need of help yet and therefore he declined this charitable aid.[3]

Finally, in the autumn of 1706, Short was able to get into touch with the refugee himself and prevailed upon him to accept. He told him of his admiration for his work, the *Moral Reflections*, and of his desire to own a copy of the edition in eight volumes, a desire which Quesnel was only too happy to gratify. One finds him writing to Mademoiselle de Joncoux, that resourceful friend of the declining Port Royal, requesting her to have the *Reflections* bound for Dr Short, "le plus proprement qu'il se peut, en veau doré sur tranche avec tout ce qu'on a coutume d'y mettre d'ornements".[4] To Short himself he wrote with gratitude, told him of the doctors that had been friends of Port Royal, M. Hamon and M. Dodart, commended his admiration of the *Provinciales*, spoke of Nicole's Latin Wendrock notes on these letters, recently translated into French by Mlle de Joncoux, and said he wished the notes could be translated into English.[5]

1 *Recueil*, pp. 108–9.   2 MSS. coll. at Ushaw College, 1, No. 96.
3 *Ib.*   4 Quesnel, *Correspondance*, 11, pp. 267–9, Nov. 4, 1706.
5 *Ib.* pp. 272–4, Nov. 6, 1706.

Their correspondence continued up to the year 1711, though possibly the last letter or letters were written after Short's death. Some of these letters brought the promise of books, others brought news of Port Royal persecuted and finally destroyed; yet others spoke about the state of ecclesiastical affairs in Holland.[1] Quesnel was touched by Short's deference —"Vous me parlez, mon très cher Monsieur, comme si j'étais un grand personnage, ôtez-vous cela de l'esprit....Le mal qu'on m'a fait a fait dire du bien de moi, beaucoup plus qu'il n'y en a".[2] In August 1708 Short even invited Quesnel to come and live with him, but Quesnel, an old man of seventy-four, believed, though deeply moved by this kindness, that Providence had ordained otherwise.[3]

During this time his *Réflexions morales* were being put into English under Dr Short's supervision. The *Réflexions* on the Gospel of St Matthew were translated in 1706 by a gentleman named Whetenhall,[4] though not immediately published. The translator seemed to realize that he must walk warily, for he safeguarded himself by saying that in order to make the translation conform to the original no alterations had been made in any of the expressions "which do not suit with the opinions commonly receiv'd in England".[5] Whetenhall dying about 1706, his work was carried on by his nephew Francis Thwaites and by Dom Thomas Southcote; the *Réflexions* on St Mark and St Luke were translated by the former and published in 1707, those on St John were translated by the latter, appearing in 1709 with the above-mentioned *Réflexions* on St Matthew. But the publication was suddenly stopped when the prohibition of the

1 *Ib.* pp. 281–2, 290, 296, 297–8, 301–2, 303–4, 307–8, 313–14, 366–8.
2 *Ib.* p. 290, see also pp. 281–2.   3 *Ib.* pp. 297–8.
4 Perhaps the "Wetenhal" who corresponded with Van Erkel.
5 "The sheets of this part of the work were sent to Mr Jenks who hastily revised and corrected them as he was then leaving London for Shropshire. He says 'As for the Preface to it, I made bold to burn it and took care to have the first sheet printed without it'....Mr Jenks had made considerable alterations, but he says 'there are still faults left in the English notes upon St Matthew which are enough to deserve the Pope's censure'." Gillow, under "Jenks". The B.M. copy of this St Matthew does contain Quesnel's preface so that Jenks must have been alluding to a preface by Whetenhall. Or perhaps Dr Short, the "Jansenist without restriction", restored Quesnel's preface.

book became known.[1] "Quesnel's book has bin formerly esteemed by many good men,...and particularly by Bp. Leyburn", says a writer, "but y^t since the condemnation itt has bin put into hands of people is fals."[2]

When an Anglican, Richard Russell, began to translate the *Réflexions* ten years or so later it was some time before he discovered to his dismay that an English translation had been made.

"I question very much whether this edition was ever published", he says, "and am rather inclined to think that it was sold privately among those of the romish persuasion....I am creditably informed this edition was quickly suppressed, before any more than fifty copies of it were got abroad: which I suppose was done by the influence of the Jesuits."[3]

Short also corresponded with Van Erkel, the canon of Utrecht, whom we have already mentioned, and Van Erkel availed himself of his English correspondent to secure information about the English chapter whose situation, it seemed to him, was analogous to that of the chapter of Utrecht. The London chapter had been created in 1623 by Dr Bishop, Bishop of Chalcedon, and confirmed by his successor, Dr Smith, also Bishop of Chalcedon, but it had been attacked by the regulars who insisted that as "neither the bishops were ordinaries, the institution of the chapter was an illegal act, and that the authority which it assumed was null".[4] The chapter of Utrecht was a very ancient one, but on account of some of the changes it underwent during the Reformation, it was held by the regulars to have ceased to exist.[5]

The Church of Utrecht was also interested in the struggle of the English Catholics to obtain a diocesan bishop, for the adversaries of Utrecht maintained that the Archbishop of Utrecht, Sasbold Vosmeer, and his successors were not ordin-

1 Gillow, under "Jenks", "Short", "Southcote", "Thwaites". Kirk, *Biographies*, under "Southcote", "Thwaites".
2 MSS. coll. at Ushaw College, 1, No. 83. Feb. 20, 1710/11. J. Coles.
3 Russell's translation of Quesnel, 1, pp. viii–ix.
4 Berington, *Supplement to Panzani's Memoirs*, p. 276. Cf. Sergeant, *Account of the English chapter, passim.*
5 Neale, *History of the so-called Jansenist Church of Holland*, pp. 64, 143, 396–7

aries, but vicars-apostolic with a title *in partibus.*[1] Since the death of Bishop Smith in 1655, the English chapter had applied for an ordinary, but when Dr John Leyburn was appointed bishop in 1685, it was with the title of vicar-apostolic only, greatly to the consternation of the chapter, and the same was true of the other bishops appointed later.[2]

"The bookseller from Holland", writes Short, "sent me a paper of an Ecclesiastic who desires to know what Books we have of the undertaking of the Padri to make themselves masters of the Church of England 100 years ago by establishing an Archpriest."[3]

Short complied very gladly with Van Erkel's request for information about the chapter, said he was able to gain access to its archives, and in 1708 sent a lengthy document in French which seems a partial and adapted translation of Sergeant's *Abstract of the transactions relating to the English Secular clergy.* "Je souhaite de tout mon cœur", he concludes, "qu'il y eut quelque chose icy dont le clergé d'hollande put profiter ou que je puisse leur être en quelque chose utile. Je m'estimerois heureux de mourir après leur avoir rendu service."[4]

This document was translated into Latin and was printed first in Van Erkel's *Protestatio asserta* in 1710, and again in his *Defensio Ecclesiae Ultrajectinae* in 1728.[5] The *Recueil de divers Témoignages* relates that there was at this time a secret correspondence between some members of the English chapter and the Dutch clergy. "M. Rshort...en a été comme le canal et le Médiateur durant plusieurs années."[6] There is still extant a short manuscript treatise on Jansenism written by Short addressed to the English Jesuits, whom he makes responsible for the trans-

1 *Ib.* pp. 121, 393–5, where the question is discussed.
2 Berington, *op. cit., passim.*
3 MSS. coll. at Ushaw College, 1, No. 98.
4 Letter in the archives of the Chapter of Utrecht, see also *Recueil de divers Témoignages*, p. 109.
5 In the 1738 edition this is on pp. 503–12.
6 P. 379, where the chapter is described as follows: "L'Eglise catholique d'Angleterre gémit encore aujourd'hui de l'anéantissement de l'Episcopat et de la Hierarchie dont tout le monde sait que les Jésuites sont cause. Il s'est néanmoins conservé à Londres un Chapitre de 30 Chanoines qui se perpetuent, quoique le malheur des tems ne leur permette pas d'exercer leurs droits et leur jurisdiction".

lation and diffusion of *The Secret Policy of the Jansenists*, a "lyeing book", a "slandering libel"—they had not only had a finger but a whole hand in this "Pye".[1]

In England he was naturally often looked upon as a Jansenist[2]—a gentleman was heard to say that in case of illness he would not send for Dr Short because he could not expect help from him without turning Jansenist, and an Irish capuchin remarked that "he had some difficulty in letting ye Dr come to a sick penitent of his for fear of being perverted".[3] He was denounced by the Jesuits, but made a public protestation after receiving communion, reading over each of the five propositions and affirming that "it was not his".[4] This, it may be pointed out, did not commit him in any way to the condemnation of Jansenism, since many Jansenists also rejected the propositions which, so they said, were not to be found in the *Augustinus*.

Another who was denounced as a Jansenist was a certain Gerald or Gerard Saltmarsh,[5] who had been chaplain to the Duke of Norfolk, and it is true that Van Erkel corresponded with him and sent him books, "Il me paroist toujours beaucoup occupé de tous ce que vous regard", writes the Duchess of Tyrconnel to Van Erkel,[6] and another time she wishes Van Erkel could read the letter Monsieur Saltmarsh had written—only it was in English—and see with his own eyes the esteem and friendship which Saltmarsh entertained for him.[7]

In January 1707 Saltmarsh came near being appointed bishop; the Roman agent of the English Catholics, Mr Laurence Mayes, was given to understand that all was well and that the Bulls would be dispatched within four days when a letter arrived which put a stop to everything. Charges of rigorism and Jansenism had been brought against the intended bishop:[8] Bussy,

1 MSS. coll. at Ushaw College, 1, No. 90, no date.
2 *Ib.* No. 93, Feb. 4, 1707/8, Short to ——, No. 95, no date, Short to C. Towneley.
3 *Ib.* No. 71, March 1708, letter from Fr. Mannock copied by A. Giffard.
4 *Ib.* No. 83, Feb. 20, 1710/11, from J. Coles.
5 *Ib.* No. 75, June 1708, Ralph Postgate to A. Giffard.
6 Sept. 9 (1705), letter in the archives of the Chapter of Utrecht.
7 Dec. 29 (1705), letter in the archives of the Chapter of Utrecht.
8 MSS. coll. at Ushaw College, 1, No. 60 (Fragment of a diary), No. 63 (p. 233).

the Internuncio at Cologne, had written to say that he suspected Saltmarsh of being a friend and favourer of the Jansenists.[1]

It is doubtless of Saltmarsh that a certain missionary priest by name of Marison wrote to Van Erkel in 1714. The Pilgrim (i.e.Marison) had been to see one of the chief doctors (i.e. priests) in London, the one who had had the happiness of being Van Erkel's guest for some days. "Il a soutenu vos intérêts noblement devant le grand Medecin [i.e. Internuncio] de Bruxelles qui a fait tant de bruit, et aux dépens de sa propre promotion à la place d'un premier Medecin [i.e. bishop]." Saltmarsh sent Van Erkel a whimsical message reminding him of his loss: "Il m'a dit agréablement de vous bien saluer et remercier, mais de vous faire souvenir qu'il vous pardonne et remet de bon cœur la restitution que vous lui devez de cette charge qui lui est échappée pour avoir maintenu votre bon droit".[2]

With regard to the formal charges which the bishops had to face—Bishop Smith, returning from a three months' visitation of the Northern district in the summer of 1709, said he had made it his business to inquire and he could affirm that there was "nothing of Jansenism in all these parts...everyone entirely, interiorly and without any mental reservation submitting to the Apostolic Constitutions of Inn. X, Alex. VII and Clem. XI". He hoped he had satisfied some zealots in these particulars.[3]

A letter sent in November of this year by the secular clergy in London to their brethren in the country reported that a most diligent investigation of the matter had shown all accusations false. Even the Provincial of the Jesuit Fathers declared that he knew of no one addicted to Jansenism.[4]

In this same year the English, Scotch and Irish Catholics were urged to adhere to the Bull *Vineam Domini*. A brief, dated August 17th, 1709, was addressed to them by Clement XI; the faithful were warned against the reading of Jansenist books and

1 Brady, *Episcopal Succession*, III, p. 290, Gillow and Kirk, under "Saltmarsh".
2 *Recueil de divers Témoignages*, pp. 122–3 (original in the archives of the Chapter of Utrecht).
3 Brady, *op. cit.* III, pp. 246–7, August 5, 1709.
4 Dodd, *Church History*, III, pp. 524–5.

the intimacy with persons of doubtful orthodoxy; they were also exhorted to caution in their choice of spiritual directors.[1] This brief aroused bitter resentment among some ecclesiastics, who considered it levelled against themselves. It contained in substance, they said, "ye very same accusation wich our unjust adversarys have bin endeavouring for many years to disperse amongst the people, and now they obtain a Bull from ye Pope to confirm men in ye same bad opinion of us". If the Pope thought it his duty to caution the Catholics of England against the cunning arts of some men, whom would the world believe these men to be, but those who for these last years had been defamed as Jansenists? It was at least plain that many and great accusations had been brought to Rome against the clergy in England. If a caution were given not to read books infected with Jansenism, it was because it was said that the English clergy permitted "ye reading of Kenel's book", nay, commanded and encouraged it. And so on.[2]

A reply from England was not immediately forthcoming. Months later one finds Cardinal Caprara writing that he has been expecting a document from England for over a year, "une certaine déclaration que je dois avoir d'Angleterre, souscrite par nos evesques vicaires apostoliques". Aware of the difficulties besetting concerted action among the Catholics in England he adds: "Ils auront eu peine à s'assembler pour faire cet acte d'une soumission aveugle que les catholiques d'Angleterre doivent aux déclarations pontificales contre le Jansénisme".[3] Shortly afterwards, however, he received the expected declaration, according to which the Bull *Vineam Domini* was accepted, as well as the Bulls previously given in condemnation of Jansenism by Innocent X and Alexander VII.[4] A letter from

1 Polidori, *De Vita et Rebus gestis Clementis Undecimi*, p. 215; *Bullarium Pontificium S. Congregationis de Propaganda Fide* (Rome, 1839), Appendix, 1, p. 384 (quoted in Hunter Blair's translation of Bellesheim, *History of the Catholic Church in Scotland*, IV, pp. 200–1).

2 MSS. coll. at Ushaw College, 1, No. 68, July 1710, from A. Giffard.

3 Dodd, *Church History*, III, p. 522, April 1710. This must refer to some correspondence that preceded the brief.

4 *Ib.* pp. 522–3. One declaration was dated Feb. 22, 1710, another Sept. 23, 1710.

Cardinal Paulucci informed the clergy in England of the Pope's great satisfaction.[1]

A little work appeared in 1710, *A short Review of the Book of Jansenius*, by Sylvester Jenks, who declared the *Augustinus* to be one of the worst books he had ever read. "I was past the three and fiftieth year of my Age, before I could prevail with myself to look it in the Face,"[2] but for fear of the mischief that Jansenist books might do to a friend of his—Dr Short—he took pains to write this *Review* as an antidote.[3] He remarked, however, in his preface, "Notwithstanding all the confident Reports of a Jansenian invasion from Holland, we have hitherto been more afraid than hurt".

Two books that embittered the controversy followed in 1713 and 1715; both were by Dodd, the author of the *Church History*. Dodd's real name was Hugh Tootell, and he was a nephew of the Tootell who had been harried with accusations of Jansenism in 1686. This may in part account for the extraordinary animosity which Dodd's books display against the Society of Jesus, though, as regards his lack of impartiality, Gillow observes that an examination of Bishop Dicconson's diary at Douay and of other original letters and documents written by the leading actors in the dispute[4] showed that Dodd had faithfully drawn his facts from these sources.[5]

The first of these books in 1713 was a *History of the English College at Doway* purported to be written by an outsider, a chaplain to an English regiment, giving *inter alia* an account of the charges made both against the college and the secular clergy of England. An answer, *A modest Defence* by Father Hunter, was published in the following year and called forth in 1715 a violent retort by Dodd, *The Secret Policy of the English Society of Jesus*, in which he accused the Fathers of bestowing the name of Jansenists on those whom they wanted to ruin.

Most of the Roman Catholics in England had heard of the Name of Jansenists, but few were thoroughly instructed what sort of cattle

1 Dodd, *Secret Policy*, pp. 269–70, Feb. 17, 1711. A copy of the letter is in the Ushaw collection, 1, No. 86.
2 *A Short Review*, pp. 1–2. 3 Gillow, under "Jenks".
4 Preserved in the Ushaw coll. 5 Gillow, *op. cit.* III, p. 179.

they were. So it was the Jesuits' Business first to set this matter right.[1]...If you insisted much upon the Example of the Primitive Times in your Moral Instructions; if you complain'd of the extravagant Opinions of loose Casuists or were anything Cautious in the Precept of Fasting, if you were either one of the Faculty of Sorbon, or offer'd to enlarge upon the Praises of that celebrated Body of Men, your Business was done. You were tainted, and your Name handed about as a Person pernicuously bent, and by no means to be rely'd upon in Spirituals.[2]...Speak but half a word in Praise of a Port Royal writer, tho' it be but in regard of his Stile and you are a Jansenist.[3]

The whole story of the accusations was rehearsed. "Childish observations", said Dodd, "were taken from the Words and Practises of Clergymen which served to engross the Grand Calumny and make the World believe that many were disposed to catch the Distemper though they were not actually infected. ...Several Clergymen were namely attack'd and traduced as Jansenists".[4] He reverted to the old charge that the Jesuits had opposed the establishing of bishops in England.

What opposition has been made against adding Two New Prelates to those that are deceas'd 'tis too fresh in our Memory to want any place in this story. 'Tis not long since the Twenty Ninth of January 1707 when the useful imputation of Jansenism was of singular service in this respect. Was not notice given legally from Rome that a worthy Member of the Clergy might expect his Bulls, in order to be consecrated, but the business dropt on a sudden?[5]

—an obvious reference to Saltmarsh. Father Hunter again answered Dodd's book, but it was deemed the better part of wisdom not to publish the reply.[6]

1 Dodd, *Secret Policy*, p. 262.
2 *Ib.* p. 264.   3 *Ib.* p. 202.
4 *Ib.* p. 665. Some who were accused: John Savage, fifth and last Lord Rivers (Gillow, under "Mannock"), Christopher Piggott (Kirk, see also under "Gumblestone"), William Crathorn (Kirk, under "Robert Bowes"), Thomas Mainwaring (Gillow), Vane (Ushaw coll. 1, No. 75), Thomas Witham (Kirk). Some of the accusers: Thomas Eyre, S.J. (Gillow), Richard Gumblestone or Gomeldon (Kirk, Gillow), Francis Mannock, S.J. (Gillow), James Rigby (Gillow), Lewis Sabran, S.J. (Gillow).
The bookseller John Lewis took an active interest on the side of the Jesuits in their controversy about Jansenism (Gillow).
5 Dodd, *Secret Policy*, p. 218.   6 Kirk, under "Hunter".

The Bull *Unigenitus* condemning Quesnel's work was promulgated in 1713. Bishop Giffard mentions receiving it in 1714, but the situation of the English Catholics, so he explained, did not permit of much action on his part.

Monsignor Santini sent me the Constitution from Brussels; and it happened to come just as the Proclamation came forth, so that all I could do was to signify it to the Superiors of the regulars and to some of the clergy. When circumstances permit I will proceed further. At least nothing shall be wanting that prudence allows of. Too forward a zeal in such things may provoke the state and occasion great mischief.[1]

Was the bishop lukewarm in his acceptance of the Bull? Some were inclined to think that he was. The bookseller Lewis who took an active part against the Jansenists in this controversy reported that when

Mr Sutten (an Irish capucino) coming from Brussels brought with him the condemnation of Quesnel's book...he waited here sometime before he could speak with ye Bishop to deliver the same...it was believed y^t ye Bishop kept out of the way on purpose; when ye bull of condemnation was delivered it was a long time before ye Bishop would give notice of ye said bull or prohibit the clergy from using it (the book).

Lewis also added that after the prohibition several clergymen continued to recommend the book to their penitents.[2]

Bishop Giffard, an old man of seventy-two, was certainly not filled with any hostility to the Jansenists, for when a certain Marison, an Irish missionary priest saw him in August 1714 and told him of the plight of the Church of Utrecht, none being willing to ordain priests for this church, now declared schismatic, he was moved to pity,[3] and in November of this year one finds Marison telling Van Erkel of the gladness with which Giffard heard of the zeal of the Dutch clergy for the Gospel.[4]

1 Brady, *Episcopal Succession*, III, p. 153.
2 MSS. coll. at Ushaw College, I, No. 69 (accusation transmitted to E. Dicconson by J. Coles).
3 *Recueil de divers Témoignages*, pp. 122–3 (original in archives of the Chapter of Utrecht).
4 *Ib.* p. 125 (original in archives).

In spite of possible reluctance the Bull was ultimately accepted. The Cardinal de Bissy in his collection of documents *Temoignages de l'Eglise Universelle en faveur de la Bulle Unigenitus* (1718) gives short extracts from the letters of three of the English vicars-apostolic according to which the Bulls *Vineam Domini* and *Unigenitus* were gladly received by the faithful.[1] A letter written in 1720 by Bishop Giffard to the Pope, Clement XI, said that he had accepted the Constitution *Unigenitus*.[2] That some resistance was encountered may be inferred from a declaration signed in 1718 by several of the former "appellants" of "the Province of Canterbury", signifying that they accepted the Bull.[3] The Appeal of the Cardinal de Noailles against the Bull had been instantly translated and circulated. A letter from Cardinal Gualterio in 1723 desires full information of any unwillingness on the part of the English clergy to receive the Bull, and he is informed in return that:

the work of Quesnel is in general circulation among the English catholics, under the direction of the clergy, one of whom translated and printed the said work with the consent of the Bishops. Although their approbation was afterwards withdrawn, many copies of the book were put into circulation. It is only too common to hear people speak in praise of Philip le Bel, of the nuns of Port Royal des Champs and of all measures tendants a depouiller les Papes et a avancer le pouvoir des eveques particuliers....The chief agent of the party in England is one of the clergy who has crossed the sea many times to visit the Jansenists. Celuy-ci est en etroite liaison avec nos eveques et dix ou douze des principaux du clergé qui ne peuvent ignorer ses sentiments.

The writer has heard such people say that the Jesuits have been the cause of the loss of more souls than Calvin and Luther, etc.[4]

In the meantime the partisans of the Bull did not remain

1 It may, however, be noted that the names of the English vicars-apostolic are not given, and that the letters are not dated.

2 Brady, *op. cit.* III, p. 153.

3 *Downside Review*, IV (1885), p. 199 (Archives of St Gregory's Monastery, Downside).

4 *Ib.* V (1886), pp. 281–2 (Archives of St Gregory's Monastery, Downside). The curious thing about this letter is that it seems to have been written by the Father Southcott who had himself translated Quesnel on St John fifteen years previously. Cf. Kirk, *Biographies*. Kirk spells the name Southcote.

inactive. In 1714 appeared another translation from the French, *Familiar Instructions about Predestination and Grace.* "What is Predestination? What is Jansenism? Are all Jansenists hereticks?" inquired "the Lay Person", and "the Divine" made suitable answer to these and other questions. Another translation followed in 1724, *An Abstract of what is necessary to be known concerning the Constitution Unigenitus.* The translator thought these Instructions not unseasonable for the Catholics of England, even though some believed that the English Catholics should not be enlightened in these matters.

In ten years time and more since the Constitution came out first, 'tis very hard that even the publick News Papers should be full of those matters and that the Catholicks should know nothing of them. England is not so far from France and Holland, but that the Infection of Jansenism may easily be convey'd over in an English dress, especially since that forreign Commodity is no Counterband in a Protestant Country. It is not long since the Gentlemen of the Party have taken pains to send whole Chests of Jansenist Books even into China some Thousands of Miles off, and amongst several others 60 volumes against the Constitution Unigenitus. And shall we think they would forget to supply England so much nearer them, and at so much less charges with plenty of this modish Ware?

A polemical tract of 1729 was entitled *The Bull Unigenitus clear'd from Innovation and Immorality.* "The Decree Unigenitus", said the writer, "is almost as well known to the Town as the Beggar's Opera. Tradesmen and Mechanicks give us long Lectures of it. In all Coffee houses it is a celebrated Topick. It is the daily Exercise of Wit. And it has been lately advanc'd so high, as to help on the learned Chat of the Tea-table."

On the Jansenist side the so-called *Montpellier Catechism,* often attributed to Bishop Colbert, but written by the Oratorian Pouget, was translated in or about 1722 by Sylvester Lloyd, and condemned by a decree of the Index in 1725.[1] An earlier translation by a Dr Hall had never been published.[2]

Now and again one comes upon propaganda in France seemingly destined for the English, perhaps the English residing

1 Reusch, *Der Index,* II, pp. 410, 762, see also Vacant, *Dictionnaire de Théologie Catholique,* under "Catéchisme".
2 The Translator to the Reader.

in France, though in this age of the *Lettres persanes* foreign atmosphere is a convenient device, and foreign dress a safe cloak for criticism. The Jesuit organ, the *Journal de Trévoux*, publishes a *Lettre écrite à un Milord à Londres par un Anglois voyageur en France*, in which the situation is explained in terms of Whigs and "Toris". "Les Déistes, les Sociniens, les Esprits forts, les Huguenots, les Républicains, tous ceux qui souffrent avec peine le gouvernement civil et Ecclésiastique, se cachent sous le nom de Jansénistes, comme chez nous sous le nom de Whigs." We are even introduced to the "Dames de la Grâce", the "Miladys Janséniennes".[1] In the *Nouvelles Ecclésiastiques*, the Jansenist publication, we read of a series of periodical *Lettres d'un Catholique François à un Anglois sur les Miracles de M. Pâris*, prohibited indeed by the Lieutenant de Police, but appearing all the same. "L'auteur continue à l'occasion des miracles de Monsieur de Pâris à faire connaître les Jesuites à son Anglois."[2]

The pamphlet *The Bull Unigenitus clear'd* was not unknown to the Jansenists in Holland, and the abbé d'Étemare remarks in a letter of July 30th of this year, 1729, that M. de Maupas (i.e. the abbé Le Gros) must not forget to send Mr Wauchope a short and solid answer to this little book. "M. Wacop" was also to receive a copy of the history of the Constitution *Unigenitus* which served as an introduction to the *Hexaples* or *Écrit à Six Colonnes*, and this copy was to be a present from Étemare, to be charged to his account. Nor must M. Wauchope's nephew be forgotten—he was coming to Holland, and news could be had of him from the bookseller Van den Walther. M. Herbert must also be remembered. "Il est à désirer que l'on soit attentif à envoier quelques livres en Angleterre à M. Herbert"—Arnauld's *Letters*, these a present from Étemare, the Bishop of Senez' *Pastoral Instructions*, les *Apologies* de M. l'Évêque de Babylone, and several copies of the *Mémoire aux Plénipotentiaires touchant les Jésuites*.[3]

1 *Journal de Trévoux*, Jan. 1715, pp. 108–16.
2 *Nouvelles Ecclés.*, 22 août, 1733, p. 172; 3 oct. p. 197; 9 nov. p. 228; 21 déc. p. 256, etc.
3 Amersfoort Archives, Carton L, Cat. number 3786. The spelling Wauchope and Wacop occur in the same letter.

Now it is known that Étemare and Le Gros went to England in 1729, and one is left with the impression that this letter was written after their return, when they had come to know "M. Herbert" and "M. Wauchope". M. Herbert, described elsewhere as a canon of the London chapter, had been in correspondence the year before, in 1728, with Quesnel's friend, the canon Ernest de Brigode,[1] a Jansenist who, as early as 1722, is accused of having "fort à cœur le projet de Réunion avec la Religion anglicane et cela pour fortifier le parti janséniste".[2] Le Gros and Étemare had come to England with a very definite mission—they had been sent by the Archbishop of Utrecht, Barchman, "afin de prendre une connaissance détaillée de l'Eglise Catholique de ce Royaume, dont l'état et la cause avoient tant de rapport avec l'Eglise de Hollande et pour tacher d'établir entr'elles une correspondance qui pouvait leur être fort utile à l'une et à l'autre".[3]

From this visit Étemare and Le Gros seem to have brought back not only *The Bull Unigenitus clear'd* but "a book of M. H.'s" which, they considered, should be translated into Latin or French, *An abstract of the transactions relating to the English secular clergy*[4]—"il ne faudroit rien négliger pour le faire imprimer"—and along with this book might be printed the letter of the Bishop of Chalcedon (Richard Smith) of October 16th, 1627, to lay people on the approbation required by regulars— a letter requiring regulars to obtain his licence for hearing confessions.[5]

The mission as a whole was not as successful as was hoped, but the correspondence between members of the two Churches continued during the lifetime of Archbishop Barchman.[6] The

1 Reference to a letter offering help, Feb. 15, 1728, *Recueil de divers Témoignages*, p. 379.
2 Archives of the Ministère des Affaires Étrangères, Hollande, Corr. Pol. Vol. 350, f. 300. (Reference from Préclin, *Union des Églises*, p. 21.)
3 *Nouvelles Ecclés.*, 1771, p. 32.
4 The *Abstract of Transactions* is by a certain John Sergeant (London, 1703, reprinted by W. Turnbull, 1853) who also went by the name of Holland. We have already seen that Short's French translation of this Abstract had been translated into Latin.
5 Amersfoort Archives, Carton L, Cat. number 3786, July 30, 1729.
6 *Nouvelles Ecclés.*, *loc. cit.*

Jansenist Petitpied, one of the Sorbonne doctors who had signed the famous *Cas de Conscience*, had friends in London who sent him in 1733 a copy of a treatise proving that the Constitution *Unigenitus* could and must be accepted, and Petitpied wrote back from Utrecht expressing his disapproval.[1] In 1734 "M. Wauchope", whom one discovers to have been a London doctor, ventured to reason with Bishop Petre on the subject of the Bull, and Petitpied was not surprised to hear of the "espèce de mépris" with which the bishop had received the "solid remonstrances" of the "virtuous layman". Bishop Petre's answer was transmitted to Petitpied at Utrecht, and Petitpied sent a memoir of some twenty pages to Wauchope to fortify him against the writings in favour of the Constitution *Unigenitus*, "dont s'appuyoit M. Piter".[2] From Petitpied M. d'Étemare also heard news of England—that Bishop Giffard had died and also M. Herbert, the London canon, and again one feels that Étemare had met these ecclesiastics during his visit to England.[3]

From London too a Mrs Daly corresponded with a cousin of M. d'Étemare, Mlle de Théméricourt, a former pupil of Port Royal, who now spent her life copying and publishing Port Royal manuscripts. Through Mlle de Théméricourt Mrs Daly obtained, to her great joy, a letter from the aged "prisoner of Jesus Christ", as he called himself, Soanen, the appellant Bishop of Senez, over ninety years old, who had been condemned by the so-called Council of Embrun for his Pastoral Instructions, deprived of his functions and relegated to a remote monastery. After his death Mrs Daly received a relic which, so she reported to Mlle de Théméricourt, performed a miraculous cure on one of her servants.[4] Letters, relics, hero-worship—a few friends lingered on in ardent veneration of the past, and then they too went their way.

1 B.N. f. fr. MS. 24876, pp. 259–61.
2 *Ib.* pp. 421–44, and Arsenal MS. 5784, f. 171 (reference given by M. Préclin in *L'Union des Églises*, p. 171).
3 Arsenal, *ib.* (*Anecdotes de M. d'Etemare ou se trouve la Relation de ses conferences avec M. Petitpied*). Among the MSS. of the Arsenal is also a notebook that evidently was once the property of an English ecclesiastic, opposed to the Jansenists. It contains notes in English, French and Latin, and extracts from various authors including Arnauld's *Fréquente Communion* and the *Montpellier Catechism* (MS. 2177).
4 *Lettres de Messire Jean Soanen, Ev. de Senez*, II, pp. 750–1.

Some allusions have been made to Douay College as having been very naturally involved in the controversies of the period, and a few details may be added here.

Dr Guilday in his book *The English Catholic Refugees on the Continent* stresses the important rôle played by Douay College and remarks that the research worker in the Roman archives "gains the impression...that the conditions in England, and in the other Colleges, Convents and Seminaries established abroad for the English exiles were never given more than a secondary place in English affairs in comparison to Douay".[1] But he also points out that outside of Rome there is a regrettable lack of material for certain important years. The fifth *Douay Diary* ends in 1654, the sixth *Diary* covering the years 1676–92 is lost, the seventh *Diary* does not begin till 1715; there are therefore no diaries for the years 1654–1715,[2] and the narrative is perforce fragmentary.

One of the earliest to be mentioned as a sympathizer of Jansenism was possibly Dr Kellison, who died in 1642 after being President of Douay for twenty-seven years. Dodd accuses the Jesuits of saying that Kellison "all along struck in with Saint-Cyran and other Abettors of Jansenism".[3] The internuncio at Brussels received protestations of orthodoxy from Douay in 1652;[4] but about this time the vice-president, Dr Edward Daniel, was not promoted to the presidency of the college, partly because he did not take a definite enough position against Jansenism, and partly also, no doubt, because he had studied under Blackloe, though he disclaimed his "novelties".[5] The fifth *Douay Diary* mentions another friend of Blackloe, Thomas Carr (*alias* Miles Pinckney), as one who "to the best of his power promoted Jansenism".[6]

A note on a President of Douay, Dr John Leyburn, preserved in the Archives of the Propaganda Fide, says in 1672 that it is feared he tends to favour the opinions of Jansenius,[7] and Dodd,

1 Guilday, *English Catholic Refugees*, pp. 307–8.
2 *Ib.* pp. 306–27.
3 Dodd, *Secret Policy*, p. 32, cf. Hunter, *A modest Defence*, p. 92.
4 R.O. *Roman Transcripts*, vol. 131. April 5, 1652, cf. Guilday, p. 327, *n.* 1.
5 Dodd, *Church History*, III, pp. 294, 380.
6 *Cath. Rec. Soc. Publications, Douay Diaries*, II, p. 545.
7 R.O. *Roman Transcripts*, vol. 99. Aug. 12, 1672. Leyburn was President from 1670 to 1676.

though what he affirms must be accepted with caution, relates that when Dr Leyburn was upon the point of being promoted to Prelacy "an original letter was produced from a certain English Regular and Superior which advised their Agent at Rome to press Home the Accusation of Jansenism".[1]

At any rate Leyburn does not seem to have been hostile to the Jansenists—he corresponded with Arnauld's friend Neercassel, the Archbishop of Utrecht, he approved of Neercassel's book, the *Amor poenitens*,[2] and Neercassel heard with joy of Leyburn's promotion to a bishopric. Both Neercassel and Arnauld believed that Leyburn would be consecrated in Flanders and looked forward to seeing him; but the consecration took place in Rome, Leyburn went to England through France, and Neercassel never saw him again.[3]

Arnauld knew Leyburn well enough to send him a copy of his *Fantôme du Jansénisme* to London. Leyburn, then vicar-apostolic of all England, replied cordially to the Jansenist, Ernest Ruth d'Ans, who had forwarded the book. " Je suis infiniment obligé à l'Auteur qui par votre moyen m'en a fait présent. Vous le remercierez, s'il vous plait, de ma part; lui témoignant l'estime particulière que j'en fais." He had already seen a copy of the work.

M. Genet me le fit voir quelques jours auparavant, et j'ai eu en le lisant la satisfaction que me donnent tous les autres ouvrages du même Auteur. Il semble que la Divine Providence a voulu permettre à son adversaire de lui donner cette belle occasion pour faire paraître à toutes les personnes raisonnables que ce monstre terrible qu'on a tant combattu sous le nomen de Jansénisme n'est en effet qu'un pitoyable fantôme.[4]

But Arnauld was sorry to learn from some English priests that Leyburn was " un zéro en chiffre" over against the English Jesuits. Leyburn was not firm and resolute enough, said Arnauld's

---

1 Dodd, *Secret Policy*, p. 266.
2 Arnauld, *Œuvres*, IV, pp. 177–8.
3 *Ib.* pp. 58, 182–3, Aug. 10 and Oct. 7, 1685.
4 *Ib.* XXIV, p. 602, March 4, 1687. There seems no reason to doubt its authenticity. Note *ib.* "M. Genet, Auteur de la Morale de Grenoble étoit pour lors à Londres. Innocent XI l'avoit donné à M. Dadda, Nonce auprès du Roi d'Angleterre, pour son Théologien".

informants, and Arnauld wondered whether one could not prevail on the "Cardinal de Norfolck" to write to Leyburn to exhort him to greater courage.[1]

To return to Douay, however. It was in the eighteenth century that the college was most seriously indicted. The first to bear the brunt of the attack was Edward Hawarden, one of the professors of divinity. About 1704 it became known that "several hands were engaged in making affidavits or subscriptions against Dr Hawarden, insinuating that he was teaching the doctrines of Jansenius". Gradually the charges were made to include the other professors with one or two exceptions. It is said that the hostile rumours against Hawarden had their origin partly in professional jealousy of his ability, partly in the rancour of a student who had been dismissed from Douay that year, the "turbulent gentleman", as writers of the time call him, Austin Newdigate Poyntz.

This young man complained to the Jesuits that his superiors at the college were rigorists and Jansenists, said he had heard that Hawarden's attitude to the famous *Cas de Conscience* would be the same as that of the forty doctors of the Sorbonne, and he handed over Dr Hawarden's Dictata, the notes given to students. These were examined, but nothing incriminating was found. The charge was renewed in 1707[2] when Bussy, the nuncio at Cologne, sent information to Rome against Douay College, "naming more especially Dr Hawarden", accompanying this information with insinuations against the bishops of England. Dr Hawarden withdrew from Douay in September of that year to take up work in England. He affirmed he had condemned the *Cas de Conscience*, had declared his acceptance of the various Constitutions and had always detested the errors of Jansenius, but it was still maintained that he would not condemn those who did not condemn Jansenius.

Every one hoped that his departure would restore quiet, "but this proved a mistake, for no sooner had he gone than the war

1 *Ib.* II, p. 719, Oct. 7, 1686.
2 Cf. Kirk, *Biographies*, p. 184: "I find a Father Pigott, a Jesuit, at Douay in 1707, very busy with Poynts in bringing the charge of Jansenism against Dr Hawarden".

was renewed. It was reported that he had fled through fear, and that the college would very shortly be placed under the supervision of the Jesuits ". Gillow explains that the English Jesuits were amongst the most zealous opponents of Jansenism and their fears that the schism might spread to their country "made them excessively sensitive on the subject, and the action of some members of their society was construed by the seculars into an attack on the whole body of clergy in England and into an attempt to obtain possession of the administration of Douay College ".[1]

On October 31st, 1709, a letter from George Witham, one of the vicars-apostolic of England, to Dr Paston, President of Douay, brought news of definite charges.

Cardinal Paulucci has lately writ to me that his holiness has been inform'd that notice is come to him that many and divers readers and scholars in your college publickly teach and learn the false doctrine of Jansenius; and has commanded the said Paulucci to signify to us that we should with all diligence possible procure them to be removed; that others may be substituted in their room...to the end the see apostolick be not necessitated to suspend the pension or rents usually allowed the college.

No one was mentioned by name. "Mr H. is not now there who displeased some persons", and Paston was desired to tell "who now they are that displease".[2]

Here was serious news indeed. In this crisis the college seems to have appealed to the Court of St-Germain for help. "James III"[3] and Lord Caryll[4] wrote letters to Cardinal Caprara, Protector of England, desiring justice to be done; the Duke of Berwick, the Duke of Perth, and others of the court wrote and signed a declaration that they were persuaded of the falseness of these accusations,[5] though one wonders how a master of the

---

1 This and the whole preceding account of Hawarden is based on Gillow's article "Hawarden" in his *Biographical Dictionary*. See also Kirk, *Biographies*, article "Hawarden".
2 Dodd, *Church History*, III, pp. 520–1.
3 *Hist. MSS. Comm., Stuart Papers at Windsor*, I, p. 236, March 10, 1710.
4 Dodd, *Church History*, III, p. 522, March 10, 1710.
5 *Ib.* p. 521, Feb. 28, 1710.

wardrobe, for instance, should be qualified to judge in doctrinal matters.

Caprara replied to Caryll that all these letters and attestations were no doubt very honourable, but "on les croira mendiez"; they would not suffice to allay the suspicions of the cardinals whose displeasure might cause the suspension of the pension, nay would already have caused it, had he not intervened. He advised the president, Paston, to come to Rome in spite of his age—he was over seventy—to clear the college of all diffamations; then the whole matter could be dispatched in a fortnight, and Paston could vouch for his orthodoxy and that of his college.[1]

In April 1710 Bishop Giffard and Bishop Witham again wrote to Dr Paston. Each had had a letter from Grimaldi, the internuncio at Brussels, who through Cardinal Paulucci renewed the Pope's orders "assuring that his Holiness does not build upon uncertain names, but authentick testimonys and depositions of persons worthy of credit who leave no doubt of ye truth...that the doctrine of Jansen is taught and learned in your house". The names of five persons were given, but Bishop Witham told Dr Paston he was writing to the cardinal to acquaint him that "4 of ye persons accused have been a long time ago from yr house", he would also transmit Dr Paston's assurance that "since ye year 1707 and month of September... yt Mr Hawarden went from ye house nothing has been done, sayed or writ wch could give the least shadow of offence in matters of doctrin". Bishop Giffard too marvelled at the "strange information" the cardinal had.[2]

The letters written to Paulucci must have seemed unconvincing and the journey to Rome not feasible, for a visitation of the college was held in 1711.[3] The two visitors examined "from ye President downwards to ye end of ye Divines". They spent "two dayes in asking questions, two dayes in examining Dr Hawarden's dictates and two writing over fair ye answers of ye house

1 *Ib.* p. 522.
2 MSS. coll. at Ushaw College, I, No. 65, p. 247. (Copies.) The persons named were "Mr Hawarden, Mr Plummerden, Mr Crathorn, Mr Stafford and Mr Allers".
3 Burton, *Life of Challoner*, I, p. 31 *n.*

...and two more swearing all of ym".[1] All the persons in the house and their writings were found free from the suspected doctrine, and Bishop Witham remarked that he hoped such a solemn justification would serve *ad obstruendum ora loquentium iniqua*.[2] The Bull *Unigenitus* was subscribed by the superiors of the college on July 16th, 1714, and a letter written to Dr Paston by Cardinal Paulucci in March 1715 cleared the college of all aspersions of Jansenism.[3] Nevertheless Dr Paston's successor, Robert Witham, did not escape the charge of Jansenism.[4]

[1] Letter of Nov. 20, 1712, printed in the *Ushaw Magazine*, xiv, pp. 19–20.
[2] *Ib.* p. 21.
[3] Dodd, *Church History*, iii, pp. 523–4.
[4] Guilday, *The English Catholic Refugees*, pp. 334, 338 (from documents preserved in the archives of the Propaganda). Charges were also laid against the English College at Rome. See Gasquet, *History of the Venerable English College* (1920), pp. 171–2, and also against the whole of the English Benedictine Congregation: Taunton, *History of the Jesuits in England* (1901), p. 468. Since we have been speaking of Douay a little incident may be recounted here, though it is not connected with the college itself. It is related by a certain Beauvoir, the Anglican chaplain of the ambassador, Lord Stair. Beauvoir, of whom more will be said hereafter, frequented Jansenist society and was on friendly terms with the Church historian Du Pin. "One Hutchinson, a Franciscan of Douay", he writes in 1716, "maintain'd lately some Theses that showed up the Pope's Power and Infallibility to the height and vindicated the Constitution Unigenitus. The Parliament of Douay hath censured those theses and Dr Dupin complain'd of them to the Sorbonne. The Faculty appointed Comm^rs to examine y^m and they have extracted 8 or 9 Propositions to be condemn'd by the Faculty."
"But", continues Beauvoir, "the Pope's Nuntio hath bellow'd so loud at the Palais Royall that the Regent to be rid of that din hath forbid the Sorbonne to proceed farther. They are not, however, disheartened and hope to have again leave to speak." B.M. Add. MSS. 22880, ff. 8–9, Aug. 27 (O.S.), 1716. Beauvoir to (?Anthony Hammond). Cf. J. Carreyre, *Le Jansénisme durant la Régence* (Louvain, 1929), i, p. 115.

CHAPTER XIII

L'Affaire des Hibernois. Friends at Rome

WADDING AND NOLAN

IN the eighteenth century one finds scarcely any Irish Jansenists; in the seventeenth century they are a little more common, especially before 1660. We have seen, in the very early days, how Conry at Louvain shared many of the ideas of Jansenius long before the name of Jansenism was evolved, and how Dr Sinnich, at Louvain also, wrote much in defence of the *Augustinus*. We have also seen how Dr Kelly acted as a kind of intermediary between Port Royal and the Stuart refugees, and how Dr Callaghan was violently attacked for his Jansenism by le Père Brisacier.

Another Irish friend of the Jansenists was a certain "Philippe Olonergan, docteur hibernois", who had furnished a "magnificent" approbation of La Lane's book *De la Grâce victorieuse*;[1] yet another was a certain "sieur Clonsinnil", also a doctor of the Sorbonne,[2] who wrote in defence of the Irish Jansenists. According to him the Irish living at the Collège des Lombards were Jansenists, "les plus scavants et les plus considérables de la Nation adherent à la doctrine de Saint-Augustin",[3] which is another way of saying that they were Jansenists. The Jesuit Father Rapin mentions several Irish Jansenists in his *Mémoires* besides Kelly and Callaghan, ecclesiastics by the names of

---

1 Gerberon, *op. cit.* I, p. 477. The Syndic Hallier complained of the approbation, and this in turn called forth another book, *Défense d'une approbation donnée par Mre Philippes Olonergan, Hibernois, Docteur en Theologie de la Faculté de Paris, au livre de la grâce victorieuse.* Gerberon, *op. cit.* I, p. 491; *Histoire du Cas de Conscience*, III, pp. 357–8; Saint-Amour, *Journal*, p. 136.
2 Gerberon, *op. cit.* I, p. 479.
3 Clonsinnil, *Défense des Hibernois*, pp. 4, 11.

Hyfernan, Butler, Poerus, Mulrian and Cahill.[1] Rapin says the first four of these and Callaghan were sent to Ireland to spread Jansenism, but that they were promptly made to return by Rinuccini, which is not exact as far as Callaghan is concerned.[2] Port Royal records tell of la Mère Angélique giving alms to an Irish priest who had come to see her before he returned to Ireland.[3]

In 1651 there appeared a little pamphlet *Défense des Hibernois Disciples de Saint Augustin*. The writer, the aforementioned Clonsinnil, complains of the harshness with which the Irish Jansenists are treated: "On veut empescher les Hibernois qui résident dans Paris et qui n'ont pas voulu souscrire à la Déclaration Molinienne de retourner en leur patrie pour y estre employez au service de l'Eglise quoy qu'ils fussent des plus capables pour travailler à la vigne du Seigneur—on les retient dans ce pays en usant d'une grande dureté à leur égard."[4]

In this pamphlet we are introduced to the so-called *Affaire des Hibernois*, one of the most extraordinary episodes of the campaign waged to obtain the papal condemnation of the five propositions. Incidentally an interesting sidelight is thrown on a page of academic life, and on the lack of amenity existing between the various members of the University of Paris which was indeed a house divided against itself.

For the better understanding of the significance of this episode

1 Rapin, *Mémoires*, i, p. 411. The annotator of the *Mémoires* gives a certain amount of information about these ecclesiastics:
(1) Patrice Hifferman, du diocèse de Cashell, ordonné prêtre à Paris le 23 février 1641, mort à l'Hôtel Dieu le 1er février 1683.
(2) Edmond Butler, prêtre, licencié en théologie, habitait encore le collège des Irlandais en 1683.
(3) Poerus—the annotator is puzzled because Poer was anything but a Jansenist.
(4) Jean Moulrian, Irlandois, ordonné prêtre à Paris au mois de décembre 1637.
(5) Hugues Cahilh ou O'Cahil du diocèse de Cashell, ordonné prêtre le 10 août 1648.
2 Rapin, *Mémoires, loc. cit.* That Rapin is not always reliable can be seen from the following. On p. 130, vol. i, he says that Lady Hamilton and Lady Muskerry introduced Callaghan to the abbé Mazure; on p. 410 he says that they had known each other as fellow students, i.e. long before the ladies came to France.
3 M. A. Arnauld, *Mémoires et Relations*, p. 221; Mlle Poulain, *Nouvelle Histoire abrégée*, iii, p. 26.
4 Clonsinnil, *Défense*, p. 17.

it should be remembered that in July 1649 Cornet, then Syndic of the Faculty of Theology, had formulated the five propositions that were to attain to such renown, and a commission had been appointed to examine them, but on account of an appeal made by some sixty or seventy doctors, including Arnauld, the Parlement of Paris put a stop to these proceedings in the Sorbonne in October 1649, naturally without pacifying the hostile camps— no censure was to be promulgated by the commission, no discussions of the proposition were to take place, no writings dealing directly or indirectly with these controversial matters were to be published until the Parlement should decide otherwise.[1]

The matter was carried on outside the university. Eighty-five prelates sent a letter to the Pope in May 1650, urging him to examine the propositions. Inside the university feelings ran high, and each party watched the other narrowly.

The Jansenists charged Saint-Amour, a former Rector of the University of Paris, then in Rome, with the defence of the *Augustinus*. Three other deputies came to join him in December 1651, while Hallier and two other doctors arrived in May 1652 to uphold the other side.

Our immediate concern, however, is with the *affaire des Hibernois*. Clonsinnil gives an account of the first part of the episode, and in relating the story after him we are, of course, using a source frankly Jansenist, though the incidents are in the main confirmed by two documents published on the other side, viz. the *Conclusions de la Faculté de Theologie pour les Hybernois* and the *Factum pour les Hybernois*; these, however, take up chiefly the later part of the story.

In June 1650 an Irish priest of the Mission of Father Vincent de Paul, Duygine by name, visited some of the Irish who were at the University of Paris, professed great compassion for their poverty and advised them to apply to a certain M. de la Bidière who was anxious to do something to alleviate the distress of the nation. They went to see this M. de la Bidière who informed them of his intention of founding a community where they

1 Jourdain, *Histoire de l'Université de Paris*, pp. 173–5.

might live, and he asked them to draw up some rules and regulations for this establishment.

These rules were gladly framed and brought to the benefactor who now began to lay down some conditions—they must have as their superior a Jesuit or a priest of the Mission, and also, since the Irish were accused of being Jansenist in their sympathies, they must renounce all Jansenism, promise obedience to the Pope and receive all his Bulls, especially those directed against Jansenius and his followers. The Irish replied that as for the first point, not belonging to an order themselves, it would be better for them to be directed by a secular priest, and moreover, since several of them had the honour of being members of the University of Paris which looked upon the Jesuits as adversaries, the university would object to their being governed by a Jesuit. As for Jansenism, they did not know what it was, they were Catholics and disciples of St Augustine, and like all disciples of St Augustine in entire submission to the Holy See.

M. de la Bidière, however, insisted on a written and signed declaration condemning Jansenius and promising in particular to receive all papal Bulls. The Irish withdrew before this request, and all their fellow-countrymen who heard of this approved of their conduct, especially a certain Nicolas Poer and his friend Mollony, and another one of them, Richard Nugent by name, declared vehemently that he would rather thrust his hand into a burning fire than sign such a declaration.

M. de la Bidière having failed in his object two Jesuits next went to see the above Poer who taught at the Collège de Lisieux, and in spite of his professed conviction they dazzled him with promises of a college for the Irish, if he and his companions would only sign. Poer broached the subject to the Irish at the Collège des Lombards, but they declared indignantly that it should never be said of the Irish that they sold the doctrines of the Church for temporal advancement. Poer then applied himself to the younger Irish "qui étudient encore leur philosophie"—they were to come and consult with him about the matter at the Collège de Lisieux, but were to keep it very secret from the Irish at the Collège des Lombards. The latter, however, heard of it and sent word to the Rector of the University, Courtin, begging him to put a stop to the proceedings of Poer who was stirring up unrest among the Irish, and holding assemblies in his room to pronounce upon questions of doctrine as if he were a pope or a bishop.

The rector at once dispatched one of the beadles of the University to Poer's room, ordering him and his friends to refrain from such conventicles and from presuming to judge doctrinal matters, and the assembled students disbanded obediently enough—this was on February 13th, 1651.[1] In the meantime the Jesuits, so our Jansenist author tells us, had also applied to the Congregation of the Priests of the Mission for aid in this matter of obtaining signatures from the Irish. The Irish students were in the habit of meeting at the Collège des Bons Enfants on Sunday afternoons, when they carried on discussions "in their own language" under the guidance of one of these priests, "Vuhite" by name—he was also known as le Père Le Blanc. In these meetings Father White would storm against the Jansenists and would even fall upon his knees praying that none who held these opinions might ever go to Ireland, especially not Messieurs..., naming them all by name. During the week he went about the university and also daily visited some of the Irish trying to obtain their signatures to a declaration which he presented, though the Irish sent two fruitless deputations to Father Vincent de Paul, the founder of the order, begging him that he would restrain the zeal of his missionaries.

In the end Father White obtained a few signatures from the younger men who were impressed by his promises and by his solemn warnings, the latter to the effect that Father Vincent de Paul had credit enough to prevent any of those who did not sign from obtaining a living in Ireland. Even the heroic Richard Nugent, who was going to let his hand be consumed by fire rather than accept the declaration, yielded in the end. The declaration was to the effect that in these calamitous times, when new dogmas were taught by certain persons, there was great danger lest some of the Irish studying in Paris be imbued with

1 Saint-Amour, *Journal*, Part III, ch. 9.

these doctrines and spread them in the Irish Church. The undersigned therefore promised—*firmiter statuimus promittimusque*—to fight this peril with all their might, to adhere to all œcumenical councils, to all papal decrees and censures, especially those directed against Baius and Jansenius, and to refrain from defending, teaching and preaching any propositions suspected of heresy, especially the following—and the five propositions were given in full.[1]

Twenty-seven had signed, the greater number of them were students, having "no rank or degree in the University, some of them having scarce studied Philosophy or Grammar",[2] yet by April 1st the Jesuits printed the declaration in their *Triumphus Catholicae Veritatis*[3] and also in their *Iansenius Damnatus*, as if it had come, remarks Clonsinnil, from the majority of the Irish doctors and priests. They also published the news in Ireland, while Hallier, the Syndic of the Faculty of Theology, said in his letters that the Irish doctors and priests who were in Paris had drawn up a declaration against "les propositions de la grâce".

The Irish who had not signed, upwards of sixty ecclesiastics, according to our Jansenist authority, took counsel with "Monsieur Tyrell", Doctor of Theology of the University of Paris and Superior of the Irish in Paris,[4] with "Monsieur O'Moloy", a celebrated professor,[5] and other Irish theologians, and, in order to save the honour of the country, they presented a petition to the Rector, the Deans and the Procurators of the Nations, begging that the declaration signed by a few Irish, "un petit nombre d'Escholiers pour la plupart", might not be imputed to the whole nation.[6]

1 *Apologetical Memoires* (printed at the end of Saint-Amour's *Journal*), p. 136, where the declaration is printed in full, including the signatures. Also printed in Boyle, *The Irish College*, pp. 22–4.
2 *Apol. Memoires*, p. 126.   3 *Ib.* p. 134.
4 Dr Edward Tyrrell, Boyle, *Irish College*, pp. 7, 15.
5 Professor of Philosophy in the Collège de Beauvais, Boyle, *Irish College*, p. 14.
6 The petition was signed by "M. Olonergan, Docteur de la Faculté de Paris, M. Maurice Poerus, Licentié en Théologie, M. Hifernan, Bachelier en Theologie, M. Macnamara, Bachelier en Théologie et Professeur en Philosophie". (An Irishman by the name of Macnamara was professor of philosophy in the Collège du Cardinal Lemoine, Boyle, *Irish College*, p. 14.)

So much for Clonsinnil's story, as it was written down in the year it happened, 1651. His little pamphlet seems the source from which all Jansenist historians draw their information. There is nothing equally full on the other side. What took place next can be put together from Saint-Amour's *Journal* and the *Mémoires Apologétiques de l'Université de Paris*[1] on the one hand, and the *Conclusions de la Faculté de Théologie pour les Hybernois* and the *Factum pour les Hybernois* on the other.

When the rector, greatly astonished, heard of "this enterprise against his authority", that the Irish had signed a doctrinal declaration contrary to his orders, he summoned four of the offenders, those who had university degrees, before the usual assembly of the three Deans of Faculties and the four Procurators of Nations, the latter representing the Faculty of Arts. The assembly, held at his house on March 4th, decided that the Irish had committed an act of temerity and insolence in passing judgment on a question on which the Faculty of Theology, the Archbishop of Paris and the whole clergy of France had refused to commit themselves. It nullified their declaration as prejudicial to the authority of the university, contrary to the customs and rights of the Gallican Church, and ordered them to revoke it within a week, failing which those who were members of the university were to be deprived of their degrees and rights, and the others were to be expelled from their colleges and debarred from ever receiving any degrees. The four Irishmen promised in writing to comply with this judgment. All copies of the declaration were to be brought to the rector to be torn up. They said they had signed three or four copies, one of them had been handed over to M. Vincent de Paul, but they did not know what had happened to the other copies.

At this same meeting was read the petition already mentioned in which the Irish who had not signed begged that they might not

1 These *Mémoires* were first published separately, and later as an appendix to Saint-Amour's *Journal* in 1662, and are very likely by Saint-Amour himself. In quoting from this document I use the English translation published in London in 1664 as an appendix to Saint-Amour, viz. *Apologetical Memoires in behalf of the Rector, Deanes, Proctors and Deputies of the University of Paris Against the Enterprises of certain Irish, for the most part Students in the University.*

be "branded with so shameful a blot to their reputation" as if they had all consented to the fault of some. The rector's decree embodying the decisions of the assembly was solemnly published by the Grand Beadle of the Nation of France and was signified to all the principals of colleges. There the matter rested for the moment, but not for long.

On March 21st the usual General Assembly of the University was held at the convent of the Mathurins. At the General Assembly, so we read in the *Factum pour les Hybernois*, the rector gives the university as a whole an oratorical account of what he has done in the last three months with his council, and asks to have his actions confirmed. This is a mere matter of form, says the author—the Dean of the Faculty of Theology speaks first and says, *Facultas probat ea quae praeclare gessisti in tuo Magistratu, litteras commendatitias decernit, pollicetur Amplissimum Comitatum.* Then the other two deans say the same thing, the Dean of the Faculty of Canon Law and the Dean of the Faculty of Medicine, but the Doctors and Masters of Arts often do not know what the rector has been talking about—one gathers they only came to walk in the academic procession! The rector, it should be added, was chosen from the Faculty of Arts and represented that faculty.

But this meeting, instead of being a drowsy confirmation of the rector's actions, developed into a very noisy affair. M. Hallier, Syndic of the Faculty of Theology, an ardent adversary of the Jansenists, rose to protest and was "mighty hot" in defence of the Irish, while other doctors rose from their seats, and would not let him talk, because he said he spoke in the name of the Faculty of Theology, and they cried that they had given him no orders! The dean alone spoke in the name of the Faculty! Let the syndic have the dean take the votes of the doctors! The dean, M. Messier, tried several times to take their suffrages, but he was hindered by other doctors, and M. Hallier "clamor'd much that none should speak". The meeting ended in general din and confusion, so that one wonders how the Jansenist author of the *Apologetical Memoires* can speak of a "solemn" confirmation.

"After this solemn confirmation 'twas hoped the Irish would

betake themselves to their duty", but they were "possess'd by other spirits than their own." Hallier, not having been allowed to remonstrate at the General Assembly, went this same day, March 21st, and protested before some notaries, and on the next day Poer and some of the Irish too went before notaries and not only made a declaration of what had happened, but also appealed from the rector's decree to the Parlement of Paris. The Parlement on March 24th retained their cause for judgment, and ordered the university to refrain from enforcing its decree until further notice,[1] much to the joy of those concerned.

A week later, on April 1st, it was the turn of the Faculty of Theology to hold its monthly assembly, and here too, of course, the *affaire des Hibernois* came up. Poer and another Irish ecclesiastic appeared before the meeting, told their story, and said that they would willingly submit to the judgment and correction of the Faculty of Theology. In the meantime, they added, it was hard for innocents to be ejected from the university like criminals, and they craved the protection of the faculty. They had decided and defined nothing with regard to doctrinal matters, they had merely made a resolution not to teach certain doctrines condemned by the Popes.

When Poer had finished his harangue, M. de Sainte-Beuve, Doctor of the Sorbonne and Professor of Theology, a vehement opponent of the Molinists, invited him to name those professors of the University of Paris who taught these pernicious doctrines —the declaration of the Irish had implied the existence of such professors. An ominous silence followed his words. Poer, taken aback by his ponderous adversary, hesitated—some of the doctors advised him not to answer, but to withdraw.[2] "They who had inspir'd this Batchelor with the boldness to come upon the stage and kindle the flame of Division", writes a Jansenist, "hinder'd him from answering to the Question and immediately

1 "...la Cour reçoit les dits Supplians Appelans, ordonne que...les parties auront Audience en premier jour, cependant fait deffenses de rien executer contre iceux Supplians jusques à ce qu'autrement par la Cour en ait esté ordonné." *Arrest de la Cour de Parlement* printed at the end of the *Conclusions de la Faculté de Théologie pour les Hybernois.*
2 *Conclusions de la Fac. de Théol.* p. 15.

got him away.... M. Hallier said he should answer with advice, *respondebit ex consilio.*"[1]

After the Irish had gone Hallier gave the faculty his account of the past events, told how he had been hindered from protesting at the General Assembly where he had wished to point out that the rector, the deans and procurators could not conclude or decide anything in this affair without consulting the Faculty of Theology, nor could they deprive Doctors and Bachelors of Theology of their degrees—they had given a judgment in doctrinal matters which was quite beyond their province. The uproar at the General Assembly had been such, he reported, that the rector had been obliged to go off to his procession without having had his decree confirmed.

Here M. de Sainte-Beuve rose to protest indignantly—the decree was a very just one, and duly confirmed in the General Assembly; he had an authenticated transcript of the confirmation which he offered to read to the faculty.

After some heated discussion as to whether or not the five propositions were being taught at the university, the Faculty of Theology adopted the following emphatic conclusion: that they disapproved of the rector's decree, they disapproved of the consent given by the sub-dean of the Faculty of Theology, M. Hennequin, at the rector's council-meeting, they approved of what had been done by M. Hallier at the General Assembly, and they seconded the appeal of the Irish to the Parlement. Four doctors were appointed to prosecute the business *ubicunque* and *quomodocunque*, though upwards of thirty doctors objected and said "that they stood for the whole University to make good its Decree against the Irish". The terms *ubicunque* and *quomodocunque* were judged very extraordinary and as meaning that the matter if necessary should be carried as far as Rome.

The resolution of the Faculty of Theology gave the Irish such confidence, we hear, that they had their original declaration printed with all the signatures appended, though the four that had been summoned to the rector's council-meeting had given

1 *Apologetical Memoires*, p. 128.

an undertaking in writing that they would revoke their declaration.

At the May assembly of the Faculty of Theology the resolution or conclusion was read again in spite of "very great contest", nay more, during this month M. Hallier had it printed, and not only in its original Latin form, but also in French so that all the unlettered could read and understand it—*Conclusio Facultatis Theologicæ Parisiensis pro Hibernos adversus Decretum . . . Dom. Rectoris Academiæ . . . et Jansenistas* and *Conclusion de la Faculté de Théologie de Paris pour les Hybernois contre le Decret de Monsieur le Recteur . . . et contre les Jansenistes.* And on the eve of Pentecost these pamphlets, of twenty odd pages each, suddenly appeared all over Paris, affixed "at all the Turnings of the University and the City and that with an injurious title".

The rector could not brook this monstrous insult to his authority. He instantly summoned his council to meet on the first day after the festivals, May 31st, and here a second decree[1] was drawn up, to the effect that the rector and the deputies had not gone beyond their power in what they had ordained against the Irish, who by their declaration transgressed against the discipline of the university and violated the rights and safety of the king and kingdom—great words for small doings—and that since the Irish had appealed from the rector's decree to the Parlement which had received them as appellants they could not also put their case before the Faculty of Theology, nor could the Faculty of Theology have taken up their case without doing wrong to the authority of the Parlement.

In order that the Faculty of Theology "might not pretend ignorance of all the Contents of this new Decree",[2] it was affixed to the gates of all the colleges next day, and the Grand Beadle of the Nation of France, accompanied by the Petty Beadle of the Nation of France, the Beadle of the Faculty of Canon Law and the Beadle of the Faculty of Medicine, carried a copy of the decree to the monthly Assembly of the Faculty of Theology meeting on that day, June 1st.

1 Printed in full in *ib.* pp. 138–9.
2 Saint-Amour, *Journal* (Engl. transl.), p. 108.

Not only this, but the university drew up and published certain *Memoires Apologetiques pour les Recteur, Doyens, Procureurs et Supposts de l'Université de Paris contre l'entreprise de quelques Hibernois, la plupart étudians en l'Université*,[1] this document being addressed to the Parlement of Paris. "The University found itself in so deplorable a passe", it said, "as to be put to uphold its Authority against its own children and to render an account of its proceedings." "The quality of the persons lately employed to divide it was a thing of sufficient wonder and 'twas scarce credible either that a small number of Irish, circumvented by strange Artifices, could raise against it the Syndic of the Theological Faculty, or that so many Doctors could be brought to favour so temerarious an enterprise."[2]

The *Memoires* gave an account of past events, justified the rector and criticized both the manner of the Irish, who wrote as if endowed with the authority of the Archbishop of Paris, and the matter of their declaration—while the university did not pronounce itself, either for or against the five propositions condemned by the Irish, it objected to the presumptuousness of the Irish in passing judgment on a matter that not even the Faculty of Theology had judged, and it declared it unlawful for private persons to make declarations of faith. But above all it took exception to "the stone of stumbling", their undertaking to obey *all* papal Bulls, since this was wholly contrary to the liberties of the Gallican Church and the authority of kings.

Some Irish residing in France, oblig'd by the publick hospitality of this Courteous Nation, and though Strangers, yet admitted to Study with perfect liberty in the University of Paris are so presumptuous as to make Conventicles about points of doctrine and our Religion; they subscribe Declarations against the Authority of Kings, the Arrests of Parliament, the Censures of the University and the Faculty...they promise to maintain the Bull of Boniface the VIII upon which Sanctarel and all the Sanctarellists chiefly found their pernicious doctrine of deposing Kings.[3]

"But let us not", say these *Memoires*, "lay the blame upon these scholars who no doubt had not malignity enough to frame such a

1 Orig. 36 pp., 4to, reprinted as an appendix to Saint-Amour's *Journal*.
2 *Apologetical Memoires*, p. 126.   3 *Ib.* p. 132.

dangerous Conspiracy out of their own heads...'tis plain on one side that the Jesuites were the promotors of it, and that the Declaration of the Irish was contriv'd by those Fathers, who always retaining the poison of their evil Doctrine against Kings, spread the same in all places where they come; and on the other 'tis as clear that M. Hallier Syndic of the Faculty was in the plot of this Declaration, since he became the Defender of it."[1]

In conclusion it was hoped that the Parlement of Paris would judge "the enterprise of the Irish an insolent action, and the conspiracy of the syndic and many doctors with them an effect of blind passion deserving to be repell'd by the publick authority of Justice".[2]

The Faculty of Theology, nothing daunted, retaliated by another publication, *Factum pour les Hybernois Appelants du Decret de Monsieur le Recteur...Pour servir de réponse aux Mémoires Apologétiques*. This pamphlet of some forty pages was also addressed to the Parlement and was written by the advocate Pucelle to show that the Irish were not guilty of any of the wrongs of which the rector accused them—they had never defined any doctrine, they had not been disobedient to him, for when he forbade them to hold conventicles and pass judgment on doctrinal matters they had separated, nor was their declaration a public document, it was merely a promise to accept the judgment of another and was not a judgment in itself.

The major part of the pamphlet consisted of an attack on the rector who was guilty of judging matters outside of his province —it was for the Faculty of Theology to judge the declaration of the Irish, if the rector thought it involved doctrinal matter; it was for the Parlement to judge it if the rector thought it contrary to the interests of the state. But it was as clear as daylight that the rector's decrees were the work of the Jansenists who wanted to show the world at large that the University of Paris upheld the doctrine of Jansenius, and as these decrees had been published widely the Faculty of Theology in its turn had to publish its *Conclusion* to show that it had no part in the rector's decrees. It was hoped that the Parlement of Paris would revoke

1 *Ib*. pp. 131–3.   2 *Ib*. p. 135.

both these decrees and restrain the rector from intervening in matters of doctrine.

The Jansenist historian Gerberon relates that Hallier and Cornet attacked the rector's second decree in the July meeting of the Faculty of Theology, but the faculty would not take action, so Amiot, one of the four doctors charged with the business of the Irish, appealed to the Parlement on behalf of the faculty which called forth another Jansenist polemic, *Faussetez contenues dans une Requête faite et présentée au Parlement par M. Amiot Docteur, sous le nom de la Faculté de Théologie.*[1]

As for the end of the story, writers on the Molinist side conclude with a triumphant allusion to the decree of the Parlement of March 24th[2] which, as we have seen, merely retained the cause for judgment, ordering the rector not to enforce his decree in the meantime, while the Jansenist writer Saint-Amour relates, with Gerberon bearing out his narrative, that the Faculty of Theology and the Irish were obliged to yield to both of the decrees, and that the *Conclusion* in which the Faculty had defied the rector was "reform'd by an accommodation to which they were glad to submit in a conference held for that purpose in the Colledge of Navarre, July 28".[3] At this conference appeared Hallier and Amiot with the Irish on one side, and the rector and some doctors on the other.[4]

But they did not perform what they had promised, continues Saint-Amour, for in September of this year, 1651, a Cordelier appeared in Rome, a man for whom even Rapin has no good word, a Father Mulard who said he had been sent from France as a deputy of the Faculty of Theology. He presented the afore-mentioned *Conclusion* as well as the *Memoires Apologetiques*, and gave out that the four doctors named to prosecute the business of the Irish had appointed him for this employment. M. Hallier "had been decry'd at Paris indeed", he said, "but if he was ill represented to the Parliament for having protected

1 Gerberon, *op. cit.* 1, pp. 477–8.
2 E.g. Rapin, *Mémoires*, 1, p. 414; Jourdain, *Histoire de l'Université de Paris*, p. 183; Boyle, *Irish College*, p. 17.
3 Saint-Amour, *Journal* (Engl. transl.), p. 109.
4 Gerberon, *op. cit.* 1, pp. 478–9.

poor strangers, he should be reveng'd at Rome for the wrong done him at Paris".[1]

"This business hath insensibly rested till the present time", writes Saint-Amour in his *Journal* toward 1653, "without being regulated one way or another."[2]

But the five propositions were condemned by Innocent X in May 1653, and no more pressure was likely to be put on the Irish students who were on the side of orthodoxy.

Before concluding this chapter in which we have frequently spoken of Saint-Amour, a brief mention may be made of two Irishmen whom Saint-Amour met at Rome where he was with other Jansenist deputies in the interests of the *Augustinus*. In the summer of 1651 a special congregation was appointed to examine the five propositions, a congregation consisting of five cardinals and thirteen consultors. One of these consultors was the famous Luke Wadding whom the Jansenists looked upon as not hostile to their cause.

The Jansenist Bourgeois sent to Rome in 1645 in defence of Arnauld's *Fréquente Communion* had already come to think of him as a kind of friend.

"Il ne me reste qu'un mot à dire de mes autres amis de Rome", he writes in his *Relation*. "Le R. P. Luc Wadding, Religieux de S. François, Irlandois, âgé de 80 ans, Fondateur à Rome du Monastère de Saint-Isidore pour les Religieux de son Ordre et de sa nation et l'un de mes juges, m'a témoigné toujours tant de bienveillance et défendu partout toutes les causes où j'avais interest avec tant de zèle et par le seul amour qu'il avoit pour la vérité que sa mémoire me sera toujours en singulière vénération."[3]

In the matter of the *Augustinus* the Jansenist deputies arrived in Rome much earlier than the deputies on the other side, and Rapin relates that they spent their time paying court to all kinds of people, especially to three or four ecclesiastics one of whom was Wadding, "un homme assez singulier dans ses sentiments et d'un caractère propre à s'entêter des nouvelles opinions sous prétexte de la doctrine de Saint-Augustin". Saint-Amour won

1 Saint-Amour, *Journal*, pp. 109–10.
2 *Ib.*
3 Bourgeois, *Relation*, p. 112.

him over by his "civilities", we are told, for he consulted him like an oracle.[1]

The congregation of cardinals and consultors held meetings from September 1652 to April 1653. In giving his opinion Wadding was throughout inclined to be favourable, or at least lenient, to the Jansenists, either suggesting that the proposition was not by Jansenius, or that it was orthodox in the sense that Jansenius had meant to give it. The fourth proposition alone he judged severely.[2]

After the five propositions had been condemned in May 1653 Wadding rejected them whole-heartedly, though he said that he had at one time believed they might be maintained in a certain sense.[3]

He was, however, as it would seem, excluded secretly from the Congregation of the Inquisition for his leniency to the Jansenists[4] and his adversaries circulated all kinds of rumours at Rome about him—that he was so favourable to the Jansenists, because they paid him well and that he sold them his suffrage for 300 pistoles d'or which were used to build the fine library at St Isidore's, or at least were a kind of contribution towards it. He served the Jansenists well for their money, says the Jesuit Father Rapin, for besides expressing an opinion almost always favourable to their cause, he had the "audacity" to maintain that there was no trace of the fifth proposition in Jansenius, and thus was the first to embolden the Jansenists to say the same of the other propositions.[5]

The other Irishman in Rome whom the Jansenists considered a friend of theirs was the Dominican Father John Nolan. An account of a conference held between the Dominicans and the

1 Rapin, *Mémoires*, I, p. 459.
2 Saint-Amour, *Journal*, pp. 74, 132–3, 136, 205, 249, 364, 380 and *Appendix*, pp. 175, 178, 180, 182, 184 (Engl. transl. pp. 59, 106, 109, 161, 194, 283, 294 and *Appendix*, pp. 144, 148, 150, 152, 154); Gerberon, *op. cit.* II, pp. 46, 51, 57, 61, 64, 93, 124, 137; Rapin, *Mémoires*, I, p. 492; II, pp. 6, 15–17, 24, 31, 33, 53, 63, 67, 69, 71, 72, 83, 84, 102; Dumas, *Histoire des Cinq Propositions*, I, pp. 22, 27, 29.
3 Dumas, *op. cit.* p. 79; *Défense de l'Histoire des Cinq Propositions* (Liége 1701), pp. 188, 199–202.
4 Saint-Amour, *Journal*, p. 74 (Engl. transl. p. 59); Rapin, *Mémoires*, II, p. 50. Quite possibly this was due to his great age.
5 Rapin, *Mémoires*, I, p. 328; II, p. 40.

Molinist deputies at Rome early in 1653 on the question of efficacious and sufficient grace shows Nolan present and inclined to side with the Jansenists.[1]

A few months later came news of a startling nature. A letter from Rome dated November 23rd, 1653, reported, "Here is a Dominican fryar that taught in the Minerva divinity committed to the inquisition for being a favourite to the Jansenists"[2] and writing a few days later to Bellings Hyde confirmed the news, "An Irish Dominican, Father Nolan has been put into the Inquisition at Rome for writing somewhat in favour of Jansenius".[3]

Saint-Amour heard the news from "a good priest" who said that the imprisonment could be attributed to nothing but an absolute persecution by the enemies of Christ's grace.[4] Rapin, as usual, is ready with some details—according to him Nolan had distributed papers for the Jansenists after they left Rome, and had also written to the provincials of his order in France and in Flanders, saying that certain Jansenist interpretations of the five propositions were acceptable.[5] He died in the prison of the Inquisition in 1656.[6]

1 Saint-Amour, *Journal*, pp. 386–93 (Engl. transl. pp. 298–304). An account furnished to Saint-Amour by one of the Dominicans present: cf. Gerberon, *op. cit.* II, pp. 31, 97–120.
2 *Thurloe Papers*, I, p. 586, cf. p. 618.
3 *Cal. Clarendon Papers*, II, p. 282, Paris, Dec. 12, 1653. See also Des Lions, *Observations sur le Jansénisme*, quoted in Sainte-Beuve, *Port-Royal*, III, p. 592.
4 Saint-Amour, *Journal*, pp. 566–7 (Engl. transl. pp. 440–1) (Saint-Amour himself does not think that Nolan was imprisoned for his views on efficacious grace).
5 Rapin, *Mémoires*, II, pp. 138–9.
6 *Ib.* p. 64 *n.*

CHAPTER XIV

Ireland and Jansenism

T H E previous chapter has dealt with some of the Irish abroad. If we now come to Ireland itself we shall above all gain the impression that the Irish Catholics were much more on their guard against the "perils" of Jansenism than their brethren in England and Scotland. The general attitude is one of caution and watchfulness.

From January 8th to 11th, 1660, the Synod of Tuam met *in quodam refugii loco dictæ diœcesis,* and drew attention to the pitfalls of Jansenism. *Caveant omnes a Jansenismo, et novis aut suspectis opinionibus.* None might engage in any writings upon these without permission from the Bishop.¹ In October 1660 the provincial Synod of Armagh decreed that any who were suspect of Jansenism were excluded from all benefices, and, lest any might enter the fold like ravening wolves, the clergy requested with all due submission to the Holy See that none might be promoted without a recommendation from the Primate and the ordinary.²

At the time of the Restoration the question of Jansenism came up in a curious episode. It was thought advisable by a certain section of the Irish Catholics that they should come forward with some protestation of loyalty, and that by declaring unreserved allegiance to the king and rejecting the ultramontane principle of the Pope's right to temporal power they might dispel some of the prejudice engendered by their share in the Rebellion of 1641.³

This movement emanated from one who had been hostile to the Nuncio Rinuccini and the ultramontane party, Father Peter Walsh. A document known as the Irish Remonstrance or the

---

1 Renehan, *Collections*, p. 502.   2 *Spicilegium Ossoriense*, II, p. 197.
3 Butler, *Historical Memoirs*, III, p. 417; Bagwell, article on Peter Walsh in *D.N.B.*; Bagwell, *Ireland under the Stuarts*, III, ch. 43.

Loyal Formulary, not unlike the Oath of Allegiance in substance, was drawn up by Bellings,[1] another adversary of Rinuccini, and was signed by a small number of Irish priests and laymen. The Remonstrance was condemned by the Internuncio Vecchiis, Cardinal Barberini, the Theological Faculty at Louvain and others, because it contained propositions already condemned by the Holy See.[2]

Just about this time, or a little later—in 1663—the Sorbonne drew up a declaration in six articles which foreshadowed the later declaration of Gallican liberties.[3] We may note here incidentally, though it takes us away from Ireland for the moment, that Arnauld and his friends heard with interest of the English Catholics being made to swear "certains articles conformes à ceux de la Faculté de Paris touchant le pouvoir des rois indépendamment du pape". But they also heard that certain Cordeliers having accepted these articles, their superior in Flanders had sent one of the order to those in England, enjoining them to revoke their oath, and that the Lord Chancellor, hearing of this conduct "so contrary to royal authority", had let it be known that the Cordelier would be hanged as a spy unless he left London.

"Voilà ce que l'indiscretion de quelques personnes animées d'un faux zèle produisait en Angleterre", said the Jansenists, "au préjudice non seulement de l'État, mais même de la religion catholique qui n'y a jamais trouvé de plus grands obstacles que par la témérité de ces dévots indiscrets qui ne faisant point de scrupule de violer les justes bornes de la royauté et du sacerdoce, ont empêché dans ces Iles Britanniques la réunion des esprits, la réconciliation des cœurs autant de fois qu'il s'est trouvé des occasions favorables pour le rétablissement de la religion catholique."[4]

1 He adopted the Declaration inserted by Father Cressy in his *Exomologesis* (1647); Butler, *op. cit.* III, p. 418.

2 At the time that Bellings, the author of the Formulary, was soliciting a cardinal's hat for Aubigny a memorandum was drawn up at Rome enumerating Charles' services over against Roman Catholicism, "Quand fut publiée cette protestation des Irlandais, si contraire à l'obéissance due au Siège apostolique, il ne consentit jamais à la recevoir, ni à l'approuver" (quoted in *Études*, v, p. 202). What, one wonders, was the attitude of Bellings to this?

3 Lavisse, *Histoire de France*, VII[2], p. 18.

4 Hermant, *Mémoires*, VI, p. 300.

We resume our main narrative. A history of the Remonstrance would be out of place here; it will be sufficient for our purposes to remember that Walsh ultimately resolved to bring the matter before a national assembly of the clergy of Ireland. This congregation met in June 1666 and the Lord-Lieutenant, Ormonde, urged the assembled ecclesiastics to adopt not only the Remonstrance but the Gallican declarations of the Sorbonne. The original Remonstrance was, however, not acceptable to the Assembly, nor the last three declarations of the Sorbonne. The sixth one, "that it is not the Doctrine or Dogma of the Faculty that the Pope without the consent of the Church is infallible" was considered especially objectionable. "The Jansenists", said the Irish clergy, "held that way." As far as the Pope's infallibility in matters of religion and faith went, they were "loath that Forraign Catholick Nations" should think they wavered and that they treated of so odious and unprofitable a question in a country where they had neither University nor Jansenists, "if not perhaps some few Particulars whom they conceived to further this dispute in an underhand way".[1]

To this allusion to Jansenism Walsh took exception. He deprecated any reference to the Jansenists which brought in only irrelevant matter. No one but himself, Ormonde and Bellings, "that catholick and virtuous grave gentleman of quality", had "furthered the dispute". All they had done was above-board and not underhand. He had never heard of a single Jansenist among the Irish, nor anyone as much as suspected for such, except a chaplain to a lady of great virtue and quality who seemed to have been bred with those that were now by some called Jansenists, though he did not maintain their doctrine.

Did they mean Bellings? he asked. Though peradventure he might be the mark they aimed at, because he was known to have been befriended during his exile in France by one of those called Jansenists, though of his own country—a manifest allusion to Callaghan—Walsh was sure he was not a Jansenist, if by Jansenist was understood an abettor of the five propositions,

1 Walsh, *History and Vindication*, the Second Part of the First Treatise, pp. 689–90.

condemned in the sense in which they were condemned by the Church, and not one who had merely a good opinion of the many excellencies which he saw in those abusively called Jansenists, and so called only because they spoke reverently of the person of Jansenius and "wrote severely against many wicked Aphorismes of some Casuistes".

Did they mean him, Walsh? He had indeed the honour of some little personal acquaintance in his youth with that most illustrious and most reverend person Jansenius himself at Louvain some twenty-nine years ago. He had dedicated his theses to Jansenius, then Bishop-elect of Ypres, and Jansenius had honoured his philosophical public disputes with his presence at St Anthony of Padua's College there. He had made himself thoroughly acquainted with those opinions now called Jansenism, but this was in the writings and school dictates of Father John Barnewel, uncle of the present Lord of Trimlestown, some years before Jansenius wrote on the subject. Father Barnewel had taken up this matter by the advice of that great Augustinian Florentius Conrius, the titulary Archbishop of Tuam, the greatest Augustinian of the age, and by whom Jansenius was indoctrinated first in these principles, as they said. He admitted that he, Walsh, was one of the first that read the *Augustinus*, before it was bound and as it came from the Louvain press, yet he declared he was never concerned with Jansenism beyond wishing to know what was said on both sides, and he himself had never had the least tincture of a Jansenist.[1]

But all his protestations have not saved Walsh from being condemned as a Jansenist by Catholic historians[2] who see in his efforts to induce the Irish clergy to accept his Remonstrance "an attempt to realize in practice the teachings of Jansenius",[3] and indeed even Ormonde remarked in speaking of Walsh's book, "The doctrine is such as would cost him his life, if he could be found where the Pope has power".[4]

1 Walsh, *History and Vindication*, Fourth Treatise, pp. 52–76. The fourth treatise does not seem to be found in all copies of the *History*. The copy, 186, c. 4, at the B.M. does not contain it, the copy G. 5429 does.
2 E.g. Cardinal Moran.   3 Moran, *Memoirs of Plunket*, p. 251.
4 Bagwell, *Ireland under the Stuarts*, III, p. 65.

Two or three years later, in 1668, one finds an appeal addressed to Clement IX to have bishops appointed to the vacant sees in Ireland, especially at this time when "there were some who now sought to Introduce and disseminate Jansenism".[1] All possible precautions were taken to hinder the spread of the heresy. In 1669 it was rumoured that Dr Kelly, whom we have seen as the friend of Bernières and Singlin in Paris, was aspiring to a bishopric in Ireland, but unfavourable reports from the nuncio in France ended the matter. Kelly was a rabid Jansenist, he said, he had always upheld the party of the four bishops and was one of the most hostile to the Holy See. The Jansenists in Paris thought they could introduce Jansenism into Ireland, hence they were trying to get Kelly made a bishop, and money and recommendations from the Jansenists were forthcoming. According to the nuncio one of Kelly's relatives and a sharer in his beliefs, Daniel Rion, was also aspiring to a bishopric.[2] The Synods of Clones in 1670 and of Ardpatrick in 1678 thought it necessary to take up the question of Jansenism.[3]

Dr Plunket, Primate of Ireland, wrote in March 1677 to Cardinal Altieri, Cardinal Protector of Ireland, asking for some remedy *ne Regnum hoc Jansenistarum deliriis inficiatur*.[4] Though the edicts of the English Parliament filled them with alarm, yet the Irish Catholics were far more terrified, he said, "by the spiritual calamities which seemed impending from the remains of Jansenism, and the novelties which continued yet to spread in France and Belgium", for it was from various parts of these countries that spiritual labourers came to cultivate this vineyard.[5]

News must have reached the Irish priests in France that the spread of Jansenism was attributed to some of them, for already before this date they had protested against the accusations. *Non sine gravi animi dolore intellexerint se traductos, ac tam in urbe quam extra insimulatos Jansenismi*.[6]

1 Moran, *Plunket*, p. 250. The appeal was made by Gerard Ferrall, afterwards Vicar-Apostolic of Ardagh, when agent of the Archbishop of Armagh in Rome.
2 Bellesheim, *Geschichte*, ii, p. 609.   3 *Ib.* p. 608; Moran, *Plunket*, p. 251.
4 Bellesheim, *op. cit.* ii, pp. 608–9; Moran, *loc. cit.*   5 Moran, *loc. cit.*
6 *Spicilegium Ossoriense*, ii, pp. 219–21, Aug. 26, 1676, 38 signatures.

PLATE V

THE COLLÈGE DES ÉCOSSAIS

In the letter we have just mentioned Plunket enumerates the teachings of the innovators which fill him with such anxiety, their doctrines

concerning the infallibility of the Roman Pontiff—the authority of St Augustine, as if it were superior to the definitions of Rome—the invalidity of absolution without the perfect love of God—the necessity of reforming in many things the worship of God, of the Blessed Virgin, and the saints—reproving frequent recourse to the sacraments of penance—deferring absolution solely on account of relapse or any grievous sin (which gradually defers the faithful from approaching this sacrament)—reproving the custom of seeking absolution of mere venial sins—declaring that invincible ignorance of the natural law can never excuse from sin—and that works of virtue, unless they proceed from the pure love of God, are never free from sin, and not only do not tend to our salvation, but are absolutely vicious.[1]

A letter from Dr Brennan, then Bishop of Waterford, written about this time from his "place of refuge in Ireland", voices the same complaints.[2] Inquiries were made from Rome, particularly with regard to possible Jansenist books in circulation in Ireland, and Dr Brennan, now Archbishop of Cashel, sent back an interesting reply in 1678.

We find here the New Testament, printed in France in the French language, and having various errors contrary to the Vulgate and to the Catholic religion. Another work is also met with, entitled 'On frequent Communion', printed in French, and translated into English, having errors contrary to true devotion, and the practices of Holy Church. There is also the Mass, printed in French and newly translated into English.

The New Testament in French has not as yet come into my hands; I had, however, the Mass in French, and I made a seizure on it. I saw the book on frequent Communion, and though I could not get possession of it, yet I prohibited its being read. It is true however that these books are but very few in these parts, and I am not wanting in being ever on my guard, lest they should be introduced or published here.

As to the followers of the errors of Jansenius, thanks to God they

---

1 Moran, *Plunket*, p. 251.   2 *Ib.* p. 253.

are but few in this country. There was one regular who was deeply tinged with these errors, but I acted severely with him, and imposed silence on him, so that he retracted, and has become observant.

For this reason, and because he was a foreigner, Dr Brennan refrains from giving his name, nor does he give the names of another religious and two secular priests " of the same hue ", they having already departed this life. "For the future", he concludes, " in consequence of the great vigilance and circumspection which are used, we hope that God may be served here *in veritate et sinceritate doctrinæ.*"[1]

Accusations were also brought against Cornelius Daly, a doctor of the University of Paris; however, at Dr Plunket's desire, he signed a formulary condemning Jansenism in 1678.[2]

The Synod of Cashel in 1685 still drew attention to the dangers of the new opinions,[3] but for the next few years little or nothing is heard of Jansenism in Ireland, though when the question arose of the famous Michael Moor becoming provost of Trinity College, Dublin, it was said that he was "a person suspected for Jansenism and twice forced to abjure that heresy".[4]

As in all other countries Jansenism comes to the fore again at the beginning of the eighteenth century with renewed outcries, renewed vigilance, renewed protestations of orthodoxy. Some of the Irish clergy living at Prunay near Chartres send a letter to the Pope in 1704 rejoicing in their security under the Bishop of Chartres—*nulla hic Janseniana lues, nulla Quietistarum corruptela, nullus satan aut occursus malus,*[5] yet about this time, so it was said, the perils that beset the Catholic Church in Ireland arose from Jansenist rather than from Protestant sources, for there came some to Ireland imbued with the doctrines of Jansenius, and translations of Jansenist books began to circulate afresh.[6] A papal brief warned the English, Scotch and Irish in 1709, as we have seen, of the dangers of the innovations

1 Moran, *Plunket*, pp. 253–4.
2 *Ib.* pp. 254–5, see also p. 92.
3 Renehan, *Collections*, p. 463.
4 *Hist. MSS. Comm., Stuart MSS. at Windsor Castle*, VI, pp. 26–7 (1687).
5 *Spicilegium Ossoriense*, II, p. 379.
6 Burke, *Hibernia Dominicana*, pp. 160, 168–9; Polidori, *De Vita et Rebus Gestis Clementis XI*, p. 215: cf. Moran, *Plunket*, p. 256.

and drew attention to the Bull *Vineam Domini* recently promulgated.[1]

We come now to a very curious episode that has sometimes been declared impossible by Roman Catholic writers,[2] namely the ordination of twelve young Dutchmen by Luke Fagan, Bishop of Meath. Codde, the Archbishop of Utrecht,[3] had been deposed for Jansenism at the beginning of the eighteenth century by Clement XI who gave his place to Theodore de Cock.[4] After Codde's death in 1710 the Chapter of Utrecht, which had supported him throughout, considered the see vacant and governed the diocese. The Church was regarded as schismatic, and it proved wellnigh impossible to find anyone on the continent willing to ordain their priests. For almost fifteen years there had been no ordination in the Church of Utrecht. A certain Irish ecclesiastic by the name of Marison,[5] who had visited some of the chief members of the Chapter of Utrecht, Van Heussen and Van Erkel, in 1714, thought he could procure relief from Ireland. Various obstacles and "dangers" prevented him from getting to Ireland at once, but in the summer of 1714 he was, as we have related, in London and saw Bishop Giffard who, according to him, was touched by the plight of the Church of Utrecht. He also saw another member of the Roman Catholic clergy—Gerald Saltmarsh in all probability—who had been Van Erkel's guest in Holland and who sent him his greetings.[6]

In November of this same year Marison was at Antwerp, not yet successful in his enterprise, though hopeful of its outcome.[7] He must have persevered in his negotiations, for in the spring of

---

1 *Bullarium...S. Congregationis d' Propaganda Fide*, I, App. p. 384 (quoted in Bellesheim, *op. cit.* III, p. 72).

2 E.g. Moran, *Plunket*, p. 258; Bellesheim, *op. cit.* III, p. 88.

3 Under the title of Archbishop of Sebaste.

4 Subsequently exiled by the States-General.

5 It is sometimes said that Marison and a certain Paul Kenny are one and the same person, but this is not the case.

6 *Première Lettre de M. Marison, Prêtre Missionnaire d'Irlande à M. Van Erkel*, London, Aug. 13, 1714, *Recueil de divers Témoignages*, pp. 122–3 (original in the archives of the Chapter of Utrecht).

7 *Deuxième Lettre du même au même*, Antwerp, Nov. 11, 1714, *ib.* pp. 123–5 (original in the archives of the Chapter of Utrecht).

14-2

1715 three young Dutchmen were ordained in Ireland[1] upon letters dimissory from the vicar-general of the Chapter of Utrecht, Van Heussen, and other ordinations were to follow. But Marison, who was in Dublin in the winter of 1715–16, found it not altogether easy to prevail on "the Merchant"— the name used for Bishop Fagan in this correspondence—to continue his "business" with the Dutch "merchants". The Merchant had made inquiries and had been misinformed by some one not well versed in the affairs of the Dutch merchants. "Il en est si frappé qu'il n'y a pas moyen de le guérir de sa crainte." It might even be necessary to have recourse to another merchant "de meilleure composition", only he lived far away and it was difficult to reach him in winter.[2]

This last letter from Marison was opened unbeknown to him, and Bishop Fagan's secretary, Paul Kenny, added a postscript: Marison was zealous but indiscreet. "Il témoigne beaucoup de passion et cela gâte tout." There were certain things which the Chief Merchant did not wish him to know.[3]

In April of this year, 1716, Kenny wrote again from Dublin. The Merchant was displeased because others had been informed of the affair, in particular M. Barnaval who is presumably the Matthew Barnewall liberated a short time previously from the Bastille where he had been imprisoned for spreading Jansenist books.[4] Kenny had begged and besought the young merchants not to talk, he had impressed them with the saying *frustra sit per plura quod potest per pauciora*. His advice had not been followed, "d'où vient que toute notre affaire est gâtée". After declaring several times that he would do nothing whatever without the formulary, the Merchant had at last consented to accept the signature modified by the following explanatory clause: *nimirum sensum ab autore intentum esse sensum verborum ut jacent, vel sonant; et extractas ex Libro Jansenii, vel esse in Libro Jansenii non cadere sub*

1 See a letter of ordination on p. 276 of this book.
2 *Troisième Lettre du même au même*, Dublin, Feb. 11, 1715/16, *Recueil de divers Témoignages*, pp. 125–6 (original in the archives).
3 *Ib.* This Paul Kenny is variously called Paul Kenny van der Cruys or de la Croix, and is described as Prior of the Discalced Carmelites of Dublin.
4 More will be said of him in another chapter.

juramento, sed tantum supponi. Any who came must be prepared to subscribe the formulary with this addition.[1]

In June things were no further advanced and Kenny thought of applying to another Merchant. *Valde enim timidus et scrupulosus est Mercator noster.*[2] Nor had any progress been made in July.[3] But a fourth and last ordination did take place in September. Altogether twelve ecclesiastics had been ordained at four different times.[4] A little manuscript diary preserved in the archives of the Chapter of Utrecht tells of the experiences of one of the groups—*Reisverhaal van den Hr Priem met andere Geestelijken naar Ierland.*[5]

Among those ordained in Ireland was Jerome de Bock, later Bishop of Haarlem, another was Peter John Meindaerts, a future Archbishop of Utrecht. Young Meindaerts was one of those who went to Ireland in the late summer of 1716. The voyage was very rough and fraught with all kinds of dangers, and hardly had they landed when they were arrested as spies in the service of the Pretender. They were closely questioned and the object of their expedition was in danger of being discovered, "et cet aveu n'était pas de nature à les tirer d'embarras dans un pays comme celui-là". Fortunately the officer who examined them had been at Louvain and he recognized by their answers that they had really studied there. Meindaerts, the only one of the company who knew French and a little English, was the spokesman and he talked to the officer of the various customs of the town of Louvain, especially of the honours shown to the student who carried off the prize of "Premier de Louvain", a distinction which had befallen one of his companions a few years before. The officer was satisfied, took them to be young men travelling to satisfy their curiosity, and let them go. Other obstacles were

1 *Deuxième Lettre de Kenny à Van Erkel*, Dublin, April 4, 1716, *Recueil de divers Témoignages*, p. 127.
2 *Epistola tertia*, A Dublin Junii die 2, 1716. *Ib.*
3 *Ib.*
4 *Ib.* p. 128, where the names of the twelve are given. From a deeply grateful letter of thanks from Van Heussen to Fagan, dated Oct. 26, 1715 (in the archives of the Chapter of Utrecht) one gathers that a group was sent about this time.
5 Sixty-six closely written pages. Begun by H. Stalderwijk who died, continued by G. Priem.

encountered, but the expedition was finally crowned with success.[1]

Bishop Fagan continued to be haunted by fear and scruples. He was well, wrote Kenny about a year after the last ordination, *sed in magna anxietate propter timorem*, and he entreated them that the promise—of secrecy no doubt—might be kept.[2] A few months later Fagan himself wrote to Van Heussen in some agitation. Letters had come to the principal Merchants of the kingdom ordering an investigation, and if the Merchant guilty of having perpetrated a certain crime could be found he was to be punished. The Merchant, although he believed he had performed a thing acceptable to God, was deeply perplexed and begged Van Heussen to let him know whether there was any danger of discovery. He had acted in all good faith, desiring only the preservation and propagation of the clerical state. God grant that it had been accomplished by legitimate means, as he thought.[3] "Vous voyez ce que le marchand a écrit de sa propre main", writes Kenny on the same sheet of paper, and he urges that the utmost secrecy be observed.

By way of conclusion to this episode a curious anecdote is often related, but even Jansenist writers give it as a mere rumour. A report went abroad that an Irish bishop had consecrated some Dutch Jansenists, and Fagan, then Archbishop of Dublin, so the story goes, was ordered to make inquiries. He assembled all his suffragans, questioned them, and was able to report to Rome that none of them was guilty.[4]

An allusion to the ordinations is also found in a non-Jansenist source—a manuscript account of the Jansenist clergy in Holland referring to them in 1753. The anonymous author who is hostile to the Jansenists relates that an Irish priest travelling in Holland pointed out that Jansenism and the five propositions

1 *Nouv. ecclés.* 1768, p. 77 (Nécrologe de Meindaerts).
2 *Recueil de divers Témoignages*, p. 127, Sept. 1717.
3 Archives of the Chapter of Utrecht. Letters to Van Heussen. Latin autograph letter, unsigned, but endorsed in another hand "Mercator magnus". Dated by Kenny in his postscript Feb. 11, 1717/18. Catalogued as being from Fagan.
4 Besides the various authorities already given see for the whole of this episode Du Pac de Bellegarde, *Histoire abrégée de l'Église Métropolitaine d'Utrecht*, pp. 445–8.

were unknown in Ireland, and that all the clergy needed to do was to send their candidates to Ireland where they would be ordained without the slightest difficulty. "Caravans" of young ecclesiastics went across, but the great expense incurred proved an obstacle.[1] Now Jansenism was known in Ireland, as we have seen, and the ordinations could not have taken place as casually as the author suggests, but the fact that he does speak of the ordinations shows that the story was common knowledge in Utrecht where he lived for some months.

But to return to Ireland. In 1719 the prelates were urged through the Internuncio Santini of Brussels to make a stand and to signify their acceptance of the Bull *Unigenitus*. The Archbishop of Cashel, Christopher Butler, replying to this letter expressed his conviction that not one of them would be found who would not subscribe to the constitution without any mental reservation. "Neither by us, or by our clergy, or by our people", he writes, "have any of those profane and novel terms, *religious silence* or the *question of right and fact* been adopted; nor have those infamous books been known...unless perhaps by name to the greater part of our nation."[2] His Pastoral entitled the *Psalter of Cashel* deals with the Bull *Unigenitus*.[3]

No doubt the general orthodoxy in Ireland was closely connected with the marked orthodoxy of the Irish College in Paris. A report sent in by the Nuncio Dolci in 1736 expresses distrust of the superiors of the Scots College, but affirms that in the Irish College, composed of about a hundred persons, none but the most sound doctrine is taught. Of some two hundred Irish priests in the city and diocese of Paris scarcely two or three have appealed, and these are held in execration by all the others of the nation.[4]

1 Bibliothèque Mazarine, MS. 2504, pièce 21, p. 4.
2 Burke, *Hibernia Dominicana*, App. p. 819. See also Moran, *Spicilegium Ossoriense*, III, p. 132, where Archbishop MacMahon of Armagh speaks of the universal acceptance of the Bull *Unigenitus*.
3 Renehan, *Collections*, p. 305.
4 Archiv. Vatic. Nunz. di Francia, vol. 261 (quoted in Bellesheim, *op. cit.* III, pp. 113, 745–6). One finds the Cardinal de Noailles exclaiming impatiently in 1706 that the nuns of Port Royal ought to have as their confessor "quelque Irlandois qui n'entendît pas le français de peur qu'il ne se gâtât avec elles",

The Jansenist Carré de Montgéron, chronicler of the miracles, declares that most of the priests at the Hôtel-Dieu are Irish and "Constitutionnaires outrés".[1] The lists of appellants published in the three folio volumes of *La Constitution Unigenitus déférée à l'Église Universelle* scarce have an Irish name.[2] One rarely finds an Irishman believing in the Convulsionaries as did the Abbé Matthew Barnewall,[3] or one who, like the appellant "M. [Malachie] Magerraghty, Irlandois", is described by the *Nouvelles ecclésiastiques* as "attaché de tout temps à la vérité".[4] On the other hand there are frequent hostile references in this Jansenist paper to the Irish students and their Sorbonne theses "se déchainans contre Jansenius et les Appellans",[5] "infectées du plus pur Molinisme.... Déclamations contre Jansenius et les Appellants",[6] "traitant d'une manière indigne la Doctrine de St Augustin",[7] "déclamant contre les Appellants, contre M. de Pâris et les Miracles",[8] "accusations contre Jansenius et Quesnel",[9] "Macperlant, Prêtre Irlandois... d'une théologie aussi mince que sa figure.... Esclave des Jésuites".[10]

The Irish ecclesiastics adhere throughout to the Bull *Unigenitus* and every now and again they encounter the hostility of the Parlement of Paris, for now Jansenism was becoming increasingly political in nature and linked with Gallicanism.

[Pinault] *Histoire abrégée de la dernière persécution* (1750, 3 vols.), 1, p. 344, a statement which the Jansenist Guilbert takes literally, for he writes with some irritation in his *Mémoires*, "Un Hibernois étoit en effet un homme très-propre à ergotiser l'infaillibilité mais peu propre à entendre le langage des Religieuses. Cet idiome lui auroit été plus étranger que celui de la Cochinchine. Il fallut... abandonner cette idée Hibernique", v, p. 23.

1 Carré de Montgéron, *La Vérité des Miracles*, II, Observations sur les Convulsionnaires, Deuxième Partie, p. 43.

2 There is a "Petrus Butlery" who appealed in 1718, "Hiberniæ Presbyter ad præsens pro fide catholica profugus" (*La Constitution Unigenitus déférée*, I, p. 234); a certain Flannery, "Irlandois", who appealed in 1717 with other doctors of the Faculté Théologique de Nantes, but he ultimately revoked his appeal (I, pp. 178-9). Possibly the appellants "Mackivorly" and Macarty were Irish too (I, p. 257; Suite au Tome Premier, p. 72).

3 See p. 251 of this book.

4 *Nouv. ecclés.* 1748, p. 110; 1749, p. 99. For his appeal see *La Constitution Unigenitus déférée*, I, pp. 90, 550; Suite au Tome Premier, p. 59.

5 Heli, "Prêtre Ibernois", *Nouv. ecclés.* 1733, p. 106.

6 Fitzgerald, Kearney, Hanharan, *ib.* 1734, p. 141.

7 Hanharan, Madgett, *ib.* 1733, p. 158.   8 Hanharan, *ib.* 1733, p. 22.

9 Finaughti, *ib.* 1731, p. 207.   10 *Ib.* 1757, p. 120, see also 1747, p. 87.

"Le sieur Finaughty, Hibernois" was obliged to withdraw a thesis in 1731 for his reference to the Bull.[1] A thesis presented to the Sorbonne in July 1732 by le Sieur Madgett, "prêtre hybernois", was denounced in August to the Parlement by a zealous magistrate as dangerous and contrary to the decisions of the Parlement concerning the Bull.[2] In the following year another thesis by Madgett was stopped by order of the Chancellor who took exception to what was said about the infallibility of the Pope.[3] Some of the French students inquiring of the Irish why they did not in their theses uphold the four famous propositions of the clergy affirming the liberties of the Gallican Church, they replied that they would no longer be considered Catholic in their own country, were they to do so.[4] Madgett excused himself by saying that he had not had time to study these matters. "Cela pourrait être," assents the Jansenist paper, "car cet étranger, ennemi pour ainsi dire par état de nos Libertés, est pourvu d'un emploi qui peut lui dérober beaucoup de temps"—he had been entrusted with the instruction of the young at the Collège de Sainte-Barbe, now reformed and no longer Jansenist.[5]

A move was made to oblige all Irish students to uphold the four propositions of the clergy in their theses, but was defeated.[6] In 1733 the Parlement of Paris suppressed a thesis defended by "Jean Hanharan, Prêtre Irlandois de Nation" as dangerous and capable of fomenting discord, a thesis also not in keeping with the liberties of the Gallican Church. The Syndic of the Faculty of Theology, Romigny, the Dean Leuillier and Hanharan were summoned. The Irishman attempted to justify his thesis, but fortunately for him, so the *Nouvelles ecclésiastiques* report, his "baragouin hybernois" was not understood.[7]

A new storm arose when the Parlement declared in 1755 that the Bull *Unigenitus* had neither the character nor the consequences of a tenet of faith, and enjoined all ecclesiastics to observe silence with regard to the Bull.[8] An Irish priest was imprisoned at the

1 *Ib.* 1731, p. 207.   2 *Ib.* 1732, pp. 162–3, 165–6, 173.
3 *Ib.* 1733, p. 158.   4 *Ib.*   5 *Ib.*
6 *Ib.* p. 159.   7 *Ib.* pp. 22–3.
8 Cf. Lavisse, *Histoire de France*, VIII², p. 241.

Conciergerie this year for having "tormented a woman with the formulary and the Bull without understanding the matter himself", but he was liberated on declaring his submission.[1]

In 1758 M. de Jarente, Bishop of Orleans, was set to deal with some of the "docteurs fanatiques" who had contravened "la Loi du Silence". Three Irish doctors—their names are given as "Brady, Heneguand et Stafort"—were among those summoned to the Louvre. The prelate asked them whether, having found a place of refuge in the kingdom of France, they did not think themselves obliged to conform to the laws established there? They replied that since they sent out missionaries to remote regions, especially to Ireland—one infers that they were connected with the Irish College—they had to form them in the Catholic faith and instruct them in the Bull *Unigenitus*. "Remarquons bien cette conséquence", exclaims the Jansenist chronicler, "et souvenons-nous que la Bulle Unigenitus ne peut avoir ni la dénomination ni le caractère ni les effets de Règle de Foi. L'Irlande ne sera-t-elle pas bien instruite par de tels Missionnaires avec une pareille Bulle?"[2]

Some doctors of the Sorbonne, partisans of the Bull and unwilling to conform to the so-called law of silence, refused to let students proceed to the theses called "majeures" and "Sorboniques" until Baïanism, Jansenism and Quesnellism could be freely mentioned again.[3] They hoped thereby to force the king to revoke the edict, but orders were sent by him to have all students and professors proceed with their work.[4] One finds an Irish student, "le Sieur Hallarang, Hibernois", and another young man, distributing letters to their fellow-students, urging them to refrain from all "exercices de licence", in spite of the king's orders, and this for the good of religion and the honour of the faculty ("c'est-à-dire pour la Constitution Unigenitus" is the explanation). The students were exiled from Paris, but the *Nouvelles ecclésiastiques*, finding that their action had had some effect, think the punishment very slight.[5]

A thesis to be defended in 1760 by an Irishman called Ferris

1 *Nouv. ecclés.* 1756, p. 30.   2 *Ib.* 1758, p. 62.
3 *Ib.* p. 81.   4 *Ib.* p. 89.   5 *Ib.* pp. 89–90.

was not admitted on account of its references to Jansenism. The professor who was to have presided over this exercise was summoned before the magistrates and was forbidden to let the candidate proceed, for the Parlement still showed itself hostile to those who would not keep quiet on controversial questions.[1]

The Irish in Paris with hardly an exception belong to the party that the *Nouvelles ecclésiastiques* call the *zelanti*, and the contemptuous attitude of the paper with regard to the Irish is explained by the fact that throughout the century they are practically always to be found on the side of the Bull *Unigenitus*.[2]

1 *Ib.* 1760, p. 109. Other hostile references to Irish ecclesiastics: Macarti, *ib.* 1730, pp. 166, 210; Brisland, *ib.* 1751, p. 156.

2 Very many years later, however, in the time of Scipione dei Ricci, some young Irish ecclesiastics came under the influence of the Italian Jansenist Tamburini who "appeared to have infused the poison of his errors into their minds". "The return of these young men to Ireland", writes Cardinal Moran, "excited considerable alarm.... Great vigilance was adopted with regard to these young men, and when Pius VI had published in 1794 his Constitution *Auctorem Fidei*, in which he condemned the acts of the synod of Pistoja the bishops of Ireland...hastened to return their thanks to the Holy See for its final condemnation of the pestiferous errors of Jansenism", Moran, *Plunket*, pp. 391–2. Préclin, *Les Jansénistes du 18e siècle*, mentions a certain Dom Étienne O'Sullivan who is doubtless of Irish origin (p. 408). At Louvain, at the end of the seventeenth and beginning of the eighteenth century, the adversaries of the formulary, especially the well-known Dr Hennebel, encountered as an opponent a certain Dr Martin, an Irishman, but there seem also to have been Irishmen who sided with Hennebel. The Archbishop of Malines forbade the following book: *Amici Hiberni ad Amicum Doctorem Martin Hibernum correptio fraterna, super imprudentissimis e audacissimis reflexionibus, quas nuper edidit in Declarationem Doctoris Hennebelli*, Leodii...1701 (*Hist. du Cas de Conscience*, II, p. 335, see also I, p. 319; VII, p. 222; *Dictionnaire des Livres Jansénistes*, I, p. 347; Arnauld, *Œuvres*, III, pp. 205, 304, 346, 347, 385, 639).

CHAPTER XV

Arnauld and England

THE ROYAL FAMILY AT SAINT-GERMAIN

"Sr,
Your kind advertisement of the 18th is the first notice that ever any French author had mentioned my name", writes Sir Robert Southwell in November 1682 to Thomas Henshaw, the King's "Under-Secretary of the French tongue". He did not seem greatly concerned by the news that the author spoke ill of him. "If I never have any other Accuser then a French Papist and my crime lye not on this side Dover I may live long Enough without holding up my hand at the Barr." Since the French book was concerned with the Popish Plot, Southwell could scarcely expect to avoid notice. "Indeed, the Name of Monsr Arnold if He be the Author of the Book you mention is considerable and if He Involve the whole English Nation, the Parliamt, Judges and Kings Council in a depraved Infatuation as to the late Plott, it were hard if I only should Escape." However, there was one consolation—Arnauld was a Jansenist, "'tis to be hoped that the Jesuits at least will not believe him".[1]

Other Englishmen too had noticed the book,[2] and the pious Mr Nelson, who was to achieve a reputation during the reign of Queen Anne for his religious writings, heard about the work from Dean Tillotson, the future Archbishop of Canterbury. The dean had not read it yet, but wondered that "so wise a man should think fit to intermeddle in the affairs of another country and of which he could but have a partial information".[3]

1 B.M. Add. MSS. 38015, f. 278 (Nov. 22, 1682).
2 R.O. *S.P. France*, vol. 144, f. 50, Lord Preston to Sir Leoline Jenkins, June 7, 1682.
3 Birch, T., *Life of Dr John Tillotson, Archbishop of Canterbury* (1752), pp. 94–5, July 5, 1682.

The book in question was Arnauld's *Apologie des Catholiques*, a reply to Jurieu's *Politique du Clergé de France*. Jurieu had imputed a seditious spirit to the Catholics, had expressed his belief in the genuineness of the Popish Plot and had spoken with hostility of the Catholics of England. Arnauld therefore rushed into the fray and wrote to show that the Plot was a mere invention of Titus Oates.

Arnauld had withdrawn to Holland by this time, and it was to Utrecht that M. de Pontchâteau had brought him various pamphlets concerning the English Catholics. The first volume of the *Apologie* was finished here about Easter 1681. In summer he moved to Delft where other "Mémoires" reached him, in particular translations of English books which were sent from Amsterdam, and here he composed the second part of his book,[1] amid all the rigours of exile, as his friends said, *vix habens ubi caput reclinet*.[2] His friends also admired the generosity with which he defended the Jesuits of England, and Leibniz, writing to the Landgrave of Hesse, remarked that surely nothing but the love of truth could have induced Arnauld to undertake this work, for it was not incumbent on the Jansenists to justify the Jesuits;[3] and others remarked later ironically that the Jesuits had repaid him well for his trouble.[4]

Arnauld had planned a third part to his *Apologie*, giving new details about the Plot, and he was anxious to obtain further documents. M. de Neercassel transmitted his request to a French ecclesiastic living at The Hague, and he in turn passed it on to the comte d'Avaux from whom it finally went to Barillon, then ambassador in England, but Barillon regretted his inability to send any *éclaircissements*. "J'honore infiniment la personne dont l'ami vous a parlé," he replies, "mais les matières dont il est question, sont si difficiles à expliquer à fond que cela même

1 Guelphe, *Relation de la Retraite de M. Arnauld*, pp. 33–5.
2 Arnauld, *Œuvres*, XII, p. lix (Neercassel to Bossuet).
3 *Ib.* p. lx.
4 *Ib.* IV, p. 186; Quesnel, *Histoire abrégée de la vie et des ouvrages de M. Arnauld*, pp. 184–8: cf. Dodd, *Secret Policy*, p. 24: "Arnauld the very reverse of a Jesuit was so charitable as to plead eloquently in a learned Book, in Defence of your Fathers accused of the Popish Plot (for which he was well repaid by you)". For the fate of the book in France see Arnauld, *Œuvres*, XII, p. lxv.

222 ARNAULD AND ENGLAND

ne peut se bien faire que de vive voix."[1] Nor was Cardinal
Howard able to help Arnauld.[2]

Southwell, naturally curious, procured himself the *Apologie*,
and was somewhat amazed by the allegations brought against
him; in view of "Mons[r] Arnold's high Fame in the World for
learning and veracity...it looks almost unmannerly in mee to
differ from him", he writes, "yet I am encouraged herein by a
Suspition that he's not the Author of the Book, for he's not
versed in the ways of scurrilous language that becomes not a
gentleman. He always contents himself with demonstration and
observes the rule of Suaviter in Modo et Fortiter in Re".[3]

When Southwell discovered that the author was really
Arnauld, and finding himself "very coarsely handled", he spoke
to the Duke of York who advised him how to proceed "with
the old gentleman". "He doubted not", says Southwell, "that
if I fairly undeceived him he would make me reparation."[4] A
complaint was put before the learned Justel, then in London,
and he sent it on to Arnauld through the intermediary of a
friend. Arnauld declared himself very ready to set matters right,
if he had been misinformed, and upon Justel's sending him
copies of certain documents[5] he printed an *Éclaircissement* to
correct his book.[6] A number of these *Éclaircissements* were dispatched to London, and almost two hundred copies went to
Sir William Trumbull in France. "I wish", says Southwell,
"that this justification should be read at Paris where the book
has been much discussed."[7]

Arnauld wrote Southwell a letter of apology, remarkable for
its beautiful simplicity and dignity, a letter which Southwell
acknowledged with as much pleasure as surprise, it being, he
said, most extraordinary to find people who preferred the love

1 Arnauld, *Œuvres*, pp. lxviii–lxix, and IV, pp. 169–70. 2 *Ib.* XII, p. lxix.
3 B.M. Add. MSS. 38015, ff. 283–4, Jan. 9, 1682/3, to Mr Henshaw.
4 *Hist. MSS. Comm.*, *MSS. of the Marquis of Downshire*, I, Part I, p. 158: cf.
Quesnel, *loc. cit.*; Racine (abbé), *Hist. ecclés.* XI, pp. 377–8.
5 Arnauld, *Œuvres*, II, p. 528; XII, p. lxiii.
6 *Addition à l'Apologie*, 38 pp., bound with vol. I of the copy of the *Apologie*
at the Bibliothèque Nationale.
7 *Hist. MSS. Comm.*, *MSS. of the Marquis of Downshire*, I, Part I, pp. 156, 158
(Southwell to Sir W. Trumbull, April 22 and 24, 1686).

of truth to their reputation. The Duke of York, now become king, asked to see the letter, kept it for a whole day, and on returning it said it was a beautiful letter and such as one would expect from Monsieur Arnauld.[1] He read Arnauld's pamphlet with much satisfaction and sent him expressions of his friendship through a certain "Mr Fraiser", who was also commanded to thank Arnauld for the various books and "petits traittez" he sent the king from time to time. One wonders whether the king's spiritual adviser knew of this friendship, and whether he was aware that the king read Arnauld's books "with the pleasure and satisfaction that everything coming from Arnauld's pen merited". Nay more, James was going to provide for Arnauld in England. "Sa Majesté fait son possible de trouver une condition et un établissement digne de l'estime qu'elle a pour vous et en peu de tems ne doute pas de vous en pouvoir faire la proposition." In the meantime he was having a search made for some papers and documents to be sent to Arnauld, for he intended to put his pen to use.[2]

Arnauld declined the offer of an establishment on account of his advanced age, but continued to show an almost touching devotion to James whom he probably knew since the early days when Port Royal had befriended the Stuart exiles. He noted with anxiety the clouds gathering on the horizon and the coming of the storm.[3] In his eagerness one even finds him exclaiming, "Que l'on crie tant qu'on voudra contre la France, mais je ne saurais souffrir ces injustes plaintes contre S.M.B.!"[4] He gave up writing for a time to the Landgrave of Hesse, because the latter did not share his feelings for the King of England.[5] In his eyes James had all the virtues, and perhaps his only failing was the number of unwise favours accorded to the Jesuit Father, "le P. Peters"[6], which, so Arnauld understood from some English priests, was extremely prejudicial to reunion with the Protestants.[7]

1 Letter printed in *Addition à l'Apologie*, p. 36.
2 Arnauld, *Œuvres*, II, pp. 669–70, April 18 (O.S.), 1686. For Arnauld's reply see pp. 670–1.
3 *Ib.* III, pp. 150, 152–3, 155–9, 161, 163–7, 170–7, 182, 184–6, 188, 190, 192, 194, 199, 202, 204, 206, 208–9.
4 *Ib.* p. 203, May 13, 1689.   5 *Ib.* p. 174, cf. p. 220.
6 *Ib.* pp. 146, 167, 171, 208–9, 222.   7 *Ib.* II, p. 719.

At length the disaster was complete and William established on the throne of England. With a fire unusual in an old man of seventy-seven, but perhaps less astonishing in one to whom polemics and controversies were second nature, Arnauld turned upon William and produced a violent diatribe in which the usurper was made to play the combined parts of the most horrid monsters of history—*Le Prince d'Orange, nouvel Absalon, nouvel Hérode, nouveau Néron, nouveau Cromwel.*[1]

The book itself brought further trouble on the exiled and ever undiplomatic author. "Ce fut alors qu'il se trouva dans la plus grande extrémité où il se fut trouvé de sa vie", exclaims Racine. He had to leave Holland and went into hiding in a little village near Liége, while the Prince of Orange, so we are told, demanded of his allies not to tolerate the doctor in their dominions. France was closed to him. Brussels was possible for a year with the connivance of the governor-general, but even here safety came to an end.[2]

Yet amid his own tribulations Arnauld continued to be pre-occupied with the fate of James. His possible abandonment by the French filled him with consternation and incredulity. When M. du Vaucel told him that according to many people France would not make much difficulty "de laisser là le Roi Jacques" if an advantageous peace could be made with Spain and the Empire, he was bewildered. If it meant that the French would not make the restoration of James an essential condition of peace, he understood after a fashion, but if thereby was meant that France would undertake not to help James and would recognize William, that was unbelievable. "C'est ce que je ne croirai jamais que je ne l'aie vu",[3] he protests vehemently.

1 In vol. xxxvii of the *Œuvres.*
2 Racine, *Port-Royal* (éd. Gazier), p. 95; Quesnel, *Histoire abrégée de la Vie...* *de M. Arnauld,* pp. 438–40; Arnauld, *Œuvres,* xliii, p. 276 (Life by le P. Noël de Larrière).
3 *Œuvres,* iii, p. 406, Nov. 30, 1691. A very interesting article by M. Gustave Charlier in the *Mercure de France* for July 1, 1931, suggests that *Athalie,* written by that friend of Arnauld and Port Royal, Racine, in 1691 is full of allusions to the contemporary history of England, and it quotes that other friend of Arnauld, Quesnel, writing to M. Vuillart, "Nous relisons de temps en temps Athalie et nous y trouvons toujours de nouvelles beautés...et il y a des portraits où l'on n'a pas besoin de dire à qui ils ressemblent" (p. 91).

PLATE VI

DR JOHN BETHAM

A curious little incident links James II and one of the solitaries, Lancelot. After the death of M. de Barcos, nephew of Saint-Cyran, Lancelot, accused of Jansenism, had been removed from the abbey of Saint-Cyran and had been relegated to the remote abbey of Quimperlé. In March 1689 the king was on his way from France to Ireland. He passed through Brittany and a brief halt was made at Quimperlé one evening. A supper had been prepared for the king at the abbey, and M. d'Avaux who was with the expedition made Brother Claude Lancelot, an old man of over seventy, sit down at table beside the king. "Qui auroit cru", says Arnauld, "qu'un religieux exilé au fond de la Bretagne auroit eu l'honneur de manger avec un roi?"[1]

A few years later James, now definitely established at Saint-Germain, was hunting near Versailles and came upon a convent unknown to him. With his usual piety he would not pass by, but alighted. His visit is recorded in the annals of Port Royal.

1693. Le mardy 1er septembre. Le Roy d'Angleterre arriva icy en chassant un cerf. Il s'informa ce que c'étoit que cette Abbaye; decendit de cheval pour aller à l'église dont on luy ouvrit toutes les portes et demanda N.M. au Parloir à qui sa Mté parla avec beaucoup de bonté s'informant de nostre Institut et du temps de nre fondation. Il partit ensuite et n'attendit pas que le cerf fut pris qui estoit alors dans l'étang poursuivi par des chiens et de ceux qui etoit dans le bateau....On présenta du pain et du vin au Roy. Il fallut donner la petite charette pour emmener le cerf a Versailles avec le cheval gris et un de Mr Tero.[2]

Mme de Maintenon was rather shocked to discover that the King of England read Port Royal authors, and she was perturbed to find that if he read all the books of "ces messieurs", it was because the new Archbishop of Paris, M. de Noailles, had given him permission.[3] M. Ernest Ruth d'Ans, at one time a confessor of Port Royal and later Arnauld's companion in exile, counted the king among his friends and protectors.[4] James, so utterly bereft of all critical faculty, never seems to have been fully aware

1 Ib. p. 176, see also p. 177: cf. Sainte-Beuve, Port-Royal, I, p. 439.
2 B.N. f. fr. MS. 17779, f. 341.
3 Maintenon, Correspondance générale, IV, p. 262, Oct. 13, 1698.
4 Nécrologe des Appelans, p. 351.

of the "perils" of Jansenism—not so his consort, Mary of Modena, who was always on her guard and told Mme de Maintenon that she did not wish to read any of these books.[1] One imagines therefore her consternation when it was discovered in 1703 that her son's preceptor, Dr John Betham,[2] inclined to Jansenism.

"Poor King James" had died in 1701, and the young "king", a boy of fifteen, had been exposed to hearing all kinds of pernicious doctrine. The queen herself wrote out a statement concerning Dr Betham's wrongs. The doctor admired Port Royal books so much that, in speaking to the king, he had put them before all other spiritual books, even before St François de Sales, and if he had his way the king would read no other books of devotion. He taught the king that Port Royal was one of the most regular and holy communities of France, that Arnauld and Nicole were great men and worthy reformers of the clergy of France, and, hearing of a saint who was to be canonized, he remarked that Arnauld too deserved to be made a saint. As for Quesnel he declared that he was unjustly persecuted and he rejoiced in Quesnel's escape from imprisonment.

Furthermore Dr Betham had blamed the *ordonnance* of the Bishop of Chartres against the *Cas de Conscience*, he had spoken against the infallibility of the Pope, he had thrown aspersions on the Jesuits whose veracity could not be trusted, and he had criticized the King of France for imprisoning people—presumably Jansenists—without hearing what they had to say in their justification. At the same time he had made the young king understand that he must say nothing about all this to his confessor or to the queen, "car la Reyne est délicate sur ces matières et si elle venoit à me soupçonner d'estre favorable à ces gens-là, nous aurions bien du bruit".[3]

How the matter reached Mary's ears we do not know, but when she discovered the state of affairs she had the "king"

---

[1] Maintenon, *Correspondance générale*, IV, p. 262, Oct. 13, 1698.
[2] A portrait of Dr Betham is reproduced in vol. 19 of the *Catholic Record Society Publications* (1917).
[3] *Hist. MSS. Comm., Stuart Papers at Windsor*, I, pp. 190-2.

write out a statement[1] and made inquiries of others who said that Mr Betham had always been suspected of Jansenism and other bad principles, he had been heard to maintain that the *Provinciales* had never been refuted and had given some one at Saint-Germain a copy of the edition in which the French, Latin, Italian and Spanish texts appeared side by side, but the informer hastily added that he had never read more than the title. Certainly Dr Betham had always favoured the factions that supported "innovations", nor did he appear to be in the interests of France, for people of merit had heard him say "he would like better to live under the tyranny of the usurper Cromwell and of the Prince of Orange than under the government of France".[2]

In her concern the queen consulted Mme de Maintenon who, in turn, asked advice of the Bishop of Toul, one of the most ardent opponents of Jansenism and later, as Cardinal de Bissy, a zealous promoter of the Bull *Unigenitus*. She transmitted to him two statements drawn up by the queen, and the bishop wrote back a long letter in his own hand so that inviolable secrecy might be preserved. He considered the king too young and the preceptor too old for simple warnings—Dr Betham was about sixty—but he suggested the presence of a third person whenever Dr Betham was with the king. In this way the queen would not have to resort to anything as drastic as the dismissal of the preceptor, and if she had to do it ultimately, she would at least have given proof of her moderation.

The bishop felt it deeply that Jansenism should be endeavouring to establish itself at the court of England, but he was not surprised. It was a holy court, he said, and the Jansenist party had always tried to cover itself with the appearance of piety and to seek the support of good people. The sainted king in heaven and the queen still upon earth, aided by the wise counsels of Mme de Maintenon, would preserve the English court from that contagion which was only too widespread among the Catholics in Holland.[3]

1 *Ib.* II, p. 520.   2 *Ib.* I, p. 192; II, p. 520.
3 *Ib.* I, pp. 188–9, Dec. 16, 1703.

Mme de Maintenon sent this letter on to the queen, but thought the bishop's advice difficult to carry out. The natural third person to be present at all intercourse would be the governor, the Duke of Perth, but the governor was believed to be somewhat favourable to Jansenism himself. Nor did it seem very useful to give advice to Dr Betham, as the Curé of Saint-Sulpice proposed. She thought that the queen should wait until Providence supplied some opportunity, and in the meantime she had the confidence of the young king, and the king also had an enlightened confessor—it was impossible that he should change without its being noticed.[1]

Finally the matter was referred to the Cardinal de Noailles. He had two long conversations with Dr Betham and declared he had reason to be satisfied.[2] One doubts whether this would have been the outcome, if Dr Betham had been summoned before the Bishop of Toul. Knowing what was Noailles' attitude to the Jansenists one may assume that he dealt leniently with the preceptor.

Yet this did not close the incident. Presently Dr Betham received a *lettre de cachet* ordering him to withdraw from Saint-Germain. The "Queen-Regent", it was said, "was prevailed upon to make use of yt arbitrary way to remove him". "But being afraid it should be known and so do prejudice to ye young King's affairs", she sent for Dr Thomas Witham, superior of St Gregory's Seminary, Paris, and for Dr John Ingleton, under-preceptor to the king, and ordered them to signify the matter to Dr Betham, adding that the reason for his going must be kept very secret. "It gave a fresh instance of ye power ye Fathers had over her and made it credible she had vowed obedience to ye society."[3] Dr Betham retired to St Gregory's Seminary where he died in 1709.[4]

Certainly "James III" showed no particular leanings to Jansenism in after years—the Cardinal de Tencin, a notorious

1 *Hist. MSS. Comm., Stuart Papers at Windsor*, i, p. 189.
2 *Ib.* pp. 192–3.
3 Ushaw Collection MSS. i, No. 65 (p. 246). A memorandum signed "E. Dicconson".
4 *D.N.B.* article on John Betham.

enemy of Jansenism and in particular of Soanen, Bishop of Senez, was often said to owe his promotion to him[1]—and the queen continued a steadfast adversary. One finds her lending a little book containing the condemnation of Quesnel's New Testament to one of the religious at Chaillot, and she is very glad to hear that Quesnel's books are no longer to be found in the hands of the sisters. "Je prie bien qu'ils n'y retournent jamais ni aucuns autre de la mesme espèce."[2] Another time she hastens to send on to Chaillot an admonitory letter from the Cardinal de Noailles to the remaining nuns of Port Royal, "aus filles du Port Royal qui ne sont pas encore soumises.... Il faut bien prier pour ces 4 brebis qui sont encore esgarées".[3] If there were any Jansenists in the Saint-Germain colony it was not the queen's fault.

1 *Mémoires pour servir à l'histoire de M. le Cardinal de Tencin jusqu'à l'année* 1743 (B.N. Ln²⁷ 19421), cf. *Nouvelles ecclésiastiques*, July 25, 1728, p. 2, July 30, p. 9, "Le bruit s'est répandu ici de toutes parts que M. de Tencin avoit fait compter ou prêté une somme de cent mille écus au Roy d'Angleterre pour obtenir sa nomination. Nous ignorons si M. d'Ambrun a eu recours à de telles voyes pour avancer sa promotion; mais ce que nous savons certainement, c'est que le Roy d'Angleterre tiendroit a grand injure qu'on le soupçonnât d'une telle bassesse.... M. de Tencin a connu très particulièrement le Roy d'Angleterre à Rome".
2 *Roxburghe Club Publications, Stuart Papers*, I, p. 185, "ce 11me Novembre".
:*Ib.* p. 147, "ce 18 Janvier 1711".

CHAPTER XVI

The Innes Family and the Collège des Écossais

SCOTTISH JANSENISTS

"LE MARDY 23ᵉ. On chanta Tierces et la Messe et le Libera. Ce fut M. Innesse qui officia"—thus we read in a Port Royal manuscript record for 1695.[1] That same month of August "M. Innesse" had been one of the ecclesiastics present at the anniversary mass held for Arnauld at Port Royal des Champs.[2] The Bibliothèque Mazarine possesses a large manuscript volume containing a copy of Lancelot's Memoirs and various letters and papers concerning Saint-Cyran.[3] "Recueil", says a note, "qui nous est venu de M. Thomas Innes, très digne Prêtre du Collège des Ecossois." In Cerveau's *Nécrologe* of eminent Jansenists one may read a short biography of Thomas Innes, Ami de la Vérité,[4] and the Jansenist weekly, the *Nouvelles ecclésiastiques*, commemorates his passing away in 1744 in his eighty-third year.[5]

"M. Thomas", for so, we read in the *Nouvelles ecclésiastiques*, he was always called in Paris, came to France at the age of fifteen, lived at the Collège des Écossais, studied at the Collège de Navarre and was attached to the clergy of Saint-Étienne du Mont, where he conceived a great admiration for the abbé Colbert, later bishop of Montpellier, one of the four appellant bishops. After a brief stay in Scotland as a missionary he was recalled to the Collège des Écossais to help the principal, his brother Lewis, who was frequently away at Saint-Germain-en-

1 B.N. f. fr. MS. 17779, f. 367, Aug. 23, 1695 (Port Royal des Champs).
2 *Ib.* Aug. 9, 1695. Arnauld had died in August 1694.
3 Bibl. Mazarine, MS. 2481. Innes has put his initials T.I. at the beginning and at the end of the book. It would hardly have been prudent to write out his name in full.
4 *Nécrologe des plus célèbres Défenseurs du Dix-huitième Siècle*, Seconde Partie (vol. III of the whole *Nécrologe*), pp. 72–3. An account largely based on that of the *Nouvelles ecclésiastiques*, as is also that of Guilbert, *Mémoires*, VII, p. 543.
5 *Nouv. ecclés.* 1745, pp. 69–71.

Laye. He had become acquainted at an early date with Port Royal through M. Le Noir, canon of Notre Dame, and his brother, M. Le Noir de Sainte-Claude, a solitary whose attachment to Port Royal was to cost him eight years in the Bastille. In the pilgrimages to Port Royal which Innes undertook from time to time he used to meet the famous Santeuil and asked him to write some hymns in honour of the saints of England. Duguet, Rollin and other Appellants were among his friends, and he joined them in an appeal against the Constitution *Unigenitus*; his name, however, does not appear in the lists because his friends, especially Duguet, thought it might be prejudicial to the work in Scotland, if certain adversaries were aware of his being an Appellant. He was known personally to the Cardinal de Noailles who held him in great esteem.

His historical work took him back to Scotland to collect material, and we catch a glimpse of him at the Advocates' Library in Edinburgh, "in the hours when open, a monkish, bookish person who meddled with nothing but literature".[1] A curious accident happened to him on the voyage—when embarking he fell into the sea, he was rescued, but indifferent to all that concerned the body, he neglected to take off his dripping garments and was always hereafter slightly paralysed on one side. When he returned to France in 1726 he took up his abode again at the Collège des Écossais, but complaints had been brought against him. A young Scotch priest, crossed in his ambitions, so the *Nouvelles ecclésiastiques* relate, imagined that Innes had put obstacles in his way and spoke against him, both in Paris and in Rome. This was perhaps a certain Colin Campbell who reported various sayings of Innes—that the Bull *Unigenitus* was a contrivance of the Jesuits, that the five condemned propositions were not to be found in Jansenius, that the Council of Trent was a mere academic assembly, etc.[2] "M. Thomas" was denounced as a Jansenist who infected the young, and upon advice received from Rome he withdrew from the college in

1 Woodrow, *Analecta* (quoted in the *Miscellany of the Spalding Club*, vol. II).
2 Bellesheim, *History of the Cath. Church in Scotland* (Hunter Blair's transl.), IV, pp. 209–10.

order that his presence might not embarrass the establishment[1] and went to live with a worthy Scottish gentleman by the name of Panton. He was interdicted by M. de Vintimille, the new Archbishop of Paris, successor in 1729 to the Cardinal de Noailles who had died.

He found it however impossible to continue his historical work deprived of the resources of the college library, and the difficulty of his situation being put before " James III", he was enabled to return to the college. He chose a small remote room where he could live quietly without rousing his enemies, and here he remained till his death in 1744, working at his history. "Ceux qui ont connu ce vénérable vieillard", says our chronicler, "n'ignorent pas que son caractère dominant étoit un grand amour pour la vie obscure, une profonde humilité et une gravité vraiment sacerdotale." His simplicity of speech, his quiet bearing, filled those who met him with sudden and in- voluntary respect. In all his conduct, we read, he showed himself a true disciple of Port Royal. After the Scriptures he loved best to read the works of Saint-Cyran and of Singlin. His library included all the principal works written in defence of the Appeal and of the Miracles, and the *Nouvelles ecclésiastiques* were a great solace to him in his solitude.

He was fortified in his last hours by Saint-Cyran's *Con- sidérations sur la Mort* and Quesnel's *Bonheur de la Mort chrétienne*. And having been unknown all his life he desired to be no less unknown in his death and to be buried like a pauper. At his request no one was invited to his funeral, and he was laid to rest very quietly in the cemetery of Saint-Étienne du Mont. The *Nouvelles ecclésiastiques* found it difficult to procure the necessary facts for his obituary—"ceux qui auroient pu être en état de nous fournir des Mémoires capables de faire connoître suffisam- ment ce grand serviteur de Dieu, ont suivi trop littéralement ses humbles et pieuses intentions".[2]

1 Cf. Gordon, *Eccles. Chronicles*, IV, p. 249.
2 *Nouv. ecclés.* 1745, pp. 69–71. A biographical account of Innes by his grand-nephew Alexander Innes can be read in vol. II of the *Miscellany* of the Spalding Club, pp. cxiv–cxix, where Alexander Innes endeavours to clear his relative from the charge of Jansenism which "gave the good old gentleman much pain".

The Jansenist M. d'Étemare had visited the good old man a few months previously, and wrote on hearing of his peaceful death, "Assurement il y a bien lieu de penser que M. Thomas Inesse a part au bonheur de ceux qui meurent dans le Seigneur. ...Sa mort porte le caractère de celle des Patriarches". He thought of him as of one who had preceded him with others to a better country. "Ils sont parvenus au port d'où ils nous considérent au milieu des flots dont nous sommes battus. Notre situation depuis douze ou treize ans ressemble encore plus à une tempête que les temps ordinaires de cette vie."[1]

This Thomas Innes, priest, historian and antiquary,[2] prefect of studies at the Scots College in Paris, was brother to Lewis Innes, principal of the College, as we have seen, and uncle to George Innes who later succeeded him as prefect of studies and finally himself became principal. For seventy years, from 1682 to 1752, the Innes family was thus very intimately connected with the Collège des Écossais[3]; other members of the family carried on the tradition, and since many of the students of the Collège des Écossais went as missionary priests to Scotland later on, we must doubtless attribute to the influence of the Innes dynasty the fact that Jansenism gained what would seem a much stronger foothold in Scotland than in England or Ireland. Thomas Innes himself was for a short time a missionary in Scotland, from 1698 to 1701,[4] after having served for two years at Magny, the parish of Port Royal des Champs.[5]

Already at the end of the seventeenth century one comes across the suggestion that those of the Scots College are Jansenists,[6] but the chief accusations are made, as elsewhere, in the eighteenth century. The Nuncio Lercari reported that before the

1 Amersfoort Archives, *Lettres de M. d'Etemare*, Carton H, Feb. 10, 1744, Cat. number 5400.
2 His chief works are *A Critical Essay on the Ancient Inhabitants of the Northern Parts of Britain or Scotland* and *The Civil and Ecclesiastical History of Scotland*.
3 Lewis Innes, principal 1682–1714, when he resigned; Thomas Innes, prefect of studies 1701–27; George Innes, prefect of studies 1727–about 1738, principal 1738–52 (*Spalding Club Miscell.* II, pp. cxiv–cxix; Gordon, *Eccles. Chronicles*, IV, pp. 248–9).
4 Gordon, *op. cit.* IV, pp. 629–30.   5 *Spalding Club Miscell.* II, p. cxvi.
6 Daumet, *Notice sur les Établissements religieux, anglais, écossais et irlandais*, p. 245.

promulgation of the Constitution *Unigenitus* pure Jansenism was taught at the college, and that since the Constitution was published the superiors of the college had appealed against it in 1718, when Charles Whiteford was principal and Thomas Innes prefect of studies.[1] This had the effect of depriving the college of a pension of 1600 livres from the French clergy, for when the principal of the college or Thomas Innes (there is some confusion in the mind of the author of this anecdote, the abbé Dorsanne) came to solicit the continuation of the pension, the Bishop of Châlons, one of the presidents of the Assembly of the Clergy, at once asked him whether he accepted the Constitution. The principal hesitated and did not wish to commit himself. The bishop drew his own conclusions and moved that the pension be suppressed. "On eut beau représenter que ce n'étoit point à ce Principal que la pension étoit accordée, mais à de pauvres Boursiers qui n'avoient pas de pain et ne scavoient ce que c'étoit que la constitution. On n'écouta rien et la pension fut retranchée."[2]

Accusations were doubtless often made without foundation.[3] According to the abbé Macpherson when a certain priest by the name of James Carnegie, a connection of the Earl of Northesk, was on his way in 1726 to Rome to see the Pretender concerning some political affairs, the Scottish Jesuits in Paris thought he had been sent by the clergy that he might be named bishop. "They formally accused him to the Nuncio of Paris of favouring the Jansenists, and made the Nuncio understand that the Jansenistical party in Scotland which they represented as numerous designed getting him made Bishop to establish the Heresy on a solid bottom in that country: The Nuncio was mightily alarmed and informed the Cardinal Prefect of Propaganda of the intelligence which he had received." Cardinal Sacripanti who had already been informed of the reasons for Carnegie's journey sent

1 Report printed in Bellesheim (Hunter Blair's transl.), IV, pp. 408-13.
2 Dorsanne, *Journal*, II, p. 170.
3 Thus a certain Robert Strachan who died in 1725 was "peculiarly persecuted by the Jesuits and openly accused of Jansenism. So much noise was made that Bishop Gordon deemed it necessary publicly to examine into the whole business. Upon the strictest scrutiny the whole accusation...appeared to have been founded on misrepresentation and slander". Gordon, *Eccles. Chronicles*, IV, p. 618.

for the agent Mr Stuart, put the letter into his hand and said smiling, "Observe the artifices of our Scots Jansenists and mark the zeal and Charity of our Scots Jesuits".[1]

We have seen that a papal brief of 1709 had urged the Scottish Catholics with the English and Irish Catholics to adhere to the Bull *Vineam Domini*.[2] As the years went on some of the Catholic clergy in Scotland evidently considered the situation serious, for at a meeting in the Highland district in 1733, Bishop James Gordon was urged to oblige all the missionaries to accept the Constitution *Unigenitus* and other bulls directed against Jansenism, since they suspected some of their number of adhering to the errors of Jansenius and Quesnel. A formulary, drawn up with reluctance, was subscribed by all present, met with approbation from the Congregation of Propaganda, and a brief issued by Clement XII in September 1736 directed the bishops to require all priests entering the mission to subscribe it.[3] The formulary was now made to cover a catechism that had appeared some ten years before and was condemned as Jansenist in its tendencies,[4] and this amplified formulary was to be subscribed by the Scottish vicars-apostolic and all their clergy.

A few months before this brief was issued unfavourable reports about the Collège des Écossais had been received by the Congregation of Propaganda. This news came from Germany, from Abbot Bernard Stuart of Ratisbon. He spoke with great concern of the ravening wolves in sheeps' clothing who, under the pretext of purer doctrine and primitive discipline, were creating factions among the Catholics, spurning those who were not with them as lazy, stupid and addicted to super-

1 *Ib.* p. 533.
2 Bellesheim (Hunter Blair's transl.), IV, pp. 200–1, from *Bullarium Pontificium S. Congregationis de Propaganda Fide* (Rome 1839, 8 vols.), Appendix, I, p. 384.
3 Bellesheim (Hunter Blair's transl.), IV, pp. 202–3, from *Bullarium Pontificium S. Congregationis de Propaganda Fide*, II, p. 240.
4 Bellesheim, *loc. cit.*; Reusch, *Der Index*, II, pp. 410, 415; Vacant, Mangenot et Amann, *Dictionnaire de Théologie catholique* under "Catéchisme." *A catechism for those that are more advanced in years and knowledge* (1724), *Instructions and prayers for children* (1724), *Catechism of abridgement of Christian doctrine* (1725), all condemned in 1734–5. Judging from Lercari's report printed in Bellesheim, IV, pp. 408–13, this catechism is by Andrew Hassett and Robert Gordon. See also Gordon, *Eccles. Chronicles*, IV, p. 564.

stitious practices, especially if they were educated in Rome or Germany.[1]

An investigation was naturally ordered and the nuncio in France, Lercari, charged with the visit, sent a very damning report to Rome in 1737. It had been extremely difficult to secure information on account of the great secrecy and caution observed by the superiors, but he was convinced that the college was in great need of reform, and the first thing to do was to remove the three Innes.[2] They were all three Jansenists and Appellants, they always resided at the college and governed the community absolutely. Charles Whiteford, the present principal, had also appealed with them,[3] and while it was true that he had revoked his appeal, this was not generally known in Paris where he should have been obliged to repair the scandal he had created.

It was not known that George Innes and Alexander Gordon,[4] the present prefect of studies, had ever accepted the Bull, and therefore the paper signed by them in 1735, and sent to the Congregation of Propaganda to justify themselves, deserved no consideration, all the more since their relations continued the same with the Jansenists. In the opinion of all the Catholics in Paris Jansenism was taught at the college as much as ever it was.

A note on Thomas Innes follows—when he was prefect of studies at the college not only had his teaching been contrary to the Catholic doctrine, but being also confessor at the College of Sainte-Barbe, he used to conduct his own students thither to perform their spiritual exercises and to receive the instructions in Jansenism given there.

As for Lewis Innes, he had perverted the Scotch who lived at the Palace of Saint-Germain, and at present he was director of all these families who looked upon him as their apostle. Among his followers were Milord Milton[5] and especially Milord

1 Bellesheim (Hunter Blair's transl.), IV, p. 204. 2 *Ib.*
3 Cf. *La Constitution Unigenitus déférée à l'Église universelle*, I, p. 134.
4 In the list of Appellants printed in *La Constitution Unigenitus déférée*... one finds the name of "A. Gordon, Docteur de Sorbonne" twice. See I, pp. 304 and 549.
5 I.e Middleton, one of the sons of Charles, second Earl of Middleton. Lord Edward Drummond, afterwards sixth Duke of Perth, married Lady Elizabeth Middleton.

Édouard Perth, Milord Milton's brother-in-law, who was so openly declared in favour of Jansenism that he refused to be present at a mission held a few months before by the Jesuit fathers at Saint-Germain and during this time withdrew to Paris to the Scots College. From all this it might be inferred what evil had been done by this Lewis and was still being done in the college where he was held to be an oracle.

Two or three students, it was true, had been expelled from the college for talking openly against the Constitution, but it was universally believed that this was merely an act of outward show, and not a sincere proof of submission.

It may be noted here incidentally that we find a certain Stuart excluded for some reason or other from the Scots College in 1744, and that he turns to the abbé d'Étemare for help. Étemare was not in Paris at the time, but some financial assistance was given through Jansenist friends.[1]

But to return to Lercari's report. The superiors of the college, we read, sent their students to be ordained outside of the diocese of Paris, to be ordained, for instance, by Mgr Gordon, one of their party, and when students came to them from the college at Rome to be instructed in matters necessary for the exercise of their mission in Scotland, they managed to retain the students for at least a year, and sent them out imbued with the errors of Jansenism. The missionaries to Scotland[2] were few in number, and most of them tainted with the heresy.

Mgr Gordon, vicar-apostolic of the Lowlands, was not

1 Amersfoort Archives, *Lettres de M. d'Étemare*, Carton H, Oct. 13, 1744, Cat. number 5475.
2 Lercari enumerates the best known—Alexander Drummond who had refused to sign the formulary, Andrew Hassett and Robert Gordon, authors of a catechism condemned in Rome, George Gordon of Scanan, Patrick Leith, George Duncan, and John Gordon who had refused to sign the formulary and went about in Scotland publishing the pretended miracles of the abbé Paris. Elsewhere he mentions John Tyrie, but there is some confusion here. Other missionaries accused were James Leslie and Robert Strachan (Gordon, *Eccles. Chronicles*, IV, pp. 574, 618). Some of those who accused the Scotch of Jansenism were George Gordon, Gregor MacGregor (*ib.* pp. 555, 592), Colin Campbell (Bellesheim, IV, p. 209), John Tyrie (*Scots College, Rome*, p. 32), Sempill, Melfort, Alexander Lawson (*ib.* p. 36). Bishop James Grant, who spent a year in Paris after studying at the Scots College in Rome, was opposed to Jansenism (Gordon, *op. cit.* IV, p. 10).

believed to be free from Jansenism. It was said that he had perverted many Catholics, he had brought into the mission refractory ecclesiastics, and, far from assuring himself of their submission to the Constitution, he showed the utmost partiality for these suspected priests. He permitted the reading of Jansenist books; he corresponded with Thomas and Lewis Innes; he sent young men to the college, though he could not have been ignorant of the errors taught there; he had examined and approved the aforesaid catechisms, already condemned by Rome; more than anyone else he was opposed to the signature of the formulary sent from Rome, and finally he had selected as his coadjutor Alexander Smith.

As the new coadjutor was suspected of favouring Jansenism, Mgr Gordon, fearing opposition, had had him appointed, and had consecrated him secretly. There was no record of Smith's appeal against the Bull,[1] but it was known that while at Paris he was regarded as a Jansenist, and since his departure he had continued to correspond with many of the refractory doctors excluded from the Sorbonne. If he succeeded Mgr Gordon as vicar-apostolic the greatest harm would be done.

As for the formulary sent to Scotland from Rome, it had not yet been enforced universally—it was said that this would draw the attention of the government to the Scottish Catholics, but Lercari believed that these so-called difficulties were promoted

[1] According to Dorsanne (*Journal*, 1, p. 255) there was a Smith who first appealed, but then withdrew his appeal. Bishop Smith had the utmost difficulty in getting his catechism published. Such violent opposition was encountered that for a time publication was deferred, and when at last the little works were printed and circulated he incurred "the most marked and indecent opposition from a few persons who held his orthodoxy in most unjust suspicion". Gordon, *Eccles. Chronicles*, iv, pp. 9–10.

Of this, or another Scottish catechism, the *Nouvelles ecclés.* (June 25, 1760) relate the following: "Le Catéchisme à l'usage des Missionnaires Ecossois ayant déplu aux Jésuites, leur Général a présenté à la Congrégation du Saint Office un Mémoire accompagné d'une traduction de ce Catéchisme pour le faire condamner. Mais avant que de prononcer la Congrégation a pris la sage précaution de faire vérifier la fidélité de la traduction et l'on a reconnu qu'elle altéroit l'original et lui prétoit des propositions censurables qui n'y sont point. En conséquence le Decret du Saint Office déclare ledit Catéchisme exempt d'erreur et permet aux Missionnaires de continuer à s'en servir". This is, of course, a very biased account and not to be taken literally, but may serve as an echo of the prolonged strife.

by the artifices of the Jansenists. Mgr "Magdonol", however, was to be considered orthodox.[1] Lercari's report was to a certain extent confirmed, or perhaps even inspired, by two Scottish priests, John Tyrie and Colin Campbell, who accused all the vicars-apostolic of Scotland in 1738 of being infected with Jansenism and of being unwilling to take and administer the oath prescribed against the so-called heresy. These two priests were alumni of the Scots College at Rome, and the abbé Macpherson believed that the Jesuit rectors of this college were responsible for the charge and fomented the discord, but a document preserved at Blairs College mentions two secular priests by the name of Sempil and Melfort as instigators of the charge, as well as a cleric, Alexander Lawson, catechist in the *ospizio dei convertendi* at Borgo.[2]

News also reached the Congregation of Propaganda that Thomas Innes was Bishop Gordon's spiritual adviser, although Gordon knew that Innes was opposed to the Constitution *Unigenitus*.[3] A fresh brief was therefore issued in 1738 by Clement XII, calling on the Scottish missionaries to subscribe the formulary, and another work was added to the former list of condemned writings, the so-called *Montpellier Catechism*.[4]

The Catholic clergy of Scotland was for long divided into two antagonistic parties, the party of Paris, trained at the Collège des Écossais, favoured, so it was said, by Bishop Gordon, a party

---

1 Archiv. Vatic. Nuntiatura di Francia, vol. 262. Italian text printed in Bellesheim, *Geschichte der Katholischen Kirche in Irland*, II, pp. 540–3, English translation in Hunter Blair's translation of Bellesheim, IV, pp. 408–13. The superiors of the college made a reply to this and said that they had always defended the Constitution *Unigenitus* (Bellesheim (Hunter Blair's transl.), IV, p. 209). In his report Lercari mentions that the famous Law had given the college many shares or banknotes, but that doubtless these had met with the general fate. It must not, however, be inferred from this that Law was inclined to Jansenism—on the contrary. See Dorsanne, *Journal*, II, p. 7.

2 *The Scots College, Rome*, pp. 22, 32, 33, 35, 36, 49, 50. The Rev. W. E. Brown, one of the authors of this book, considers that the vicars-apostolic did lay themselves open to suspicion by postponing the taking of the oath or ordering their clergy to take it, but that on the other hand "though the Vicars Apostolic were somewhat rigorist in their moral discipline, they were never guilty of teaching any of the condemned propositions" (p. 33).

3 Bellesheim (Hunter Blair's transl.), IV, p. 210.

4 *Bullar. Prop.* II, pp. 238–43 (quoted in Bellesheim, IV, p. 208).

holding liberal views, and the party of Rome which consisted of the strictly orthodox, for the most part alumni of the Scots College at Rome.[1]

The 1736 formulary was once more imposed shortly after 1745, and was signed only after much delay by the Paris party.[2] From 1739 to 1764 the college furnished no priests to the mission. Some of the scholars entered the army, others returned as laymen to their country. A report submitted to the Congregation of Propaganda as late as 1782 still speaks of the suspicion of Jansenism attaching to the superiors of the college and of the consequent attitude of the missionaries who formed a strong party against the ecclesiastics trained in Rome.[3] Serious disagreements arose between the superiors and Bishop Hay who refused to send any more boys to the college—"it is better for us to send none there than to send and have them ruined"— but the coming of the French Revolution swept everything away.[4]

1 Bellesheim (Hunter Blair's transl.), IV, pp. 210–11.
2 *Ib.* p. 252. Among those reluctant to sign were Alexander Gordon, principal of the college, James Macdonald, Alexander Geddes.
3 *Ib.* pp. 251–2.
4 Gordon, *Eccles. Chronicles*, IV, pp. 249–52 (Life of Bishop Hay).

PLATE VII

ELIZABETH HAMILTON, COMTESSE DE GRAMONT

CHAPTER XVII

The Saint-Germain Colony

HOWEVER much the queen disapproved of "innovations", at Saint-Germain itself there was a distinct undercurrent of Jansenism. Dr Betham was not the only one who thought well of Port Royal, and, if Queen Mary's informer had not read the *Provinciales*, others had. How some of them came to read the book is told by Sainte-Beuve, who takes his story from the manuscript letters of Racine's friend, M. Vuillart. When le Père Daniel wrote his answer to the *Provincial Letters—Les Entretiens de Cléandre et Eudoxe*—an attempt was made to circulate this book at Saint-Germain, but the result was not altogether what had been anticipated. A copy came into the hands of the Duke of Berwick who had never read the *Provinciales*. The brief quotations from Pascal interested him so much that it made him anxious to read the rest of the work, which was procured and read with much enjoyment. Berwick's pleasure proved infectious, the other "mylords" wanted to have copies and sent to Paris for them and the booksellers were hardly able to supply their wants fast enough. "Cela est vrai à la lettre."[1] The learned Latin notes which Nicole had contributed to the *Provinciales* under the name of Wendrock were translated into French by Mlle de Joncoux for the court of Saint-Germain.[2]

The Duke's good will was valued by the Jansenists, for one of their party writes a few years later from his hiding-place in Brussels to Mlle de Joncoux, that interesting friend of Port Royal,[3] "La protection de M. de Berwick est bonne. J'ay de bons amis à la Cour de St Germain",[4] and another time the

---

1 Sainte-Beuve, *Port-Royal*, III, p. 223 (Jan. 26, 1697).
2 Information from Mademoiselle Gazier.
3 For Mlle de Joncoux see an article by Mlle Gazier in the *Revue de Paris*, April 15, 1929.
4 B.N. f. fr. MS. 19731, f. 55, Feb. 5, 1704, unsigned letter.

writer asks Mlle de Joncoux to get some one from the court of Saint-Germain to see an Irish dominican provincial for him, with a view to passing on some papers to a Spanish grandee.[1] Quesnel in exile heard with interest of Lord Middleton's conversion at Saint-Germain, the news evidently being transmitted to him by Jansenist friends.[2] At the funeral of the venerable Prior of Chambourcy, M. Arnoul, interdicted and suspended for Jansenism, his friends observed with satisfaction the presence of a "gentilhomme du Roy d'Angleterre".[3]

Mary of Modena regretted that the English living at Saint-Germain did not send their children to the Jesuit colleges, though she had urged them to do so. She was quite aware, she said, of the dislike many had of the Jesuits, for it was extended to her, not only by the "heretics", but by some of the Catholics.[4] The Duke of Berwick sent his elder children to the Collège du Plessis, but if the abbé Dorsanne, a writer with a Jansenist bias, may be believed, he found it expedient to withdraw them and to send them to a Jesuit school. He desired some favour for one of his sons from the King of Spain, and had written to the very influential Père d'Aubenton, but had not even received an acknowledgment of his letter. On complaining to some Jesuits at Bordeaux he was told "Your children are at the Collège du Plessis; send them to the Collège de Clermont". The duke dismissed a preceptor, because he was opposed to the Jesuits, transferred his children to the Jesuit college, and all was well, his requests were granted. But the story is a somewhat dubious one.[5]

We have seen elsewhere that the Nuncio Lercari attributed the Jansenism of the court of Saint-Germain to the influence of Lewis Innes. There was another person who doubtless served as a link somewhat earlier, and this was one who had been brought up at Port Royal, Elizabeth Hamilton, now for many

1 B.N. f. fr. MS. 19731, f. 103, July 12, 1704.
2 B.N. f. fr. MS. 19730, f. 139, Sept. 23, 1702.
3 *Histoire du Cas de Conscience*, VII, p. 285. This was in 1706.
4 *Roxburghe Club Publications, Stuart Papers*, II, p. 385 (1712).
5 Dorsanne, *Journal*, II, p. 118. The author of the life of Fitzjames, Bishop of Soissons, one of Berwick's sons, says that the children were transferred at the request of the Cardinal de Fleury (Fitzjames, *Œuvres Posthumes*, p. xvii).

years Madame de Gramont.[1] She was often at Saint-Germain where she had two brothers—Richard Hamilton, once in command of the Irish armies, now Master of the Wardrobe, and Anthony, the future author of the *Mémoires de Grammont*, who was to end his days in piety, but for the present was not enamoured of the heavy devotion of the king or of the superabundance of Jesuits lodged in the palace.[2]

Mme de Gramont had sent one of her daughters, Marie-Elisabeth, to be educated at Port Royal, and the little girl of eleven was one of those who were turned out in 1679,[3] nor was the abbess of the neighbouring convent of Gif allowed to take her in, for Gif was considered too friendly to Port Royal.[4] It was on this occasion that Mme de Gramont took it upon herself to approach Louis XIV openly on the subject of these persecutions, saying that it was hard to understand why the nuns of Port Royal should be treated thus. As for herself, the nuns had clothed her, fed and educated her for seven or eight years out of pure charity—they were admirable. "So every one says", was the answer, "but it is a place of assemblies and cabals."[5] Mme de Gramont was often proud and overbearing in manner—"Angloise insupportable" said those who disliked her—yet she was never ashamed to speak of her poverty-stricken youth and of the unbounded kindness she had received from Port Royal in the days of exile.

The influence of Port Royal had, it is true, paled somewhat before the splendour of court life, but throughout Elizabeth Hamilton remained loyal to her old friends, and this at a time when she was constantly in the king's society, at Versailles, at Marly, at Fontainebleau, at Compiègne, and well aware of his intense dislike of Port Royal. Later years brought a return to piety, and though at first Fénelon, no friend of what he called "la cabale des Jansénistes", was her director, his influence waned necessarily as he became involved in the controversy of

1 For Mme de Gramont see Clark, *Anthony Hamilton*, pp. 109–23.
2 Hamilton, *Œuvres* (1812, 3 vols.), II, pp. 399–402, cf. III, p. 237.
3 B.N. f. fr. MS. 17779, ff. 36, 42.
4 *Ib.* f. 22.
5 *Ib.* f. 33. Cf. Besoigne, *Histoire*, II, p. 540; Guilbert, *Mémoires*, II, pp. 247–8.

Quietism and, as Archbishop of Cambrai, exchanged Versailles for his diocese.

From this time on her relations with Port Royal grew much more marked. "Madame la comtesse de Gramont ne garde plus de mesures la-dessus," writes Mme de Maintenon in 1696, "elle a et montre sans façon (dans une chambre qu'elle a au couvent de la Madeleine) tous les portraits de Jansénius, de M. Arnauld, de Saci."[1] The friends of Port Royal were her friends, Pomponne, du Charmel, Nicole, du Fossé, M. Vuillart, Mlle de Joncoux, Boileau, and in particular Racine.[2] She was evidently considered an influential ally. "Il n'est pas necessaire que ie vous exhorte a agir auprés de madame la comtesse de Grandmont", writes a Jansenist from Holland to Mlle de Joncoux.[3]

M. de Harlay, Archbishop of Paris, had died in 1695 and his successor, M. de Noailles, was considered far more lenient to the Jansenists, therefore in 1696 Mme de Gramont requested Mme de Maintenon to ask the king whether she might spend the Easter week at Port Royal. According to Saint-Simon, Mme de Maintenon, very jealous of Mme de Gramont, always hoped that this veneration for Port Royal would discredit the countess,[4] and indeed the king was extremely annoyed that anyone should have dared to make such a request,[5] but still she continued in favour. At the risk of royal displeasure, however, she went quietly now and again to Port Royal till one day the king discovered where she had gone. He was incensed by her disregard of his wishes. In the case of anyone else, says Saint-Simon, it would have been a crime past remission. Mme de Gramont apologized—her apologies were not received, her name was struck off the list of the ladies who were to accompany the king to Marly, for the king remarked that Marly and Port

1 Maintenon, *Correspondance générale*, IV, p. 90.
2 B.N. f. fr. MS. 17807, f. 41; Arsenal MS. 6038, no. 783; MS. 6040, no. 1118; Du Fossé, *Mémoires*, IV, pp. 235–7; Mme de Caylus, *Souvenirs* (1889), pp. 128–9; Racine, *Œuvres*, VII, pp. 105, 106, 140, 185, 186, 243, 244, 297, 313, 318, etc.; Quesnel, *Correspondance*, I, 391; Sainte-Beuve, *Port-Royal*, IV, p. 511 (Letter from M. Vuillart); Gazier, "Françoise Marguerite de Joncoux", *Revue de Paris*, April 15, 1929, p. 832.
3 B.N. f. fr. MS. 17807, f. 41, Dec. 30 [1700]. The letter is signed "L'Abbé".
4 Saint-Simon, *Mémoires*, XI, pp. 111, 112.
5 Maintenon, *Correspondance générale*, IV, p. 90.

Royal were incompatible. Nor was she invited to the next "voyage de Marly", she who always went. Mme de Gramont, said the king, could not possibly have been in ignorance of his dislike of a community openly Jansenist, a sect which was an abomination to him like all other novelties in matters of religion.

"Elevée à Port-Royal", she writes about this time, "ce que j'ay de sentimens de piété m'a été inspiré par les grands exemples de pénitence que j'y ai vus et par les instructions Chrétiennes que j'y ai reçues. Le désir de ranimer ces sentimens me porte à y aller de temps en temps et à y faire quelques jours de retraite. Je n'aurois pas prévu que ceux que j'y ai passés en cette dernière rencontre fussent capables de m'attirer cette disgrâce."[1]

The incident was the talk of the town. Quesnel read about it in the *Gazette de Bruxelles*, though letters from Paris had already informed him of it and of the king's remark "qu'elle avoit d'autant plus tort qu'elle ne pouvoit ignorer qu'il avoit en horreur cette maison".[2]

Peace was finally made and though Mme de Gramont refused to "abjure" Port Royal, it was understood that she was to indulge in no more *disparades*.[3] Even after Mme de Gramont's death in 1708, the second Madame, mother of the future regent, remarked that all her sympathies were for Port Royal des Champs; the countess had said so much to her about its inmates that she was appalled by the injustice done to them, and she believed that the misfortunes overtaking France were a just retribution.[4]

As for Anthony Hamilton who had related with such consummate art and enjoyment the "Histoire Amoureuse de la Cour d'Angleterre" in his *Mémoires de Grammont*, we learn from Saint-Simon, that his sister finally brought him to a state of

1 Guilbert, *Mémoires*, III, p. 268.
2 Quesnel, *Correspondance*, II, pp. 61, 63.
3 Saint-Simon, *Mémoires*, VI, pp. 216–8; XI, p. 112; XVI, pp. 71–3; Dangeau, *Journal*, VII, pp. 104, 106, 120; Guilbert, *Mémoires*, III, p. 268; Fénelon, *Correspondance* (1827–9, 11 vols.), I, p. 81: cf. Sainte-Beuve, *Port-Royal*, VI, pp. 163–5.
4 Sainte-Beuve, *Port-Royal*, VI, p. 166 *n*.

great piety in which he renounced the ladies for whom he had so often composed elegant stories and graceful verse.[1]

> Grâce au ciel! je respire enfin
> Au bord fatal du précipice
> Où m'avaient entrainé le désordre et le vice
> Qui règnent dans le cœur humain;
> Le Sauveur m'a tendu la main.... [2]

This latter day religion is probably in a way the work of Port Royal, for apart from his sister's influence it must not be forgotten that in his destitute childhood he had been befriended by the Messieurs.

One of the Ladies of the Bedchamber at Saint-Germain was for a while the Duchess of Tyrconnel, the "little Jennings", the famous beauty of the Grammont *Mémoires*. A firm friend of the Hamiltons—her first husband, killed long ago in the French service, had been their brother George—she too was deeply attached to the cause of Port Royal and in later years acted as an intermediary between the Catholics in England and the Dutch Jansenists.[3] Berwick's first wife was a daughter of the Hamiltons' cousin, Helen Muskerry, brought up like Elizabeth Hamilton at Port Royal, and at one time Berwick was said to be governed by the Hamiltons,[4] all of which may help to account for the duke's friendliness to the cause of Port Royal.

Mention has already been made of the Jansenism of Lord Middleton, one of the sons of Charles, second Earl of Middleton, whose conversion Quesnel noticed, and of the Jansenism of his brother-in-law, Lord Edward Drummond, afterwards sixth Duke of Perth, so pronounced that he withdrew to the Collège des Écossais, the Innes stronghold, when the Jesuit Fathers came to hold a retreat at Saint-Germain. Lord Edward's father, the first Duke of Perth, had already been supposed to favour Jansenism, as we have seen.

1 Saint-Simon, *Mémoires*, xiv (éd. Chéruel), pp. 210–11. Saint-Simon here confuses Anthony and Richard Hamilton, or at any rate gives a composite picture of the two brothers.
2 Hamilton, *Œuvres* (1812, 3 vols.), iii, p. 308.
3 See her letters of 1705, from Aix-la-Chapelle, to Van Erkel, in the archives of the Chapter of Utrecht.
4 Avaux, comte de, *Négociations en Irlande* (1830, privately printed), *passim*.

With Milord Édouard, as he is often called, we approach a new phase of Jansenism, and not an attractive one. The diacre Pâris had died in 1727, greatly venerated for his virtues. He was buried in the cemetery of Saint-Médard, and, soon after, it began to be rumoured that miracles were taking place there—those that lay down on his grave recovered their health. Mobs invaded the cemetery, rich and poor, lord and beggar. The excitement reached a state of frenzy, people were seized with fits and fell into convulsions, they entered states of trance in which they were insensible to pain inflicted on them at their request by their friends. "There are strange things done at St Medard", writes Bishop Atterbury from Paris in 1731. "However my faith is not strong enough to pronounce them miracles. They even decline in my opinion since the violent agitations that appear in all those that frequent the tomb for the cure of their maladies and I am at a loss what to say or think of that matter."[1]

Testimonials were drawn up in favour of those who were miraculously healed, and one finds in 1731, among those bearing witness that "Don Alphonse de Palacios" had recovered his eyesight, "Très Honorable Sir Edouard Aston, fils ainé du Très Honorable Milord Aston, Pair d'Ecosse".[2] This same year there is in a Jansenist correspondence an allusion to the convulsions of the "gentilhomme anglais qui se porte bien",[3] but it is far more likely that this refers to Lord Edward Drummond[4] than to young Aston. Carré de Montgéron, the historian of the convulsionaries, tells us that Lord Edward was converted on

[1] Folkestone Williams, *Memoir and Correspondence of Bishop Atterbury* (1869, 2 vols.), II, p. 244.

[2] Carré de Montgéron, *La Vérité des Miracles*, I, pièces justificatives, p. 1. This was evidently Edward Richard, son of Walter, 4th Lord Aston of Forfar, born in 1713, and therefore only about 18 years old. See Sir J. B. Paul, *Scots Peerage* (Edinburgh 1910), p. 412.

[3] Arsenal MS. 5784, f. 316 (417).

[4] Lord Edward Drummond was born in the Castle of Stirling in 1690, during the imprisonment of his parents there. He was brought to France in his youth, but was in Scotland during the rising of 1715. He returned to France, where he was a gentleman-in-waiting at the court of Saint-Germain, and a colonel in the French cavalry. *Scots Peerage*, VII, pp. 56–7, where it is said that he was a general in the French army, but he was really only a colonel.

beholding the miracles and "le surnaturel évident des convulsions".[1]

In 1732 the cemetery was closed by the police, but the convulsionaries continued to meet in secret. One of them, a certain Charlotte La Porte, being accused of fraud, divers persons felt constrained to testify to her innocence, so the *Nouvelles ecclésiastiques* relate, and among those who wrote to her judge was "Milord Droumond de Perth". "Je saisis avec reconnoissance l'occasion", he says, "de vous demander votre bonne justice pour Charlotte la Porte par le canal de qui j'ai lieu de croire que Dieu m'a fait des grâces très particulières."[2] With Voltaire's brother, Armand Arouet, and Carré de Montgéron, "Milord Edouard de Rumond de Perth" testified on another occasion that a certain Marie Sonnet had remained for thirty-six minutes stretched across a roaring fire, only her head and her feet supported at either end by a stool![3]

Another time, in 1737, he was at the house of a Mme de Vieuxpont where some thirty people, priests and laymen, were engaged in prayer with Jeanne Mouler or Moulère, a convulsionary. The police burst into the room and at first those present refused to give their names, but finally a list was made out and carried to the Lieutenant de Police, Hérault, while the prisoners were closely guarded. After two hours the messenger returned with orders to convey twelve of the prisoners to the Bastille. "Milord Perth Comte de Drummont" was liberated this time,[4] but two years later, on October 30th, 1739, he was actually imprisoned.

On that morning at six o'clock the police entered the country house of M. d'Angervillers at Lardy. Everyone was still in bed, but they arrested the convulsionary Gabrielle Mouler, a sister of Jeanne Mouler, Lord Edward Drummond and three other persons, piled them on a cart, and sent them to the Bastille.[5]

1 Carré de Montgéron, *Vérité des Miracles*, II, Observations sur les Convulsionnaires, Deuxième partie, p. 32.
2 *Nouv. ecclés.* 1735, p. 174.
3 Carré de Montgéron, *op. cit.* II, Observations sur les Convulsionnaires, Deuxième partie, p. 32.
4 *Nouv. ecclés.* 1737, pp. 194-5.
5 Arsenal MS. 11422, f. 100 (Bastille, dossier Drummond. A few of these papers have been printed in Ravaisson, *Archives de la Bastille*, xv, pp. 33-40).

One of Lord Edward's first thoughts was to reassure his wife, and he wrote her the next morning a little letter which never reached its destination at Saint-Germain, since to this day it reposes among the papers of the Bastille.

samedy matin.

Nous avons été arretés hier au matin a la Campagne par ordre du Roy et j'ai couché cette nuit à la Bastille, ne soiez nullement en peine de moy et tenez vous en repos, je n'ai jamais passé une mellieure nuit, et je me trouve par la misericorde de Dieu dans une paix que je ne puis vous exprimer. Je vous embrasse de tout mon cœur.

E. D.[1]

Lady Drummond on hearing of her husband's imprisonment left Saint-Germain at once and came to Paris. A note from her which was probably never shown her husband is also among the papers of the Bastille.

ce dimanche 1ᵉʳ 9ᵇʳᵉ

ie suis venue ici aujourd'hui, mon cher my Lord pour être plus a portée de scavoir de vos nouvelles, vous me coñoissez assez pour imaginer que ien suis inquete ie vous coniure de men donner aussi souvent qu'il vous sera permis et de me dire sincerement comment vous vous portez et si vous n'avez point besoin de linge ou d'habits ie vous souhaite le bon soir mon cher my lord.[2]

At his examination Lord Edward declared that it was useless to question him since he had nothing to say beyond the fact that he respected the orders of the king, that no one could be more attached to His Majesty than he was, but that he regarded the convulsions as the work of God.[3]

A letter from his wife must have reached him at length, for on November 10th he writes to her, moved by her anxiety, but this letter too remained at the Bastille.

Je suis plus penetré que je ne puis vous l'exprimer, Madame, de la situation ou vous vous trouvez, j'espere que Dieu dans sa misericorde sera votre consolation...j'ai été tres attendri en lisant votre lettre, et je vous avouerai que contre votre intention elle a été une forte tentation pour moi, je dis contre votre intention, parce que j'ai eu la

---

1 *Ib.* f. 110. Addressed: "Madame, Madame la Comtesse de Drummond au Chateau a St Germain en Laye".
2 *Ib.* f. 112. Addressed: "Monsieur, Monsieur le Comte de Drummond". Not signed, but the writer is obviously Lady Drummond.
3 *Ib.* f. 76. Signed: "E. Drummond de Perth".

consolation d'y voir que vous seriez fachée que je fasse aucune demarche contre mon honneur et ma conscience, et il est vrai que si dans la conjoncture presente je me determinois a promettre la moindre chose, je croirois prononcer ma propre condamnation...le moindre faux pas peut conduire dans l'abyme et après y avoir été comme englouti pendant tant d'années, je dois plus trembler que tout autre.[1]

But deliverance was at hand, and three days later he was set free, though relegated to Saint-Germain.[2] He continued to be regarded as a suspicious character, for when he asked in 1741 to be allowed to go to Paris, he was told that it would be very dangerous to give him such permission.[3]

In 1747 he seems to have taken things into his own hands, for it was rumoured that he and his wife were in Paris, and the Lieutenant de Police, Hérault, received instructions to find out where they were—"ils sont convulsionnaires et on aurait une signification à leur faire".[4] Various places were investigated, the "hotel imperial rue Dauphine" where lived Milord Édouard's nephew, "Milord Jean Durmonde Duc de Perth", the "Cartier Ste Genevive", where Milord Édouard was well known, the Collège des Écossais, but all that could be learned was that he had returned to Saint-Germain-en-Laye after a stay of two months somewhere in Paris.[5]

About fifteen months later Hérault was informed that Lord Edward Drummond was living in the "rue popaincourt"— "très connu pour Grand Convulsionnaire tient chez lui des assemblées où il s'y trouve ce que nous avons de plus fameux dans le party".[6] Yet nothing seems to have been done at the time, and the report forgotten, for two years later the Lieutenant de Police, Berryer, was ordered to find out who was the foreigner, the lord, living in a certain house, "rue popincourt", and who were the people he saw. "Il importe au service du roi que je

1 Arsenal MS. 11422, f. 128. Addressed: "A Madame, Madame la Comtesse de Drummond".
2 Ib. ff. 29, 118. See also MSS. 12483, 12491, f. 44, 12581. This episode is also mentioned in Barbier's Journal, IV, p. 63; Luynes, Mémoires, XIV, p. 17; La Bastille dévoilée (1789, 3 vols.), I, p. 94; Funck-Brentano, Les Lettres de Cachet à Paris, p. 273.
3 Arsenal MS. 11422, f. 141.   4 Ib. f. 161.   5 Ib. f. 163.   6 Ib. f. 165.

sois informé", says the Ministre des Affaires Étrangères, the Marquis de Puyzieulx.[1]

Nothing very alarming was learned about the "foreigner", le Comte de Drummond. He was sixty years old, very pious, and kept his gardener very busy—"il aime extremement les fleurs". He and his wife saw very few people, and when they first came to this house which belonged to a Monsieur Racine, they never went out, never received anyone and had even forbidden their servants to mention their name. But a cook whom they had dismissed had boasted that her master's name was Stuart and that he was closely related to Prince Charles Edward—the young Pretender—which showed, so the police thought, that the prince might have stayed here when he came to Paris.[2] The young Pretender, it will be remembered, had been obliged to withdraw from France in 1748. The government, more interested at that time in the whereabouts of the young Pretender than in the doings of Lord Edward, seems to have left him in peace to cultivate his flowers and go to mass.

Since we are dealing with the subject of miracles and convulsionaries, we may note that among others cured by the intercession of "M. de Pâris" one finds a nun of English or Irish origin, born at Saint-Germain, Charlotte "Kearnen",[3] while a certain Lord Kingston was also said to frequent the convulsionaries.[4] Another whom one finds in their society was the abbé de Barneville of Dublin who seems to have been of the family of the Barnewalls, Viscounts Kingsland.[5] He had been imprisoned in the Bastille for a year and a half in 1712–13, for having distributed Jansenist books and tracts, and was again arrested at Port Royal des Champs in 1736, in the company of convulsionaries, an old man of over eighty. He died in the prison of the Conciergerie in 1738, protesting to the last against

1 *Ib.* ff. 174, 177, 186.
2 *Ib.* ff. 181–2.
3 *Nouv. ecclés.* 1732, p. 198.
4 Ravaisson, *Archives de la Bastille*, xv, p. 32.
5 This Matthew Barnewall who admitted that he had changed his name to "de Barneville" in France said that his father was a "gentilhomme", and that he himself was born at Gracedieu near Dublin, a property which belonged to the Barnewalls of Kingsland (Lodge, *Peerage of Ireland*, 1754, vol. III).

the formulary and the Bull *Unigenitus*. His letters from the Conciergerie were signed "prisonnier pour Jésus Christ", perhaps in imitation of Soanen, Bishop of Senez, with whom he corresponded.[1]

With Lord Edward Drummond we also encounter another curious phase of the Jansenist struggle, the open warfare between the Gallican Parlement of Paris and the Church. In 1749 the Archbishop of Paris, Christophe de Beaumont, had ordered his clergy to refuse the sacraments to all those suspected of Jansenism, unless they could produce a "billet de confession", i.e. a letter showing that they had made their confession to a priest accepting the Constitution *Unigenitus*. The Jansenists complained of this measure to the Parlement of Paris which retaliated by punishing the clergy either by imprisonment or banishment. The king sided now with the bishops, now with the Parlement.[2]

In 1755 Lady Drummond fell dangerously ill, and the curé of the parish church, Sainte-Marguerite, being asked to administer the last rites to her refused because Lady Drummond would not tell him to whom she had made her confession. No English or Irish "porte-dieu" of the parish would administer her. It was supposed that she had confessed to one of the Scotch Jansenists who were often at the house.

Milord Édouard complained to the Premier Président of the Parlement of Paris, and went again, accompanied by a huissier, to the curé. Three "sommations" were made without result and the Parlement took up the case. The curé escaped imprisonment by flight, and another priest, Coquelin by name, complied with the order of the Parlement and administered the sacraments to Lady Drummond, but he in turn was interdicted by the Arch-

1 Arsenal MS. 10602 (Bastille, dossier Barneville et Pardiac), ff. 90. 92, 130, 132, etc.; Arsenal MS. 11314 (Bastille, dossier Chopin), f. 323; Arsenal MS. 11462 (Bastille, dossier Frion), ff. 248, 256–62, 275, 277–8; *Nouv. Ecclés.* 1728, seconde suite du Supplément, p. 292; Ravaisson, *Archives de la Bastille*, XIII, pp. 24–6 (correspondence concerning him); *Vie et Lettres de M. Soanen*, II, p. 480; Funck-Brentano, *Lettres de cachet*, p. 167. His niece "Marie Anne de Barneville" of Dublin was also imprisoned for frequenting convulsionaries, Arsenal MS. 11462 (Bastille, dossier Frion), ff. 105, 131, 132, 134, 138.
2 Préclin, *Les Jansénistes du dix-huitième Siècle*, pp. 236–50.

bishop of Paris for his disobedience. The clergy were in an extremely difficult situation—if they obeyed the archbishop they were punished by the Parlement and if they obeyed the Parlement they were punished by the archbishop. The incident caused a great sensation.[1]

Eventually Lady Drummond recovered, but a somewhat similar incident took place when Lord Edward Drummond, now Duke of Perth, died in 1760—the priest who administered the last rites to him was interdicted by the Archbishop of Paris. The duke was buried in the church of Sainte-Marguerite amid the sorrowing poor who looked upon him as their friend, their benefactor and their father.[2]

When the Parlement of Paris took up the case of Lady Drummond there was among her witnesses "le Comte Rothe neveu de la dame de Perth".[3] This was Edward Rothe, son of Lieutenant-General Michael Rothe and Lady Katherine Middleton—very likely he too belonged to the circle of Saint-Germain Jansenists.

To the same group doubtless belonged the abbé Francis Plowden, son of Francis Plowden, comptroller of the household of Saint-Germain and his wife Mary Stafford, maid of honour to Mary of Modena. He left St Gregory's Seminary without taking the doctorate on account of some scruples concerning the Constitution *Unigenitus* and gave up all hopes of preferment, though it is said that the Pretender wished to nominate him for the cardinalate. He went to England, somewhat uncertain whether his services would be accepted, all English priests being required to subscribe the Bull. His surmise proved correct and he returned to France after three years, worked with the Pères de la Doctrine Chrétienne, and died regretted by the Jansenists of the *Nouvelles ecclésiastiques*, and no doubt by many others.[4]

1 B.N. f. fr. MS. 20959, ff. 13–17; f. fr. MS. 23459, ff. 64–5 (I owe both references to M. Préclin); Arsenal MS. 11422, ff. 190–3; *Nouv. ecclés.* 1755, pp. 37, 40, 41, 61; Barbier, *Journal*, pp. 62–3; Luynes, duc de, *Mémoires*, XIV, pp. 11, 15, 16, 17.
2 *Nouv. ecclés.* 1760, pp. 126–7; Cerveau, *Supplément au Nécrologe*, IV, pp. 159–60.
3 *Nouv. ecclés.* 1755, p. 41.
4 *Ib.* 1789, p. 97; Gillow, *Biographical Dictionary*, v, p. 327; Kirk, *Biographies*, p. 185; *Catholic Record Soc. Public., Miscellan.* (1917), XI, p. 132; Lart, *Jacobite Extracts* (1912, 2 vols.), pp. 114–15.

Another who had spent his youth at Saint-Germain was the abbé Strickland, later Bishop of Namur, a not altogether attractive personality and much of an intriguer. Various charges were brought against him at different times, among them the charge of Jansenism.[1]

Born at Saint-Germain in 1709 Francis Fitzjames,[2] one of the sons of the Duke of Berwick, entered the Church, and eventually became Bishop of Soissons. He was trained at the seminary of Saint-Sulpice, and accepted both the formulary and the Constitution *Unigenitus*, but treated with leniency and even with esteem those who thought otherwise and was considered favourable to the Appellants, while the Jansenists professed great admiration for him. Twice he was recommended for the cardinalate by his uncle, the Pretender, but the court of France was opposed because he was represented, as he himself wrote to the Pope, Benedict XIV, "un homme suspect dans sa doctrine et accusé de jansénisme". It was said that after his death the Jesuits spread the report that M. de Soissons had died "en vrai Anglican" without wishing to receive the sacraments.[3] He was buried in the convent of the English Benedictines at Paris. "Gare les Miracles!" exclaimed a Jesuit. "Il va en pleuvoir aux Bénédictins anglais, autant qu'à Saint-Médard."[4]

It must not be inferred, however, that all those who grew up at Saint-Germain were admirers of Jansenism. One finds, for instance, Catherine Dillon, sister of Arthur Richard Dillon, Archbishop of Narbonne, chosen to reform the convent of the Carmelites at Saint-Denis, the Carmelites having refused to accept the Constitution *Unigenitus*. "Prieure par Lettre de Cachet", the *Nouvelles ecclésiastiques* call her disdainfully[5]—and as for the

1 Du Pac de Bellegarde, *Mémoires historiques sur l'affaire de la Bulle Unigenitus dans les Pays Bas autrichiens* (1755, 4 vols.), II, p. 282 *n.*; Dorsanne, *Journal*, I, p. 498; Panzani, *Memoirs* (Berington's Supplement), pp. 408–9.

2 An interesting portrait of Fitzjames is to be found in *El Mariscal de Berwick* by the Duque de Berwick y de Alba (Madrid 1925).

3 Fitzjames, *Œuvres posthumes*, I, pp. xv, xvii, xviii, lxxxi–lxxxiii, lxxxvi, cvi; *Nouv. ecclés.* 1764, p. 153, 1789, p. 97; Racine (abbé), *Hist. ecclés.* XII, p. 51; Gazier, *Histoire du mouvement janséniste, passim*, especially II, pp. 91–7.

4 Gazier, *op. cit.* II, p. 97 *n.*

5 *Nouv. ecclés.* 1747, p. 185.

archbishop himself, one gathers from the Memoirs of his grand-
niece, Mme de la Tour du Pin,[1] that he was very far removed
from being a Jansenist, not only in matters of doctrine but also
in his manner of living.

1 Mme de la Tour du Pin, *Journal d'une femme de cinquante ans* (1913, 2 vols.).

CHAPTER XVIII

Latter day Friends

THE condemnation of Jansenius, of Jansenism in its earlier stages and of the five propositions, had interested Protestant England chiefly in so far as it offered evidence of dissension within the Catholic Church or seemed another proof of the machinations of the Jesuits. Much greater personal interest was taken in Quesnel.[1] No one except a few theologians had read the *Augustinus*, the five propositions were beyond the comprehension of the lay mind, and who could fathom the subtle distinction made by the Jansenists between fact and right? But here was a kindly old man whom some had visited in Holland,[2] here was a New Testament accompanied by a plain commentary, a commentary written by one who had "a great talent in speaking to the heart".[3] What he said about the futility

---

1 Quesnel's family lived for a time in Scotland (Quesnel, *Correspondance*, II, p. 394). One finds him described in the *Nécrologe des Appelans* (p. 86) as "fils de Jacques Quesnel, Libraire à Paris et petit-fils de François Quesnel, Gentilhomme Ecossois". This François Quesnel is doubtless the painter born at Holyrood, "François Quesnel, peintre et dessinateur français, né à Holyrood en Ecosse, vers 1543, mort à Paris en 1619. Son père Pierre Quesnel...était attaché à la cour de Marie de Lorraine,...mère de Marie Stuart" (*Grande Encyclopédie*). There was a Quesnel who wrote letters in English for the English embassy in Paris (R.O. *S.P. France*, vol. 122, f. 68).

2 An Englishman who visited Quesnel in Holland in 1714 and had a great deal of talk with him *de Primata Papae* was so charmed, as he said, with his very good company that he wished all Papists were like him. Quesnel was then about 80 years old and was living "with four very great scholars, Pères de l'Oratoire de Paris in a house of Prince Gracht...and had a free and easy way of shaking off prejudices established by Popes and Councils". *Hist. MSS. Comm., MSS. of the Duke of Portland at Welbeck*, v, p. 456 (by the "house of Prince Gracht" is doubtless meant a house on the Prinsengracht, Amsterdam).

3 G. Horne (Bishop of Norwich), *Works* (1818, 6 vols.), 1, p. 231. From a letter written to a lady in 1758. "The Portroyalists were the first, we believe, whether among Roman Catholics or Protestants, who distinctly conceived, and executed consistently and intelligently the plan, familiar enough to us of a 'plain commentary' without any shew of learning and intended simply for practical instruction and simple explanation." Dean Church, *Occasional Papers* (1897, 2 vols.), 1, p. 278.

of human effort and the saving power of grace, of the life hidden in God, and Christ above all things, was very familiar and acceptable, and in the Bull condemning him they saw "the unanimous sense of the Holy Evangelists condemn'd as Devilish and Damnable"[1]—"that diabolical Bull Unigenitus", said Wesley, "which destroys the very foundations of Christianity",[2] a Bull which had put an end to all attempts "to bring about a reconciliation between the Protestant and Romish Churches".[3] As early as 1706, some years before the Bull, there were rumours of Quesnel's going over to the Anglican Church, and one who returned from England reported that Quesnel was said to be there, seeking employment from the Archbishop of Canterbury.[4]

The Bull was promulgated in 1713 and had one result interesting for England, namely a movement to bring the Gallican and Anglican Churches together. The chaplain to Lord Stair, English Ambassador in France, a certain Beauvoir, seems to have consorted with Appellants and Jansenists,[5] especially Dr Du Pin, the Church historian, who informed him of the appeal of the four bishops in 1717—"voilà des nouvelles qui ne vous seront pas indifférentes".[6] In December of that year Beauvoir dined with Du Pin, with Dr Hideux, the Jansenist Syndic of the Sorbonne, and two other doctors, doubtless Jansenists also. "They talked as if the whole Kingdom was to appeal to the future general council. They wished for an union with the church of England

---

1 *The Pope's Bull* (see p. 286 of this book), Preface.
2 Wesley, *Journal*, III, p. 451.
3 Wesley, *A concise Ecclesiastical History* (1781), IV, pp. 158–61 (an adaptation of Mosheim's *Ecclesiastical History*).
4 "Je...le questionnai sur ce qu'il avoit veu en Angleterre, il me dit qu'il y avoit esté pris avec Mr leveque de Quebeck et mené prisonnier à Londres. Il me raconta les honnestetes que Mr l'Archeveque de Cantorbery avoit fait à Mr de Quebeck, qu'il le traitoit comme son confrère, qu'il lui avoit fait presenter un habit violet et de très beau linge et une croix d'or avec permission de la porter...je luy demandé s'il n'avoit point ouy parler en ce pays la du Pere Quesnel, il me dit qu'il en avoit ouy beaucoup parler et qu'on disoit qu'il estoit venu en Angleterre demander de l'employ à l'Archevesque de Cantorbery." (The abbé Delagarde to the abbé Despinay.) B.N. f. fr. MS. 19736, f. 87, July 23 [1706], cf. f. 81, June 28 [1706].
5 B.M. Add. 22880 (Beauvoir Correspondence), *passim*.
6 Lupton, *Archbishop Wake and the Project of Union* (1717–1720) *between the Gallican and Anglican Churches*, p. 48.

as the most effectual means to unite all the Western Churches."[1] The story of this Project of Union is well known to English students. It was fully told by Lupton[2] in 1896, and again with additions by Dr Préclin in 1928,[3] and it will suffice to say a few words only about it here.

A letter from Du Pin to Archbishop Wake on February 11th, 1718, expressed desire for union between the Gallican and Anglican Churches. In March an address was made by a certain abbé de Girardin to the doctors of the Sorbonne commending a possible reconciliation.[4] In summer Du Pin drew up a kind of document called a *Commonitorium* showing in what way the Churches might be united. The Cardinal de Noailles was said to approve of the project. Letters passed back and forth, and the matter began to be noised abroad.[5] Du Pin was known to correspond with the Archbishop of Canterbury. "D'abord on supposa que ce commerce étoit un devoir de pure civilité. Dans la suite on y soupçonna du mystère; il en transpira quelque chose, on y eut l'œil. Enfin on parvint à la connaissance du plus abominable complot qu'un Docteur Catholique ait pu tramer en matière de religion."[6] This plot was what adversaries called the "Projet pour unir à l'Église Anglicane le Parti des Jansénistes opposans".[7] Du Pin's papers were seized in February 1719, and in June of this year he died. Matters were at a standstill for the present though some half-hearted attempts continued to be made by the abbé Girardin and others.[8]

But Girardin had a friend who was becoming increasingly interested in the validity of Anglican ordinations, and who in turn became the correspondent of Archbishop Wake. This was

1 Maclaine's ed. of Mosheim's *Ecclesiastical History* (1825, 6 vols.), III, pp. 642–3, Beauvoir to Wake.
2 See p. 257 n. 6.
3 *L'Union des Églises Gallicane et Anglicane.*
4 He thought that the English Church might be more easily reconciled than the Greek. The possibility of reconciliation between the Greek and the Gallican Churches was at this time under consideration.
5 See e.g. *Gazette de la Régence* (éd. E. de Barthélemy, 1887), p. 301.
6 Lafiteau, *Histoire de la Constitution Unigenitus*, pp. 413–15.
7 *Dictionnaire des Livres Jansénistes*, III, pp. 320–2.
8 For these see Préclin, *op. cit.* pp. 16–21.

the famous Père Le Courayer who published in 1723 the *Dissertation sur la Validité des Ordinations des Anglais*, "une suite de ce malheureux projet d'union que le docteur Dupin avoit projeté quelques années auparavant avec l'église anglicane", says the Bishop of Sisteron, Lafiteau.[1] Withdrawing to England in 1728 Le Courayer lived there till his death in 1776, and was buried in the cloisters of Westminster Abbey.

Now although Le Courayer was an Appellant, and though his work is often classed as Jansenist,[2] he himself affirmed that he was anything but a Jansenist, and Queen Caroline remarked that the Jansenists were "his utter enemies and would consent to burn him if they had him in their power because of some of his opinions".[3] An account of him is therefore rather beyond the scope of this work, but in connection with the question of the validity of Anglican ordinations it is interesting to note that in 1925 the Old Catholic Church of Utrecht, formerly often designated as the Jansenist Church of Holland, recognized this validity, and that there exists a society for the reunion of the Anglican and Old Catholic Communions, the Society of St Willibrord.[4] The Archbishop of Utrecht, Mgr Kenninck, and the Bishops of Haarlem and Deventer attended the Lambeth Conference of 1930.

As for the abbé Piers de Girardin, who has been mentioned several times, he was of Irish extraction. Queen Caroline who knew him said that his true name was Price, but that he pretended to be of the Fitzgerald family in Ireland and hence took the name of Giraldon (*sic*).[5] Beauvoir calls him "Abbot Pearse" in one of his letters.[6] He was an Appellant and Reappellant, and was excluded from the Faculty of Theology for

---

1 *Histoire de la Constitution Unigenitus*, pp. 493–4.
2 E.g. *Dictionnaire des Livres Jansénistes*, 1, pp. 486–93. His work is condemned by the "mandements de plusieurs évêques...qui en prennent occasion d'invectiver contre les Jansenistes mettant sur leur compte la doctrine perverse de ce Genovefain sur le libre arbitre et la gràce", complains the Jansenist publication, the *Nouvelles ecclésiastiques*, 1728, p. 16.
3 *Hist. MSS. Comm., Egmont MSS., Diary*, 1, p. 396.
4 C. B. Moss, *The Old Catholic Churches and Reunion, passim*, especially pp. 57, 62.
5 *Egmont MSS., loc. cit.*
6 B.M. Add. 22880, f. 8.

his Jansenism.[1] He went to England more than once, probably in 1721–2, as the guest of Archbishop Wake,[2] and again in 1732 when he fled to England "being a busy Jansenist", to avoid the anger of Cardinal Fleury, but at the desire of Queen Caroline he had permission to return unmolested. "For which I have great obligations to the Cardinal", said the queen, "but it was on condition that if he should play the fool again I should never mediate more for him, for he would certainly send him to the Bastille."[3]

Girardin also corresponded with Dutch Jansenists, and especially with the canon Ernest de Brigode who was greatly interested in union with the Anglican Church.[4] He associated with Bishop Atterbury too, living in exile in France, another Anglican who evidently saw much of Jansenist society, for after he had been visited by some officers of justice on account of his having supposedly helped Le Courayer in his flight, he also received a letter from the Lieutenant de Police, Hérault, to notify him of the king's desire "que les Jansénistes ne trouvassent auprès de vous ny ressources ni conseils, et que vous éloignassiez surtout de votre hostel quelques prêtres dont la doctrine est contraire à celle de l'Église Romaine".[5]

Let us return to England, and to some of the books and pamphlets of the time. The Bull *Unigenitus* was issued in 1713, as we have seen; in 1714 appeared a translation of the Bull with a preface directed "to all English Protestants by one of the Reform'd in France". Quesnel, they were told, was called by many good people the second Luther, though "whether he may advance the Blessed Work of the Reformation so far as to Merit that glorious Appellation God only knows". Three editions of this pamphlet were published in the year 1714. Between 1714 and 1753 the Bull was printed at least eight times

1 *La Constitution Unigenitus déférée*, I, pp. lxii and 306; *Nouv. ecclés.* 1730, pp. 9, 131; Préclin, *op. cit.* p. 161.
2 Lupton, *op. cit.* p. 105 *n.*
3 *Hist. MSS. Comm., Egmont MSS., Diary*, I, p. 396.
4 Préclin, *op. cit.* p. 21. His source is the *Corr. Politique de Hollande* at the Affaires Étrangères.
5 Folkestone Williams, *Memoirs and Correspondence of Bishop Atterbury* (1869, 2 vols.), II, p. 258.

in England, either alone or with other works, all bitterly opposed to the Bull and designed to show up once more the "errors of Popery". The appeal of the Cardinal de Noailles, opposed to the Bull, was observed with keen interest. In 1720 came *A short History of the Constitution Unigenitus*, "thunder'd out against that Incomparable Work, *Moral Reflections upon the New Testament*".

"I here present you with the Translation of a small Treatise", said the publisher, "sent some little time ago to a Gentleman in London by his Correspondent in France. It has run thro the Fire there, and the Custom House here; Two great Escapes!...I need not mention the Thousands of this Treatise in the Original that have, as I am informed, been Privately Printed, and handed about over the whole Kingdom of France: For if the Secret Springs of Great Actions and Revolutions are justly accounted the most valuable Part of History, this Little Piece may upon that Score claim some Regard, since it opens the First Scene of a probable Reformation in France; where there seems nothing wanting but an Henry the Eighth to finish so great and desirable a Change and to unite us as happily in our Religion as we are at present in our Politicks."

Boyer's *Parallèle de la doctrine des païens avec celle des jésuites et de leur constitution* was translated and published as soon as it appeared in 1726. "The Original was no sooner printed in a neighbouring Kingdom, than it was suppress'd, and even smothered by the Flames of Authority, but after having been brought over to England with great Hazard and Difficulty was directed to be translated into English."[1]

From 1719 to 1725 appeared, from the pen of Richard Russell, an Anglican clergyman who had been obliged to give up his living on account of the new oath of allegiance, the first complete English translation of Quesnel—with the omission of "a few popish errors". A Roman Catholic translation had been suppressed, as we have seen. This new translation contained a short biography of Quesnel, as well as a reprint of the Constitution *Unigenitus*. The translator had planned to add a short historical account of the controversy, but wisely refrained "since the controversy is newly broken out with greater violence

1 *A parallel...*, Dedication, p. iii.

than ever".[1] His translation was reprinted twice in the eighteenth century, at Bath in 1790 and at Glasgow.[2] The "Presbyter
of the Church of England" responsible for the 1790 edition
said that "though an Englishman he hoped he would not offend
any by declaring that he knew of no exposition in his mother
tongue so well calculated to do good as this one". He would
rather die, he said, with Quesnel's faith in the most desert
regions, than in the faith of the Council of Trent in the Pope's
palace. We are told that Dr Horne, the Bishop of Norwich, who
was a constant reader of Quesnel, had adopted Quesnel's method
of writing in his *Commentary on the Psalms*.[3] When another
edition of Quesnel appeared in the nineteenth century,[4] the
editor remarked that the work might be considered as already
naturalized in England.

    Among Quesnel's admirers is Wesley, who possessed all his
works and had chosen his *Commentary on the Gospels* as one of the
books to be studied at the school at Kingswood.[5] Duguet is
another of the later Jansenists to whom he feels drawn, and he
translated some of his writings. The earlier Jansenists are not to
his liking—their doctrine was not his, but approximated rather
to that of Whitefield—and in his *Ecclesiastical History*, partly
translated from Mosheim, partly adapted from M'Laine's translation of Mosheim, he goes even further than Mosheim in his
severe judgment and speaks harshly of Saint-Cyran.[6] The
manuscript notes on Wesley's copy of Nicole show that he did
not care for him either.[7]

    He took a keen interest in the so-called miracles wrought at
the tomb of the diacre Pâris, and it has been suggested, rather
unkindly, that the fanaticism of the convulsionaries had features
closely resembling those of contemporary Methodism in Eng-

    1 *Moral Reflections*, 1, p. xiii.   2 Preface to the 1842 edition.
    3 Preface to the 1790 edition, pp. ix, xi, xvi. "All who love divine truth must
delight to read and cannot but admire so spiritual, so holy, so sensible, so
judicious a writer as Quesnel."
    4 In 1842.
    5 Gounelle, *Wesley et ses rapports avec les Français*, p. 79, see also *Journal*, 1,
p. 269.
    6 *A concise ecclesiastical History* (1781, 4 vols.), IV, pp. 50–3.
    7 Gounelle, *op. cit.* p. 81.

land.[1] We may point out here, leaving Wesley for a moment, that Bougeant's comedy, intended to show up what he considered the impostures of the Jansenists, is entitled *Les Quakres François*.[2] Wesley did not share the scepticism of Queen Caroline who thought that the Jansenists helped their cause "by craft and lying wonders". "I cannot forgive their playing tricks to support themselves", she says, "and pretending to be cured of distemper by praying to Abbé Paris."[3]

One finds the following entry in Wesley's *Journal* in 1750:

> I read, to my no small amazement, the account given by Monsieur Montgeron both of his own conversion and of the other miracles wrought at the tomb of Abbé Paris. I had always looked upon the whole affair as a mere legend, as I suppose most Protestants do, but I see no possible way to deny these facts without invalidating all human testimony. I may full as reasonably deny that there is such a person as M. Montgeron or such a city as Paris in the world....If it be said "But will not the admitting these miracles establish Popery". Just the reverse. Abbé Paris lived and died in open opposition to the grossest errors of Popery.[4]

Wesley's conviction excited the scorn of Bishop Warburton who remarked that "Mr Wesley chooses to let Popery share with him the glory of divine communications and expressly vouches for the Miracles wrought at the tomb of Abbé Paris",[5] to which Wesley replied: "As to the affair of Abbé Paris, whoever will read over with calmness and impartiality but one volume of Monsieur Mongeron, will then be a competent judge. Meantime I would just observe that if these miracles were real, they strike at the root of the whole Papal authority, as having been wrought in direct opposition to the famous Bull Unigenitus".[6]

1 *Times Lit. Suppl.* Nov. 14, 1929, "The later Jansenism" (a review of Dr Préclin's books).
2 Bougeant, *Les Quakres François ou les Nouveaux Trembleurs* (Utrecht 1732).
3 *Hist. MSS. Comm., Egmont MSS., Diary*, I, p. 396.
4 *Journal*, III, p. 451.
5 Warburton, *The Doctrine of Grace* (1763), p. 162. These miracles are also discussed in A. A. Sykes, *A brief discourse concerning the credibility of Miracles and Revelations* (1742). Warburton admired Arnauld and called him "that shining ornament of the Gallican church". J. S. Watson, *Life of Warburton*, cf. Arnauld, *Œuvres*, v, p. lxvi.
6 Wesley, *Works*, IX, pp. 127-8.

Another eighteenth-century reader of Jansenist books was William Law (1686–1761), the famous author of the *Serious Call to a Devout and Holy Life*. In his library one finds a number of books by authors such as Saint-Cyran, Pascal, Arnauld d'Andilly, Hermant, Du Pin, Le Nain de Tillemont, as well as the Montpellier *Catechism*.[1]

As for Port Royal itself, comparatively little was known of it in England in the seventeenth century, but the publication in 1677 of the " *Moral Essays* written by Messieurs du Port Royal", the translation of Mme Périer's *Life* of Pascal in 1688, of their logic and their text-books, had begun to familiarize the public with the existence of the Messieurs. It should also be noted here that the vast majority of Port Royal books were not published till the eighteenth century, the *Mémoires pour servir à l'histoire de Port-Royal*, the *Mémoires* of Fontaine, Lancelot, du Fossé, the various *Nécrologes*, the *Recueil d'Utrecht*, the *Histoire des Persécutions*, Racine's *Abrégé*,[2] etc. A fragment of this last-named book was translated in 1785.

Claude Mauger, a seventeenth-century teacher of French in London, returning to England after an absence of some years boasted that in France he was every day with some of " the Ablest Gentlemen of the Port Royal", who assured him that his grammar was in their library, as well as his French Letters translated into English. He therefore informed his English readers—who were no doubt less startled than we are by the unexpected result of association with the Messieurs—that there were no words or phrases in his grammar but were "very Modish".[3]

In the eighteenth century readers of the *Spectator* learned from Addison himself that the gentlemen of Port Royal were more eminent for their learning and their humility than any other in France.[4] "Inform yourself what the Port Royal is"

1 *A catalogue of the Library at King's Cliffe founded by William Law* (1927).
2 Cf. a very interesting article by Mlle Gazier on "Les Sources de Sainte-Beuve", *Revue bleue* (*Revue politique et littéraire*), July 17, 1926.
3 Mauger, *French Grammar*, 16th edition (1694). Cf K. Lambley, *The Teaching and Cultivation of the French Language in England during Tudor and Stuart Times* (1920), pp. 310–11, and Charlanne, *L'influence française en Angleterre au dix-septième siècle* (1906), p. 193.
4 *Spectator*, July 2, 1714 (No. 562).

comes from so worldly a writer as Lord Chesterfield addressing his son.[1] Less unexpected is the testimony borne by a Quaker, Dr John Rutty. One finds him recording in 1754 in his *Spiritual Diary*, "Now and not until now, even in this evening of the day as at the eleventh hour, even in my fifty-sixth year, did God first favour me with this new irradiation of gospel light (and by means of those truly Christian writers the Messrs du Port-royal)", viz. "that it is criminal not to hate this life comparatively and not to desire the happiness of another life",[2] and two days afterwards "the picture drawn of the miseries of this life in the Messrs du Port Royal, never to be erased: for surely this gaudy scene is but a deceitful one".[3] Somewhat later he returns to the same subject: "Days without number have I idolized natural knowledge, in pursuing it as the chief good which it is not, a truth I was never thoroughly enlightened in till I lately read Messrs du Port Royal; so dwarfish have I been".[4]

But no one in eighteenth-century England seems to have admired Port Royal and its writers as Hannah More did. Her predilections were known to Dr Johnson who liked to tease her about them in his own way:

"Saturday I went to Mrs Reynolds", she writes, "to meet Sir Joshua and Dr Johnson....Our conversation ran very much upon religious opinions, chiefly those of the Roman Catholics. He took the part of the Jesuits and I declared myself a Jansenist. He was very angry because I quoted Boileau's bon mot upon the Jesuits that they had lengthened the creed and shortened the decalogue, but I continued sturdily to vindicate my old friends of the Port Royal."[5]

On another occasion he reproved her "with pretended sharpness" for reading "*Les Pensées* de Pascal or any of the Port Royal authors", alleging that as a good Protestant she ought to abstain from books written by Catholics. "I was beginning to stand on my defence", she tells us, "when he took me with both hands, and with a tear running down his cheeks. 'Child,' said he with the most affecting earnestness, 'I am heartily glad

1 Chesterfield, *Letters* (1892, 3 vols.), I, p. 73.
2 Rutty, *Spiritual Diary*, p. 13.
3 *Ib.*   4 *Ib.* p. 26, cf. p. 362.
5 Roberts, *Memoirs of Hannah More*, I, p. 278 (incident of 1783).

that you read pious books, by whomsoever they may be written.'"[1] Dr Johnson, it may be added, had a copy of the *Pensées* himself, and we have an entertaining picture of the book being given to the talkative Boswell on Good Friday 1779 to keep him from disturbing the doctor. "In the interval between morning and evening service, he endeavoured to employ himself earnestly in devotional exercises", says Boswell, "and...he ...gave me *Les Pensées de Paschal* that I might not interrupt him. I preserve the book with reverence. His presenting it to me is marked upon it with his own hand and I have found in it a truly divine unction."[2]

Hannah More's enthusiasm proved contagious—one summer in Oxford, in 1781, she happened to say so much about her favourite book *De l'histoire de Messieurs de Port Royal*[3] that it excited great desire in several reverend doctors to see it, no one there having ever met with it except Dr Horne, the future Bishop of Norwich, and reader of Quesnel ("Vous savez qu'il a une petite teinture du mystique", she explains, as she speaks of Dr Horne's extreme admiration for the story of Port Royal). The libraries were searched, but no such book could be found. Her friend Mrs Kennicott repeated to the Bishop of Llandaff, Bishop Barrington, what she had said about the book, and the bishop resolved at once to get it and accordingly sent to Holland for two sets, but in vain, for he was told that the book was quite out of print and never could be got but by chance in a catalogue. One finds Hannah More writing to her friend Mrs Boscawen to borrow a copy for the Kennicotts, though not for the bishop who, she thought, would doubtless call her an enthusiast and a thousand bad names for so warmly recommending a book in which there was a little mystical rubbish.[4]

She herself bought Port Royal books wherever she could, and finally, after a search of nearly twenty years, she put herself in possession of "almost all those excellent authors, Messieurs de

---

1 Roberts, *Memoirs of Hannah More*, I, p. 211 (1781).
2 Boswell, *Life of Johnson* (Oxford 1887, 6 vols.) III, p. 380.
3 Possibly Fontaine's *Mémoires*? or Besoigne's *Histoire*? ("*deuxième partie: histoire des messieurs*").
4 Roberts, *Memoirs of Hannah More*, I, pp. 204-5.

Port Royal".[1] She did not hoard her treasures, however, as some of us might have done. One day she sent a parcel of her precious books to a friend in trouble, Mrs Mary Anne Schimmelpenninck, originally a Quaker, later a Moravian, and finally very much attracted by the Church of Rome. Mrs Schimmelpenninck read the books with the greatest interest—this was in 1809; she obtained others, and took a particular pleasure in Lancelot's *Voyage d'Alet*, also lent by Hannah More. She found that this book "was not to be easily procured", and noted down extracts, first for her own edification, but later on she translated them and, with additions of her own, put together a kind of compilation published in 1813 under the title of *Narrative of a Tour to la Grande Chartreuse and Alet*.[2]

She regretted that Port Royal was so little known to English readers.

"It is surprising", she remarks, "that a society which engaged so much attention scarcely a century ago, should now be so little known, in a country which daily enjoys the fruits of its labors. Whilst English youth owe the rudiments of ancient literature to Lancelot Arnauld (*sic*), the formation of their taste to Racine and Pascal; whilst our countrymen derive learning from the labors of Tillemont and piety from the works of Pascal, Nicole and Quesnel, surely no English reader ought to be indifferent to the untimely fate of Port Royal."[3]

After the peace of 1814 Mr and Mrs Schimmelpenninck went across to the Netherlands and here they formed an acquaintance with the famous Bishop Grégoire, the constitutional Bishop of Blois, and with him they visited the tomb of "the holy Jansenius".[4] They also visited Port Royal de Paris where la Mère Angélique is buried, Saint-Étienne du Mont where Pascal and Racine lie, they saw M. de Saint-Cyran's tomb at Saint-Jacques du Haut Pas, and the chapel there which before the Revolution contained the remains of Mme de Longueville.[5] But above all they went out to Port Royal des Champs. The description which

1 *Ib.* iii, p. 281 (this was in 1809), cf. pp. 216 and 238.
2 Hankin, *Life of Mary Anne Schimmelpenninck*, pp. 361–2.
3 Schimmelpenninck, *Narrative of a Tour to...Alet*, p. 243.
4 Hankin, *op. cit.* p. 362.
5 Schimmelpenninck, *Narrative of the Demolition of Port Royal*, pp. 344–5.

Mrs Schimmelpenninck left of her visit is exceedingly interesting, and some of it may well be quoted here; it is interesting too in that it shows the condition of Les Granges and Port Royal in 1814. To-day a tiny museum in the form of a chapel, erected in 1891, stands on the former site of the high altar of Port Royal, and La Solitude has been reconstructed. Much more remains of Les Granges, and the estate is fortunate in its present owner, M. Ribardière. A modern wing was built by a former owner, but the old part of the house with the cells of the solitaries is kept in a state of pious preservation.

Our visitors spent the night at Versailles to be within easy reach of Port Royal. They left early next morning. Their carriage soon turned from the highway, and they drove along a rather dreary road past two or three villages.

"At length", writes Mrs Schimmelpenninck in her *Journal*, "the tabled plain over which our road had generally extended, seemed suddenly to terminate just before us, as though we were arriving at the brow of a precipice extending across the whole plain. About a hundred yards to our right was a large old-fashioned farm-house, which the coachman informed us was Les Granges, the former abode of the recluses. He advised us to drive there first for directions, as the descent into the valley of Port Royal was exceedingly steep; and that he was unacquainted with the roads, one of which was very unsafe....

Accordingly we turned into the cart-track which led to the house, and which was bounded by a high garden-wall, till we came to a lofty archway, which having passed through, we found ourselves in the farmyard of the celebrated Les Granges, the abode of the Le Maîtres, the Fontaines, the Arnaulds, etc.

Here were the farmer and all his men at work, and the mistress busy feeding her poultry. In a moment our carriage was surrounded by master, mistress, men, maids...who all seemed equally amazed at the sight of a carriage in so remote a place.

They however told us...that we were perfectly welcome to see the whole house; that they would then conduct us by the foot-way down the steep, to see the remains of Port Royal des Champs, and that if we liked to take a farm-house dinner, they would with the greatest pleasure get us whatever their house afforded.

"I must now introduce you to Les Granges. More than half the original building, we were told, is demolished; but what is left, has yet the appearance of a very large and old-fashioned farm-house, built of rough stone....

The entrance to the house is from the farm-yard. A considerable part of the lower floor was formerly appropriated to the refectory of the recluses, but as it is now partitioned into several rooms, I could not judge of its size.

We then went up a staircase which is of brick or stone, to visit the chambers of the recluses: they are all floored with the small hexagonal tiles which are so common in France and Flanders. We first met with them in the bed-room of Jansenius at Louvain....

The physician Hamon's room was one of the first we saw. It was small, and must have been inconvenient. The furnace, oven, mortar and various other utensils for preparing medicines for the poor still remained. Through this room was a little light closet, in which he used to sleep on a board, instead of a mattress. The staples which held his bookcase yet remain, as well as the alarum by which he called himself to midnight prayer.

From this room we went to those of Arnauld, which are rather large, and open into each other. From the windows, which, like all the others in the house, were only the size of casements, the prospect is delightful....Here we saw the stone table on which M. d'Andilli wrote many of the lives of the Saints; and here our kind hostess, Madame Methouard, pointed out with much regret, the devastations of the Cossacks, who had pilfered a set of prints of Don Quixote, with which [Mrs Schimmelpenninck is able to record this without a smile] she had replaced the ecclesiastical library of Arnauld.

We then visited several of the other cells; after which, leaving our baggage in M. le Maitre's room, where we were to dine, we set out under the auspices of Madame Methouard, by the short path-way down the steep, to the Monastery; leaving our carriage...to meet us near the church-yard of St Lambert....

Our way lay through the farm-yard, where a door opened upon a space, which extended under the wall, along the brow of the hill. Here we distinctly perceived there had been a terrace, where the recluses walked to meditate. On the outside, the slope towards the brow of the hill was planted at intervals with fruit-trees, and was formerly their orchard.

On reaching the verge of the steep descent, we, for the first time, beheld Port Royal. Imagine the hill forming a complete steep or precipice, extending in an amphitheatrical form, and shagged with forest trees,...and in the bottom a beautiful level plain, watered by a brook, and terminated by an opposing range of wooded hills; in the midst, and almost directly under our feet, covered with a profusion of creepers and wild flowers, are the silent remains of the Monastery of Port Royal des Champs. The view...is one of the most completely beautiful it is possible to conceive. I could scarcely imagine, whilst contemplating it, that the view I was looking at was the same place which Madame de Sévigné describes as '*Un désert affreux et tout propre à inspirer le désir de faire son salut*'....

The monastery itself is so completely destroyed, that at the distance at which we stood, the ruins of its foundations, especially as they are grown over with shrubs and field-flowers, are scarcely perceptible, except as roughening the verdant plain....Just below us, at the foot of the hill, was the road winding between it and the boundary wall to the grand gothic entrance gate, which still remains entire. Close by it, to the right, is the house of the venerable M. De Saint Marthe now converted into a barn.

On the left, the road remains flanked with eight towers, built during the civil wars. Near them appears another grand gateway, which formerly led to the Hotel of the Duchesse of Longueville. The terrace of her garden still remains elevated above the level of the valley....The dovecote too remains, the mill also and the house of the miller,...and the solid stone-work constructed by the recluses, to draw the waters from the meadow, and render the naturally marshy valley healthy....In front of the place where we stood, and just at the foot of the opposing wooded hill, is a sort of amphitheatre hollowed out; it is carpeted with turf, and formed with rude stone-work like a grotto; it is overshadowed by the wide umbrage of the forest trees around, and above; and the remains of long stone seats show the place where the nuns of Port Royal used formerly to work together, and to hold their conference. This place was called the Desert; and many remaining pathways leading from it...still mark *la solitude*, where the nuns used to walk....All else is so completely ruined and demolished, that unless we had taken the plans and drawings, we could not possibly have distinguished the various parts of the buildings....

After contemplating the view for some time, we prepared to descend the hill....Accordingly, we began cautiously to descend the steep, by a rude zig-zag path, or track, which is, however, so precipitous, that it is by no means easy to keep a firm footing, even by holding the boughs of the trees and shrubs....

On reaching the bottom of the hill, we found ourselves in the private road, formerly bordered by an avenue, which turns out of the Chevreuse road, and runs between the foot of the hill and the north monastery wall to the Abbey door. This is a noble gothic gateway, of the style of the thirteenth century. On the right was a door for foot-passengers. In front is a little plain, where the poor used to assemble to receive food and alms. The traces of the stone benches yet remain....

Some way to the left of the entrance, extends a long range of ruined foundations, which, on consulting the description of the buildings of Port Royal, by Besogne, Clemencet and Racine, and comparing them with Mad. Horthemel's plans and drawings, is, I find, the long range of buildings appropriated to guests, which were divided into separate houses for men and women, and which had a very pretty garden behind it, extending as far as the wall of the monastery, and a solitude....

After crossing what was the grand entrance court...we came to what was formerly the site of the church. Nothing of this church now remains, but one vast pile of ruins....Amidst the heaps of stones and rubbish lying about them, we often traced the heads of angels...or broken columns or capitals, peeping out under the rich profusion of wild flowers which covered them....Cattle were quietly grazing on the green expanse of what was once the church. At the farther end, where once the high altar stood, is now a spreading walnut tree....

On one of the rude stones some visitor probably has deeply but rudely scratched with a knife the words: 'By the waters of Babylon we sat down and wept, when we remembered thee, O Zion'. The yellow lichen was beginning to deface some of the letters of this inscription, and many years are probably now passed by, since the individual who wrote it, has rejoined the saints he mourns.

Immediately behind the church which formed one side of the square, were the cloisters and burying-ground: at present grass and bright field flowers cover the whole expanse, yet the unevenness of the ground still records the barbarous exhumation of 1711, and the remains of the stone cross in the centre is covered with the names of pilgrims who visit the spot."

After spending some time wandering about the ruins and trying to identify the various places, our visitors walked to the village of Saint-Lambert. On their way they beheld the ruins of the Château de Vaumurier, once the country house of a friend of Port Royal, the duc de Luynes, and later the property of the convent, a house of reception to strangers and visitors. Near the church they came upon the house formerly occupied by M. Le Nain de Tillemont, and in the little church itself they found beside the high altar another altar which was taken from Port Royal at the time of the demolition, so they were told.

Then, searching for some time amongst the grass and nettles with which the churchyard was overgrown, they discovered the four stones which marked "the wide pit or grave in which were interred the mangled remains of the saints of Port Royal". They learned that remote as the little church of Saint-Lambert appeared, they were by no means the first who visited it. "Since the destruction of Port Royal it has always been esteemed a consecrated spot; and during the summer season, the ruins of Port Royal have constantly attracted numbers of visitors."

"Port Royal", so Mrs Schimmelpenninck writes in 1814, "is still held in such veneration that on the second of November (All Souls day), and on the twenty-ninth of October (the anniversary of its dispersion) there are multitudes of persons who...visit this consecrated spot; and many of them make, what is termed, the pilgrimage of Port Royal. That is, they take a regular tour, divided into ten or twelve stations, of all the places most remarkable as the scenes of the lives, or deaths, or burial places of the Port Royalists; and at each they spend some time in prayer, meditation, or other devotional exercises."

And Mrs Schimmelpenninck goes on to describe the little *Manuel des pèlerins de Port-Royal des Champs*, and doubtless she had brought her own copy with her[1], a copy given to her, as the fly-leaf records, by Bishop Grégoire.

"The country people, whose parents benefited by the piety or charity of Port Royal, are particularly assiduous and devout in visiting its ruins, and the common grave of their benefactors at St Lambert", she continues. "We were told, that both in the October which completed the century of its destruction, and on that of the remarkably hard winter two years ago, many aged people were seen kneeling, and some of them for hours, with their white locks exposed to a pouring rain, both amongst the ruins of Port Royal, and on the site of the interment in the church of St Lambert."

Our travellers now drove back to Les Granges where Mme Methouard gave them dinner in M. Le Maître's room. What pleased them most was a plate of pears from a tree planted by M. Arnauld d'Andilly and some peaches from a tree planted, so

1 To-day at Sion College Library.

they were told, by Pascal. After dinner they were taken to see "the celebrated well dug...under Pascal's direction"; it stood exactly in the middle of the farmyard, just opposite the house, but was "not discernible to those unacquainted with it", because it had been completely surrounded by piles of firewood, faggots and hay-stacks. This had been done to prevent accidents, as the Cossacks, during their abode at Port Royal, broke down the wall which formerly guarded the top. The machine for drawing the water had ceased to exist some years before.

On one side of the farmyard they were shown "a sort of dismantled hovel, or seed-house, the remains of a cell which Pascal used as a study, and where he was continually accustomed to retire during his visits at Port Royal, when he wished to be in perfect and uninterrupted solitude".

Then they went to the garden behind the house "very spacious...surrounded by a high wall, and planted with abundance of fruit trees". From space to space were little green arbours which served as places of retirement and meditation to the recluses during their work. Among the fruit trees they saw several of a great age, completely covered with moss and lichen, and of which only a very few branches still bore any fruit. Some of the trees planted by the solitaries were completely withered, but they were "left untouched and fenced round, out of respect to the memory of the saints of Port Royal". "These are holy trees", said Mme Methouard.

A last lingering look at the ruins of Port Royal, and the visitors took leave. As they passed Versailles on their way back to Paris, "Versailles where the decree for that demolition was signed", and as they beheld Saint-Denis next day "where the ashes of that sovereign who ordered it, were torn from their long sepulture", they reflected on the "just retribution from God".[1]

Returning home Mrs Schimmelpenninck set to work again, and wrote a *Narrative of the Demolition of Port Royal* which appeared in 1816, along with a much enlarged edition of the

---

[1] Schimmelpenninck, *Narrative of the Demolition of Port Royal des Champs*, pp. 313–51, viz. "Account of a visit to the ruins of Port Royal des Champs".

274 LATTER DAY FRIENDS

Tour to Alet.[1] These books were again published in 1829 with many additions, under the title of *Select Memoirs of Port Royal*.[2] In the preface Mrs Schimmelpenninck remarked that while a few of the moral and literary works of the Jansenists had attained just celebrity in England, their religious and biographical authors had been comparatively little known, and the history of "the celebrated Institution of Port Royal" itself still less so. A fourth edition followed, and a fifth edition appeared in 1858 after Mrs Schimmelpenninck's death.

Hannah More was keenly interested in these publications. "I am glad to see that you have so much contributed to make Port Royalism known in this country", she writes to her friend. "Even religious readers are in general ignorant of the treasures of religion and learning possessed by these devoted people. I was, even at an early period of my spiritual reading, so warm in their praise that Dr Johnson used to call me 'the Jansenist'."[3]

With the help of Bishop Grégoire Mrs Schimmelpenninck collected a small library of Port Royal books, many of them published anonymously or under pseudonyms, most of them out of print long ago, and therefore rare and valuable, none of them to be procured in England; and, indeed, without the assistance of one so versed in this literature it would have been difficult to achieve such a library.[4] The collection, comprising a little over four hundred volumes, practically all relating to Port Royal, is to-day at Sion College, London.[5] The books have a special book-plate, "Port Royal Library...", a catalogue of their own,[6] and are kept apart. Sion College also possesses

1 Contains biographies of Saint-Cyran, Jansenius, and a short sketch of Port Royal.　　　　　　2 In 3 vols.

3 Hankin, *Life of Mary Anne Schimmelpenninck*, p. 363.

4 *Ib*. See also the catalogue of the Port Royal Library at Sion College, Introduction, p. ix.

5 It was bequeathed by Mrs Schimmelpenninck to the Rev. Robert Aitken, vicar of Pendeen, who edited the 5th edition of her *Select Memoirs*. From his widow the collection came to Sion College.

6 *A complete Catalogue of the Sion College Port Royal Library* (Aberdeen University Press 1898). An old catalogue of Sion College Library, dated 1724, includes a certain number of Jansenist books. Of these the *Augustinus*, the *Fréquente Communion*, the *Pensées*, Nicole's *Essays* and Arnauld d'Andilly's *Pères des Déserts* all belonged at one time to Edward Waple's, London, Vicar of St Sepulchre's, Archdeacon of Taunton, and President of Sion College. A number of Jansenist books were also to be found at Dr William's Library, London.

Mrs Schimmelpenninck's set of the very rare Port Royal engravings by Madeleine Hortemels, and eighteen engraved portraits of persons connected with Port Royal. In the library itself hang the portraits of Jansenius, Saint-Cyran, and la Mère Angélique.

Another collection of Port Royal books is preserved at Oxford, in the library of Keble College.¹ These books, "the patient, intelligent accumulation of years", were brought together by the Rev. H. T. Morgan who died in 1910. All his life long he had been interested in the story of Port Royal, and he wrote a number of essays on its more theological aspects.²

The library of the London Oratory, Brompton Road, South Kensington, has the best collection in London, if not in England, of Jansenist books and pamphlets.³

Mrs Schimmelpenninck always rejoiced, we are told, that she had been the means of enabling her generation to know Port Royal.⁴ The nineteenth and twentieth centuries have continued her work, and a number of studies bear witness to the abiding interest which Port Royal has called forth in the country of Little Gidding.⁵

1 About 175 volumes—information kindly given me by Mr W. H. V. Reade, Librarian of Keble College.
2 H. T. Morgan, *Port Royal and other Studies* (1914), see p. 144, Postscript.
3 R. A. Rye, *Guide to the Libraries of London* (1927), p. 418. The Library is a private one, but the librarian has consented to admit male post-graduate students. (This collection is included in the above list for the sake of convenience, and naturally not as one emanating from a *milieu* favourable to Jansenism.)
4 Hankin, *op. cit.* p. 363.
5 While it is not proposed to give a full bibliography of English 19th- and 20th-century studies of Port Royal, the following should be mentioned: Charles Beard, *Port Royal*, 1861, 2 vols.; A. K. H., *Angélique of Port Royal*, 1905; E. Romanes, *The Story of Port Royal*, 1907; M. E. Lowndes, *The Nuns of Port Royal*, 1909; H. C. Barnard, *The little Schools of Port Royal*, 1913; H. T. Morgan, *Port Royal and other Studies*, 1914; H. C. Barnard, *The Port Royalists on Education*, 1918. Accounts of Jansenism are given by Neale in his *History of the so-called Jansenist Church of Holland*, 1885, by Viscount St Cyres in vol. v of the *Cambridge Modern History* (1908) and by Mr David Ogg, both in his *Europe in the Seventeenth Century*, 1925, and in a collective work, *Christianity in the Light of Modern Knowledge*, 1929. Jansenism is also studied in many books on Pascal, e.g. by Viscount St Cyres in his biography of *Pascal*, 1909, by Dr H. F. Stewart in *The Holiness of Pascal*, 1915 and in his edition of the *Lettres provinciales*, 1920, and by Mr R. H. Soltau, in *Pascal, the Man and the Message*, 1927.

A LETTER OF ORDINATION FROM BISHOP
FAGAN OF MEATH
(see p. 212)

Nos Lucas Fagan, Dei et Sanctæ Sedis Apostolicæ gratia, Episcopus
Middensis in Regno Hiberniæ, fidem facimus et attestamur dilectum
Domnum ac Magistrum Joannem Libon Archidiæcesis Ultrajectensis
a Domino Hugone Francisco van Heussen, Capituli Romano-
Catholici prædicti Archidiæcesis, sede vacante, Vicario Generali, ritè
dimissum, Litteris ab eo expeditis Lugduni Batavorum, 25. Martii
1715 ac præmissis cæteris de jure præmittendis, juxtà facultatem nobis
concessam ordinandi extrà tempora et non servatis interstitiis, fuisse
anno 1715 Dominicâ tertiâ post Pascha Resurrectionis, ad Diacona-
tum, et subsequente Dominicâ ad Presbiteratum a nobis ritè et
canonicè promotum et ordinatum; In quorum fidem præsentes
Litteras, manu sigilloque munitas, necnon Chirographo Secretarii
nostri subscriptas dedimus. In loco refugii nostri, die 25. Maii anno
Domini 1715.

Lucas Middensis.

De Mandato Illustrissimi Domini mei

Paulus Kenny.

(*Recueil de divers Témoignages*, p. 128.)

A NOTE ON A PSEUDO M. DE LUZANCY

One is surprised to find at the British Museum sermons by an Anglican clergyman bearing the Jansenist name of de Luzancy, the real M. de Luzancy being one of the sons of M. Arnauld d'Andilly, and thus brother of M. de Pomponne and of la Mère Angélique de Saint-Jean, and nephew of le grand Arnauld. This "M. de Luzancy" was known by name to Arnauld and Nicole who considered him an impostor, as indeed he must have been, if he really gave out that he was the son of M. Arnauld d'Andilly.

His real name was Hyppolite Châtelet de Beauchâteau, they said. He was the son of an actor and an actress, had entered the Congrégation de la Doctrine Chrétienne which he left to enter the Society of Jesus which he also left. He next went to the Jansenist abbé Le Roi at Hautefontaine, but finally, toward 1675, he proceeded to London where he abjured Catholicism. In London, so Arnauld and Nicole learned, he assumed the name of "M. de Luzancy", said he was M. de Pomponne's brother and Arnauld's nephew, a doctor of the Sorbonne and well known to the Gentlemen of Port Royal; he had worked at the *Perpétuité de la Foi* with his uncle, but had come to recognize his uncle's errors and had resolved to leave the Church of Rome. The author of Nicole's life, the abbé Goujet, learned that Luzancy had had an encounter with the Jesuits in London who had forced him to retract, but that Luzancy had thrown himself on the protection of Charles II.[1]

This is borne out by a proclamation of Charles II, dated November 10th, 1675, in which a reward of £200 was offered for the apprehension of the French Jesuit who had offered violence to "Monsieur Luzancy alias Chastelet". His Majesty, it was said, had taken M. Luzancy "in a more special manner under his Royal protection".[2]

Ultimately "M. de Luzancy" became vicar of Dovercourt and Harwich.[3]

1 Nicole, *Œuvres*, XIV (vie de M. Nicole) (Liége 1767), pp. 212–15.
2 A copy is preserved at the B.M. See also *Cal. S. P. Dom. Charles II*, 1675–6, pp. 389–93, 398, 1676–7, p. 261, 1674–8, *Addenda*, p. 614; Dodd's *Church History*, III, pp. 271–2 (based on Wood's *Fasti Oxonienses*) and Lingard, *History of England*, IX, pp. 278, 280, 377.
3 *A Sermon preached at Colchester June 2, 1697...before the Bishop of London at a Conference with his Clergy upon H.M. late Injunctions...by H. de Luzancy, B.D., Vicar of Doverc. and Harwich* (at the B.M.).

A LIST OF BOOKS CONNECTED WITH
PORT ROYAL AND JANSENISM

Being seventeenth- and eighteenth-century English books, or translations from French into English, or books published in England.

(NOTE. This bibliography does not contain translations of Port Royal text-books, such as *The Port Royal Logic or the Art of Thinking*, 1685, 1693, 1696, 1702, 1717, 1816, 1851, 1861, 1872, etc.; *The Art of Speaking*, 1676, 1696, 1707; *The General and Rational Grammar*, 1753, etc. For these see the British Museum Catalogue and Arber's *Term Catalogues*. Nor does it contain a complete list of translations of the *Provinciales* or the *Pensées*; only the earlier ones are given. Arnauld's controversy with Claude is not included, nor the writings of the Church historian Le Nain de Tillemont or of the historian Rollin.

Abbreviations used: B.M.—British Museum; Arber—Arber's *Term Catalogues*; Gillow—Gillow's *Biographical Dictionary of the English Catholics*.)

1653 Mens divinitus inspirata Sanctissimo Patri Domino Nostro Innocentio Papae X Super quinque Propositiones Cornelij Jansenij Authore P. Fr. Francisco Macedo....Londini... 1653.

  B.M. (Not by an English author, but interesting as one of the first books printed in England with a view to stifling Jansenism there.)

1657 Les Provinciales: or the Mysterie of Jesvitisme. Discover'd in certain Letters, written upon occasion of the present Differences at Sorbonne, between the Jansenists and the Molinists. Displaying the Corrupt Maximes and Politicks of that Society. Faithfully rendred into English. London, Printed by J.G. for R. Royston. 1657.

  B.M.

1657 The 16 of Octob. 1657 Entred for his copie under the hand of Master Lee warden a booke called Additionalls to the mistery of Jesuitisme vizt: *An advice of the pastors of Rouen to the pastors of all other places in and through France, concerning the pernicious maximes of some late casuists etc.* Translated out of French by a pson of quality...vj^d.

  (In the margin: Richard Royston.)

  Registers of the Stationers' Company, II, p. 150. (This may possibly be a notice of the Additionals that are printed with the second edition of the *Provincial Letters*, though both title and content are not quite the same.)

1658 Les Provinciales, Or the Mystery of Jesvitisme.... The second
Edition corrected; with large Additionals.... London, Printed
for Richard Royston... 1658.

B.M. The Additionals have a separate title-page and pagination: Additionals to the Mystery of Jesvitisme. Englished
by the same hand. London, Printed for Richard Royston,
1658. They consist of the following:

1. [Nicole, Arnauld, Pascal—see Maire's *Bibl.* 11², p. 300.] The Repre-
sentation of the Curez of Paris to the Reverend the Curez of other
Diocesses of France, upon occasion of certain corrupt maximes of some
late Casuists.

2. [Nicole, Arnauld, Pascal—see Maire, *ibid.*] A Copy of the Petition
presented by the Reverend the Curez of Rouen to the right reverend
Father in God the most illustrious and most religious the Archbishop of
Rouen, Primate of Normandy.

3. [Nicole, Arnauld, Pascal—see Maire, *ibid.*] A Catalogue of the
Propositions, contained in an Extract of some of the most dangerous
Propositions of diverse late Casuists....

4. [Du Four, Charles—see Maire, p. 306.] A Letter from a Curé of
Rouen to a Curé in the Countrey giving an account of the procedure of
his brethren the Curez of the said City against the doctrine of certain
Casuists.

5. A Petition of the Curez of Rouen to Monsieur the Officiall presented
October the 26, 1656.

6. A Remonstrance of the Reverend the Curez of Paris to their Lords
of the Assembly General of the Clergy.

7. The Principles and consequences of Probability, explicated by
Caramuel.

8. The Resolution of S. Thomas upon the contrariety of opinions
concerning the same matter of fact.

9. A Catalogue of the Propositions... collected by the Reverend the
Curez of Paris and presented to the honourable the Assembly Generall of
the Clergy of France. Nov. 24, 1656.

10. The Censure of the Books of Caramuel.

11. An Extract of certain Propositions out of... Mascarenhas.

12. A list of many dangerous propositions taken... particularly out of
... Escobar.

13. A letter written by the Archbishop of Maechlin.

14. Propositions that ought not to be tolerated.

15. Advertisements to Confessors.

16. The Judgement of the Theological Faculty of Lovaine.

17. [Pascal—see *Œuvres*, VII, p. 277.] Factum or a Remonstrance of the
Curez of Paris by way of answer to a Book intituled An Apologie for the
Casuists against the Calumnies of the Jansenists.

18. [Pascal—see *Œuvres*, VII, p. 308.] The Answer of the Curez of Paris
maintaining the Factum presented by them... to demand the censure of
the Apology of the Casuists.

19. The names of some of the most eminent Casuists.

1658 A further Discovery of the Mystery of Jesuitism in a Collection of severall Pieces representing the Humours, Designs and Practises of those who call themselves the Society of Jesus. London 1658.
> B.M. (The "pieces" are: (1) P. Jarrigius, The Jesuits upon the Scaffold. (2) By the same, The Calumnies of James Beaufes refuted. (3) Secret Instructions for the Superiours of the Society of Jesus. (4) A Discourse of the Reason why the Jesuits are so generally hated. (5) A Discovery of the Society in relation to their Politicks. (6) The Prophecy of Saint Hildegard fulfilled in the Jesuits.)

1659 [Nouet, S.J., (Jacques), Annat, S.J., (François).] An Answer to the Provinciall Letters published by the Jansenists under the Name of Lewis Montalt against the Doctrine of the Jesuits and School Divines made by some Fathers of the Society in France. There is set before the Answers in this Edition, The History of Jansenisme and at the end A Conclusion of the Work where the English Additionalls are shewed to deserve no Answer; also an Appendix, shewing the same of the Book called A further Discovery of Jesuitism. Printed at Paris in the year 1659.
> B.M. (The translator is Martin Grene or Green. See preface to the 1704 edition of *The Discourses of Cleander and Eudoxe*.)

1659 [Arnauld in all probability; possibly with the collaboration of Pascal. See Pascal, *Œuvres*, VIII, 81–2 and Maire 11², p. 302.] A Journall of all Proceedings between the Jansenists and the Jesuits: From the first coming abroad of the Provincial Letters to the Publication and the Censures of the Clergy of France and Theological Faculty of Paris passed upon a Book entituled An Apology for the Casuists. Together with the Censure itself of the said Faculty. Publish'd by a well wisher to the distressed Church of England. London, 1659.
> B.M. (Translated and published by H.H.)

1659 The holy Life of Philip Nerius...to which is annexed A Relation written by S. Augustine of the Miracles in his dayes.... And a Relation of sundry Miracles wrought at the Monastery of Port Royall in Paris A.D. 1656....Translated out of a French Copie published at Paris 1656. At Paris 1659.
> B.M.

1662 [Arnauld.] The new Heresie of the Jesuits publickly main-
      tain'd at Paris in the Colledge of Clermont by Conclusions
      printed 12. December 1661. Denounced to all the Bishops
      of France. Translated out of the French Original.... London.
      Printed in the year of our Lord 1662.
      B.M.

1664 [Arnauld, Nicole, etc.] τὸ μυστήριον τῆς ᾽Ανομίας. Another
      Part of the Mystery of Jesuitism or The new Heresie of the
      Jesuites, publickly maintained at Paris in the College of Cler-
      mont the XII of December MDCLXI. Declar'd to all the Bishops
      of France according to the Copy printed at Paris. Together
      with The Imaginary Heresie in three Letters with divers other
      Particulars relating to this Abominable Mysterie. Never before
      published in English. London... Printed for Richard Royston
      ...1664.
          B.M. (Translator: Evelyn. The volume contains: (1) The
          new Heresie, translated from Arnauld. (2) Four of
          Nicole's Lettres de l'Hérésie imaginaire. (3) Extracts
          translated from White's *alias* Blackloe's Exetasis sive
          Tho. Albii Purgatio. (4) An Extract from La Chaîne
          du Hercule Gaulois. (5) The censure of the Faculty of
          Paris concerning the Jesuites. (6) The sense of the
          French Church touching the Pope's Infallibility.)

1664 Saint-Amour, Louis Gorin de. The Journal of Monsᵣ de Saint
      Amour, Doctor of Sorbonne, containing a full Account of all
      the Transactions both in France and at Rome, concerning the
      Five Famous Propositions Controverted between the Jan-
      senists and the Molinists, from the beginning of that Affair
      till the Pope's Decision. Faithfully rendred out of French. A
      like Display of the Romish State, Court, Interests, Policies etc.
      and the mighty influences of the Jesuites in that Church, and
      many other Christian States being not hitherto extant....
      London...1664.
      B.M. (Translator: G. Havers.)

[1665 or 1666 (Nicole). The pernicious Consequences of the new
      Heresy of the Jesuits against Kings and State.]
          (Translator: Evelyn. I know of no extant copy of this book,
          but Evelyn himself tells us that he presented a book
          with the above title to the King in 1666. See *Diary and
          Correspondence*, II, p. 3; III, pp. 149, 192.)

1667 [Dechamps or de Champs, Etienne Agard.] The secret Policy of the Jansenists and the present State of the Sorbon. Discovered by a Doctour of that Faculty who having learnt Iansenisme when he studied Divinity, under a Master that taught it there publickly, has been since disabused and follows the Catholick party. Translated out of the French Copie. Printed at Troyes, By Christian Roman, at the Sign of true Faith near the great Church. 1667.
B.M. (The author of the above is given as Etienne Deschamps by Dodd in his *Secret Policy of the English Society of Jesus* and as Agard de Champs by Barbier. From a note by M. Gazier in Hermant's *Mémoires*, 1, p. 301, it would seem that these two are identical. Cf. Catalogue of the B.N. The translator is Thomas Fairfax, S.J., according to Gillow.)

1668 [Le P. Zacharie de Lisieux.] Fontaines, Louys. A Relation of the Country of Jansenia; wherein is treated of the Singularities founde therein, the Customes, Manners, and Religion of its Inhabitants. With a map of the Countrey. Composed in French by Lewis Fountaine, Esq; and newly translated into English by P.B. London...1668.
B.M.

1669 [Gale, Theophilus.] The true Idea of Jansenisme, both historick and dogmatick. By T.G. London...1669.
B.M.

1670 [Pontchâteau, Sébastien de Cambout de.] The Moral Practice of the Jesuites demonstrated by many remarkable Histories of their Actions in all Parts of the World....By the Doctors of the Sorbonne. Faithfully rendred into English. London...1670.
B.M. (A work continued by Arnauld. The above being part of it is printed in Arnauld's *Œuvres*, vol. 32.)

1670 [Perrault, Nicolas. Preface by Alexandre Varet.] The Jesuits Morals collected by a Doctor of the Colledge of Sorbon in Paris....Written in French and exactly translated into English. ...London...1670.
B.M. (Translated by Tonge according to Evelyn, and according to the preface of the 1704 ed. of *The Discourses of Cleander and Eudoxe*.)

1677   Omnes qui audiunt Evangelium idque vere agnoscunt sunt
       Gratiæ et Salutis capaces. Thesis in Academia Oxon. explicata
       Jun. 13. 1662. Cui accesserunt Animadversiones in aliqua
       Jansenii atque etiam Calvini Dogmata veritati prædictæ ad-
       versa. Per Eccl. Angl. Presbyterum....Sold by R. Clavell at
       the Peacock in St Paul's Churchyard.
           Arber, I, p. 291.

1677–78 [Nicole.] Moral Essays contain'd in several Treatises on
       many important Duties. Written in French by Messieurs du
       Port Royal. Faithfully rendred into English by a Person of
       Quality. First volume...printed for R. Bentley....London...
       1677.
       Of the Education of a Prince. Divided into three Parts.
       Useful for all Persons whatsoever. Written in French by
       Messieurs du Port Royal and intended as a second volume of
       the Moral Essays. Rendred into English by the Author of
       Ars Cogitandi. Printed for R. Bentley. London...1678.
       B.M.

1679   [Pascal.] The Mystery of Jesuitism discovered in certain
       Letters....London...Richard Royston...1679.
           B.M. (A reprint of the second English edition of the
           Provincial Letters, including the Additionals.)

1680   [Nicole.] Moral Essayes....Written in French by Messieurs du
       Port Royal. Third Volume, printed for R. Bentley....London
       1680.
           Arber, I, p. 397.

1688   Monsieur Pascall's Thoughts, Meditations and Prayers, touch-
       ing Matters moral and divine. As they were found in his Papers
       after his Death. Together with a Discourse upon Monsieur
       Pascall's Thoughts, wherein is shewn what was his Design [by
       Filleau de la Chaise]. As also another Discourse on the Proofs
       of the Truth of the Books of Moses [by Fillcau de la Chaise].
       And a Treatise wherein is made appear that there are Demon-
       strations of a different Nature, but as certain as those of
       Geometry, and that such may be given of the Christian
       Religion. Done into English by Jos. Walker. Licensed by
       R.M. London, printed for Jacob Tonson at the Judge's Head
       in Chancery Lane near Fleet-street 1688.
           B.M. (This edition also contains a translation of Mme
           Périer's Life of Pascal.)

1696 [Nicole.] Moral Essayes...written in French by Messieurs Du Port Royal. Done into English by a Person of Quality in Four Parts....Printed for S. Manship at the Ship in Cornhill.
       Arber, II, p. 583. (The B.M. copy consists of two volumes bound into one. First Volume: The Third Edition with Amendments...1696. Second Volume: The Second Edition...1696.)

1701 [Nicole.] Moral Thoughts upon the Mysteries of our Lord and Saviour Jesus Christ; being devout contemplations upon the remarkable[s] of his Life from his conception to his Ascension. Written in French by Messieurs du Port Royal, Authors of the Moral Essays, and done into English: proper for the Holy time of Lent.
       Arber, III, p. 224.

1701 [Daniel, Gabriel.] The Discourses of Cleander and Eudoxus upon the Provincial Letters. By a lover of Peace and Concord. Translated out of a French Copy. Printed at Cullen. 1701.
       B.M. (The translator is William Darrell, S.J., according to Gillow. Gillow mentions a possible earlier edition of 1694, but he gives particulars of this edition in quotation marks and in small print, *after* the 1701 edition which would show that he felt dubious about its existence.)

1703 [Doucin, Louis.] A brief Abstract of the Memorial concerning the State and Progress of Jansenism in Holland....Printed in the year 1703.
       Ushaw College. (The translator is probably Thomas Fairfax, S.J.—see Gillow, under Fairfax.)

1703 [de Champs or Dechamps, Etienne Agard.] The Secret Policy of the Jansenists and the present State of the Sorbon. Discover'd by a converted Doctor of that Faculty. The Second Edition. To which is premis'd A brief Abstract of the Memorial concerning the State and Progress of Jansenism in Holland.... Printed in the year 1703.
       Ushaw College. (A reprint of the 1667 edition with additions.)

1703 A case of Conscience Proposed to and Decided by Forty Doctors of the Faculty of Paris, in Favour of Jansenism. As also, what has been done on this occasion by the Pope, Archbishop of Paris, and the King. Together with a Collection of Records containing what former Popes and Prelates have

done and writ concerning the Fact of Jansenius, and some of the famed Books of his Party, abetted in the Case. With some Remarks upon it, proper to clear this whole matter. Printed for A.B. 1703.
> Gillow (under Fairfax; a translation attributed to Thomas Fairfax by Sylvester Jenks).

1704 [Daniel, Gabriel.] The Discourses of Cleander and Eudoxe upon the Provincial Letters. To which is added An Answer to the Apology for the Provincial Letters. Translated out of a French Copy. London, Printed in the year 1704.
> B.M. (The translator is William Darrell, S.J., according to Gillow. This edition contains a long preface not in the 1701 edition.)

1704 Thoughts on Religion and other Subjects by Monsieur Pascal. Translated from the French. London 1704.
> B.M. (Translator: Basil Kennet.)

1706 Animadversiones in aliqua Corn. Jansenii, Gulielmi Twisse, Ric. Baxtero et Gerardi de Vries, dogmata quæ doctrinæ Evangelicæ de Benevolentia Divina Hominibus per Christum exhibita advertantur....Prostant venales apud R. Wilkin...in Cæmeterio D. Pauli.
> Arber, III, p. 504.

[1709 (Quesnel.) Moral Reflections upon the Gospel of St Mark. Moral Reflections upon the Gospel of St Luke.]
> Gillow. (The translator was Francis Thwaites, according to Gillow who says that this edition was suppressed.)

1709 [Quesnel.] Moral Reflections upon the Gospel of St Matthew. To make the Reading of it more Profitable, and the Meditating on it more Easie. Translated from the French by T.W. Printed in the year 1709.
> B.M. (Translator: Thomas Whetenhall, according to Gillow. This edition was probably also suppressed, but a few copies seem to have escaped.)

[1709 (Quesnel.) Moral Reflections upon the Gospel of St John.]
> Gillow. (The translator was Thomas Southcote, O.S.B., according to Gillow who says that this edition was suppressed.)

1710 Memoirs for Rome concerning the State of the Christian Religion in China. London 1710.
> Gillow. (Under Lewis. Gillow says that these Memoirs were by Le Comte. The B.M. has the following book. Memoirs and Observations...made in a late Journey through the Empire of China and published in several Letters. By Louis Le Compte, Jesuit. Confessor to the Dutchess of Burgundy....Translated from the Paris Edition. London...1697. The "Introduction to the English Translation" attacks "the subtle Jesuites", but is well disposed to "Monsieur Arnaud and many other worthy clergymen of the Church of Rome".)

1710 [Jenks, Sylvester.] A short Review of the Book of Jansenius. ...Printed in the year MDCCX. Permissu Superiorum.
> B.M.

1713 [Dodd, Charles, *alias* H. Tootell.] A History of the English College at Doway....By R. C. Chaplain to an English Regiment that march'd in upon its surrendering to the Allies. ...London...1713.
> B.M.

1713 The Constitution of his Holiness Pope Clement XI Condemning a great number of Propositions taken out of a Book Printed in French....At Rome 1713. From the Printing House of the Camera Apostolica.
> B.M. (The Constitution Unigenitus. Latin and English texts.)

1714 [Hunter, Thomas, S.J.] A Modest Defence of the Clergy and Religious in a Discourse directed to R.C. Chaplain of an English Regiment....Printed in the year M.DCCXIV.
> B.M.

1714 The Pope's Bull, condemning the New Testament, with Moral Reflections, done by Father Quesnel, the Present Luther of France....Faithfully translated from the French....London 1714.
> B.M.
> The third Edition corrected....London 1714.
> B.M.

1714 [Hugot, Nicolas.] Familiar Instructions about Predestination and Grace. By way of Question and Answer. Translated from the French. London, printed for W. Lewis...1714.
> Ushaw College.

1715 [Dodd, Charles, *alias* H. Tootell.] The secret Policy of the English Society of Jesus...in Eight Parts and Twenty-four Letters. Directed to their Provincial....London...1715.
    B.M. (Part VII is "An Exact History of Jansenism, with the turn given to it by ill-minded Men, and the late Informations against Doway College and the Clergy from Original Depositions".)

1717 The Act of Appeal of His Eminence the Cardinal of Noailles, Archbishop of Paris of the Third of April MDCCXVII to the Pope Better Advis'd and to the Future General Council, from the Constitution of our Holy Father Pope Clement XI of September the 8th MDCCXIII. London. Printed for J. Roberts ...1717. Price Three Pence.
    B.M.

1718 The Mandate of his Eminence Monseigneur the Cardinal de Noailles...for Publishing the Appeal which he brought the 3rd of April 1717 to the Pope better advised....Together with the very Act of the Appeal...to which is added the Extract from the Registers of the Chancery of the Church and University of Paris....As also the Extract from the Registers of the Conclusions of the Chapter of the Metropolitan Church of Paris. From the Paris Edition put out by the Cardinal's Orders. ...Faithfully translated into English and printed together with the genuine French (for the Benefit of the Curious), with the Cardinal's marginal Notes, Quotations and References relating to this famous Controversy which already has been and will be the Subject of so much Speculation to the learned World. London...(1718). Note, what has hitherto been published on this Subject is absolutely spurious.
    B.M.

1719–1725 [Quesnel.] The New Testament with Moral Reflections upon every verse....London 1719–1725, 4 vols.
    B.M. (Translator: Richard Russell. In vols. II, III and IV one finds the additional statement "written in French by Father Quesnel and now translated into English".)

1720 A short history of the famous Constitution Unigenitus thunder'd out by Pope Clement XI against that Incomparable Work, call'd Moral Reflections upon the New Testament.... Done from the French....London 1720.
    B.M.

1720 Mandate of Cardinal Noailles concerning the Bull Unigenitus in french and english 1720.
Catalogus Bibliothecæ Harvardianæ, 1790.

1723 The Lives of Picus and Pascal Faithfully Collected from the most Authentick Accounts of them. To which is subjoin'd a Parallel between those two Christian Worthies. By Mr Jesup. London...1723.
B.M. (The Life of Pascal has a separate title-page: The Life of the celebrated Monsieur Pascal collected from the Writings of Madame Perier his Sister. By Mr Jesup. London...1723.)

1723 [Pouget, F. A.] General Instructions by Way of Catechism.... Translated from the Original French, and carefully compar'd with the Spanish Approv'd Translation. First Part. The second Edition, corrected and amended. By S[ylvester] Ll[oyd]. London...1723.
B.M. (The so-called Montpellier Catechism. The English translation condemned by a decree of the Index in 1725. Gillow says that only Part I appeared.)

1724 An Abstract of what is necessary to be known concerning the Constitution Unigenitus the better to avoid the Errours and Snares of the Modern Innovators. Address'd to the Faithful who are in Danger of being seduced by them. Translated from the French Copy printed at Luxembourg 1719. Anno MDCCXXIV Permissu Superiorum.
Ushaw College.

1724 [Nicole.] Moral Essays...written in French by Messieurs du Port Royal....Fourth Edition, London, for Parker at the Bible and Crown. 1724. 4 vols.
Edition mentioned in the introduction to Locke's translation of Nicole published 1828.

1726 [Boyer, P.] A parallel of the Doctrine of the Pagans with the Doctrine of the Jesuits and that of the Constitution Unigenitus....Translated from the Original printed in France. To which are added Copies of the said Constitution and of the 101 Propositions of Father Quesnel thereby condemned. London...1726.
B.M.

1727 Thoughts on Religion and other curious Subjects. Written originally in French by Monsieur Pascal. Translated into English by Basil Kennet, D.D., late Principal of Corpus Christi Coll. Oxon. Monsieur *Pascal* in his most excellent Discourse of the *Misery of Man*, tells us, *That all our Endeavours after Greatness proceed from nothing but a Desire of being surrounded by a Multitude of Persons and Affairs that may hinder us from looking into our selves, which is a view we cannot bear.* Had that incomparable Person Monsieur Pascal been a little more indulgent to himself, the World might probably have enjoy'd him much longer: whereas through too great an Application to his Studies in his Youth, he contracted that ill Habit of Body, which, after a tedious Sickness, carry'd him off in the Fortieth Year of his Age: And the whole History we have of his Life till that time, is but one continued Account of the Behaviour of a noble soul struggling under innumberable Pains and Distempers. *Vide Spectator* ii, No. 116. The Second Edition. London. Printed for Jacob Tonson ...1727.
B.M.

1728 A true and impartial Account of all that has pass'd between the Court of Rome and Cardinal de Noailles in Relation to the Constitution since the Promotion of Benedict XIII. Taken from Authentick Papers and Original Letters. Done from the French. London...1728.
B.M.

1729 The Bull Unigenitus clear'd from Innovation and Immorality. London, Printed in the Year of our Lord MDCCXXIX.
Ushaw College.

1733 Memoirs of John Gordon of Glencat...who was thirteen years in the Scots College at Paris amongst the secular Clergy...the History of Baianism, Jansenism and the Constitution Unigenitus impartially related....London. 1733.
B.M.

1734 The famous Bull or Constitution Unigenitus...against Father Quesnelle's Translation of the New Testament in the Vulgar Tongue...the whole impartially related in these Memoirs of John Gordon, who was thirteen years in the Scots College... but being accused of teaching the Principles condemned by the Bull he made his Escape to Scotland where he renounced Popery....The Second Edition....London...[1734].
B.M.

1740 The Institution of a Prince or a Treatise of the Virtues and
Duties of a Sovereign. Translated from the French of the Abbé
Duguet. London...1740. 2 vols.

1741 Thoughts on Religion...by Monsieur Pascal....Translated
into English by Basil Kennet....The Fourth Edition. London.
1741.
B.M.

1744 The Life of Mr Paschal with his Letters relating to the Jesuits,
in two Volumes. Translated into English by W[illiam]
A[ndrews]. London 1744.
  B.M. ("I have been induced to give the public a new translation, because the old one is now out of print, in very
  few hands and in a dress not so modern: defective likewise,
  as the translator has not inserted the defence of the
  twelfth letter, and has omitted the letter to father
  Annat.")

1749 Thoughts on Religion...by Monsieur Pascal....Translated
into English by Basil Kennet....London, 1749.
  Lowndes' *Bibliographer's Manual*. ("The 1741 edition re-
  issued with a new title.")

1749 [Duguet.] The Principles of Christian Faith....London 1749.
Edition described in the preface to the 1754 edition.

1751 Thoughts on Religion...by Monsieur Pascal....Translated
into English by Basil Kennet....Edinburgh 1751.
Lowndes' *Bibliographer's Manual*.

1753 The famous Bull Unigenitus in English with a short History of
its Rise and Progress. Portsmouth...1753.
B.M.

1754 [Duguet.] The Principles of the Christian Faith. In two
Volumes. Newly translated from the French. Edinburgh...
1754.
B.M.

1785 Letters from Mons. Racine the Elder to his Son...to which is
added a short account of the Abbey of Port Royal ("taken from
Mons. Racine's own abridgment of the history of Port Royal").
London 1785.
B.M.

1790 The Four Gospels with a Comment and Reflections both Spiritual and Moral. By Pasquier Quesnel. Translated from the French. Revised, corrected and the Popish Errors expurged by a Presbyter of the Church of England. Bath 1790. 2 vols.

> B.M. (A partial reprint of the 1719–1725 edition. This edition was also reprinted at Glasgow in the 18th century. See the preface to the 1842 translation.)

1828 Discourses: translated from Nicole's Essays by John Locke, with important variations from the Original French....Now first printed from the Autograph of the Translator....London ...1828.

> B.M.

NOTE. Lowndes' *Bibliographer's Manual* (and Maire after him) give an edition of the *Provincial Letters* for 1688 as being a reprint of Evelyn's 1664 edition. But Evelyn published no edition of *The Provincial Letters* in 1664, only some translations o Jansenist tracts, and there does not seem to be a 1688 edition of the *Provincia Letters* in existence.

Maire, following Lowndes, also gives a 1795 edition, but the "1795" in Lowndes is the number of the item in Bindley's sale.

The edition of the *Provincial Letters* given under 1759 by Maire (II^r, p. 336), viz. McCrie's translation, should be transferred to 1859.

Authorities

A. MANUSCRIPT

PUBLIC RECORD OFFICE.

State Papers, Foreign, France: vols. 98–105, 113–55 were examined with occasional results.

News-letters: Bundles 13–24 gave a few results.

Roman Transcripts: vols. 52, 95–103, 130–2, 137 were examined and some use was made of them.

(State Papers, Foreign, Flanders: vols. 31 and 32, 1601–59, gave no results.)

BRITISH MUSEUM.

Add. MSS. 22880 (Beauvoir Correspondence).
25043 (Port Royal Nécrologe).
38015 (Letters of Sir Robert Southwell).

ST CUTHBERT'S COLLEGE, USHAW, DURHAM.

Manuscript Collections, vol. 1 (various letters of the early eighteenth century, dealing with accusations of Jansenism).

ARCHIVES DU MINISTÈRE DES AFFAIRES ÉTRANGÈRES.

Correspondance politique, Angleterre: vols. 72–87 were examined and gave some information about the abbé Stuart d'Aubigny.

Mémoires et Documents, Angleterre: vols. 27–28 (as above).

BIBLIOTHÈQUE NATIONALE.

(The following catalogue is most useful: Delisle, L., Inventaire général et méthodique des manuscrits français de la Bibliothèque Nationale, vol. 1, Théologie, Paris 1876, pp. 145–70, section XIV: Traités sur la Grâce, le Jansénisme, le Quiétisme et Port-Royal).

Fonds français 17774 (Journal de Port-Royal d'avril 1661 à avril 1662).
17776 (Journal de Port-Royal du 5 juillet 1664 au 4 mai 1672).
17779 (Journal de Port-Royal du 5 mai 1679 à déc. 1694).
17797 (Relations).
17807 (...Lettres écrites à Mlle de Joncoux...).

Fonds français 17808 (Lettres originales adressées la plupart à l'abbesse de Port-Royal par...le P. Archange...) (printed in Ubald d'Alençon).

19730 (Lettres originales du P. Quesnel et autres).

19731 (Lettres écrites de Bruxelles à Mlle de Joncoux).

19736 (Lettres de Quesnel...).

20945 (...Extraits concernant Port-Royal).

20959 (Journal du Parlement sur l'Affaire de la Constitution Unigenitus, t. ii. Concerning Lady Drummond).

23459 (Extraits des Registres du Parlement sur les Refus de Sacrements, t. i. Concerning Lady Drummond).

24876 (Lettres de M. Petitpied).

25045 (Nécrologe de Capucins. Father Pembroke).

25046 (Éloges historiques des illustres Capucins de la province de Paris).

Mélanges Colbert 106 (Correspondance de sept. 1661 à déc. 1666. Letters concerning Stuart d'Aubigny).

131 *bis* (Correspondance d'août à sept. 1665. Letter from Stuart d'Aubigny).

BIBLIOTHÈQUE DE L'ARSENAL.

Manuscrits 5784 (Pièces concernant les Convulsionnaires).

6034–6040 (Correspondence of the Arnauld family).

11422 (Bastille—dossier Drummond).

10602 (Bastille—dossier Barneville).

11314 (Bastille—dossier Chopin—for Barneville).

11462 (Bastille—dossier Frion—for Barneville).

BIBLIOTHÈQUE SAINTE-GENEVIÈVE.

Manuscrit 1480 (Mémoires de M. du Ferrier).

BIBLIOTHÈQUE MAZARINE.

Manuscrits 2465–2466 (MS. copy of Fontaine's *Mémoires*, fuller than printed copy).

2481 (Port Royal papers having belonged to Thomas Innes).

2504, pièce 21 (Mémoires pour servir à l'histoire du clergé Janséniste d'Hollande).

4535 (Histoire littéraire de Port-Royal by Dom Clémencet).

Bibliothèque de la Ville de Troyes.
Manuscrit 1689 (Recueil de lettres de M. Nicole, Arnauld, etc.).

Archives of the Oud Katholiek Seminarie, Amersfoort.
Lettres de l'abbé d'Étemare. Carton L.

Archives of the Chapter of Utrecht (temporarily transferred to the Rijksarchief at The Hague).
(Consult the following Catalogue: J. Bruggeman, Inventaris van de Archieven bij het Metropolitaan Kapittel van Utrecht van de Roomsch. Katholieke Kerk der Oud Bisschopelijke Clerezie. 'S Gravenhage, 1928.)
Letters addressed to Van Erkel, Canon and later Dean of the Chapter of Utrecht, by " J. Wetenhal" (copy); by the Duchess of Tyrconnel; by Dr Richard Short; by — Marison; by Paul Kenny.
Letter addressed to Bishop Fagan of Meath, by H. Van Heussen, Vicar of the Chapter of Utrecht.
Letter addressed to Van Heussen, by Bishop Fagan.
Reisverhaal van den Hr. Priem met andere Geestelijken naar Ierland, 1715–1716.

B. PRINTED DOCUMENTS, SOURCES AND CONTEMPORARY HISTORIES

(See also the list of books on Jansenism (p 278).)

Note. Only such sources are here given, as were definitely utilized, though many more were consulted. Information about books to which only a passing reference is made is usually given in the footnotes.

This is naturally not an attempt to give a bibliography of the history of Port Royal and Jansenism. Various bibliographies will be found in the following, and elsewhere.

Sainte-Beuve, Port-Royal, iii (cf. C. Gazier, Les Sources de Sainte-Beuve, Revue bleue, 17 juillet 1926, and Giraud, La valeur historique du Port-Royal de Sainte-Beuve, Revue hebdomadaire, 12 octobre 1929).

Beard, C. History of Port Royal. 1861.

Maulvault, A. Répertoire alphabétique des personnes et des choses de Port-Royal. 1902.

Gazier, A. In Racine's Abrégé de l'Histoire de Port-Royal. 1908.

Vacant, Mangenot et Amann. Dictionnaire de Théologie Catholique, vol. 8. 1924. Article " Jansénisme".

Maire, A. Bibliographie des Œuvres de Pascal. 1925–7. 5 vols. (Covers more ground than the title implies.)

Dedieu, J. L'agonie du Jansénisme (1715–1790), Revue d'histoire de l'Eglise de France, avril 1928.

See also at the Bibliothèque Nationale the Catalogue de l'Histoire de France, vol. 5, 1858. Histoire religieuse.

For the period in English history see especially G. Davies, Bibliography of British History, Stuart Period, 1928, and J. H. Pollen, Sources for the History of Roman Catholics in England, Ireland and Scotland, 1921.

A Letter from a Gentleman to his Friend in London in Confutation of the scurrilous Libel of an Anonymous Blackloist, 1660.

Apologetical Memoires in behalf of the Rector, Deanes, Proctors and Deputies of the University of Paris. Against the Enterprise of certain Irish for the most part Students in the University [1651]. See Saint-Amour's Journal where they are reprinted (cf. p. 281 of this book).

Arber, E. Term Catalogues, 1668–1709. London, 1903–6. 3 vols.

Arnauld, Antoine. Œuvres. Paris-Lausanne, 1775–83. 43 vols. Especially vols. 1–4, Letters; 14, Apologie pour les Catholiques; 20, Relations with Dr Holden; 29 and 30, the Brisacier-Callaghan affair; 37, Le véritable portrait de Guillaume Henri de Nassau.

Arnauld, la R.M. Jeanne-Catherine-Agnès de Saint-Paul (la Mère Agnès). Letters. Paris, 1858. 2 vols.

Arnauld, la R.M. Jacqueline-Marie-Angélique de Sainte-Madeleine (la Mère Angélique). Mémoires et Relations sur ce qui s'est passé à Port-Royal des Champs. 1716.

—— Lettres. Utrecht, 1742–1744. 3 vols.

Arnauld d'Andilly, la R.M. Angélique de Saint-Jean. Relations sur la Vie de la Révérende Mère Angélique de Sainte-Magdelaine Arnauld. See Mémoires pour servir, vol. 3.

Barbier, E. J. Journal. Paris, 1847–56. 4 vols.

Barrow, Isaac. Theological Works. Cambridge, 1869. 9 vols.

Baxter, Richard. A Key for Catholics to open the Jugling of the Jesuits. London, second edition, 1674.

—— Reliquiæ Baxterianæ or Narrative of his Life and Times. London, 1696.

[Besoigne, J.] Histoire de l'Abbaye de Port-Royal. Cologne, 1752. 6 vols.

Birch, Thomas. A Collection of the State Papers of Thomas Thurloe. London, 1742. 7 vols.

[Bissy, Thiard de.] Témoignages de l'Eglise Universelle en faveur de la Bulle Unigenitus. Bruxelles, 1718.

Blackloe. See under White.

Boislisle, J. de. Mémoriaux du Conseil de 1661. Paris, 1905-7. 3 vols.

Bourgeois, docteur de Sorbonne. Relation...contenant ce qui s'est passé à Rome en 1645 et 1646.

Boyle, Robert. Works. London, 1772. 6 vols.

[Brisacier, J. de.] Le Jansenisme confondu dans l'advocat du Sr Callaghan. Paris, 1651.

—— L'Innocence et la Vérité reconnues dans les preuves invincibles de la mauvaise foy du Sr Jean Callaghan. Ibernois, 1653.

Brown, T. Miscellanea Aulica. London, 1702.

Burke, T. Hibernia Dominicana. Cologne, 1762.

Burnet, Gilbert. History of My own Time. Part I, Reign of Charles II, ed. by O. Airy. Oxford, 1897-1900. 2 vols. Vols. 3-6. Oxford, 1833. A Supplement, ed. by H. C. Foxcroft. Oxford, 1902.

Calamy, Edmund. An historical Account of my own Life. London, 1829. 2 vols.

Calendars of State Papers, Domestic.

Callaghan, J. Lettre à un docteur de Sorbonne de ses amis (1652) (also attributed to Arnauld).

Camden Society Publications. See Nicholas Papers.

Carré de Montgéron, L. B. de. La Vérité des Miracles. Cologne, 1745. 3 vols.

Catholic Record Society Publications, especially vol. 9, Miscellanea VII. London, 1911; Vols. 10-11, Douay Diaries. London, 1911.

[Cerveau, R.] Nécrologe des plus célèbres Défenseurs et Confesseurs de la vérité des XVIIe et XVIIIe siècles. 1760-78. 7 vols.

Clarendon State Papers. Oxford, 1767-86. 3 vols.

Clarendon State Papers preserved in the Bodleian Library, Calendar of, ed. by W. D. Macrae and F. J. Routledge. Oxford, 1869-1932. 4 vols.

Clarendon. See also Roxburghe Club Publications.

[Clémencet, Dom Charles.] Histoire générale de Port-Royal. Amsterdam, 1755-7. 10 vols.

—— Histoire littéraire de Port-Royal. Paris, 1868. (Only one vol. published.)

Clonsinnil. Défense des Hibernois, Disciples de S. Augustin. Paris, 1651.

Collins, A. Letters and Memorials of State. London, 1746. 2 vols.

[Colonia, le P.] Dictionnaire des Livres jansénistes ou qui favorisent le Jansénisme. Anvers, 1725. 4 vols.

Conclusion de la Faculté de Théologie de Paris pour les Hybernois contre le Décret de Monsieur le Recteur de l'Université du 4 mars 1651 et contre les Iansenistes. Ensemble l'arrest de la cour du 24e mars 1651 pour les mesmes Hybernois. Paris, 1651.

Constitution Unigenitus, la, déférée à l'Eglise Universelle. Cologne, 1757. 3 vols. [By G. N. Nivelle?]

Dangeau, Marquis de. Journal. Paris, 1854–60. 19 vols. (Vol. 19 contains the Index.)

Dictionnaire des Livres Jansénistes. See under Colonia.

Divers Actes, Lettres et Relations des Religieuses de Port-Royal... touchant la persécution. 1725.

Dodd, Charles (H. Tootell). Church History of England. Brussels, 1737–42. 3 vols.

Dorsanne, J. Journal pour servir à l'Histoire de la Constitution Unigenitus. Rome, 1753. 2 vols.

Douay Diaries. See under Catholic Record Society.

Du Fossé, Pierre Thomas. Mémoires pour servir à l'Histoire de Port-Royal. Rouen, 1876–9. 4 vols.

[Dumas, H.] Histoire des cinq Propositions de Jansenius. Trévoux, 1702. 3 vols.

[Du Pac de Bellegarde, G.] Histoire abrégée de l'Eglise Métropoli-taine d'Utrecht. Utrecht, 1765. Recueil de divers Témoignages en faveur de l'Eglise de Hollande. Utrecht, 1763.

Evelyn, John. Diary and Correspondence. London, 1850–2. 4 vols.

Factum pour les Hybernois. See under Pucelle.

Fitzjames, François de. Evêque de Soissons. Œuvres posthumes. Avignon, 1769. 2 vols.

Fontaine, Nicolas. Mémoires pour servir à l'histoire de Port-Royal. Utrecht, 1736. 2 vols.

Funck-Brentano, F. Les Lettres de Cachet à Paris. Paris, 1903.

Gale, Theophilus. The Court of the Gentiles, Parts iii–iv. Oxford, 1677–8. For his True Idea of Jansenisme see list of English books on Jansenism.

[Gerberon, Dom.] Histoire générale du Jansénisme. Amsterdam, 1700. 3 vols.

Gordon, J. F. S. Ecclesiastical Chronicle for Scotland. Glasgow, 1867. 4 vols.

[Guelphe.] Relation de la Retraite de M. Arnauld dans les Pays bas en 1679. Mons, 1733.

[Guilbert, Pierre.] Mémoires historiques et chronologiques sur l'Abbaye de Port-Royal des Champs (depuis la Paix de l'Eglise). Utrecht, 1755–6. 7 vols.

—— Mémoires historiques et chronologiques sur l'Abbaye de Port-Royal des Champs depuis sa fondation. Partie Première. Utrecht, 1758–9. 2 vols.

Hermant, Godefroi. Mémoires. Paris, 1905–10. 6 vols.

Histoire de Port-Royal, Histoire du Jansénisme. See under Besoigne, Clémencet, Gerberon.

Histoire des Persécutions des Religieuses de Port-Royal écrite par elles-mêmes. Ville-Franche, 1753.

Histoire du Cas de Conscience. (By Fouillou, Louail, Mlle de Joncoux, Petitpied et Quesnel. Nancy, 1705–11. 8 vols.

Historical Manuscripts Commission Reports, *passim.* Especially Manuscripts of the Marquis of Ormonde. New Series. London, 1902–12. Stuart Manuscripts at Windsor Castle. London, 1902–12.

Jansenius, Cornelius. Lettres. Cologne, 1702.

Joly, Guy. Mémoires, éd. Michaud et Poujoulat, 3e série, vol. 2. Paris, 1838.

Lafiteau, P. F. Histoire de la Constitution Unigenitus. Besançon, 1820.

Le Maistre, Antoine. Plaidoyez et Harangues…donnez au public par M. Jean Issali. 5e édition. Paris, 1660.

L(eyburn), G(eorge). An Epistle declaratorie. 1657.

Lombard, Etienne, Sieur du Trouillas. Response a un sermon prononcé par le P. Brisacier…le 29 mars 1651.

Luynes, duc de. Mémoires, vol. 14. Paris, 1860–4. 17 vols.

Maintenon, Mme de. Correspondance générale. Paris, 1865. 4 vols.

Mémoires et Relations. See under Arnauld.

Mémoires…. See also under Du Fossé, Fontaine, Guilbert.

Mémoires pour servir à l'histoire de Port-Royal. 1733–7. 3 vols. (Vol. 3 has the subtitle Relations sur la Vie de la Rév. Mère Angélique de Sainte Magdelaine Arnauld, ou Recueil de la Mère Angélique de Saint Jean Arnauld d'Andilly sur la vie de sa Tante la Mère Marie Angélique de Sainte Magdelaine Arnauld.)

Mémoires pour servir à l'histoire de Port-Royal et à la vie de la Révérende Mère Marie-Angélique…réformatrice de ce monastère. Utrecht, 1742. 3 vols.

Moran, P. F. Spicilegium Ossoriense. Dublin, 1874–84. 3 vols.

Nécrologe de l'abbaye de Notre Dame de Port-Royal. Amsterdam, 1723. (Compiled by Dom Rivet de la Grange.) See also under Cerveau and Supplément.

Nécrologe des Appelans. 1755.

Nicholas Papers, vol. 2. Westminster, 1892. (Camden Society Publications.)

Nivelle. See under Constitution Unigenitus.

Nouvelles Ecclésiastiques, ou Mémoires pour servir à l'histoire de la Constitution Unigenitus, 1713–93. (Excellent index for 1728–60 published in 1767 by the abbé Bonnemare. Another index exists for 1761–90.)

Panzani, Gregorio. Memoires translated by Joseph Berington to which are added an Introduction and a Supplement. Birmingham, 1793.

Pascal. Œuvres. (Éd. Grands Écrivains de la France. Paris, 1908, etc. 14 vols. Especially vol. 5 (Provinciales) and vol. 11 (Écrits sur la grâce).)

[Polidori, Pietro.] De Vita et Rebus gestis Clementis Undecimi Libri Sex. Urbini, 1727.

Pucelle, Avocat. Factum pour les Hybernois, Appelans du Décret de Monsieur le Recteur du quatrième mars. 1651.

Pugh, R. Blackloe's Cabal. [Douay?] 1680.

Quesnel, Pasquier. Histoire abrégée de la vie et des ouvrages de Mons. Arnauld. Cologne, 1697.

—— Correspondance. Paris, 1900. 2 vols.

Racine. Abrégé de l'histoire de Port-Royal, ed. Gazier. Paris, 1908.

—— Œuvres, éd. Gr. Écr. vol. 7. (Correspondance.) Paris, 1888.

Racine, abbé Bonaventure. Abrégé de l'histoire ecclésiastique. Cologne, 1754. 13 vols.

Rapin, le P. R. Histoire du Jansénisme. Paris, 1861.

—— Mémoires. Paris, 1865. 3 vols.

Ravaisson, F. Archives de la Bastille. Paris, 1866–91. 17 vols.

Recueil de divers Témoignages. See Du Pac de Bellegarde.

Recueil de plusieurs Pièces pour servir à l'histoire de Port-Royal. Utrecht, 1740. (Known as the "Recueil d'Utrecht".)

Retz, Cardinal de. Mémoires, éd. Gr. Écr. Paris, 1880. Vol. 5.

Rinuccini, G. B. The Embassy in Ireland, tr. by A. Hutton. Dublin, 1873.

Roxburghe Club Publications. Notes which passed at the Privy Council between Charles II and the Earl of Clarendon. London, 1896.
—— Stuart Papers, ed. by Falconer Madan. London, 1889. 2 vols.
Rutty, Dr John. Spiritual Diary. London, 1796. 2nd ed.

Saint-Amour, L. G. de. Journal de ce qui s'est fait à Rome dans l'affaire des cinq propositions. 1662.
Saint-Évremond. Œuvres meslées. Amsterdam, 1705–6. 7 vols.
—— Œuvres mêlées, éd. Giraud. Paris, 1866. 3 vols.
Saint-Simon, Duc de. Mémoires, éd. Gr. Écr. Paris, 1878–1917. (In progress.) 31 vols. The other volumes may be consulted in Chéruel's ed. Paris, 1873–86. 21 vols.
Sergeant, J. An account of the Chapter erected by William Titular Archbishop of Chalcedon. London, 1853.
Soanen, Messire Jean, Eveque de Senez. Lettres. Cologne, 1750. 2 vols.
Stationers' Company, Transcript of Registers, 1640–1708. London, 1913–14. 3 vols.
Stuart Papers. See under Hist. MSS. Comm. and Roxburghe Club.
Supplément au Nécrologe de l'Abbaïe de Notre Dame de Port-Royal des Champs. 1735. (Compiled by Hugues Le Febvre de Saint Marc.)

Thurloe Papers. See under Birch.

Van Erkel. Defensio Ecclesiæ Ultrajectinæ. Amsterdam, 1738.
Vies intéressantes et édifiantes des Amis de Port-Royal (published by the abbé Le Clerc). Utrecht, 1751.
Vies intéressantes et édifiantes des Religieuses de Port-Royal et de plusieurs Personnes qui leur étoient attachées (published by the abbé Le Clerc). 1750. 4 vols.

Walsh, P. History and Vindication of the Loyal Formulary or The Irish Remonstrance. London, 1674.
Wesley, John. Journals. London, 1909–16. 8 vols.
—— Works. London, 1872. 14 vols.
White, T. (alias Blackloe). Sonus Buccinae. Cologne, 1659.
Wood, Anthony à. Athenae Oxonienses, ed. Bliss. London, 1813–20. 4 vols.

C. MODERN WORKS

(Well-known works of reference are not given.)

Acton, Lord. Historical Essays and Studies. London, 1907. (Secret History of Charles II.)

Bagwell, R. Ireland under the Stuarts. London, 1909–16. 3 vols.
Battifol, L. Le Cardinal de Retz. Paris, 1927.
Bellesheim, A. Geschichte der Katholischen Kirche in Irland. Mainz, 1890–1. 3 vols.
—— History of the Catholic Church in Scotland, translated with notes and additions by D. Oswald Hunter Blair. Edinburgh and London, 1890. 4 vols.
Boero, G. Istoria della Conversione alla Chiesa cattolica di Carlo II. Roma, 1863. (Reprinted from La Civiltà Cattolica, April–Sept. 1863.)
Bonney, E. Douai Papers. Ushaw Magazine, vols. 13 and 14. Ushaw, 1903 and 1904.
Boyle, P. The Irish College in Paris. London, 1901.
Brady, W. M. The Episcopal Succession in England, Scotland and Ireland. Rome, 1876–7. 3 vols.
Bremond, H. Histoire littéraire du sentiment religieux en France, vol. 4. Paris, 1920.
Bulletin du Comité flamand. See Cochin.
Burton, E. H. Life of Bishop Challoner. London, 1909. 2 vols.
Butler, C. Historical Memoirs of the English, Irish and Scottish Catholics. London, 1822. 4 vols.
Butler, D. Life and Letters of Robert Leighton. London, 1903.

Carreyre, J. Article on Jansenism (about 200 pp., excellent bibliography) in Vacant, Mangenot et Amann, Dictionnaire de Théologie Catholique, vol. 8. Paris, 1924.
Clark, R. Anthony Hamilton, his Life, his Works and his Family. London, 1921.
Cochin, Claude. Dunkerque évêché anglais. Bulletin du comité flamand de France. Bailleul, 1908. 3e fascicule.
Cust, Lady Elizabeth. Some Account of the Stuarts of Aubigny in France. London, privately printed, 1891.

Dancoisne, L. Histoire des établissements religieux britanniques à Douai. Douai, 1880.
Daumet, G. Notice sur les établissements religieux anglais, écossais et irlandais fondés à Paris avant la Révolution. Paris, 1912.

Deinhardt, W. Der Jansenismus in deutschen Landen. München, 1929.

Downside Review. London. Vol. 4, 1885; vol. 5, 1886. (Articles on Archives of St Gregory's Monastery, Downside.)

Du Boscq de Beaumont, G. et M. Bernos. Les derniers Stuarts à St-Germain-en-Laye. 2e éd. Paris, 1912.

Dumas, F. Charles II, Roi d'Angleterre, et son Fils le P. Jacques Stuart. Études. Paris, 1864, 1865.

Edinburgh Review. See Henderson.

Études religieuses, historiques et littéraires par les Pères de la Compagnie de Jésus. See under Dumas.

Faillon, abbé. Vie de M. Olier. 4e éd. Paris, 1873.

Faugère, Prosper. Introduction to his edition of the Provinciales, éd. Gr. Écr. Paris, 1886–95. 2 vols.

Gazier, A. Histoire générale du mouvement janséniste. Paris, 1923.
—— Les dernières années du Cardinal de Retz. Paris, 1875.

Gazier, C. Françoise Marguerite de Joncoux. Revue de Paris, 15 avril 1929.
—— Histoire du monastère de Port-Royal. Paris, 1929.

Gillow, J. Biographical Dictionary of the English Catholics. London, 1885–1902. 5 vols.

Gounelle, E. Wesley et ses rapports avec les Français. Nyons, 1898.

Goyau, G. Histoire religieuse (vol. 6 of G. Hanotaux, Histoire de la Nation française). Paris, 1922.

Grégoire, H. Les Ruines de Port-Royal des Champs en 1809. Paris, 1809.

Guilday, P. The English Catholic Refugees on the Continent, vol. 1. London, 1914.

Hallays, A. Le Pèlerinage de Port-Royal. Paris, 1914.

Hankin, C. Life of Mary Anne Schimmelpenninck. 3rd ed. London, 1859.

Hanotaux, G. See under Goyau.

Henderson, G. D. Foreign Religious Influences in Seventeenth Century Scotland. Edinburgh Review, April 1929.

Irish Ecclesiastical Record. See under Spelman.

Jourdain, C. Histoire de l'Université de Paris. Paris, 1862–6.

Kirk, J. Biographies of English Catholics in the Eighteenth Century, ed. by J. H. Pollen and E. Burton. London, 1909.

Le Roy, A. La France et Rome de 1700 à 1715. Paris, 1892.
Lister, Th. Life of Clarendon. London, 1838. 3 vols.
Lupton, J. H. Archbishop Wake and the Project of Union between the Gallican and Anglican Churches. London, 1896.

Maulvault, A. Répertoire alphabétique des Personnes et des Choses de Port-Royal. Paris, 1902.
Meyer, A. de. Les premières controverses jansénistes en France. Louvain, 1917.
Michel, Francisque. Les Français en Écosse et les Écossais en France. Paris, 1862. 2 vols.
Montague, V. M. The Scottish College in Paris. Scottish Historical Review. Glasgow, July, 1907.
Moran, P. F. Memoirs of the Most Rev. Oliver Plunket. Dublin, 1861.
More, Hannah. See under Roberts.
Moss, C. B. The Old Catholic Church and Reunion. London, 1927.

Neale, J. M. History of the so-called Jansenist Church of Holland. Oxford, 1858.

Ogg, David. The Cardinal de Retz. London, 1912.

Plumptre, E. H. The Life of Thomas Ken. London, 1888. 2 vols.
Préclin, E. Les Jansénistes du dix-huitième siècle et la Constitution civile du Clergé. Paris, 1929.
—— L'Union des Églises Gallicane et Anglicane. Paris, 1928.

Ranke, L. v. History of England, vol. 3. Oxford, 1875.
Renehan, L. F. Collections on Irish Church History. Dublin, 1861.
Reusch, F. H. Der Index der verbotenen Bücher. Bonn, 1883–5. 2 vols.
Roberts, W. Memoir of Hannah More. 2nd ed. London, 1834. 4 vols.

Sainte-Beuve, C.-A. Port-Royal. 3rd ed. Paris, 1867–71. 7 vols.
Schimmelpenninck, M. A. Narrative of the demolition of the monastery of Port-Royal des Champs....London, 1816. (Contains an Account of a visit to the Ruins of Port Royal.)

Scots College, Rome. A tribute of the Scots College Society. London, 1930.
Scott, Eva. The King in Exile. London, 1905.
—— The Travels of the King. London, 1907.
Sergeant, P. W. My Lady Castlemaine. London, 1912.
Sketch, A., of the History of the Benedictine Community now residing at St Benedict's Priory, Colwich, Stafford. (Privately printed.)
Spalding Club Publications. T. Innes, Civil and Ecclesiastical History of Scotland. Aberdeen, 1853. (For the editor's preface and life of Innes.)
Spelman, J. P. The Irish in Belgium, Irish Ecclesiastical Record. 3rd series, vol. 7. Dublin, 1886.

Tabaraud, M. M. Histoire critique des projets formés depuis trois cents ans pour la Réunion des Communions chrétiennes. Paris, 1824.

Ubald d'Alençon, le P. Les frères mineurs et les débuts de la Réforme à Port-Royal des Champs. Paris, 1911.
Ushaw Magazine. See under Bonney.

Vacant, Mangenot et Amann. Dictionnaire de Théologie Catholique. See under Carreyre.

Index

354 INDEX

Saint-François de Sales, *see* François de Sales, Saint

Saint-Germain, court of, asked to help Douay College, 184

Saint-Germain Jansenists, *see* Jansenism at Saint-Germain, Jansenists at Saint-Germain

Saint-Gilles d'Asson, M. de, 53

St Gregory's Seminary, Paris, 236, 253

Saint-Lambert, village, 271; cemetery, 269; dead transferred from Port Royal, 26; attracts pilgrims, 272

St Mary's Abbey, Colwich, xii, 68

Saint-Médard, cemetery of, 247, 254; closed, xviii, 248

Saint-Paul, comte de, 35

Saint-Simon, Louis de Rouvroy, duc de, quoted, 244, 245, 246

Saint-Sulpice, ecclesiastics, exclude Liancourt from sacraments, 23; threaten Miss Maitland, 28; consulted with regard to Dr Betham, 228; Seminary, 254

Saint-Vallier, Jean Baptiste de, Bishop of Quebec, 257 *n.* 4

Saint-Vincent de Paul, *see* Vincent de Paul, Saint

St Willibrord, society of, 259

Sainte-Beuve, Charles-Augustin, 69; quoted, 7 *n.* 1, 3, 19, 20, 87 *n.* 2, 97, 99, 111 *n.* 4, 122, 241; his account of the bishops, 120

Sainte-Beuve, Jacques de, docteur de Sorbonne, involved in the *affaire des Hibernois*, 195, 196

Sainte-Épine, miracles, xvi, 55, 56, 106

Sainte-Marguerite, Paris, curé of, 252

Sainte-Marthe, Claude de, confessor of Port Royal, 100; kindness to English Benedictine nuns, 72, 73; obliged to leave Port Royal, 74; death, 160; his house at Port Royal des Champs, 270

Sales, François de, *see* François de Sales

Salisbury rising, 50–1

Sall, Andrew, uses part of Port Royal preface, 145–8

Saltmarsh, Gerald, esteems Van Erkel, 170; defends his interests, 171; sends him messages, 171; receives books from him, 170; charged with Jansenism, 170; not to be bishop, 171, 174

San Clemente, Cardinal of, 156

Sanctarel, *see* Santarelli

Sanctorum Patrum de Gratia Christi et Libero Arbitrio dimicantium Trias, by Sinnich, 9

Santarelli, Antonio, 198

Santeuil, Jean Baptiste, 231

Santini, Mgr, Internuncio in Brussels, sends *Unigenitus* to England, 175; urges Irish prelates to signify acceptance, 215

Saul Exrex, by Sinnich, 9

Savage, John, Lord Rivers, 174 *n.* 4

Schimmelpenninck, Mrs Mary Anne, reads Port Royal books, 267; publishes *Narrative of a Tour*, 267, 274; regrets that Port Royal is little known in England, 267; visits the places connected with Port Royal, 267; visits Port Royal des Champs and Les Granges, 267–73; acquainted with Bishop Grégoire, 267, 268; receives a book from him, 272; her *Narrative of the Demolition of Port Royal*, 273; her *Select Memoirs of Port Royal*, 274 *and n.* 5; collects Port Royal books, 274; commended by Hannah More, 274; bequeaths books and engravings to Sion College, 274–5; rejoices in her work, 275

Schools of Port Royal, *see* Port Royal, Little Schools

Scotland, in need of charity, 50; to be submitted to Rome by Charles II, 92; missionary priests sent there, 230, 233,235,237,239,240; miracles of the abbé Pâris published there, 237 *n.* 2; Quesnel's family lived there, 256 *n.* 1; John Gordon escapes in, 289. *See also* Catholics, Scottish; Jansenists, Scottish; Jansenism in Scotland; Jesuits, Scottish

Scotland, Protestant, influenced by Jansenism, 138; by Pascal, 138

Scots College in Paris, *see* Paris, Collèges

Scots College in Rome, *see* Rome

Scottish Catholics, *see* Catholics, Scottish

Scott, James, Duke of Buccleuch and Monmouth, entrusted to Aubigny, 60; at Le Chesnay, 61; at Juilly, 61; sent for by Charles II, 61; went by name of Crofts, 62

Scriptures, as used by Jansenists, 131, 141, 145, 256 *n.* 3, 262

Scriptures, published in vulgar tongues, 145, 146, 147, 209, 289. *See also* Port Royal, Testament

INDEX

Urban VIII, issues Bull *In eminenti*, xv, 6, 17 *n.* 1; condemns Bishop Smith's proceedings, 11

Ursulines du Faubourg Saint-Jacques, 64, 65

Utrecht, Calamy studies there, 145; story of Dutch ordinations in Ireland common knowledge, 215

Utrecht, Church of, regarded as schismatic, 211; courage admired by Dr Short, 165; opposes the "exorbitant power of Rome", 165; books in defence of, 165; news given by Quesnel to Dr Short, 167; difficulties in getting priests ordained, 175, 211; priests ordained in Ireland, xvii, 211–14, 276; often visited by English priest, 176; sends emissaries to England in 1729, 179; situation considered analogous to that of the Roman Catholic Church in England, 179; corresponds with English Catholics, 179

Clergy, admired by Dr Short, 164, 165, 166, 169; appreciate his esteem, 166; correspond with English Chapter, 169; zeal for the Gospel, 175

Chapter, attacked by regulars, 168; situation analogous to that of the English Chapter, 168; governs after Codde's death, 211; its archives, xii, 164 *and n.* 6, 213, 294. *See also* Old Catholic Church

Utrum damnandus sit Jansenius, by Sinnich, 8

Validity of Anglican ordinations, 258, 259

Van den Walther, bookseller, 178

Vane, —, accused, 174 *n.* 4

Van Erkel, John Christian, Dean of the Chapter of Utrecht, corresponds with England, 164, 167 *n.* 4; excommunicated, 164; corresponds with Dr Short, 168; with the English Chapter, 168–9; prints an account of the English Chapter, 169; corresponds with the Duchess of Tyrconnel, 170, 246 *n.* 3; esteemed by Saltmarsh, 170; sends him books, 171; receives messages, 171; his interests defended by Saltmarsh, 171; hears news of Bishop Giffard, 175; visited by Marison, 211; by Saltmarsh (?), 211; his *Protestatio asserta*, 169; his *Defensio Ecclesiæ Ultrajectinæ*, 169

Van Heussen, Hugh Francis, Dean of the Chapter of Utrecht, visited by Marison, 211; gives letters dimissory to Dutch Jansenists, 212, 276; sends them to be ordained in Ireland, 276; thanks Bishop Fagan, 213 *n.* 4; hears from him, 214

Van Neercassel, *see* Neercassel

Van Rhyn, Jansenist bookseller, 165, 166, 169

Varet, Alexander, his Preface to *The Jesuits' Morals*, a translation, 112, 282

Varin, Jean, medal engraved by him, 122

Varlet, Dominique, Bishop of Babylon, 178

Vasquez, Gabriel, 113

Vatteville *or* Batteville, Baron de, Spanish Ambassador, 84 *n.* 5, 96

Vauclair, abbé de, 14

Vaumurier, country-house of the duc de Luynes, 40, 42, 271

Vavassor, François, S.J., 35

Vecchiis, Jerome de, Internuncio at Brussels, hears of English condemnation of Jansenism, 157 *n.* 5, 158 *n.* 1; condemns Irish Remonstrance, 205; in London, 94; alarmed by Aubigny's stories, 95; promises to use his influence in securing Aubigny's promotion, 95

Verney, Sir Ralph, 45

Vernon, Francis, 126

Vertus, Mlle de, 100

Vie de M. Olier, by the abbé Faillon, 78 *n.* 2

Vies des Saints Pères des Déserts, see Arnauld d'Andilly

Vies intéressantes et édifiantes, 26, 29

Vieuxpont, Mme de, 248

Villiers, Barbara, Lady Castlemaine, afterwards Duchess of Cleveland, wishes her daughter to stay at Port Royal de Paris, 66–7

Villiers, George, second Duke of Buckingham, helps to write *Sir Politick-would-be*, 86

Vincent de Paul, St, to use his credit in restraining Irish Jansenists, 191; presented with a copy of the Irish anti-Jansenist declaration, 193; priests of his Mission, 189, 190, 191

Vindiciæ censuræ facultatis theologiæ parisiensis seu Responsio ad libellum cui titulus...spongia, Petrus Aurelius, his work, xv, 11, 13 *n.* 4

Vineam Domini, see Bulls